2000

Coach of the Year

Football Manual

Edited by

Earl Browning

ISBN: 1-58518-298-2

Cover Design: V.G. Reed and Sons, Inc.
Developmental Editor: Kim Heusel
Diagrams by Steve Haag
Book Layout: Kim Heusel

Coaches Choice Books is a division of: Coaches Choice
P.O. Box 1828
Monterey, CA 93942

CONTENTS

CONTENTS

DEFENSIVE LINE TECHNIQUES AND DRILLS

UNIVERSITY OF KENTUCKY

It is a pleasure being here today representing the University of Kentucky. Kentucky is a great place to coach. I'm an Army brat and have been around the world. But Kentucky is a great place to make a home.

I'm going to go completely off my film and show you the drills we use in developing defensive linemen. We shot this film during our spring practice last year. There is about one shot of each drill. Sometimes it is a humbling experience to get what we teach in drills to show up on the field. That has to do with coaching and communicating with your kids.

The first two years at Kentucky, I coached the defensive ends. Last year I had the defensive tackles and ends. Next year I will coach the defensive tackles.

The first thing I want to talk about is *stance*. On our practice field we have some posts set into the ground. We use them as shiver-boards. You could use a flat wall. John Tenuta at Ohio State was my defensive coordinator at SMU. He kept asking me about hitting an immovable object. That's what gave me the idea about putting something in the ground. I had used a wall, but at Kentucky our field is surrounded by hedges. To get to a wall I would have to run across two practice fields. I decided to put these posts into the ground.

When we come out for practice we use these posts for punch boards. The posts are nine inches wide. They are 8 X 8 posts, with three feet above the ground. They have the same amount in the ground as you see above the ground. They are wrapped with natural fiber rope which makes them nine inches wide. It is better than working on a wall because it allows flexion in the wrist. We are working the punch with the palms of the hand. It allows us to get into the drill quicker, because we are not

working the wrist so much. We work from the knees to start with. We deliver 12 quick shots to the post. They do this on their own. We are watching for eye and hand movement with a nice flat back. We want them to get good punch from the hips. This is a quick-hands drill.

POST DRILL

After that we put them in a stance. We punch on the post from the stance. We don't try to knock the post out of the ground. We are working on stance. I tell them that the post is going to catch them when they punch. I don't want them to get hurt going too hard at the post. I have seen some of our guys get too wide with the hands and really carom off the posts.

In their stance we want their hips slightly higher than their shoulders. We want the feet about armpit-width apart. We are going to crowd the football in our stance. We are so close to the ball that they will have to back their facemask off their hands a couple of inches. In our stance we always play with our inside hand down to the football. As I get down in my stance I want my hand in front of my stagger foot, not in the center of my stance. That lets me keep my hips and shoulders even.

In the stance we want a concave effect to their backs. We want a bit of a shallow area in their back. When I don't see that, I think that is weakness in the stance. I like the other hand down so as he gets off and attacks the V in the neck of the offensive lineman, his hand is ready to get into the target area. On a passing situation, he might cock his other hand in the pass rush. I want his pads back so we can explode like he is coming out of starting blocks. Those are the things we address in the stance and punch on the post drill.

We take six shots with the right hand and six with the left hand. A lot of times we don't let them take a step. The thing that is going to deliver the blow is the hip action as he rolls his hips. I want this guy to generate a lot of force out of his hips and put it on a spot of the offensive lineman. I think we can overwhelm anyone that we meet if we put our force on a spot on half the man. We want to turn the offensive lineman. We don't attack all his body. We work on half his body.

The thumbs should be up. That insures the elbows will be in. If the elbows get turned out, you have some big problems. The offensive lineman could collapse the arms and get into the body.

Twenty years ago I did not think much about stance, but now I coach the hell out of it. That is the one basic place you start the football play from. If you are messed up there and don't know how to get out of your stance, you are useless as a football player.

When we get into a pass rush stance, we narrow the feet down. They are less than armpit-width apart. We still crowd the ball. We want the forward foot in the stance to be within five inches of

PASS RUSH STANCE

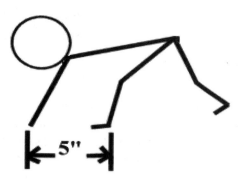

the down hand. We want all of the weight balanced between the down hand and up foot. The hips are higher than in the regular run stance. There is a bigger stagger in the stance. The back leg straightens a bit to get the hips up further. We back out the opposite hand and cock it so we can get a hell of a jump.

We tell our defensive line and show them on film how we want them to come off. What I am looking for is all four of our defensive linemen moving off the ball at the same time. When the center moves the ball, I want everyone off. If we want to check the get-off we put the tape on slow motion, watch the ball, and check the movement of the hands of the defensive lineman with the ball.

I like to use the two-man crouther sled. We teach a six-point explosion drill on this sled. To get in the six-point stance, the points on the ground are the knees, hands, and toes. We can get good teaching on hand use in this drill. This spring, since I am going to coach the tackles only, I am going to teach hands and face into the sled. The thing to emphasize in the six-point stance is to get the toes into the turf. Sometimes the kids want to get up and stand on their feet. That takes away from the hip roll.

SIX-POINT STANCE

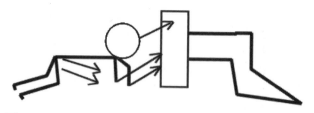

The next thing we do is get into the three-point stance against the sled. We work on explosion, drive, and escape. We explode like the six-point drill. We drive with the feet and press away. Then we execute an escape and rip through. We want the eyes on the level with our hands and dip in the hips. After the explosion and drive, I blow a whistle. On the whistle, the guy on the sled locks outs and continues to push the sled back. After that we execute the escape by ripping through.

The next thing I want to get into is tackling. At the University of Kentucky we do not tackle body on body. We tackle with apparatus only. If we get an injury, it will occur on a game day. We use the one-man sled a lot in our tackling drills We lock up on the dummy and lift. We punch our hips and put our face on the jersey. We lock up with the forearms and try to break the ribs. We take on running backs and wide receivers high on the shoulder pads above the numbers, grab cloth, and pull down as we pull our hips through. We keep our feet alive all the way through the tackle. The thing defensive linemen want to do is use their bodies in tackling. We don't want to be dragging people down with our hands. We get the body on them and arms over them in a real nice wrap. If the lineman is just reaching, he won't make many tackles.

The next drill is a simple **board drill**. This helps the tackle because he is working in a confined area. The board is 15 inches x 15 feet. This is not like running the speed ladder or running ropes. The wood is very unforgiving. If you don't do what you are supposed to do, it will put you down. In the seven years I've been using this, I haven't had any ankle injuries. (I have not had any and neither have my kids.) HA HA! We use a number of movements over the board. We make a stab step and cross the board like we are going across the face of an offensive lineman. We work lateral steps across the board. We work crossover steps across the board. We emphasis staying on the ball of the feet and not touching the board. It becomes challenging. If anyone steps on the wood the whole line rides him out for being clumsy. They work their butts off not to touch the wood. We don't want one noise coming from the wood.

RUNNING BOARDS

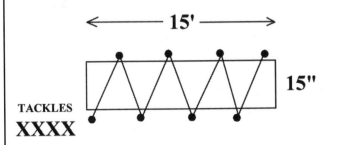

We don't practice very long so what we do in our drills is done quickly. We do a **line drill** to teach pursuit. We align and get off. We attack the offensive lineman, flatten him out, and turn his shoulders. This is basically working on getting off blocks. We get off, key the head of the offensive blocker, and flatten him out down the line of scrimmage by turning his shoulders. If the offensive lineman can't get upfield he can cut you off.

FLATTEN AND TURN

The next drill we do is called a **turn-and-run drill**. This is a pass rush drill. We align the defensive linemen on the line. They get off and rush the passes. They come in on the passer and get their hands up. The ball is thrown out and they chase the flight of the ball together. This is drill work for screens. Also I will take the ball back, pull it down, and move forward. This gives them a draw key. They stop, shout DRAW, plant the outside foot, turn to the inside and retrace their steps to the ball.

TURN-AND-RUN

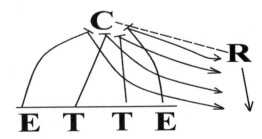

We are a basic 4-3 defense. We play a lot of even defense with our tackles. They are always moving. They are always moving to the set or away in some scheme. They are getting upfield into minimum assignment with a lot of penetration. When we move our tackle we don't lateral step on the line of scrimmage. Our defensive coordinator doesn't want anything lateral at the line of scrimmage. He wants to reset the line of scrimmage. He wants to move up the field and take ground.

This type of movement with our defensive tackle is what we call **Ears Technique**. If we are going right we step off to the right at a 45-degree angle. That removes part of the body from the contact. To get the rest of the body through, he has to put his *ear* into the body of the offensive blocker and rip through with the outside arm so he can clear the second step. He has to get his shoulder blades into the blocker and keep his pads down.

If we are going toward the strength of the set that is called **Go**. If he is going away from the strength it is called **Whip**. What they have to understand is the gap they are going into is going to move right or left. It is not going to stay there. He has to keep his head and eyes up to see which direction the gap is moving. Once they recognize which way the gap is moving, they don't have to stay square to the line. They can turn their shoulder and attack like hell in the direction of the play, flat down the line of scrimmage. The first thing the tackle should see is the offensive lineman and then the direction of the play.

GO AND WHIP

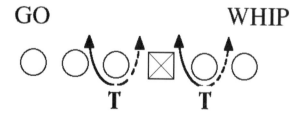

Defensive linemen think when they break the line of scrimmage, they are going to make a tackle for a loss. What they need to do is pursue to the spot where the ball is going to cross the line of scrimmage. We want them to attack without hesitation down the line of scrimmage. If the ball is going away from them we want them to stay square until they know the ball is not coming back. What we are trying to do is create thing so the tackles can play faster.

The defensive tackle has to understand that the offensive lineman is not going to lie to him. The backfield will try to fake you out. When the center blocks back and the guard and tackle pull across the center, the tackles have to recognize that. When the tackle sees the center blocking back on the other tackle, he has to know he's got to get his inside foot down on the ground and get upfield with penetration. We want him to knock down some of the blockers. The counter is a recognition play. You have to rep that until your guys know what is coming.

COUNTER

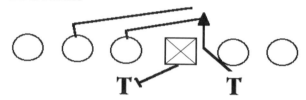

What I'm trying to do is get these guys to gain confidence that what they see is going to take them to the play. The zone play is a big play today. When we see the zone, recognition is important. As you watch this film, you see our tackle actually attacking the guy he is aligned on. That is not right. He is stepping left and should be attacking the guy in the next gap. He might have to attack the guy he is aligned on, but we want to try to get over to the far side of the gap.

The next thing we work on is the trap. We have to play the down or veer trap. The first thing I tell our tackle is any time we get a down block from the guard, we want to get our hands on him and dump him on the center. There are only three things that can happen to him. It is veer dive, play away, or trap. We try to spill the trap block. We get our shoulder pads down under the block of the trapper. We want to wrong-shoulder the blocker and see if we can't get upfield.

The next block we work on is the double team. The double team starts as a base block. We have to destroy the base block portion of this block. We want to turn our shoulder blades and hips into the double team. I don't want to touch the ground. If you get in trouble on the double team, the defensive tackle may have to touch his knee to his gap responsibility. The whole time he is touching his knee, he has to play with his hands and try to get them locked out. He drops his hips down and tries to get his hat down to hip level of the offensive blocker. If the offensive blockers get their shoulders together it is hard to beat the block. He has to keep his feet alive.

The reason I don't want my guys dropping to the ground, is we don't see the straight double team anymore. All the double-teaming now is the start of a combination block. We see two types of combination blocks. The first example is the defensive tackle in the center-guard gap. The center can't reach the tackle. The guard comes down on the tackle to keep him from penetrating. The center comes off on the tackle. The guard stays on the tackle until the center can get leverage. The guard comes off on the linebacker and the center secures his reach.

COMBINATION BLOCK

The second type of combination is one like Syracuse used on us. That is the center blocking back on the defensive tackle. The off guard comes under the center block onto the tackle and the center comes off on the linebacker.

COMBINATION BLOCK

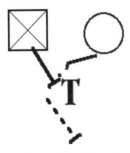

If the offensive linemen see the tackle drop to the ground to hold the double team, chances are both of them will go up on the linebacker. That is one thing we don't want to happen. That is why we don't go to the ground on the double team. He has to hold his ground knowing that one of the blocker has to release him to get to the linebacker. When that happens, he has to explode upfield.

The next thing we have to recognize is a pull inside. When the defensive tackle gets an inside pull, he cannot hesitate. He goes directly on the line he wants to take. The point of attack is in the C-Gap away from him. He can't allow the center to dictate what path he takes. Forget the center. If the center happens to get into the tackle's face, cross his face. If he gets into the hip or butt area, use the rip and go around him. If the center pin the tackle, he can't get wasted. He squeezes until he can find a way off the block. The most important thing is to *eliminate hesitation*.

PULL INSIDE

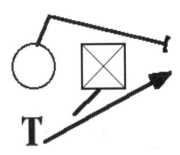

These next drills are pass rush drills. This drill is called the **Close Drill**. We want the defensive tackle to get into the offensive lineman before he gets comfortably set. If I am a defensive end I want to attack the V of the neck. The farther I want to go across his body with my inside hand is the tackle's sternum. The reason I don't go any further is so I can protect the outside shoulder from the offensive lineman. Once he puts his hand on the shoulder and shoves me away from the quarterback, that is the end of the defensive ends rush.

The outside hand is shoved into the armpit of the offensive lineman. Then I can use whatever move I have been taught. I can use the club or uppercut, rip or swim, or whatever moves you want to teach. We attack edges of linemen, never down the middle. We want to attack one half of the body to see if we can get him turned or off balance.

When we work on the Close Drill, the key things are to *break leverage and rip*. Sometimes our people think that breaking leverage is bull rushing. I want to exert so much pressure into a spot that the offensive lineman crumbles. It is that immovable object. Once I bust him, I want to get into my pass rush. A move we use in our pass rush is called *flip*. All I am trying to do is grab cloth and pull the offensive tackle toward the line of scrimmage. He then flips his hips past the offensive blocker.

This next drill is called **Scramble**. The defensive line has rush lanes to the passer. The two inside guys will attack the numbers of the offensive linemen they are lined up on. They attack the inside edge to the outside edge of the numbers. The defensive ends attack the outside edges of the numbers to the middle of the shoulder. If the quarterback moves in the pocket, we want the rush lanes to change with him. Everyone is responsible for contain. If the quarterback moves left in the pocket, the defensive tackle should move laterally to maintain his contain shoulder. If the quarterback crosses the rusher's face, he wants to move to stay in his lane. If he doesn't you have two rushers in the same lane.

CONTAIN THE SCRAMBLE

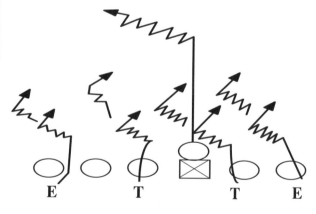

If there is a stunt, the guys work together if pass shows. The tackle comes down and picks the center. He tries to knock him in behind the guard. The nose guard takes a lead step upfield. If the guard shows high hat, the nose should be able to come up field free. If the guard closes down with the movement of the tackle, I want the nose guard to bull rush over the guard. I don't want the nose to attack wide. I don't want the quarterback to be able to step up and throw without someone in his face. If the nose goes wide, the throwing lane is created.

TWIST INTO THE RUSH

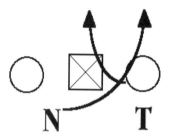

We use a **Trail Technique Drill** to stop the cutback run. The tackle closes down. As he goes down he wants to key the mesh area. That means he wants to see the football. If he doesn't see the football he attacks the naked. When we play the naked bootleg we attack straight upfield or vertical. Some people will turn and run to the sideline until they contain the quarterback.

Defensive ends should see the reverse coming. When they see it they explode vertical to the goal post. They should see it quicker than the naked bootleg. We want no hesitation. This was a big play for us against LSU. They came out on the first play and tried to run the reverse. Our defensive end did a good job of closing and exploding straight upfield. He made the play and that gave us a big boost right off the bat.

A defensive lineman has to know who can block him. The man he is lined up on is the first threat. The off guard is the second threat. The fullback or the near back is the third threat. If the defensive lineman is playing a 5 technique and gets a down block, we want him closing to the inside leg of the guard to spill the play outside. When the lineman goes down inside on a close, the linebacker is going to exchange responsibility with him. When the defensive lineman spills the play outside, I want his body north and south. I don't want him turned perpendicular to the line. I want him to be more square.

I'm not saying that Kentucky is the best defense in the league, because that is not true. But you don't see us getting manhandled or pancaked against some good offensive teams in a tough league.

COACHING THE QUARTERBACK

CINCINNATI BENGALS

What I want to do tonight is to talk about things I feel are important in coaching a quarterback. I will not get into the X's and O's so much. When you talk about the plays you run this is my feeling. We know every play is good IF it is executed well. I have a thousand plays drawn up on my computer. If the line blocks, the quarterback executes well, and the backs do their job, they are good plays. If they don't they are not good plays. After this session is over if you want to talk X's and O's we can.

I want to talk about a couple of things. First, is how to throw the football and how to drop back away from the center. Second, is how you get your quarterback ready for the season, and then how to give your quarterback a chance to be successful. That is the way I am going to start.

I know a lot of you are high school coaches. A lot of high school coaches get afraid when they get involved in a talk about coaching the quarterback. "I never played quarterback," some of you may say. "I do not have anyone on my staff that has played quarterback at any level." You do not have to be afraid of that situation. Look at Bill Walsh, perhaps one of the greatest quarterback coaches of all times. He may have played quarterback in high school, but he did not play quarterback in college and yet he was a master at coaching quarterbacks. He became a great quarterback coach because he studied football and he studied the position. He became a great teacher by studying the fundamentals and how to play the position. So, don't feel that you can't get it done because you or someone on your staff has not played quarterback.

Another important point as a high school coach is this. Do not feel that you must have a Division I prospect playing quarterback to be successful. On the college level you do not have to have a pro pros-pect playing quarterback to be successful. As Bill Walsh said in his book, "The sum of the whole is better than it parts." A classic example is to look at Joe Montana. He is one of the best quarterbacks to ever play the game. He was a third-round draft choice out of Notre Dame. No one thought he was going to be a great player. He was not big enough, he was not strong enough, and his arm was not very strong as compared to some of the other quarterbacks who were coming out that year. But Joe Montana turned out to be a great quarterback. He developed because he was smart, and he had great fundamentals. He had a great awareness for the game. So, the point I am trying to make is this. Don't think you can't be successful if you do not have a quarterback that the Division I schools are recruiting.

Next I want to talk about some general things. This is what I talk to my quarterbacks about. First, the quarterback is not going to win the game by him-self. Now, your quarterback needs to play well to give you a chance to win. But, he is probably not going to win the game by himself. Just by himself, the quarterback is not going to win the game for you. But, the quarterback can lose the game by himself. If he goes out and throws four intercep-tions, if he gets hit in the pocket and he fumbles and they pick it up and run it back for a touch-down. The quarterback can devastate your team.

We talk a lot about our quarterbacks being funda-mentally sound. We talk about them being consis-tent. We talk to them about doing their job. We are not concerned with them making the big play, but we want them to do their job. We tell them to give us a chance to win. We ask them to give our other players a chance to make our team successful. So, we do not try to put the whole ball of wax on our quarterback. We want our quarterback to do his part of the of-fense, nothing more and nothing less. We want them to blend in and make their share of plays, but do not make plays that kill us. If they can do that then we have a chance to win. Your quarterback must be consistent and blend in with your offense.

I have been reading Bill Walsh's book, *Finding the Winning Edge*. In the book he talks about football organization. He was talking about the players in general when he made this comment. "For a coach, what you have to do is to determine what skills and abilities are essential for a player, and then take the progressive steps to develop the player." That is one of the things I want to talk about. I want to cover what you need for your quarterback to be successful. Then, you must have a plan to accomplish that. The big thing I try to do is get our quarterbacks to think about the things they have to practice to make them successful.

A lot of the things I will talk about may not apply to you. I was trying to think back to the days when I was a high school quarterback in Batavia, Illinois. I can't think back that far. I can't remember much when I was playing quarterback in college. I can't even remember much about my first year in pro football. But, I think the things I am going to discuss here will apply to everyone in terms of how you are going to get your quarterback ready to play. A lot of this is what you do to develop your plan to get your quarterback ready to play. You must develop a plan to develop your quarterback.

First, I want to talk about the Proper Throwing Motion. This is how to throw the ball. The first thing is the Grip. I have my NIKE FOOTBALL up here which does not have a lot of air in it. This reminds me of a time when we were playing the Raiders. Kenny Stabler was the Raiders quarterback. Kenny had small hands. They would let some of the air out of the ball so he could grip it on a cold day. That was before refs were in charge of the balls.

I want to talk about the grip. I have seen a hundred different grips of the football. Terry Bradshaw had his finger on the top point of the ball and he had a lot of success throwing the football. Joe Kapp gripped the ball right in the middle. I think the most

important thing about the grip, is the fact it is predicated by the size of the hand of the individual. If he has a big hand. If it is a smaller hand it must come up closer to the point of the ball. This was so he could get a feel for the football. I am not so concerned about where the grip is on the ball as much as I am about it being a fingertip grip. You want the ball in your fingertips and not in the palm of your hand. There should be a space between the ball and the palm when he grips the ball.

I talk to my quarterbacks about taking a firm grip on the ball, but you do not want it to be a death grip. Again, I am not so concerned with where his hand is on the ball as I am about the fingertip grip and the space between the palm and the ball. I do feel the grip is very important.

The next area that I am big on is Pushing The Ball Back. This is putting the ball into the throwing position. We talk in terms of pushing the ball back with the left hand. I do not want them to drop and wind. We do not want to allow the point of the ball to drop below the waist. If I drop the ball and wind up, first of all it takes too long to get the ball off. Secondly, when you do all of those big motions it tends to lead into long strides. When they become big you become inefficient and you become inaccurate. So, we talk about pushing the ball back. A lot of the quarterbacks coming out of college today carry the ball high as they drop back. They have the ball high where they can push the ball back when they are ready to throw. They do this so they do not have to drop the ball down below the belt when they get ready to throw. We do not want the quarterback to drop the ball below the waist and wind up when he throws it. Pushing the ball back is a big deal. It is important in getting the ball back into the throwing position.

Next is the Release. Here is my thinking about throwing the football. Either you can do it or you can't, to a certain extent. If he can't throw the ball you are not going to make him a good passer. He either has a natural ability to throw or he doesn't. I wrote a book in 1982. It is titled, *The Art of Quarterbacking*. I was working with a friend of Paul

Brown in writing the book. When we got to the chapter on throwing they asked me how I threw the ball. I said, "I don't know, I just do it." We took a lot of film and studied my throwing motion and tried to describe it from pictures. I did not know how I threw the football. I feel to a certain extent, a kid has to be a natural thrower to be able to pass the football. A lot of the times either you can do it, or you can't. That is one of the things I look for in a quarterback. Either you can throw it or you can't.

Look at Sonny Jorgensen. He could throw the ball where he wanted it to go regardless of how he gripped it. Now, I am not saying you can't make a quarterback better with the things you do. But as far as teaching them a throwing motion, by the time you get them in high school, or certainly by the time you get them in college, you have no chance of changing a quarterback's throwing motion. A lot of it is natural ability.

It is important to let the quarterback use his natural throwing motion. Don't try to change it too much. To take someone and try to change the throwing motion is going to be more trouble than it is worth. If you take a very young kid and you tell him to throw a certain way, then you have a chance. When a kid comes to you in high school he must use his natural throwing motion.

We want them to release the ball somewhere above the shoulder. You do not want the sidearm motion. It is tough to follow through throwing sidearm. It is tough to get a consistent spiral on the ball. So, if I am looking for a quarterback, the first thing I want to see is for him to push the ball back, have a natural throwing motion, and then release the ball above the shoulder. If you get that, you can be effective.

If you are talking about a pro quarterback that drops and winds, we are not interested in him. We want consistent mechanics with our quarterback. We want a decent release, but we do not try to change it too much.

The next point is to use your whole body when you are throwing the football. You must make sure the arm strength does not come just from the arm. It must come from using your whole body in conjunction with the throw. Your legs give you balance and power. A lot of your power comes from the lower body. We want to be able to push off the back foot and step into the throw. This is what changes the momentum to get power on the ball. It is like a golf swing. Just watch Tiger Woods. It is getting the weight from the back foot to the front side. It is the same with the quarterback. You have to start it with the step into the throw. We want to push off the back foot and step into the throw. Then it is a combination of rotating the hips and shoulders. Everything has to work together. How do you do that? I am not so sure. It is timing, number 1. It is a throwing motion. It is the rotation, clearing the hip, driving with the hip, and getting the shoulders through the football. It all has to happen in a sequence. A lot of this comes back to a natural throwing motion.

Another thing you see with the good quarterback is pulling the nonthrowing arm down. For the right-hand passer it is the left arm. As you get through the throwing motion the left arm is coming down to the side as you drive through the throw. That is what happens in the throwing motion. You drive the left arm down and you come through with the release.

Next I want to discuss the Follow-Through. We do not want to kick the front leg. If we do that we have no chance to be accurate with the pass. You have to have a throwing motion with the knees flexed. As you come through, the knee has to lock. If you try to do it at the beginning of the throw, you have no chance to throw the ball accurately. You do not want to have the front leg locked when you are throwing the football. On the follow-through the throwing arm goes to the opposite hip.

The thing I talk a lot about with our quarterbacks is the wrist snap. This is part of the reason you want to grip the ball firmly, but you want your wrist to be loose. When you throw a football the tightness of the spiral comes from the snap of your wrist. I just tell our quarterbacks to see how fast they can snap their wrist straight down. We just stand in place and work on snapping our wrist down. When you get a good wrist snap you do not have to have a great arm motion with the throw. To get the tight spiral work on snapping the wrist down. When you throw the football you must understand the shape of the ball a little. It is like throwing the screwball. If you watch the way the ball comes out of your hand, it is like throwing a screwball. That is the motion. If you try to throw it like a screwball, you can't do it. So, we work a lot on the wrist snap.

I went through our film the other day and picked out some film to show you. Let me show you the throwing motion of our quarterbacks. (VIDEO)

If I had to pick one trait that I look for in a quarterback, first I want a quick release, and then I want to know if the passer is accurate when he is throwing. I can't make the passer more accurate. You can make him a little more accurate with better body balance, and with a little more anticipation. But, you are not going to make a 40 percent passer into a 60 percent passer. It comes down to this; "Either you can throw it or you can't." You have to find a quarterback that gives you a chance and then work on his fundamentals and try to make him more consistent.

Next I want to get into some Drops for the quarterbacks. One of the things you need to do is to identify the things your quarterback needs to work on. What am I going to work on to get our quarterback ready to play next season? We are going to have a 3-Step Drop, a Quick 5-Step Drop, a 5-Step Drop, and a Quick 7-Step Drop. Then we are going to have our Play Action which are all different drops for the quarterback. We will have our Out-of-the-Pocket Drops, which all have different set points. They all have different footwork and different mechanics on how they are going to come away from the center. Also, we are going to work on the Shotgun. You need to identify what you need to work on and what is in your offense. What kind of drops do you have in your offense? What are you going to ask your quarterback to do? Make sure you cover those things in an organized manner and then drill the hell out of it. You must be consistent with it. That is what we do and those are our drops.

Next I want to talk about a 5-Step Drop. About 90 percent of the passes in our offense are out of a 5-Step Drop. We do not have a 7-Step Drop in our offense. We have a Quick 7-Step Drop, but the mechanics of the quarterback is more like a good 5-Step Drop.

On the 5-Step Drop the first thing we start with is the stance. We want to be in an athletic position. The feet are about shoulders width apart and you are balanced. You want to have the weight on the balls of your feet. The weight should kind of be evenly distributed, but it should be a little toward the balls of your feet. We want the knees flexed. You want to be able to move once you get the ball from the center. You can't move if your legs are straight. How much you flex your knees depends on how big your center is. The shorter the center, the more you have to flex the knees. You want the arms bent slightly under the center. If you tighten up your muscles before you take the snap you can't be fluid. Part of playing quarterback is being fluid. By flexing the arms it allows you to ride the center on the snap.

I always talk to our quarterbacks about having the weight evenly balanced. But, I tell them to think mentally that the weight is on the left foot. The reason I say that is because I want to push off with the left foot when I am dropping back. We try to eliminate false steps. I do not want our quarterback to step in and then back. We want to eliminate the wasted motion coming away from the center.

I am real big on the First Step. Every day my quarterbacks hear "first step – kick step." The first step away from the center is the most critical step. You want to drive away from the center. It is an explosion away from the center. We should be going about 90 percent when we are coming away from the center. But, the first step should be a drive away. You are pushing and extending. When you do that your left shoulder comes up. As our quarterbacks come back on the first step I want to see the left shoulder come up as they come away from the center. That means they are getting a good first step. Your separation is going to come on your first step away from the center. If it is a 5-Step Drop I talk about depth on the first three steps and transition on the last two steps. You want a good step on the first step. You want to lengthen it out and get the shoulder up in the air. That tells me you are pushing away from the center.

Everything we do with our quarterbacks, we are working on a line. As we are coming back we want to work down the line. We want the first step to be behind our left foot. If the quarterbacks are not extending enough on that first step I will put a towel down and tell them to step over the towel on the first step. I force them to step over the towel to get depth on the first step. It is important to work on a line because I want to see where their first step is. It should be just inside the line.

After the first step we concentrate on the Crossover Steps. Again, you should be straddling the line on steps two and three. As we come back the left foot is on one side of the line and the right step is on the other side of the line. The line is not over the left guard or right guard. It is expected to be straight back. We have the quarterbacks drop back for 20 yards just to get the feel of keeping the line between the legs as they drop back.

The Crossover Steps are our transition steps. We have our momentum going back and we have to stop and get into the throw. That is where our transition comes into play. The first three steps are big steps and the last two steps are little steps. Then it is planting the foot.

We want the hips perpendicular to the line of scrimmage or parallel to the line that I am working on. When we are dropping we want the arms to swing naturally. We want the arms chest high and in a natural position. As I drop back the ball should cross my shoulders. If I try to drop back fast my arms must flow across my chest. Let the arms swing across the body as you come back. We want two hands on the ball as we drop.

In the transition portion we want two shorter, control steps. After three good steps, now the steps

have to be shorter. We must get our weight shifted back toward the line of scrimmage into our throw. I tell the quarterbacks to let their left shoulder dip. If the shoulder dips down he will have a chance to plant. We want the shoulder down when we are making our transition. We want to stick the back foot and make our transition back to the line. When that foot hits it should be on the insole of the shoe. If the weight is on the balls of the feet, the weight is still going back. We want them to stick the foot in the ground, plant, and come off the foot.

We do not throw off our back foot. There is going to be some type of hitch step to get our balance. It is tough to throw off the back foot and be successful. Most of our passes are thrown with a hitch step coming forward. There are two big things with a hitch step. Number one is not to cross the feet. Second, we do not want to bring the feet together.

You heard me talk about the first step being a Kick Step. This brings into play the going to the left and the right. When you are throwing the football you want your hips pointed toward the target so you can step into the throw. If I am throwing to my right and when I plant, basically my hips are already pointed toward my target. It is easy to the right. What we work hard on in the Kick Step is throwing to the left. Again, we work on the line. The point is, we are trying to get our hips turned so we can face our target as quickly as we can. As we come back on the drop, as we get to the last step, we want the quarterback to kick step across the line which will open the hips toward the target going to the left. To get my hips turned I have to swing my leg open. If we do not swing the leg far enough we end up throwing the ball across the body. We are trying to preset our hips toward our target. You must be working on a line to do this. It all comes down to teaching techniques.

Now I want to talk about some Drills we use with our quarterbacks. First, we put all of our quarterbacks together. We are all on a line. We may be working on a 3-Step or a 5-Step Drop. I will tell one of the quarterbacks that he has the cadence. We are all going to drop back together, but no one is going to throw. I can stand there and look at their first step. I can see if they are all getting the same depth, or if their first step is on the line. I can see if the rhythm of our drop is the same. The depths of the routes tie in with the depth of the drop. They all take their drops on one quarterback's cadence, but they do not throw the ball.

The other thing we do is to have the quarterbacks work in pairs. I will put two quarterbacks here and two over there. They throw to each other. Now, I can watch two quarterbacks on their drops and their releases.

Next we have them throw routes to stationary receivers, and that is usually me. I have them throw it to certain spots on my body. One time it will be at my head, the next time it will be at my knees. I will go to the left and then the right. We try to get them to think about the plays we are running that day and what they have to do on their drops.

One of the things we have fun with is throwing between two defenders. We put two defenders in front of the receiver and have the quarterback throw the ball between the defenders. We are trying to get the quarterback to focus with his eyes on where he wants the ball to go. I tell our guys the accuracy does not come from the arm, or lower body, it comes from the eyes. You have to focus where you want to throw the ball. It is just like shooting at the bulls eye. You want to aim at the bulls eye of the target so the shot will be as close to the center as possible. It is the same thing with the quarterback. We want him to focus to a specific spot. We want them to pick out a spot they want to throw to. We want him to be able to throw into a tight spot so he has to focus in with his eyes.

Another drill that we like is what we call "Two to the Head, and One to the Body." We have two quarterbacks playing together. They are dropping back. If they throw the pass and it is at the receivers head it counts two points. If the pass is in the framework of the upper body he gets one point. The first man to 10 wins.

Next I want to talk about Pocket Movement. Nothing ever happens like you want it to happen. How many times is everything perfect in a game? We stress to our quarterbacks to "make the routine plays – routine." When they drop back and the protection is good, and the receiver is open, they have to complete the pass. When everything happens like it is supposed to, we have to make the play. But things do not always happen the way we want it. So you have to be able to move in the pocket. First, we want two hands on the ball. I threaten the quarterbacks when I see one hand on the ball. I tell them I will take duct tape and tape their other hand to the ball if I see it again.

We want to always maintain the throwing position. Now, we are talking within the framework of the pocket. I am not talking about breaking containment or about scrambling. If I have to avoid one man, I have to slide in the pocket. We must always stay in a throwing position. As soon as I get out of throwing position that receiver will get open and I can't make the play. We stress the point of relaxing before throwing.

Some of the drills we use are what we call Slide left and right. We have them set in the pocket and then slide one man to the left or right and make the throw. We want to maintain the throwing position. Then we throw it to one of the other quarterbacks. We work to one side and then to the other side.

Another drill we call Step Up Quickly. We get to the set point and see the defender has beaten the blocker. I realize that I have to step up quickly to get the pass off. He steps up and maintains his throwing position and makes the throw downfield.

Another drill is called "Hit Them with the Dummy." We do not hit our quarterbacks in practice. So, when we are in drills we have them set to throw. As they throw the ball I take a hand dummy or a shield and hit them with the dummy. I do not hit them in the head or on the throwing arm. I will hit them in the butt, or in the legs, just to help them to get use to things happening around them.

We still use the old Wave Drill. The quarterback drops and then I motion for him to come up, or go back, go left, or go right. As the quarterback is doing the wave he has the ball in position to make the throw. He has two hands on the ball. He is ready to throw the ball when I raise my hands. This is a way for us to work on pocket movement. We try to simulate things that are going to happen in a game. If we run a skeleton pass drill we will make him move in the pocket at times before he makes his throw. We do not want to make the seven-on-seven drill perfect for the quarterback all of the time.

The other thing is Progression Footwork. We have four receivers and we have the quarterback work through the progression to the receivers. We always talk about letting the feet lead the way. We want them light on their feet. If is almost a tip toe action. We tell them to let their feet take them to where they want to throw. Unless the feet are there they can't throw it. We do not want hopping motions.

Some Odds and Ends: This all goes back to what you have to do to have your quarterback ready to play when the season starts. You want to cover all of your basics. We make a list of all of the things in our playbook that I want to cover. This is just a partial list. First, make sure your quarterbacks work with a wet ball. If you practice in the rain one day you can mark that one off. If we do not get rain we will take one practice and wet down some balls so the quarterback and center get a chance to work with a wet ball.

We do not want our quarterbacks to take hits. We work on sliding. We have too much invested in our guys to have them take the hit. So, we work on them sliding instead of taking that hit. We wait for a rainy day and we look for a puddle and have them slide into the puddle. If we do not get rain, we go to where they have the sprinklers going and work on the slide.

We work on recovering a fumbled snap. We try to simulate this and have the quarterback and center covering the fumble. Then we work on fumbles between a back and the quarterback. We show them how to cradle the ball and how to recover it.

These are things that are going to happen during the season.

Next we work on interceptions. We work on playing off the blockers. Everyone comes after the quarterback first. He has to learn to play off the blockers to buy time for the rest of our team. Also, we teach them how to use the sideline for help. We show them how to prevent the guy that intercepts the ball from cutting back. We want him to use the sideline to push him out of bounds.

We also have some tackling drills for our quarterbacks. It is a matter of putting the head in front and wrapping the arms. We do this just so they can get ready for the season.

We work on the HOT throws. They may have to throw off balance. We work on our Scramble throws. You can script some of those in practice. You must be sure you cover that in getting ready for the season.

We work on throwing long. We call it Drop In The Basket. We want them to throw it at a 45-degree angle. For us, it should be completed 42 yards from the line and 5 yards from the sideline. I put a laundry basket down there. The quarterbacks take their drop and take the hitch step and try to throw it in the basket. We use the Goal Post to give the quarterbacks a touch on throwing the ball. They have to throw the ball over the Goal Post to me after they take their drop. If they throw it over my head they have to go get it. This is used when we want to drop the ball over a linebacker's head to a receiver. We work on our Keeper action and when they get to the goal post they dump the ball to me on the other side of the goal post. This helps them develop a little touch on the ball.

The other thing we use is what we call the "Throw of the day." We pick out special situations that happen during the season that we have in on our training tapes. We script this so he will have to make a certain type of throw for the "Throw of the day." I have a video that will illustrate this to you.

"Finding The Time" is always a big factor with coaches. How can I find the time to work on everything? First is off-season. Hopefully, you can find some time during the off-season to work with the quarterbacks on some of these points. The big thing for us is prepractice. We have a 15-minute special teams period. Our quarterbacks know they must be loose before that period. They are not involved with special teams so I am working with them during that time. When the team goes to stretch the quarterbacks continue to work on individual work for another 15 minutes. So, before our practice starts I get one-half hour with our quarterbacks. Then we start our practice with a 30-minute Individual Period. A lot of that may be group work. I may send two quarterbacks to the tight ends and take two with me with the other receivers. The other thing is Post Practice. If we do not get enough work during the regular practice we stay out and work after practice.

My final session is how to give your quarterback a chance to be successful. My feeling is this: Plays are plays. You have to do the things that are in your offense. But, do the same things over and over for your quarterback. You may want to mix up the looks, change the personnel, and change protections, but let the quarterback do the same things over and over again. I am talking about mixing up the play but making it the same for the quarterback. It is a different look for the defense.

One of the first plays I learned from Bill Walsh was 76 Exit. It is a play with our X receiver doing a shallow crossing route. First we are throwing to the X man on the shallow cross. The number 2 man is the Y on the route over the ball. The H back is on a scat and the Fullback is on a swing route

and is our number 4 man. The protection is this. If the Sam Linebacker blitzes we have to throw it to the Tight End. That is the route, 76 Exit. We call this formation Weak Right.

To change it up we may call Weak Right, Y Right. Now we motion the Tight End across. We change the strength of the formation. It is still the same read for the quarterback. We may call Strong Right, Mum Across. Now we flutter the halfback across the formation. Now, we will have some runs that tie in with this. We may call Strong Right, Hum Left. We can go Far Double Wing Right. Now we have the Halfback break the formation and put him out wide. He gets to the same spot from a different formation. All of this is a different look for the defense but it is the same read for the quarterback.

We could Tag the Z and call Z Out. If the defense is camping on our crossing route we can tag it. Now the quarterback reads the Z as number 1. The things you can do are unlimited. The whole idea is to have the same read for the quarterback.

You can take the same play and go with two tight ends and two wide receivers and one running back.

2 TE'S / 2 WO'S / 1 RB

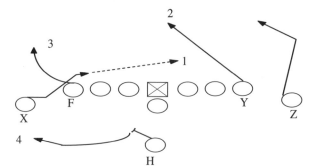

2TE'S / 1 WO / 2 RB'S

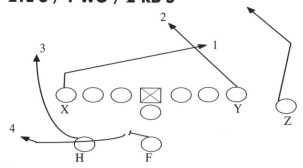

76 EXIT

It is the same routes as before but with different receivers.

You can go with two tight ends, one wideout, and two running backs. Now you just have your extra tight end run the shallow.

You can do the same thing with three tight ends. You can give them a trips look with a man in motion and run the same patterns. It is the same play with different personnel. It is a different look but it is the same read for the quarterback.

3 TIGHT ENDS

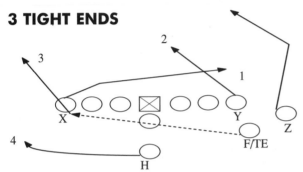

We can run it with three wide receivers. We can put the X receiver in either position and run the same route.

3 WIDEOUTS

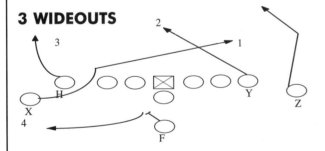

We can run the same play with four wideouts. The play is the same. It is the same read for the quarterback.

4 WIDEOUTS

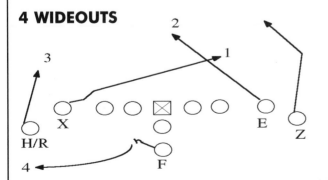

The protection is the same. The read for the quarterback is the same. But it is a different look with four wide receivers.

We can change up the pass protection. We are concerned about one linebacker making the quarterback throw the ball. We will run the same play but change the protection. Instead of having one back scat and one back blocking weak, we will block both backs on the outside linebacker. It is our Solid Protection. We call 84 Exit. It is still Exit to all of the wide receivers. Now we TAG our backs. Now they change up a little to take care of the linebacker.

SOLID PROTECTION – TAG BACKS LEFT

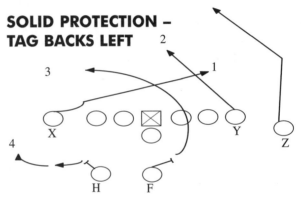

We can get real fancy and give the defense a Five Wideout look and run it off Hot Protection and tag the Fullback on a Wheel. Again, it is the same play. Now, we have a hot receiver, but it is the same read for the quarterback.

HOT PROTECTION – TAG FB WHEEL

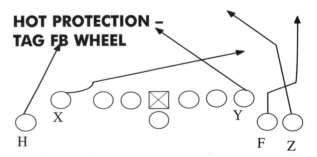

We go into a game with about 30 passes. That is our base game plan. We have another 15 in our Third-Down Package. Most of those are converted from our First-Down Package. We will put in two or three plays for special situations. But the key is this. We do a number of things over and over again from different looks so our quarterback has a chance to be successful.

MAKING THE KICKING GAME IMPORTANT

VIRGINIA TECH

I would like for you to take down these dates. On July 15 we will be having a Kicking Clinic. We will be talking about how we do things at Virginia Tech in the kicking game. If you are interested you can call the football office and we will send you an application. We would love to have you visit us.

I have always been a coach that believed in the special teams. Everywhere I have coached the head coach always stressed special teams. It was true with Mike Godfried, Bobby Ross, and Jerry Claiborne. They always stressed kicking. Then when I got the head job at Murray State it was obvious to me that the quickest way to win football games was with the kicking game. It has always been a part of me and I have continued to stress it at Virginia Tech.

The first question we get about our kicking game is this. "How much time do you spend on the kicking game?" I am going to show you how much time we spend on the kicking game. We believe in making the kicking game important and I will cover the things we do to make it important.

I want to show you a chart that we keep updated that illustrates the importance of field position. It is just a fact about football.

YARD LINE	CHANCES OF SCORING
20	1 out of 30
40	1 out of 8
50	1 out of 5
40	1 out of 3
20	1 out of 2
10	1 out of 2

You can see your chances of scoring increase within a short number of yards. The best way to get field position is in the kicking game.

We are always talking about big-yardage plays. We are always talking about momentum plays. In the Sugar Bowl this past year, if Florida State does not block one of our punts, and if they had not run back the punt on us, I am not sure they would have beaten us. In the third quarter when we made our comeback, we were establishing field position with punt returns. The kicking game was very evident in that championship game. It just makes that chart I showed you become more important because you increase your chances.

At Virginia Tech we put an importance on the kicking game. I am going to go over some things that we do that may be a little different for what other teams do. There may be some teams that do it the same way we do.

Talking about being important reminds me of a story. The Pope was visiting this country one year. He called his chauffeur and told him to get his car ready, that he wanted to take a ride to see the countryside. The Pope came down to the car and told the chauffeur that he had decided he would drive today. The chauffeur asked him if he was sure that was what he wanted to do. He told the chauffeur that it would be an easy drive in the country where there would be very little traffic. The Pope got in the car and started driving out in the country. It was not long until a police officer pulled them over. He goes up to the limousine and the Pope rolled his window down. He asked to see the license. The Pope obliged and gave him his license.

The police officer goes back to his car and gets on the phone. He calls his supervisor. He told him he had pulled over a speeder but he had a problem what to do about it. The chief asked him if he had pulled the mayor over? "No Sir! It is more important than that." The chief asked, "Do you have the governor?" "No Sir! It is more important than that." The chief asked, "Do you have the president?" "No Sir! I think it actually goes higher than that." Finally the Chief asked him, "Who in the world do you have?" The officer responded, "I do not know who he is, but he has the Pope as his chauffeur." That was an important person in the back seat.

At Virginia Tech we make the kicking game important. The first thing that happens with us is the fact that I am involved in the kicking game. I will tell you how this all came about. I came up as a defensive coach. I was a defensive coordinator most of the time when I was an assistant. When I got the head coaching job at Murray I spent all of my time on offense. I called all of the offensive plays. Then when I got to Virginia Tech I became involved in everything.

A few years later we lost a couple of coaches. Before that, our position coaches handled their phase of the kicking game. After we lost those assistants I started getting involved in the kicking game. Since that time I have decided that I would not do it any other way now. You must have an offensive coordinator and a defensive coordinator that you believe in to do this. I have no problem with that phase. But it allowed me to coach the special teams. Now I could get out of the way of the offense and defense.

As I see it now it becomes very important for the kids to play on the special teams. They know how important it is to us. Just saying it is important is not getting it done. You have to show it is important.

So you will know what I am talking about, let me give you a couple of terms. Our PRIDE TEAM is our Punt Team, our Punt Protection Team, and our Punt Coverage Team. Our Punt Block Team and Punt Return Team are called our Pride And Joy. I handled those two groups plus the Kickoff Coverage Team. I have another coach that handles the Kickoff Return Team, that has done it for a long period of time. If there was one area that I would take over that would be it. I think the Field Goals and PAT's, and blocks against those two teams fit with the offense and defense. The things on those teams

remain the same week to week. I think it sends a message to the team when the head coach is in charge of those special teams.

I think it is a more efficient way of operation to have the head coach in charge of the kicking game. Before we did it this way I would always stress to the offensive and defensive coordinators to make sure they got their kicking game covered. But now what happens is this. Those guys go study the offense and defense and I go study the kicking game. By doing it this way they get to spend more time on their area and the person working on the special teams get to spend more time on that phase of the game.

For example I will spend at least four hours looking at the Pride and Pride and Joy Teams just looking for little things that will give us an edge. I look for things like this: Some player may be mixed up on the protection. We may find one kicker that is a little slow on his steps. Another blocker may be creating too much space. How the personal protector blocks is another thing I look for. I spend at least four hours on this phase of the game. Not many assistant coaches are going to spend that much time on looking at the kicking game.

While the rest of the team is watching film on Sunday I am working on the special teams. We will add a new rush every week. Each week we will do something a little different. Whatever the opponent that week sees from past games they know they will see something a little different next week. The question will be can they handle what we do different? That is the issue.

When we start our practice I go down with the Kicking Teams. I go with the snappers, punters, and field-goal kickers. We have a competition every day. I think you have to put the field-goal kickers under the gun as much as you can. I work with them and we have competition every day. We work on the kickoffs and the onside kick. We work with the punters on the pooch kick. I think it helps to have someone with those guys to let them know it is an important part of the game.

We have our best players on our special teams. We have players that can do their very best. One reason for that may be because I am involved in the special teams. We try to convince them it will enhance their pro careers if they can play on special teams. If they have any ability in the kicking game it may make a difference in being drafted or not, or on making the last cut. If they can protect the punter, cover in open field, or return punts it is an added benefit.

We never ask anyone to stay after practice or to come out early for the kicking game. We have our kicking game in the middle of practice. We never have them come out early or stay late as a punishment. A lot of teams will send their special teams out 20 minutes early. The other teams are not out early and to some it seems like punishment to send one group out early. We would never do that at Virginia Tech.

If you come to one of our practices you would see that everything moves fast. We do not stand around during practice. Things move fast. When we do our special teams everyone stops and we all come to one field and we do all of our kicking for that practice. It may be slow for some of the players in some ways, but it is another way of telling them the kicking game is important. I can tell you something about this part of practice. This is when I start getting cranked up. I get them moving and we get things done. It is an important period in that practice and the kids know it.

If we are working on conditioning drills. We will take our Pride And Joy Teams and work on the Punt Return as far as a conditioning drill. I will promise you this, you will never see our Pride And Joy Group walking off the field. They will run off the field before the other conditioning group. We have a drill where we work our Pride Team against our Pride And Joy Team. For conditioning that day, if they are in those groups, they get half of their sprints knocked off. We do this so the players will want to be on those teams. We do not want them to feel they have to do something extra to be on those teams.

We have special awards for offense, defense, and special teams. We have an award called the BIG HIT. Anytime the offense gets an award the defense gets an award and the special teams get an award. That is just the way it is. The offense and defense selects their award winners in their meetings on Sunday. On Monday we show the Big Hits in the kicking game to the entire team. Again, it is just another way of saying the kicking game is important.

We have Goal Charts. The offense, defense, and special teams all have Goal Charts. We have special team meetings. They stay on Monday and Friday for the meetings. On Monday we show the film from the past Saturday's game. After the film we go over what we are going to do for that week. On Friday we go over all of the video each of the teams has been involved with in practice that week. Then we will show some video of the team we are getting ready to play. Those are some of the ways we try to make the kicking game more important.

Let me talk about Goals. I do not like very many goals. If you get too many goals they become too much. I like to keep goals simple and I like to make them obtainable. We like to make it a situation where we can say to the team if we make these goals we have a chance of winning.

SPECIAL TEAMS GOALS – 1999

A. PRIDE (PUNT)
_____ 1) Allow NO more than 6 yards per return.
_____ 2) Down punt inside 10-yard line.

B. KICKOFF COVERAGE TEAM
_____ 1) Average starting the opponent at the 20-yard line or less.

C. PRIDE AND JOY – PUNT RETURN
_____ 1) Average 10 yards per punt return.

D. PUNT RUSH/FG/PAT RUSH TEAMS
_____ 1) Block a punt, FG, PAT, or force a bad kick every game.

E. KICKOFF RETURN TEAM

_____ 1) For 66% of the time start our drive at the 28-yard line or beyond.

F. FG/EXTRA POINT TEAMS

_____ 1) 100% on PAT attempts.

_____ 2) 66% (2 of 3) on FG tries.

G. NO PENALTIES OR MENTAL ERRORS

H. HIDDEN YARDAGE = +20 YARDS

We add up our kickoff return and our punt return yardage against our opponent. We want to end up with those 20 extra yards. That comes out to two first downs. We look for those hidden yards. If we can just start out 20 yards more up field we have a chance to be successful.

I am going to go over our practice schedule. There are some things here that I feel are very good. Eight years ago we went 2-8-1 at Virginia Tech. After that season I took a look at every single thing in our program. We started doing something different in our practice. I will show you some of those things that came about as I went to visit other coaches to find out how they did things and to compare them with what we were doing.

During that losing season eight years ago we were ahead of six of those teams that we lost to in the fourth quarter. We were only down by six to 12 points to three other teams. So we had a chance to win nine football games. Instead we were 2-8-1. We were close but we were just not getting the job done. So I will talk about some of the changes we made in our approach to practice.

I said we have a meeting on Monday with all of the team. We give the Big Hit Awards to the offense, defense, and the kicking team.

One of the things I was concerned with when we were 2-8-1 was the number of penalties we were getting. We used to run them after practice and give them punishment during the week. We tried a lot of things but we were not getting any better.

So we started showing the entire team all of our penalties in that meeting on Monday. When you show that player blocking someone in the back to the entire squad it makes an impression. That peer pressure is wonderful. It has really helped us We have cut back on our penalties. We have really cut back on stupid penalties. I am talking about late hits and hits out of bounds. Those penalties will wear you out quicker than anything.

We show the penalties to the entire team. If they called a penalty and we do not agree with the call we tell the team that. We will tell them the penalty should not have been called. Then I will tell them when a penalty should have been called. We go through each situation and we make those guys responsible for their action in front of their teammates.

I said we have our kicking game meetings on Monday. We show the film of the game on Saturday. Then we give them a scouting report.

People ask us about spending more time on the kicking game. We do not spend more time. We spend the same amount of time each week. Each team knows exactly how much time they have each week. I think having the practice schedule organized and making it more important is the key.

MONDAY PRACTICE

Per.	Time	Minutes	Schedule
	5:10	X	- Flex
1	5:20	5	- Converge
2	5:25	5	- FG vs. FG Rush
3	5:30	10	- Individual
4	5:40	10	- Skeleton vs Var.
5	5:50	5	- Opt./Pride Protection
6	5:55	5	- Inside - Pride Joy (Rush)
7	6:00	25	- Team
8	6:25	10	- Conditioning – Scrimmage
	6:35		- Off the field

Here is one of the things that I like about our schedule. This is the way we start practice on Monday. After we have stretched and done our flexes we go to our Converge Drill. What it is is offense against the defense. We come in and run screens, draws, reverses, and the halfback pass, and plays such as that. They are plays that either turn out real good or real bad. The thing I like about the drill is that it gives the offense time to work on those plays, and it gives the defense time to work against them, but another good point is that it starts out practice fast. It does not matter if you have won or lost, I want to start out practice fast. We flex, come together, and here we go. It is a fast-paced drill.

After the Converge we come together and we kick field goals against each other. One thing I like when we kick field goals is this. We never rush the whole team. We only rush three men. But, the kicking team does not know which three men are going to rush. I do not like for everyone to rush on this drill in practice. One year we lost a player to injury because we rushed everyone. We just keep it to three men.

We take five minutes on Monday and work on our Pride Protection. We are a Zone Protection Team. We want our guys working straight back. We put the Pride Team with their backs to the camera. Then we put a light strip or a line straight back so they can see if they are working straight back. They can see it on the film.

We have the Pride And Joy guys over on the defensive side. We try to keep the two groups separated from each other because they work against each other a lot. The Pride linemen are big guys. They are tight ends, defensive ends, and big guys. On our Punt Blocking Team we have all fast guys. We have the receivers, defensive backs, and linebackers. They have to be fast to get on the Pride And Joy Team. We keep them separate so we can work against each other.

We run some of our Punt Rushes. We are in Zone Protection and it does not make any difference where they are coming from. If there is a special rush by the team that we are getting ready to play we will run that against them.

Then we go to a five-minute period with our Pride And Joy Team. We will go against the Scout Team here. Most teams protect their center one way or the other. We zone, so we just back him up. I get a scout team to run the punt against us. We work on our rush for that week. We will have two or three rushes each week.

That is all of the kicking we do on Monday. We do not stay late at night working on the schedule for the next day. If you stay late night after night you get run down after awhile and you do not make good decisions. You are tired when you get to the game on Saturday. I made a conscious effort after that to get the details done, and get the work done, and then get home and get some rest. Then we can get something done the next day. Our staff has been together for a long time and we are not going to keep them late.

After the season starts we never hit in practice. Let me tell you, Virginia Tech has always been a hard-nosed, tough football team. That is the type of kid we get at Tech. But, in that 2-8-1 year, we would get to the fourth quarter and we were soft. We could not finish it. So we made some changes and do not hit in practice like we use to.

TUESDAY PRACTICE

Per.	Time	Min.	Schedule
	4:15	10	- Flex
	4:25	4	- Central Meeting
1	4:29	9	- Individual
2	4:38	9	- Individual
3	4:47	9	- Individual
4	4:56	9	- Individual
5	5:05	10	- Perimeter - vs. Var. 3 on 3
6	5:16	10	- 1 on 1 vs. Varsity, Middle vs. Varsity
7	5:25	10	- Skel. vs. Var. – Pass Rush
8	5:35	10	- Skel. Vs. Var. Pass Rush vs. Var.
9	5:35	10	- Team vs. Scouts (Blitz)
10	5:35	10	- Kicking – Pride vs. Pride & Joy
			1. Protect
			2. Protect & Cover

			3. P
			4. P & C
			5. P
			6. P & C
11	6:05	10	- Team vs. Varsity (2 Back - Play Action)
12	6:15	5	- Team vs. Scouts (Short Yardage)
	6:20	10	- Conditioning – Pride & Joy (Return) Deep Balls
	6:30		- Off the field

On Tuesday we have a Perimeter period. I like this period. We have the tight ends, wide receivers, and backs going against the secondary. The secondary people are taking good angles to the football. They are not going to allow those long plays. On offense we work the wide receivers on blocking. We tell the tailbacks they are never to run over a defender in this drill. We tell them we want to see some moves in the drill. It is a good period both ways. We tackle to the ground, particularly early in the year.

Then we come back and do a middle drill. It is seven-on-seven, offense versus defense. Nothing is fancy in this drill. We run Isolation, Sweeps, and kick-out plays. Again, we tackle to the ground. You hold your breath in this drill because you do not want to lose a player here. I think there is something about doing things full speed at least once a week. Since we started doing this we have been a lot tougher especially in the fourth quarter.

Continuing on our Tuesday practice we get to the special teams in period 10. Here again, we all come together on one field. There are some guys standing around. I do not care.

We work our Pride versus our Pride And Joy. The first thing we work on is protection. We will run the other team's rush. I usually put a towel on the ground at a certain point. If the rushers get to that towel they can go ahead and block the kick. I do not want the rushers laying out. I do not want the punter getting hurt. It is full speed as far as protection and as far as rushing.

Next we work on Protect and Cover. First we snap the ball and punt it. We send the outside headhunters down to cover and anyone responsible for the headhunters on the return. The deep back catches the ball and we check the first group down on the punt. Then we come back and punt it again and those guys are gone. Everyone that is remaining will go to their responsibility. I like this drill because with the headhunters out of the drill it gives you a chance to see if your inside people have their lanes covered.

We will stay down at the end where we caught the punt and go the other way on the next punt. We protect on the first punt. Then we punt and cover on the second punt. We go back to the original position and punt and protect again. Then we punt again and cover. That gives us six reps with best versus best. It helps if you do not have the same people on the same teams.

Then at the end when we have conditioning the Pride And Joy guys are only running half of those sprints. They are going to be off the field before the other guys that are doing conditioning.

WEDNESDAY PRACTICE

Per.	Time	Min.	Schedule
	4:15	10	Flex
	4:25	4	- Central Meeting
	4:29	5	- Specials.
1	4:34	9	- Individual
2	4:43	9	- Individual
3	4:52	9	- Individual
4	5:01	10	- Inside vs. Scouts
5	5:11	10	- Pass Skeleton vs. Varsity (Scouts)
6	5:21	10	- Pass Skeleton vs. Varsity
7	5:31	10	- Kicking
			1, Pride (Priority) vs. Pride & Joy (Rush)
			2. Field Goals vs. FG Rush
			3. Pride & Joy (Return) vs. Pride
			4. Onside Prevent
			5. Pride vs. Pride & Joy

6. FG vs. Scouts (Rush)
7. Punt Safe vs. Pride (Priority)- (Poocher)
8. Kickoff Return (Squib, Pooch)

8	5:41	9	- Individual
9	5:50	10	- Pub (2 Deep) (5) 2 Deep (5) Blitz
10	6:00	10	- Team vs. Scouts
11	6:10	10	- Team vs. Varsity (3rd. & Long (No Blitz)
12	6:20	5	- Team vs. Scouts (Field Goals)
	6:25		- Conditioning – (Rocket, Rainbow, Lazer, Scramble – Perfect Plays – Deep Balls.
	6:30		- Off the field

Here is another thing that came from the revisions we made in our program eight years ago. Basically, we have two ways of punishing a player. We have Reminders. This is where a player does 40 seconds of Up-Downs, then 20 seconds of rest, and you continue until you think the player is *Reminded* of the violation. The other way is for serious offenses. We have Wednesday Sunrise Service. Our conditioning coach has it during the season. During the spring the position coach is responsible for the Sunrise Service.

We decided eight years ago how we would handle discipline. We said, "If you screwed up you are going to be punished." Sometimes it becomes a matter who you screwed up for as far as your position coach Some coaches may run the steps, another coach may give them Up-Downs. The punishment is not the issue. The issue is the fact that they screwed up. Our goal is to keep you from screwing up. "Do things right every time." Now, if a player screws up, he gets punished one way or the other. If it is Sunrise Service we go on with it. We are not so concerned about the punishment end of it. I think that is important. I do not think that punishment is the issue. The important thing is not to screw up and that is the issue and to do things right.

Back to Wednesday's practice. Before we start with period 1 we have a Special period. This is not so much for the punter and field-goal kicker as it is for the backups on our special teams. Sometimes those guys will go through a week's practice and not get any work. We work on all phases of the kicking game. We are spread out with each group working on a different phase.

We have the punters in one group with the punt return men at the other end. We have the snappers working with the punters. In another area we have the field-goal kickers working at one area. I have the kickoff men working at another area. I take the guys that are on the return kickoff team fielding pooch kicks.

We have our punt block drill in another area. Everyone will be involved in the punt block. That includes the Pride And Joy players, and the people on defense that would be rushing on a punt safe situation. We use that if the ball is on our 40-yard line and we do not expect the punt. We like to work on a line on this drill. We want the ball on a line. We do that so the defenders can line up as close as they can on that line and know they are on side. We get a landmark back 8 yards deep. I have a back up punter kicking in this drill. We are not going to take a chance with our starting punter.

The punter is going to make a soft kick. The defense is going to come to the landmark and take the ball off the punter's foot. We just go one at a time as the punter makes the soft kick. Everyone gets a chance to block a kick. You want them back where the punter is as much as you can get them so they will feel secure back there. When they get into a game they will know what it is like if you practice it in that manner.

We are still on that Wednesday practice schedule. Here is the kicking period. This is period 7. Everyone stops and comes to one field. The first thing is our Pride versus the Pride And Joy. The first kick is against a rush. If we do not block the punt it is an automatic punt return, one way of the other. Our punt team is covering. We have the whole operation in that drill. We will go downfield and touch the punt return man with two hands.

Next we go to our field goal versus field-goal rush. This is the period when I have the bullhorn and things really speed up. I go faster, talk louder, and we are really moving. It is a slow period because you are bringing people on and off he field but it is a fast-paced drill. Again, we only rush three players. Then we go Pride And Joy versus Pride. This time we are working on the return.

The next thing we do is to work on receiving the onside kick. We have our Hands Team on the field. I feel it is important to work on this every week. It comes down to this play a lot of the times. If you get it fine, but you have to work on it. I like for those guys to get used to handling the ball on those kicks. If the ball is kicked high we can call for the fair catch. If it is going out of bounds we can knock it out of bounds. We do all of those things but we give them a chance to practice it during the week.

We come back with Pride versus Pride And Joy again. Then we go field goal versus field goal block. Usually we go against our team and not the scout team here.

Next we work on Punt Safe versus Pride. We put the ball on our 40-yard line and we are going to kick it inside our 10-yard line. Our defense will stay in the game and we put a man back at the 10-yard line. We work on this both ways.

Then we get our kickoff return team out there and we squib or pooch the ball to them. Those are the eight things we do in a 10-minute period.

Another thing we do. We work against our best a lot more now. We do not sit there and work against the scout team for 30 minutes. All we were getting by going periods 5, 6, and 7 was this: the scout team was getting a workout and we were knocking them off the ball 4 or 5 yards. We end up practicing bad habits. All it amounts to is an assignment check. You are not going to get better going

against the scout team all of the time. What happens when you go good against good you get fundamentally better. You can improve as the season goes along. Sometimes the offense is not the same or the defense is not the same. But, to me, if you have rule blocking, this is one of the best things we do to improve our football team.

We go best against best for 10 minutes and come back the next period and go against the scout team. They are fresh and ready to go. Now you can work on special adjustments, blitzes, motion, and whatever you will be facing that week.

The next period we come back and go best against best again. Now we work on third-and-long. We make it a critical situation. We call out the Down and Distance. We run the play and see if we get the first down. We get some competition going. It is good against good.

Then we will come back and work against the scout team again and work on some other phase of the game. Most of the time that will be goal-line offense and defense. By alternating against the scout team and best against best, you save your scout team, and you get better as the season goes along. When you work good people against good people they just work harder. We never tackle them down to the ground. We do not tackle. We butt off, and we do not chop block, and we do not block low during this period. The first three steps are full speed. You can get the game momentum when you do that.

Another thing we do on Wednesday is something we like. At the end of practice we work on conditioning. I think there is a time when everyone should condition together. I think it is a part of football. You want everyone to go through something tough. We do not just run them for conditioning. We have a plan and everyone works on their aspect of the game. For example, with the quarterbacks we have we do not work on the scramble. We have an organized way of handling the situation. If you are a receiver and the quarterback starts running around, if you are running a short route you change the route when you see the quarterback scramble and go deep. If the receiver runs the Out route and sees the quarterback scramble he turns upfield. If he runs a deep post route and sees the quarterback scrambling he comes back to the ball. We want an organized way for those receivers to do that. So we work on that drill. Everyone gets their running in during the drill.

Another thing we do for conditioning is to throw the Deep Balls. You cannot get enough of this drill. We like to use it for conditioning at times.

The kickoff team does not meet with the kicking team on Monday. We meet to start the practice on Thursday to go over what they are going to do. This is a situation that we ask the group to do a little extra by having the kicking team meeting.

THURSDAY PRACTICE

Per.	Time	Min.	Schedule
	4:15	10	- Flex
1	4:25	10	- Kickoff Return
2	4:35	10	- Kickoff Coverage (1) Lanes
3	4:45	5	- Pride & Joy Rush
4	4:50	10	- Offensive 3rd & Long Skeleton vs. Scouts
5	5:00	5	- Goal Line Pass Skeleton vs. (Scouts)
6	5:05	5	- Pride (1 Fake) (2 Taking a Safety)
7	5:10	10	- 2-Minute Drill vs. Varsity
8	5:20	10	- Team (Clock) Dress Rehearsal Defense – 1st 4th Down (Punt Return of Punt Safe Offense – Barnyard (5)
9	5:30	10	- Team
10	5:40	10	- Team Field Goal (2) Field Goal Block (2)
	5:50	5	- Central Meeting
	5:55		- Off the field

The first thing we do on Thursday is to work on Kickoff Returns. That stays pretty constant as far as how you are going to return the kick. There may be a couple of things that you change, but basically it stays the same.

Next we do Kickoff Coverage. Some changes occur here but the basics do not change.

Then we have Pride And Joy. That is our Punt Block versus the scout team. If you are going to be a good punt blocking team you have to give your people chances to work on it. This is what we do. We have the second punter back deep to work on the punt block. He has a soft football to punt. Again we have our Landmark set in front of the area where he will be kicking. The landmark is at 8 yards from the center. The punter kicks the ball over that landmark. It can be a towel on the ground to mark the spot.

We are always going to block by numbers. We number our players 1 through 10 from the left to our right. We will run this drill with only one half of the line rushing. I will call out the number of the defender that I want to make the block on the kick. The offense will let that man go free. However, everyone has to come off the ball expecting to block the kick. A lot of times, what happens on punt blocks is this: the rusher is slow coming off the ball and then he realizes that he is free. He comes after the punt but just misses it because he is too late. We want them coming off the ball expecting to make the block.

We ask the front line to pull the blockers on each side of the man we are sending after the block. When a rusher gets knocked off of his course we ask him to continue his rush on the outside. What happens is this. When you do get a block inside, the ball will come rolling out on the outside. Now they can pick the ball up and take it to the end zone. Also, one of these days the punter is going to pull the ball down and run with it. If that happens we will have a man outside to make the tackle. That is why we want them to continue the rush when they are knocked off their rush lane. If they are blocked solid they need to stop and then start working outside.

Then we go to the other side of the line and do the same thing. We leave the center out of this drill. We want to give each of the rushers a chance to block the punt. After we block the kick we start working to get the ball into the end zone. It goes fast but you are working on the principles of blocking the kick. We always expect to block the kick.

After a couple of periods we come to period 6 and have our Pride period. If we are going to use a fake kick that week we will work on it at this time. We do work on taking a Safety but most of the time we do that on Friday. We usually work on something special during this session.

We work on our team offense and defense. We are going up and down the field with the different teams. If we call for the Field-Goal Block Team they come on the field immediately. When we call out a team, out they go on the field. We practice this a lot. We had better not have a penalty for too many people on the field and we do not want to end up with not enough men on the field. We work on getting the different teams on and off the field.

FRIDAY PRACTICE

Per.	Time	Min.	Schedule
	4:00		- Flex in Groups
	4:10		- Individual
	4:15		- Central Meeting
	4:20		

Pride
1. Poocher (vs. Punt Safe)
2. Kicking Out
3. Kick at (5) Sec.
4. 11-Man Rush
5. Take Safety

Kickoff Return
1. Pop Up
2. Ball blocked (behind or past LOS)
3. "Peter" or "Short" vs. Return
4. Kicker Loses Protection
5. Block Kick close to LOS
6. Fake

Field-Goal Rush
1. Jump

2. Ball blocked (behind or past LOS)

Field Goal
1. Jump on ball
2. Cover

Kickoff Coverage
1. Squib
2. Onside
3. After 15-yard penalty
4. After a Safety

Punt Safe

Onside Prevent

4:35	-1. Break to Offense - Defense
4:55	- Off the field

One thing we do now I got from Bobby Ross when he was with the San Diego Chargers. It was right after they had made the NFL playoffs. He told me one of the best things they did was to take the best plays of the last game and show them to the team before the next game. We started doing that. We show the film on Friday night. You will never see a play in the film that is not a good play. We make the session fun for the players. The players will cheer and yell and carry on. It is a good session for us. You can ask our players what is one of the things they enjoy about football at Tech and they will tell you it is Friday Night Video.

The basis for the film is that it is all positive plays. We may add some funny clips in the film. But every play that they see is a great play by their teammates from the previous week. We do it win or lose. I think this is a good thing. Sometimes when you lose you need that more than you do when you win. I believe it is important what people think when it comes to winning.

Friday is really a big kicking day. We go out and break a sweat. We go over different situations in the kicking game. We will punt from the 10-yard line and from the 1-yard line. We want to make sure we do not have any problems in this area. We work against the 11-man rush where we just want the punter to take a rocker step and kick the ball. We work on taking a safety with our punt team. We will block you up front and have the punter run out of the end zone.

When we work on our Pride And Joy we line up and tell them this punt is going to be blocked. The punter catches the ball and then throws it down on one side or the other. He may throw the ball on the other side of the line of scrimmage. If it is behind the line of scrimmage we are going to try to get it into the end zone. If it is on the other side of the line of scrimmage we are going get away from the ball. The ruling is the same on a field goal. We work on the short punt. We do not want the short punt coming down and hitting one of our linemen. That is what we do with Pride And Joy.

Next we work on field goal blocks. We do the same thing here that we did on the punt. We tell them the field goal try is going to be a blocked kick. The center snaps the ball and the holder will throw the ball down. If the ball goes behind the line of scrimmage we pick it up. If it is beyond the line of scrimmage we stay away from it. We work on this every week.

Then we work on kicking field goals. If it is a long attempt we want to make sure we cover.

We work on the kickoff coverage. We work on the squib, onside, a kick after a penalty, and kicking after a safety.

Then we go to our Punt Safe drill. After that we work on the Onside Prevent Team. Those are the things we work on for Friday. Basically this is our schedule for the week.

Some other thoughts I have on the kicking game. Most of these things apply mostly to the college level. I would strive to have at least two snappers, two kickers, and two holders. In 1992 we went down to Southern Miss and our first field-goal kicker got hurt. We had to bring in our second kicker. He kicked two field goals and we won the game. That started us on a winning streak and we have gone to seven straight bowl games. I have often wondered what would have happened if we had not had another field-goal kicker. To me it is important to work not only the starter but also the backup player.

A lot of teams do not give scholarships to kickers. They want to have them walk on and try out. I feel if the kicker is good enough you give him a scholarship.

I think it is important to develop depth in the kicking game, not only in college but in high school as well. This is true with punters, kickers, and snappers.

If I am hiring coaches I always ask about special teams experience. If they have special teams experience it is a plus for me. I have coaches on our staff that can sit down and talk about special teams and it is a good discussion because the coaches know what they are talking about.

We say this: A kicker is coached by one person. I know the fundamentals of kicking. But I do not mess with our kickers. I think the punter needs to go to only one guy. If that guy knows his swing and style that is the only guy he should go to. My point is that only one coach should be with the kicker. If he does not have a guy to go to them you may be able to help him.

I think catching the punts is the same thing. I think it is the toughest thing do in college and high school football. The more you can work on this the better off you are. Usually the punt return man is the player that catches most of them in practice.

We want our kickers to be team players. We want them to do everything the rest of the team does. We do not have a different set of rules for the kickers. The conditioning is the same and they follow the same rules. They are regular members of our team. On Saturday morning we go for a walk before the game to stretch them out. I walk with the kickers. I do not worry about it when things are going good, I worry about it when things are not going so well. I think they must fit into your team. The more they fit in, it is easier to get them through the bad times. If they miss a kick they are part of the team. You are not going to grab them by the throat. I think it is important that your specialists are treated the same as the rest of the team.

We have a Pride And Joy meeting just before the pregame meal. We ask them if they have any questions. We block a lot of punts. We usually have everyone covered. We have someone responsible for every man. It takes on a great deal of importance because it is the last thing we do before the pregame meal. We review all of their assignments in the meeting.

I am going to cover one additional thing before I stop. This started with Mike Godfried when we were together at Murray State. We have a session on the last Saturday before our opening game. We have about 80 play situations we go over. It used to be about 70 situations but it has increased to about 80 plays now. We have a scrimmage with all of the unusual things that happen in a game. It covers everything you can think of. Everyone will tell you they cover these situations, but I think it is good to physically go through these situations on the field.

When we started doing all of these different situations we realized most of them are related to the kicking game. When we come on the field we have one player calling out Pride And Joy. When we say Pride And Joy you better be out there. If you have everyone screaming when they come off the field you can't tell what is being said, so we have one player calling out the team that is going on the field. We have only one player calling out the teams. Then if something happens I am going back to that one guy.

When we score and go for two points on the PAT is another situation we cover in this session. If we score on defense we make sure the players do not come on the field or off the field until they know if we are going for 1 or 2 points.

We go through all the rules that we must cover related to those special situations. For example if a kick is blocked when we are kicking from our 5-yard line we tell the kicker to kick the ball out of the end zone and take a safety rather than giving them the ball inside the 5-yard line.

On our Pride situations we cover what to do if the punt is blocked. If it is blocked and the ball is behind the line of scrimmage we can advance the ball. We try to pick it up and run with it. We do not want them to throw the ball because we probably have players downfield.

We cover those situations that are unusual. One more situation we cover is the Field Goal Fire. If we get a bad snap we call "fire." We work on that situation. We work on the third-down field goal. If we block the kick we are going to get on the ball. We do not want the kicking team to fall on it and get another kick. If we get a bad snap on a field-goal try with eight seconds left we will throw it at the feet of the up back and kick it on fourth down.

I want to remind you of our Kicking Clinic on July 15. I always like to say something about NIKE. They have been very good to us at Virginia Tech. I think they are good for football. Anytime you can support them I would appreciate it. It has been good being with you and I hope I see you in Blacksburg. Thanks very much.

CRACK SCREEN PASS AND RECEIVER DRILLS

MARSHALL UNIVERSITY

I want to start today by telling you that I hope you leave with one or two points that will help you in your program. That is our job as college coaches. College coaches get as much out of talking with the high school coaches as we do from pro coaches. I want to thank Nike and the clinic staff for having me. The state of Kentucky has been very good to the Herd in recruiting and we hope it will continue.

The last four years Marshall University has been blessed with some great players, which helps any offensive or defensive scheme. Great players make great coaches, which I am sure you are aware of. Our Head Coach, Bob Pruett, is 50-4 over the last four seasons and is truly one of the "good guys" in this business. In our four years at Marshall, the Herd has accomplished the following:
• WON A NATIONAL TITLE.
• WON THREE CONSECUTIVE EASTERN DIVISION MAC CHAMPIONSHIPS.
• WON THREE CONSECUTIVE MAC CONFERENCE CHAMPIONSHIPS.
• BEEN TO THREE CONSECUTIVE BOWL GAMES.
• HAD TWO UNDEFEATED SEASONS.
• HAD TWO HEISMAN TROPHY FINALISTS.
• HAD TWO STRAIGHT BOWL VICTORIES.
• A BILETNIKOFF AWARD WINNER.
• A TOP 10 NATIONAL RANKING AFTER HAVING BEEN IN DIVISION I FOR JUST THREE YEARS.

The first thing I want to talk about today is a Screen Pass that I think is very underrated. It has been very productive for us. You can run the play out of any set that you want. First we will go through the technique and then I have some film to view. Like the University of Kentucky, we have 1001 Screen plays. If you want to talk about any of them I will be around and we can sit down and visit.

I want to tell you what you need to know about this one particular screen. A lot of times coaches will lecture but they will not tell you the problems on a certain play or how to solve the problems. They give you the techniques on how to run it, but they do not cover the problems you will face. I want to tell you from A to Z about the play. I do not have any secrets. Only the defensive people have secrets.

I want to talk about the Crack Screen. This play will help your Dropback Passing Game. It will help you save your quarterback and save your line and your backs. It will help your receivers as well. It is a team concept. The theory behind this play is to get leverage on the cornerback and to get the ball to the running back turned up field headed north and south. This is a different way to run the Sweep without blocking. If I could tell you we can get the ball to your running back where he will be one on one with the cornerback with 5 or 6 yards between the two, would you take it? Absolutely! That is the situation you want most of the time when you run the sweep. We are trying to create a one on one situation with someone that is a good runner.

We like to run the Crack Screen to an open end rusher. If you are an I Formation Team we like to run it to the Twin side or to the split end side. It works better because you get a wider rusher. It helps to have a wide 5 technique to that side because the running back can get out underneath him easier than he can against a tighter technique. We like to run it to the reduced side because the outside man has contain. We feel we can get underneath him.

The running back in this protection is responsible for the Will Linebacker who has the flat. If it is an 8-Man Front it is the Strong Safety, Rover type of man. If that man blitzes the running back has to chip him on the way out to the flat. You will understand this when you see it on the film. You must understand in the protection, the back to whom you are going to run the screen has the weakside Linebacker or Strong Safety type person.

You can use any formation imaginable to execute this screen. You can us any running back or you can use a motion player on the play. The best thing about the play is that it is easy to run.

The base rules are this. The widest receiver to the call cracks the first defender inside of him off the line of scrimmage. The second receiver to the call cracks the second defender inside of him off the line of scrimmage. The third receiver, if there is one, cracks the third defender inside of him off the line of scrimmage. Note: if the receivers' defender blitzes, they do not block them. They continue on to the next defender or the next lever. We do not block the cornerback, hoping to gain leverage on him by the receivers crossing the field.

It is legal to crack block in high school above the waist. You must get the head in front of the man. The first time you run the play you are going to get a high light film play on it. After you have run it a few times the defense will be aware of what you are doing and then it becomes a matter of getting in front of the defender. The key to the block is to make the man go underneath. Do not let him go over the top on the man.

The running back slips under the playside tackle out into the flat area and catches the ball one yard behind the line of scrimmage. Then he turns up field. If the weak side Linebacker blitzes it is the running backs job to chip him on the way out.

COACHING POINTS:

WIDE RECEIVERS – On the crack block – stay above the waist and keep your head in front of the defender. Never loose the defender or next

level if your man disappears. Go hard early then get under control – stay on the move. First time the block is a killer shot, after that it is a controlled stalk block.

RUNNING BACKS – Must have a clean release at all cost. Catch the ball behind the line of scrimmage. Get your head around quickly and find the ball. Chip inside pad of the weak side Linebacker if he comes and spill him outside.

OFFENSIVE LINE – Know where the ball is going. Play side tackle, invite a wide rusher up field. Play side tackle, attack the defensive end and cut him if he does not rush.

QUARTERBACK - Execute the 5-Step Drop. Make an accurate throw. Adjust on the run.

The best time to call the play is against any blitz situation. Work on zone blitz looks because they are more difficult. It is good against Man-to-Man looks and Cover 2 Man. Also, it is good when the corner starts to chase crossing routes.

We can adjust the play and run it to the tight end instead of the running back as a change up. We can game plan an Arc Scheme.

Next let me talk about the protection. First, let me talk about the running back's responsibility. The running back's key is to step under the play-side tackle. Play side is the side we are running the ball to. The offensive tackle is in a Max Protection Scheme. We are blocking Big-on-Big. The tackle is going to step back and invite the rusher outside. The running back sets back just like a normal pass play. Next, the back comes under the tackle but behind the line of scrimmage. He is one-half yard to a yard behind the line of scrimmage. All you want to do is to have the running back behind the line of scrimmage. Why do we have to have him behind the line of scrimmage? Because we are blocking downfield. That is a big key. It is the job of the running back to find a way out. It is his job to make sure he gets outside cleanly. That is why we like to run the play into a wide rusher.

This is our Protection 75. I will go over all of the positions using Max Protection. It is important to let the line know where the Screen is going. For us it is Odd numbers to the left and the Even numbers to the right. We are Big on Big in our protection. If they have a man over them they block them. If they do not have a man over them they are working with someone on the Linebackers.

A-Tackle: Max Protection – If end freezes, cut him. We tell him to invite a rusher. We want him to make the man go outside and at the same time we want him to give ground so the back can go underneath him for the pass. Again if the end does not rush we want to go cut him or we want to drive block him. Can we drive block the man downfield? Absolutely. Why? Because the pass is thrown behind the line of scrimmage. Is this the ideal situation? NO! But, why are we running this play? To slow down the rush and to get the ball to one of our best backs.

G –Guard: Max Protection

C – Center: Max Protection

O-Guard: Max Protection

B-Tackle: Max Protection

Y End: Max Protection

Quarterback: Execute 5-Step Drop. We balance on our fifth step. He is ready to throw the ball on the fifth step. We tell him to make an accurate throw because the back is not use to making great catches. We tell him to put the ball in the bread basket of the running back. We tell him to adjust on the run. We may have to check the play. The defense may call it out. He may have to throw the ball over a rusher who is running a blitz. He has to be a player at some point. It is not always going to be like we draw it up on the board.

Running back: Free release inside tackle. Stay 1 yard behind line of scrimmage. If blitzer comes, take the edge.

A Back: Crack first man inside off the line of scrimmage. Never lose man over the top. Block levels if your man is taken.

Z Back: Crack first man inside of the line of scrimmage. Never lose man over the top. Block levels if your man is taken.

X Receiver: Crack first man inside of the line of scrimmage. Never lose man over the top. Block levels if your man is taken.

MAX PROTECTION: 75

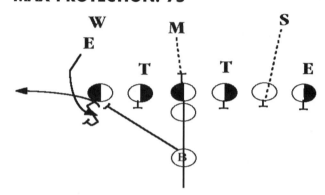

CRACK SCREEN – 1 RECEIVER SIDE

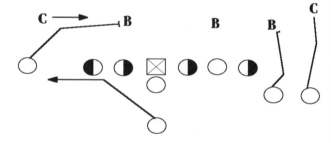

CRACK SCREEN – 2 RECEIVER SIDE

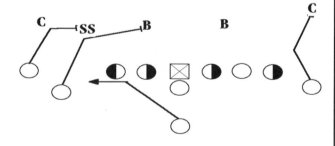

CRACK SCREEN – 3 RECEIVER SIDE

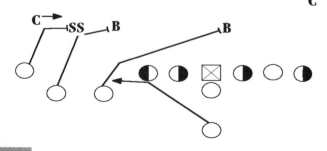

We can make adjustments on the play. We can run the Arc Scheme. This is where we block one man down inside and bring one man around the outside to block on the outside. All that is to us is a G-Scheme that we use on our Toss Sweep. Instead of sending the fullback out we bring someone else out. If the defense stops one thing we do another.

CRACK SCREEN - ARC OPTION 3 REC

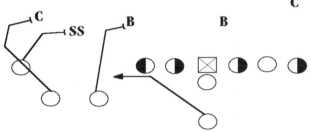

CRACK SCREEN – ARC OPTION 2 REC

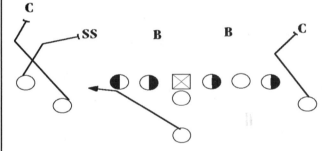

If you have a tight end that you want to get the ball to this is a good play. We are a one-back team so that tight end was our other running back in a sense. We just release him out in the flat and have him come back behind the line and we throw to him.

TIGHT END CRACK SCREEN

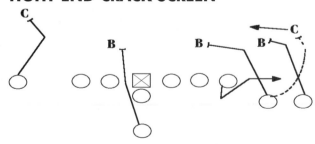

We can put the Arc Option on it by bringing the inside man out on the corner on the Arc Block.

We have used these screens against everyone. It does not matter what level you are on, you can use these plays. Now, it helps when you have superior personnel at key positions. At Marshall, we feel that because of the style of offense we run, we will always have an opportunity to attract the big time skill kids. By getting the ball into the running backs hands on the perimeter, we will always have a chance for a successful play.

I am going to show you a film of these plays and then I am going to cover the RECEIVER DRILLS. I will go quick on the overhead and then I will show them on the tape.

When Randy Moss won the Biletnikoff Award I had the time of my life. I got to go to Tallahassee, Florida, and visit with Fred Biletnikoff personally. I was with him by himself for a day and a half. I was in heaven. One, that was my idol. Anyone that could play in the NFL but could not run out of sight in a week, and then can be the MVP in the Super Bowl, is my idol. This may surprise you but he takes people that have never played football and works with them. He has coached some track players and some others that were not great football players. He goes back to the basics. That is what I want to talk about: Basic Receiver Drills.

First is the 4-Cone Drill. We set up four cones in a square 10 yards apart and 10 yards distance. This drill is used to teach the breaking point. Teach them how to plant their feet on a pass route. Teach them how to make a cut. The shoulders technique, arm movement, hands movement, and acceleration are taught in the drill. This drill is what we use to start out with.

4-CONES DRILL – RIGHT-FOOT PLANT

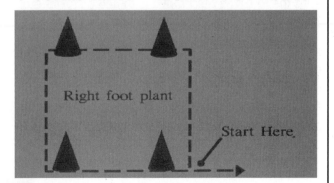

4-CONES DRILL – LEFT-FOOT PLANT

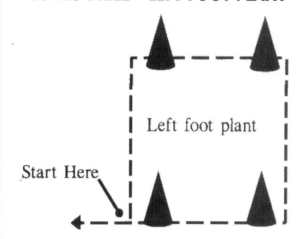

Left foot plant

Start Here

4-CONES DRILL AROUND 2ND CONE/RT

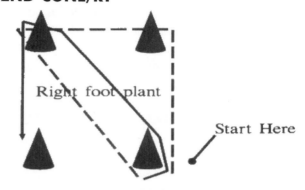

Right foot plant

Start Here

4-CONES DRILL AROUND 2ND CONE/LT

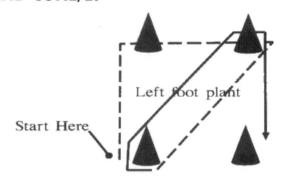

Left foot plant

Start Here

You can tell them they can go a little past the cones. They do not have to be exact. This is a square cut, not a speed cut. They have to hit on the outside foot. A lot of the receivers will give you the airplane effect. When they get ready to make that turn they want to throw the arms out. If I am a defensive back I am going to break up on that guy every time.

The next thing he does is what we call the parachute. He takes his hands and brings them straight down to his side. How many guys do you see run the 40-yard sprint with their arms down? None if they are worth a darn. Have them pump the arms. Even if you have to stop them, show them how to pump the arms. They may have to walk it a few times before they can run it with any speed. As they get better speed it up.

After they get to the point where they can run the drill with a little speed we add a football. Have his hands pop up and catch the ball and then get back into the run. The next move is to add a stutter step to the drill. It is unlimited what you can do with the drill. Use your imagination.

Next is the same drill with a variation. We use the same setup as the other drill but change the way we run it. We want them to work around the second cone back to the starting position and then back around to the second cone and then to the finish point.

Next is the One-Hand Drill. It teaches hand placement and ball concentration. Have a ball machine set to shoot at eye level and on a medium speed. Have them switch sides so they can use both hands. You can throw the ball if you do not have a ball machine.

Next is the Partner One-Hand Drill. This teaches teamwork, hand placement, and ball concentration. Have a ball machine set to shoot at eye level and at a medium speed. Each wide receiver should put up one hand to make the catch. It becomes a two-hand catch with both of them working together as one to catch the ball. Have them switch sides so they use both hands.

We teach them to catch the ball with the thumbs together and the index finger outside if the ball is up above the waist. If the ball is below the waist the pinkies come together and the thumbs go outside. We pair off the Z's together, the running backs together, the tight ends and slots together, and the

X receivers together. We make it a contest. The team that wins does not have to run. The losers have to run a sprint or a lap or whatever you agree to at the start of the drill. We do not want our guys making one-hand catches in games, but when we do, it is usually very big.

Next are the Net Drills. Hang a Net from any goal post. This will keep the footballs from going all over the place. These nets can be purchased through any major catalog. To start out, we place the receivers in front of the net of the goal post. You can do the drill with the receivers standing or running. Have the receivers switch sides after each catch. The quarterbacks throw the ball in front, behind, then right, and then left of the receivers. They mix the throws up. By doing this drill you are not running your receivers to death.

NET DRILL – STANDING/RUNNING

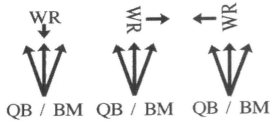

When you throw the ball to the receivers, make sure they settle a little at the end of the route. If they are coming back on a Curl route have them settle just a little as they come back to concentrate. Have them throttle down or shorten the stride down. They must watch the ball until the tuck.

NET DRILL–PLANT AND CUT

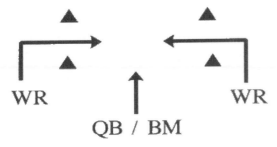

Have the receivers come down 2 or 3 yards and make a square plant and cut through the two cones across the net. The receivers come square across

in front of the net. The quarterback or coach throws the ball in various bad spots. (Low ball, high ball, behind, in front, and in any combinations of these.)

From that drill we add the Hidden Ball Drill and the Deflection Ball. We have the receiver run across in front of the net while a manager or coach or another receiver waves a pad or his arms in front of the area where the receiver is to catch the ball. The detractors should move the pads or their arms at the last minute.

Next is the Bag or Cones Drill. We set up two standup bags or two cones to simulate holes or areas to work into. We use this drill to teach coming back to the ball, working to find the "hole" or open area. We work on techniques with the break point, arms, shoulders, hands in the break point, and working around linebackers in the middle of the field.

We use the Goal Post Drill. You need a goal post or a shinny pole. Have the player straddle the post and rest his chest area on the post as he faces the passer. He extends his arms and catches the ball with both hands. This is used to teach the receivers to catch the ball with the hands and not the body.

We use the Line Drill as a warm-up type drill. We have a line of receivers facing one direction and use the 5-yard line marks as a break point. When the receivers reach the yard lines they work their feet as if they were getting ready to break down at the top of the route. We use this to work on the break point by feeling the plant in the break point. We work down the field and back. We use as much of the field as we can.

On the Ball Adjust Drill we work down a yard line and have a coach throw the ball over each shoulder, over the top of the head, and short of the receiver. This drill will make the receiver adjust to the ball while moving. The receivers can run at half speed or less. Here is a coaching point. Have the receiver make as little turn as possible when catching the ball so he can continue running down the line. On the short balls the receiver may have to slow down or even stop to catch the ball. Try to get the receiver to keep his shoulders square. This is used to teach the receiver to adjust to the ball thrown over the shoulders on deep passes.

The best way to teach catching the football is to catch the ball as many times a day as possible. A ball machine or a quarterback throwing to a receiver in as many possible situations is by far the best device to use. These are some of the drills we use. Teaching the receiver to come back to the ball is big. We have the receivers work back to the ball machine or to the quarterback. We throw the ball in different places. Have the receiver set as he comes to the ball. You can incorporate all types of cone drills and break points with the comeback drill.

COMEBACK DRILL

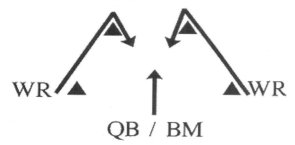

WR   WR

QB / BM

Next is our Around-the-Clock Drill. It is a good warm-up drill. Have the receivers and the quarterbacks line up 5 to 10 yards apart. We throw the ball around

AROUND THE CLOCK

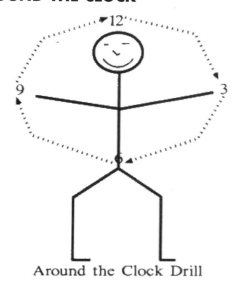

Around the Clock Drill

the clock. If you do not have quarterbacks use receivers to throw. Throw the ball at 12, 3, 6, and 9 o'clock. The head is 12 , the shoulder is 3, the groin is 6, and the other shoulder is 9 o'clock. This is a great time to practice good catching habits—eyes on the ball, tuck, four-point pressure, etc.

The Box Drill is another good warm-up drill. It is used to work on deep ball landmarks. I use this drill mainly for the Post and the Go Routes. Have the receiver start off three quarters speed and have him stick hard at the break point and adjust to the ball. Work one way then turn around and work back the other way.

With so much man-to-man defense played today this may be the most important drill you do all day. If you get the press defense as we do, you have to work against it. We work on it quite a bit as we see a lot of press defenses.

We have a drill we call the Press Drill. We have the receivers pair up. One works as a defensive back and the other is a receiver. We work on the inside release, outside release, and they switch off. You can work any or all of these combinations. Time is the big factor. Find out what the group does best and work on it more.

On the Double Move we work two short stick moves and then back to the original side. On the Speed Release we work immediately past the defensive back on the best release side. We work on Quick Hands by having the receivers slap down or up on the defensive back's hands/arms and take the best release.

The Rip Move is good for smaller receivers against physical defensive backs. The receiver takes the offside arm and rips it low and through the defensive back. He turns his shoulders slightly as he rips and gets by the defensive back.

The Swim Move is better for the taller receivers. The receiver pins the arm of the defensive back to the side he is releasing to. He then takes the offside arm over and by the defensive back. Then he gets by the defensive back.

This is what we call the NFL Cone Drill. Really, it is just a 20-yard shuttle run. It is a three-cone drill used by the NFL to test quickness and change of direction. As a receiver one must be able to change directions quickly with little or no wasted movement. This drill is a good way to get what you are looking for. We have the receivers go in pairs to get the competition effect with the drill.

NFL CONE DRILL – 20-YARD SHUTTLE

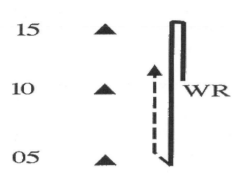

Set the cones 5 yards apart. Start either on the right or the left. Touch with the same hand all the way through.

The last drill is what I call Ball Now Drill. It is used for hand-eye coordination and quickness in the break. It is important to note that the receiver is square to the ball when he turns around. We have the receiver turn his back to the quarterback or ball machine. He gets into a squared-up and a slightly bent-knee stance. When the coach says "BALL," the wide receiver must turn around, square up, and catch the ball. First he turns to the right and the next time he turns to the left. You can increase speed on the drill as needed.

BALL NOW DRILL

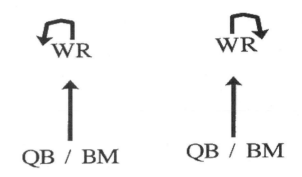

One point I want to make about catching the ball. We know we use peripheral vision to make a lot of catches. If we tell the players to catch the ball with their CHIN their eyes will follow to the ball. If we just look at the ball they will not turn their chin. If the chin turns the eyes will follow. Put your chin on the ball and the eyes will follow.

There is as little dot on the ball. We put them on every ball. You can paint the dot and put a number in the dot. Have the receivers follow that dot in catching the ball. Put the chin on the dot and the eyes will follow.

Men it has been a pleasure. MAY GOD BLESS YOU.

PUNT COVERAGE AND FAKE PUNTS

SEVIER COUNTY HIGH SCHOOL, TENNESSEE

Being from Tennessee I tend to talk fast. If I get going too fast just raise your hand and slow me down. I am going to cover two subjects today. First I will talk about our Punt Protection. However, most of my time will be spent on how we try to spread the defense in our Punting Game. I want to stress the fact that we have not taken a lot of risk, but I do want to show you how we have been able to come up with some big plays.

Few plays are as exciting as a fake punt on special teams when they are successful. A good example in Pro Football was the TD the Titans scored at the end of the game to beat Buffalo. The rest of the week after the game every time you turned on the TV you saw that play.

The best special teams story I have heard happened to a friend of mine who was coaching high school football. The coach was Louis Thompson who had played at Alabama for Bear Bryant. They scored a TD and decided to go for the kick for the PAT. Louis grabbed his center before he went out for the PAT and told him the PAT was crucial and that the team had to have it to win the game.

The center went out on the field and came up to the line of scrimmage and started talking to the defense. Soon he got over the ball and snapped it back to the holder and the kicker split the uprights with the kick. The defense just stood there and did not make an effort to block the kick. The officials signaled the PAT good and the teams went back to their benches. As the center came off the field Louis grabbed him and asked him what in the world did you tell the defense on that PAT? The center replied. "I told the defense the first snap was going to be a practice snap!" Now, what is sad about that move is this. If someone tried that on our team we would probably fall for it. How

many times in practice have you heard a coach yell out, "Take a few practice snaps."

We go to camp every year at Chattanooga Baylor Prep. We stay a week down there. Before we leave Baylor we will scrimmage 13 times and have two kicking scrimmages. I do not know what some of you can do about preseason scrimmages, but in Tennessee we are not limited on scrimmages. I play everyone that goes with us to camp. We run a kicking game scrimmage that runs for about 20 minutes and we wear them out in that session. We take another team and work on the kicking game. We run a quick whistle on all of the plays. All contact is above the waist. Every Friday at camp we run this scrimmage. We run it twice against two different teams while we are at camp. There are four teams at camp and we scrimmage all week long.

This past year I told Coach Thompson that we were going to try the "practice snap" on one of the teams in the scrimmages at camp. So when we started working on the PAT's I called the center over and told him to go up to the ball and tell the defense that this was going to be a practice snap. He did and it worked. The other coaches wanted to know why the defense just stood there. Now, we have not had the guts to call it in a real game, but I think it would probably work.

At Sevier County High School we do not have a great deal of speed. We play against teams in our region that have a lot of speed. In 1997 we were a state semifinalist team. We had 21 seniors on the team and we lost all of them. In 1998 we had one returning starter and he was a defensive tackle. We had to play kids that should have been playing JV ball. We were not athletic enough to cover anyone downfield on the kicks. We did not have the speed to get downfield and we had a freshman punter. Other than that we had a pretty good punt unit. We played the number 2-rated team in the state in our first game and they beat us 38-10. It could have been a lot worse.

We started grading the film from the game on Friday night. We took a look at our Punting Game. We found out that we had a NET YARDAGE PER PUNT of 5 yards. That was our average, a net 5 yards. Now, we are not real smart, but we are smart enough to know that you cannot be successful with those numbers. This is what led us to running the Fake Punts that we are using now.

I am going to show you a video of our quarterfinal, semifinals, and state championship games. You will see that our punts went virtually uncontested. WHY? Because we successfully faked three punts in the first two rounds of the playoffs. After that no one seemed to want to take a chance of giving up a first down by way of a fake punt. For the past two seasons we are 13-for-20 (65 percent) when you include a pass interference call. We averaged 24 yards on the fake punts. Our punter has led our region his freshman and sophomore seasons. This past year he had a 39.5-yard average.

What we are trying to do on our punting game is to take advantage of whatever the defense gives us. We have not allowed a punt return for a TD since we went to our open set. We have had two punts blocked, and that was my fault. Everything we do on the punts is signaled in from the sideline by me. On the two blocked punts it was poor judgment on my part. Neither of the blocked punts resulted in a score.

Most of the time we are going to punt the football when we line up to punt. This is the way we line up on our regular punt formation. We have two Bullets split wide. We have two contain men on the ends. Our upback will go to the ball side and the punter will become a safety. Our rules on blocking are simple. The center will help with the nose shades if he thinks he can. For outside from line from 2 to 8 they block Inside, On, Outside. This keeps them from blocking air. But, our first responsibility is the inside gap.

PROTECTION/COVERAGE – REGULAR

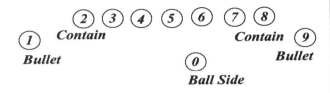

We will line up in this formation with our Bullets lined up in the Guard-Center gap. We use this when we face teams that have great speed on the corner. This helps us get the ball off and it splits the corners out more. The blocking responsibilities are the same.

BULLETS INSIDE GAPS

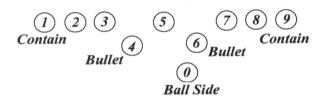

Things get a little different when we add the OPEN look. We will punt from the Open look. We ask the 2 and 8 men to keep the ball inside. We send 1 and 9 after the ball. We have the same blocking assignment with 4, 5, and 6.

OPEN – 19

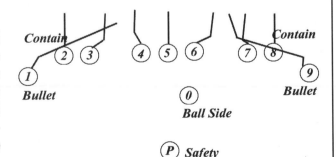

We want our 2 and 3 and 7 and 8 men to keep the ball on their inside shoulder. The inside men have the same blocking rules.

Now, here comes the kicker. If we find someone playing a 4 over 3 in the middle this is what we do. Most teams will put three men on the outside on each side and four men in the middle. They have two down linemen and two linebackers. This is where we must have a call to get back into our Regular Punt Formation. With 4 and 6 on the line and not eligible, teams will widen and come after the punt. Most of the time the defensive ends have more speed and they can get outside and come after the punt and we are stuck. So we must have a way to get back into the regular punt.

4 DEFENDER OVER 3 BLOCKERS

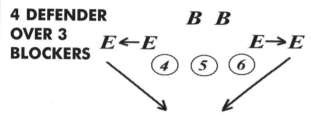

If we want to bring 2, 3, and 7, 8 back inside we call MOVE. If we call MOVE we go back inside with 2, 3, 7, and 8, and leave 1 and 9 outside just like we do on our regular punt. Now the defense has to do the adjusting. That is where I hurt us and allowed the punt to get blocked when I did not see the 4 over 3 situation.

All of the men on our punt team are skilled players. They all have ELIGIBLE NUMBERS. This makes a big difference when we start running the fakes.

Let me get to the Punt Formation Shifts and Fakes. What do we look for? First, we are always looking for any uncovered Receivers. We are looking for good matchups: #62 on our #7. On the outside we usually see three defenders on our three outside men. We usually get 4 over our 3 on the inside. Most teams will line one man deep.

OPEN – ALL SKILLED PLAYERS

Everyone except the center is off the line of scrimmage. That is our Open Set. They move up to the line of scrimmage. The signal from the sideline tells them who is to move up on the line of scrimmage. The upback gets the signal from the sideline. He will call out two numbers. Those two numbers stay where they are. Everyone else moves up. Now you have the defense scrambling to figure out who is eligible and who is not eligible.

What do we call? If we have our skilled players on defensive linemen and a 3 over 3 in the middle, we run our 78 call.

PUNT FAKE – 78

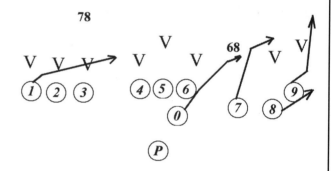

When we run the 78 Fake 1, 2, 3, 4, 5, 6, and 9 must move up on the line of scrimmage. We make a direct snap to the Punter who throws the pass. Again, if we get 4 over 3 in the middle we call MOVE and come back inside if we have 4 and 6 on the line of scrimmage.

If we have an uncovered skill person on the punt team you need to get the ball to him. We have been successful in doing this. We use tailbacks, receivers, and quarterbacks on our Punt Team. This year we had our first three quarterbacks on the Punt Team. We want to get them as much experience as possible.

If we see the defense has us covered we can punt the ball. We punt and cover just like we did in our regular punt formation.

If we have a lineman covering one of our skilled players outside we can call 78 or 68. We want to get something going outside.

We have a call where the ball is snapped directly to the punter and he throws the ball. We have a call where the ball is snapped to the punter and he punts it. We have a call where the ball is snapped to the upback and he throws the pass. It is very simple. You can use all kinds of codes to make the calls.

Most of our fakes come after we move from our Open to our Regular. If any eligible receiver is uncovered, a call from the sideline is made. The snap will go to zero who is our upback who throws to the uncovered receiver. If the ball is on the hash, the bullet into the boundary will go across to be the inside receiver on the wide side.

VS. 4 OVER 3 IN THE MIDDLE

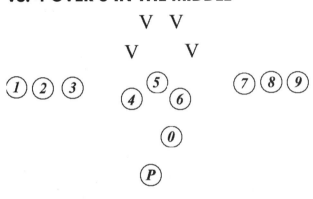

BACKED OFF – PUNT

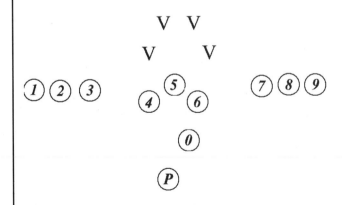

If we get four up on the line of scrimmage we can fake the punt. That is an easy throw. It is a 5- to 10-yard pass. It is like playing pitch and catch. This would be our 46.

4 RUSHING: FAKE – RUN 46 PASS

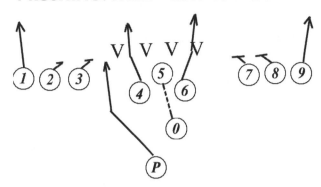

I want to go over some advantages of the Fake Punt.

ADVANTAGES OF FAKING PUNTS

1. First, is time. We work mostly on coverage. The defenses have to work on recognizing and covering the eligible receivers and adjusting to our shifts.

2. Makes setting a wall more difficult due to moving, matching up, and playing pass defense.

3. It requires more open-field blocks and it frees releases.

4. Return Team's aggressiveness is reduced. They are busy lining up and identifying eligible receivers.

5. Their defensive personnel must get on and off the field quickly.

Let me go over some Keys to Remember on the Fake Punt.

KEYS TO REMEMBER

1. Always have a way of getting back into your Best Punt Protection Formation.

2. You must spend practice time on the Punt Protection and Coverage. Don't neglect this area.

3. Some fake punts must be used sparingly depending on opponent's exposure to the play.

4. Watch for baiting. Defending teams will line up on the line of scrimmage and bail out to cover eligible receivers. If any doubt – punt.

5. All punt team members should have eligible numbers.

6. It is not so much a roll of the dice as it is being able to execute a play when the return team gives you the chance.

Let me talk about a Fake to Remember. This came in our state final. We were down 27-24 with about nine minutes left in the game. This play was called a "Backyard" football play by the broadcaster. It was a fourth-and-9 situation. We lined up in our Open Formation like we usually do. This is what it looked like.

OPEN – 28 CROSS

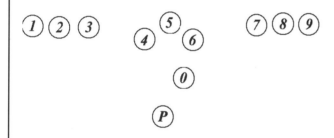

Now, when we call 28 that means the 2 man and 8 man are going to be off the ball and everyone else moves up on the line of scrimmage. We take our 2 man and we bring him across the field as we start to move. He comes across the formation and makes sure he goes back deeper than the punter. Now, we snap the ball to the punter. He throws the ball over to our 2 man.

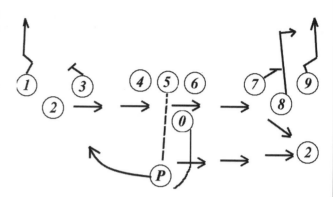

Our 2 man has three options. He can throw the ball to 8 or 9, or he can run. He can throw the ball to our upback who can run. The third option is to throw the ball back to the punter. Now, the upback and punter interchange positions after the pass over to our 2 man. The upback comes back where the punter lined up, and the punter flares up toward the line on the outside.

Our 2 man threw the ball downfield on the play and we completed it down to the opponent's 35-yard line. We ran it down to the 27-yard line.

Now, our 7 man is not eligible. We tell him if no one is rushing he is to run an Arrow route outside, but to make sure he stays on the line of scrimmage. The same is true for 3. He cannot go downfield.

That was a big play for us. It came at the right time. This is just a little of what we do with the Punting Game. It has been a lot of fun for us. It has been very successful. We only used the fake eight times but were successful on seven of them. Hopefully, I have given some of you an idea that you can play around with. Thank you very much.

THE INDIANA OPTION PACKAGE

INDIANA UNIVERSITY

Thank you. I am going to show quite a bit of video. If you have a seat where you will not be able to see you can move up a little closer. I have put together a tape for you that has three parts to it.

First, I want to show you a tape of some of the local kids that are in our program. We have seven players on our team from Kentucky. Second, I have taken the Option Package and divided it into three phases. One is our Option Game. I will diagram one of our Base Options and show you how we run it. I will cover why we run it. Then I will talk about how the fullback can fit into your offense. When you have a fullback like Jeremi Johnson (275 pounds) you want to use him. I will cover how the fullback can really fit into your offense. The next phase of that would be the option passing. I will show you how it all fits together.

You will see us at the end of the tape. We do not see ourselves as an Option football team. We are in the Shotgun throwing the football more than we are an Option Team. Those three things will be on the tape.

I just want to thank all of you for coming. We have had a lot of success in this area for the last three years. A big part of that success is because of the coach that recruits this area. It is only 1 hour and 40 minutes from Bloomington to Louisville. We have a lot of things that are pluses to this area. But, there is nothing more important than the guy that recruits the area. I want Anthony Thompson to come up here for just a minute. Anthony recruits this area for us. I have known Anthony since he was a young player. We are both from Terra Haute, Indiana. If a player comes to IU from this area it is because of Anthony Thompson. If you think anyone in your program needs a role model, and a lot of them do, Anthony is a great role model. If you

have anyone that has that problem make sure Anthony visits with that person when he comes by to see you. I mean this sincerely. Anthony Thompson was the greatest football player in the history of Indiana football. He was one of the greatest football players in the Big Ten Conference. Anthony Thompson is a better person than he was a football player. We are thrilled to have him on the staff. I would encourage all of you to get to know Anthony.

I do want to update you on one situation at Indiana. Many of you have come to our spring practices and to our games. We have an assistant head coach by the name of Pete Schmidt. Many of you know that Pete was diagnosed with lymphoma with about three weeks to go in the regular season. That is a form of cancer. He was not able to go to practice or coach the last two games of our season. After a lot of treatment I want to bring you up to date. All of the cancer except one small spot has disappeared. For those of you that know Pete, you know that he is a wonderful person. He is looking forward to being back on the field with us this spring.

We have really been fortunate at Indiana. Anytime you follow a quality coach like Bill Mallory in a program, you are fortunate to come into a program that may not be where you want it to be as far as winning and losing, but one thing I can tell you about our program. When I arrived we had great kids in our program. Two years ago we graduated 24 out of 24 players. This year we had 32 seniors on the team. Of those 32 players, 26 used up all of their eligibility. All 32 players are on schedule to graduate.

Let me give you some background on how we as a staff have evolved to this Option Offense. You have to understand that I coached at Michigan for Bo Schembechler for 10 years. That was the time when Bo had gotten away from the Option Offense. In the early '80s they had a long list of great option quarterbacks. I got there in about 1984 and that is when Jim Harbaugh was the quarterback. After Jim left we were fortunate to have some other good quarterbacks. The point is this. I had never been around an Option Offense a great deal of time. There was one exception, and that was when my father was a coach and he ran some option. But, I never really coached the option.

I left Michigan and went to coach for the Washington Redskins in the NFL. As you know, no one is going to run the option for several reasons. One thing that happened while I was in the NFL, you get a chance to go visit a lot of colleges when you are coaching in the NFL. One of the first trips to a college I had to make was to Syracuse. I had a chance to spend a day with Syracuse to see what they were doing. Syracuse had some good players. I learned quickly that they did not have as good of players as a lot of other teams around the country. But they really had an ability to create a lot of problems for their opponents with their offense. That got my wheels turning. I keep thinking if I were in college and did not have players that were as good as some of the teams we would have to play, this may be a way to neutralize the talent level.

Later I had a chance to visit Nebraska. I had a chance to sit down with Tommy Frazier and Brook Barringer. Here was one guy that was a classic option type player and one that was not an option type player. But both of these quarterbacks could run the offense and create a lot of problems for the defense. It was at that point and time that I became convinced this type of offense would be one that I would want to use if I were in a situation where we did not have the best athletes in the league. Now, If you are lucky enough to get into a school like Nebraska the offense could take you to another level.

At Indiana we have gone away from just taking the ball back 7 yards deep and hand it to a back. We have gone away from the belief that you must line up in the Shotgun. We want to sprinkle the one-back and no-back looks in, but we want to

make sure of one thing. We want teams to know that they must defend the option. We may only run the option five times in a game. But I will tell you this, if a team we play is not prepared for it we will run it every single down. It has really been good for us.

The best way to describe what we do is to describe it as the Zone Option. Everyone is familiar with the Outside Zone Play. You know, the Inside Zone and the Outside Zone. The play may be called 18 and 19, or the Outside Stretch, or other names. We had that play in our offense. Most people have a version of that play. It may be just a Toss Zone Sweep play.

So when we started talking as a staff and were talking about running the option I wanted to find a way to make sure our kids would buy into it. We wanted something where we did not have to put in a new blocking scheme and we wanted something that was simple for the quarterbacks. We want the quarterback to be able to step off the line of scrimmage, come down the line, and option the fourth man. Since that time we have evolved into two or three other options. I will not get into that today, but we evolved from this play.

OUTSIDE ZONE/TOSS SWEEP PLAY

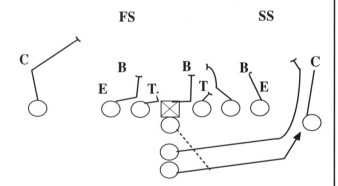

All we have done is to take that same play and run it with a one-man advantage. We have given ourselves the ability to do this. This is the same as the Toss Sweep. We have created a one-man advantage on the play. We can bring the fullback inside and seal off the inside and option off the end and kick it outside.

BASE ZONE OPTION

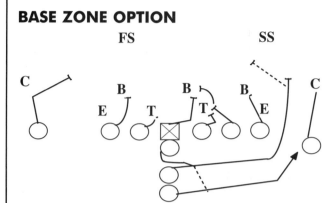

There are three or four ways to block this play. If the defensive end comes down inside we can block the play a little different. We can take our fullback and bring him inside for the fill safety. You will find as you run this option the whole play structure of the defense is going to change. If the defense starts out as a seven-man front they will get to an eight-man front when the ball is snapped. If they are an eight-man front they will bring an extra man in the alley. This is just to get even numbers with the offense.

The second thing I will show you on the tape is our ability to use our fullback. It has gotten very simple for us. As we have started to show option we have included the fullback in the offense. We run the G-Trap and give the ball to the fullback. Take a look at college football. How many teams give the ball to the fullback? There are not many. Nebraska would be the one team that consistently gives the ball to the fullback. We are the only team in our league that consistently gives the ball to the fullback inside. For us it has evolved as a result of our option.

G-TRAP

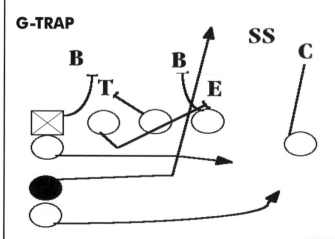

The third phase of how it all fits together is the Option Pass. We run double crossing patterns. We have had a lot of success with this play. When you start running the option the defense will get into a nine-man front on you. When they get into the nine-man fronts there are two areas that are void and that is the backside outs and the onside comebacks. Our quarterback is reading off the option. Those throws are a lot easier than you would imagine.

OPTION PASS

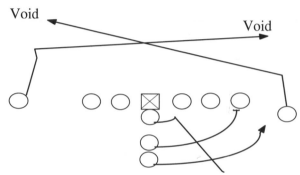

I want to show you what we see a lot of in the Big 10. We see this defensive stunt at least 10 to 25 times per game. It is the number 1 stunt in the Big 10. When we started looking at our offense we wanted something that would work against the one stunt we would see the most. You see the stunt a lot in the NFL and some high schools are using it today. Here is what the defense looks like. Especially with the hash marks, teams are using the reduced front. With the Isolation plays teams are running the defense is blitzing the gaps. They bring the strong-side tackle and end down. The nose goes opposite. The back-side tackle comes down inside. The linebackers scrape to the gaps on the strong side. They run the Zone Blitz and play Cover 3 behind them.

ZONE BLITZ

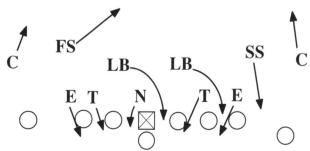

For a team that does not run the option, that blitz gives them a lot of trouble. It does more to disrupt the offense than any stunt that I know of. It takes away the bubble. Everyone is attacking the gaps. It takes away the isolation and the cutback on the Zone Play. Also, it gives the defense the ability to bring a secondary man up to cover the Toss Sweep.

As we did our self scouting we wanted to have a play that would work against the number 1 stunt in our conference. We decided we would run the Zone Option against that defense every single time. So, let me show you how we run the play if they do not blitz and then if they do blitz.

When we first started running the play the defense started zoning us and would stretch the play out. We were not blocking the tight end down. Finally, we called Nebraska and asked them what they did when teams strung the play out. The told us they sealed down with the tight end and optioned the end. Then he could make the pitch and we could block the outside. So that is what we decided to do. We brought the tight end down on the double-team on the tackle. On the back side we sealed down inside. We did not block the backside end. He would have to play the reverse or bootleg, so we did not block him.

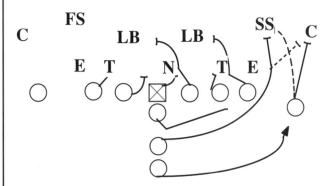

We got to the point where we could read the defense when they were going to run the Zone Blitz. If the quarterback reads the blitz he signals the tailback so he will know the ball is going to be pitched early. We call this **Angle Mike**. We kick the ball out and come outside. We have the fullback coming outside and we seal back inside.

ANGLE MIKE

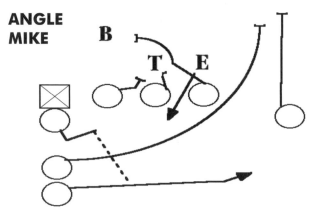

We get this a lot of the time. We spent four to six weeks talking to a lot of people about the number 1 way to attack that stunt. Now we have an answer and we do not see that stunt that much. If we see it coming our quarterback knows what play we want to get into to attack the Angle Mike.

The Zone Option is our number 1 play. We run the ball with the fullback, we run the reverse, and we are doing everything we can to keep the Zone Option Play alive. To our left the play averaged 7.2 yards per carry and to our right it averaged 8.1 per yards per carry. It has been a great play for us.

This play is good against the Bear Front or the Double-Eagle Front. This is one play they do not want to see. The offense has the ability to reach everyone on the line and to get down on the linebackers. Most of the time they are playing Cover 3 or Man Coverage.

I will give one good Option Drill that will save you some time. We are talking about getting two things done at one time. I have been to practices where they worked the fullback on the G-Trap type play for about five minutes. They work the fullback to make sure he is running the right path and that he is getting the ball properly. Then they work the option drill for about 10 minutes with the quarterback reading the end and making the pitch.

What we do on this drill is to cut our time in half by using two footballs. This drill saves us five minutes per day. That turns into 20 minutes per week. We are getting the same thing done with our drill. We have a coach playing defensive end. HE HAS A

FOOTBALL IN HIS HAND. The ball is snapped to the quarterback and he runs the Fullback BELLY. Now the quarterback continues on the option play. The coach playing defensive end pitches the quarterback the second ball. Now the quarterback options the end (Coach) and keeps the ball or pitches it. We make the fullback run 10 yards after he gets the ball. We run two plays with two footballs.

FULLBACK BELLY AND OPTION DRILL

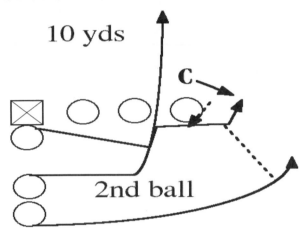

If you can run one option and run it well you are going to cut your practice time down quite a bit. The reason is because you are going to cut down on the different defenses that you see. You are going to see base defenses. You are not going to get all of the junk blitzes and stunts that other teams get. Now you have to take the skill work and their techniques and coach them because those things become the difference in the game. You have to take that option period and get as much done as you can. So what we do on the Option Drill is this.

OPTION DRILL

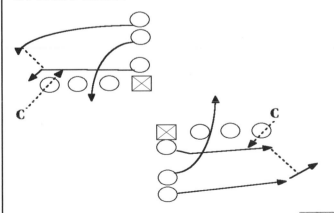

We get 10 yards apart. We run the drill in a circle. We do the same drill if we are running the Triple Option. We have two teams going at the same time. One team goes north and one team goes south.

We have a coach playing end with each unit. We have the quarterback read the 3 technique and give the fullback the ball. He runs 10 yards. Then the coach pitches the quarterback another ball. Now the quarterback continues the option. He comes down and options off the coach. He turns up or he pitches the ball.

Some of you come to clinics and see things like this and get the feeling this is what you want to add to your program. Then you go back to meet with your staff and you have a lot of doubt if you can get all of this included in your practice. That is why it is good if you can come see us practice in the spring to see how we take shortcuts to get things done. However, you are not short-changing your techniques. You are not asking your kids to go out and execute things that they have not practiced.

The question is asked about the action of the quarterback. I reversed out on one action and fronted out on the others. Let me explain what happened. We started out running the option and we had our quarterback front out and come down the line to run the option. We were watching Nebraska on TV and saw their quarterback reversing out. They did not tell us they reversed out on the option. I saw that on TV and the next week I called Nebraska and asked them why they were reversing out on the option. They said the were reversing out so they could get in rhythm with their tailback. They were buying time to get in line with the tailback. Now, you will see on one of our options that Antwaan reverse pivots one time. If you are going to run the Belly Play you want to reverse pivot. If you are in a One Back I would open up. This allows the quarterback to see what is coming at him. I would let the quarterback open up to start with just to see what is going on in front of him.

Here is something we did with our quarterback Antwaan Randel El. We took the two best running plays from Antwaan's high school (Thornton High School) tapes and his three best passing plays and added them to our offense on the first day of practice. I felt we had a special talent in Antwaan and I did not want to paralyze him mentally. We took some of the same terminology and adapted it to our offense. We said let's give Antwaan, who has special talent, the ability to go into the huddle and call the same plays that he called in high school. We put in the Belly and the Belly Option. I called it the Speed Option. One of the best plays that he ran was a Bootleg Naked. We put that play in right away. We called it the same as they did in his high school. He had success and all of a sudden our players had confidence early in his career. He started 11 games as a red-shirt freshman. Last year he was just a sophomore. There are a lot of little things you can do to create your early success in the eyes of your players.

We want to be balanced on offense. We had the ball 85 time per game. We ran the ball 42 times per game and we passed 43 times per game. The first thing we want to do is to run the option. The next thing we are going to do is to get back in the Shotgun and throw the ball.

Most of the quarterbacks that run this offense in high school are the point guard on the basketball team. We can run all of our options out of the Shotgun Formation. You can eat up some practice time for the defensive team if you can get good at running this play.

SHOTGUN - ZONE OPTION

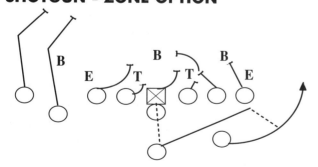

This play is especially good into the sideline. This is especially if the defense sets the defense to the wide side of the field.

The question is this, do we package our best play both right and left? Most of it is done by scouting report. If we are going to package it to both sides we are going to have two tight ends in the game. If we are only packaging it to one side we package it together with an inside run. We do not want to practice the play against every look. We package it to go right or left, and we can package it with an inside play. In the Shotgun you will have to package it with the quarterback draw, power, or a pass. Basically, you can package it any way you want. I am not giving away any secrets. I would encourage you to do that if you are not doing it. Take your base play and find as many ways to get to it as you can without having to block every single look. Package your best way with another run and then package it with a pass and it will make your practice schedule a little more fun.

The question is asked, "What do you tell your quarterback?" You will love this answer. We tell the quarterback to come down the line of scrimmage and if he can keep it , keep it. You can take a talented quarterback and just flat-out paralyze him with a lot of rules. The last thing you want is the quarterback to come down the line thinking if he is to attack the inside numbers or the outside numbers, and all of those things. We tell the quarterback if he can come down the line and keep the ball and get 5 yards to go ahead and get those 5 yards. That is a starting point. This puts him in a mode. It lets him be an aggressive athlete.

This sounds like an oversimplification, but it is not. I learned this from the passing game. Let me tell you how most teams teach the passing game. They tell the quarterback to throw the ball to the man that is open. Is he open or isn't he? That is what we do on the option. "If you can come down the line and turn up and get 5 yards, get 5 yards." If the defensive man is in a position where you can't get 5 yards we want the quarterback to kick it outside. The reason I think we are successful on the play is because this is what our kids have been doing their entire lives. That is what you do in the backyard games. That is what I did and that is what you did. In the passing game your quarterback has been throwing the ball for a long time in his back-yard. He was not throwing completions in the back-yard for the reasons you though he was. He was basically saying, "That man is open and I am going to throw him the ball." That is how it is taught in most cases in the NFL. You teach the quarterback a progression and he asks the question, "Is that man open or not?" That is the way we want our quarter-back approaching the defensive end on the option. Can he make 5 yards or not? If he can he keeps it, if he can't he pitches it. Does this make sense? I know it is simple, but you do not want to paralyze him, and that is what I am trying to say. If you want to add to it later you can, but let him get comfortable on the play first. You want him to be natural.

One award we gave this year was the Iron Man Award. It was to the player that played the most number of plays. This year we had a player play 950 plus plays. He was on all of our special teams and he played a lot for us. This encourages the players to want to get into the game and to play more plays.

The next point I want to make is probably more important than any of the X's and O's. How many of you went to the AFCA Convention in California? There are a lot of interesting things happening in our profession at this time. One thing we talk to our team about a lot is to put them in a mind-set of being a father down the road. We want to ask them what kind of fathers they are going to be. There were a couple of stories told at the AFCA this past year One, a coach from a major college football team had 31 players on his team that are fathers already. These are players in college that are fathers already. We are not encouraging players to be fathers in college, but the bottom line is the fact that we have two or three players that are already fathers. Yet these players have no example of what a father should be. I want to encourage all of you to put some thought into this. If you have a player on your team that is a father, make sure you spend some time with that player. In a lot of those cases he has no idea of what it means to be a father.

The other story that was told at the AFCA was this. Hallmark, the card company, decided to do a project. There was this prison in California near the Hallmark office. Mothers Day was coming up. There were 4,500 inmates in this prison. Hallmark offered to pay for the card and postage if the prisoners would send their mothers a Mothers Day card. The company had such a big response they actually ran out of cards. They did not have enough cards for everyone at prison.

The Hallmark people thought that was a great story but they were embarrassed by the fact they had run out of cards. They said with Fathers Day coming up they made enough cards this time so every-one that had requested cards for Mothers Day would have an opportunity to send a Fathers Day card. They made them the same offer. If they would send their father a card Hallmark would pay for the card and for the postage. NOW, what is shocking is this. NOT ONE PRISONER SHOWED UP TO SEND HIS FATHER A FATHERS DAY CARD.

The point that Bill McCartney was making when he told that story was this. A lot of the mothers in this country that are rearing these kids are really doing a great job.

There are certain things that only a male role model can do for a son or a daughter. You can imagine what the percentages say for those young men that do not have male role models. I have three boys myself. I want to stress this to all of you. Continue to stress this point with your players. Stress to them what it means to be a father. Talk to them about being a father down the road. We spend a lot of time with our guys on this subject. I feel it has a lot of benefits.

That story stresses how powerful we can be as fathers, as coaches, and as Christians or with our faith. I want to encourage all of you to try to have that type of impact on your football team. If we can do this all of us will benefit. Thanks for having us. We will see you in Bloomington.

ATTACKING WITH EIGHT-MAN FRONTS

UNIVERSITY OF PITTSBURGH

Thank you. I'm proud to be here representing the University of Pittsburgh. We are trying to take our program in the direction that you used to know it. But, you are always welcome there.

Let's start talking defense. The thing we wanted at Pitt were kids that wanted to play the game of football. I want kids that want to please their coach. For us to have a chance at the University of Pittsburgh in our defensive scheme, we have to be cohesive. Our talent level is not to the point right now where we can line up and physically whip anybody on our schedule. Our chance of winning has to come from great effort and cohesiveness.

We preach **MAD DOG FOOTBALL**. Mad Dog Football started roughly 30 years ago at the University of Houston. There was an old guy by the name of Melvin Robertson who started this. The Mad Dog Commitment was this. *"When you see one mad dog loose, you're not up too tight. If you see 11 mad dogs loose, you're going to crap a brick."* The strength of Pittsburgh is in the pack. We must have 11 players who are willing to sacrifice themselves to be a part of our defense. We must have 11 men committed to playing as one unit. We sell that to our players. Our players must have class, character, and be committed.

This is our fourth season at the University of Pittsburgh, and we are going to recommit to Mad Dog Football. Our university has won nine national championships. If you look at the Who's Who of football you will find Pittsburgh highly represented. We talk about standing on their shoulders. When you commit to Pitt, you owe it to the men who went before you to not be a Sad Sack. You owe it to them to be a football player.

When we started here in 1997 we were ranked 108th in the nation in every defensive category.

That means we were the worst defensive team in Division I football. We were unified Sad Sacks. We needed the change and needed to understand what our heritage was. When I walk out on that football field, I owe it to Coach Sherrill and Coach Majors and the people that brought tradition to Pitt football, to give them everything I've got, every step of the way every day. I believe that, and I believe our players owe it to us to give everything they've got every step of the way every day.

I think kids need to respect the privilege of playing football. Football is not for everybody. Football is not a country club. You can't pay the dues and play. You have to earn your right to play football. You have to respect the privilege you have to play the game of football, particularly if you are blessed to play in a Division I program. I believe you need to honor yourself by how you play the game. It is a true honor to coach and play football. That is why you bust your butt to be the best you can be. That's what you owe your profession and that is what a football player owes his team. You have to honor the game.

I am not a fan of bandanas and earrings. I'm not a fan of end zone dancing and mugging. I don't think that pays honor to the game. It pays honor to the individual. We don't need to honor an individual, we need to honor the game and the team we are part of. When you become part of a football team, you give up your individuality.

I believe before we talk football, we have to talk about these things with our team. We are not going to back down from anyone. I don't care who he is. If you want to play for us, this is what we believe it takes to be a part of our defensive team. We are going to insist that you do it, or you are not going to play for us. There is no player bigger than the game.

I don't care how good he is. Nobody at the University of Pittsburgh is bigger than the university. We are going to insist that the standards are met and that is how we are going to play the game.

We are going to play as many kids in the game as we can play. If we can stay fresh, it helps us to stay healthy. It also helps us to have good morale. That is what we stand for. That is where we are going to start with our program and the kids on the defense at the University of Pittsburgh. I have been blessed to work with Walt Harris, who allows us to have this type of situation and allows us to make those kinds of decisions.

Persistence is the key to success. Anyone can be successful for a couple of days. The guys that are going to be great, are going to bust their butt to be consistent, and they are going to do it over the long haul. Success is long term. You have to commit yourself on a long-term basis to achieve success. We don't want one-day wonders. We want guys who are going to do it day after day and play after play.

You can not allow yourself to be controlled by your environment. The environment in football is the scoreboard. You have to keep your eyes on the target and be committed long term. That is regardless of the environment that surrounds you. We believe this is the way we are going to play the game, and the way we are going to ask our players to play. It is in very simple plain English and our players have to understand that.

That gives you a little start of how we feel and believe. We are an eight-man front football team. This is the same defense we played at Massillon High School, Bowling Green, and the New York Jets. When you are an eight-man front team, I believe you need certain priorities. You have to have a philosophy. Our philosophy is built around the fact we want to be **fundamentally sound**. We want to be **solid tacklers**. We want to understand **leverage and pursuit**.

We want to have multiple fronts. We will never do anything to break our fundamentals. We can be multiple in looks to the offense without changing fundamentals. We are going to 1) stop the run and 2) win third down. In my experience, if we held a team to under 100 yards rushing and win 67 percent of the third-down situations, we are going to win the game.

This is how we select personnel. We play four down lineman. The letters R and E stand for our ends. We don't need to have big players at those two positions. But they must be quick, tough, and fast. They have to be aggressive and have good football sense. The E plays on air most of the time, so he can be smaller. Our inside tackles are called T and N. The 3 technique T has to be our best lineman. They need to have size also. Our outside linebackers are called SS and W. That means strong safety and Will. They have to be your best overall athletes. They also may be undersized. They are guys who are not fast enough to be corners or tailbacks, or big enough to be linebackers. They are what you call tweener.

Our inside linebackers are S and M. The Mike linebacker is a true old-time, hit-them-in-the-mouth, take-on-the-isolate, plugger-type of linebacker. Our Sam linebacker doesn't have to be as big or as physical, but he must be faster. He is in pass coverage more. He still has to have jets he can fire to take on blocks. The best player on our defense has to be the FS.

Obviously if you are going to put that many guys in the box and use your safety in run support, you better have great corners. If we can find corners that can protect up deep and make a few plays, we are going to be a good defensive team.

8-MAN FRONT

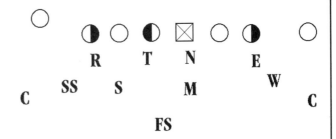

In choosing our personnel we haven't talked about being big. We have talked about having speed and tough guys. If you look at the defense against a pro-style offense, you can see we have more players in almost every situation than they have blockers. The whole idea behind the eight-man front is to have one more guy at the point of attack, than they can block.

There are certain things that an offensive football team cannot do against this defense. Outside runs against this defense are extremely difficult. It is tough to get the off tackles going to the tight-end side because the safety is reading the tight end. As soon as the tight end blocks, the safety is coming downhill into the play. Offensive football teams are going to throw to the split end and wide receivers or they are going to attack the open half of the defense. Into the boundary I think we have to defend a fullback lead and a pulling guard type of toss play. Other than the pass and those types of runs, there is not much we have to defend.

Against an eight-man front, we have found there are a lot more passes than runs. It goes back to the look. There are very few places to run the football. We see a lot of three-step passing games and a lot of play-action passes.

When we line up, most football teams will automatic. We want our kids to know that. The minute the offense automatics, we want to know what it is. We don't know their schemes for automatics, but I know that "Red 22, Red 22" is probably a run play. That quarterback is like our kids. They are taught that one automatic, which will be good for the whole game. If we are not dumb quacks, after about two times we know what "Red 22" is. I also know this. "Green 380, Green 380" is a pass. Usually they are quick slants or outs. We believe in that philosophy of football. Force them to automatic, play the automatic, and react to it. That is not complicated.

As we talk through our scheme, I'm only going to give you two or three fronts, because that is all we play. However, we want to give the illusion of playing hundreds. That's what we want the offense to think we are doing.

As we start teaching base football, we start with alignment and stance. If the football is to our inside, I want the foot toward the football back. The hand toward the ball goes on the ground. The left tackle has his right foot back and his right hand down. The stagger is slight, but will vary from player to player. We want him comfortable with the weight on the hand. We want our down people coming off the ball. We want to penetrate to the offensive side of the line of scrimmage. Each defensive guy is taught the same stance and reaction. Players lined up on the right side of the ball will have their left foot back and left hand down.

The target point on the offensive lineman is the V of the offensive lineman's neck to his gap side. We want to come off and put our eyebrows on that target. To teach getting off the ball, we put them in a stance. We back up 3 yards. We hold a tennis ball out at waist height. We drop the ball. Before the ball bounces, they have to pick it up. If I want him to move inside, I put him in his stance, move to the inside, and drop the tennis ball. If we want to work on pass rush, we move the depth of the ball back. We raise the height of the ball and drop it. The second thing you can do with the ball drop is to have him redirect after he picks up the ball.

One of the worst things that I know of occurs on third-and-10. The offense has to make 10 yards to get a first down. From the sideline someone shouts, "WATCH THE DRAW!" What is the lineman going to do? He ain't going to rush the passer. He has to watch the draw and screen. The quarterback drops back and completes a 10-yard pass for first down. If you are going to commit to getting the off the ball, do it. You want to play in the offensive backfield with the down four guys.

We don't coach with negative thoughts anymore. We want our linebackers to play with reckless abandon. We get our linebackers in a stagger with the inside foot back. We want them faking blitzes and moving around. We want to give the illusion of blitz all the time. We want an offensive lineman to think he is responsible for gaps. I don't care how you coach that tackle, if the linebacker comes up in the gap 1 yard from him, he thinks the linebacker is going to run through. The minute the tackle ignores the linebacker, he will run through the gap.

If you want the trap stopped by the down lineman they will never get off the ball. If you are going to stop the trap, it has to be done by the linebackers. We want to get off the ball and penetrate, that means the tackle is going to get trapped on occasion.

The 7 technique end is aligned on the inside shoulder of the tight end. He is coming off the ball. If the tight end releases, it is hard for the end to react to the block of the fullback coming to kick him out. We want him coming off the ball and the linebacker will have to stop the off-tackle plays. On a play-action pass we should have a damn good pass rush. The down four are coming off hard and fast. We do the same thing with our backside end. We want him coming off the ball and getting into the tackle. He will react to the bootleg, but we don't talk to him about bootleg. If we talk to him about the bootleg, he won't catch plays from behind. He would be hanging back waiting for the bootleg.

If you want to get off the ball, the talk about the trap, draw, and bootleg are counterproductive. If you want them to get off the ball, you have to be committed to it. If the tackle gets trapped, the linebacker will make the play. If the end gets kicked out, the linebacker will fill. The better we get off the ball, the better we are going to be.

If you look at our defense, you would not be thinking about running the ball a lot. You would be thinking about the three-step passing game or play-action pass with the receivers trying to get behind our corners. In this set the tight end lines up left. We give a **Left** call, which denotes strength left. The linebackers and secondary line up to passing strength. In this case that is also left, so we call **Liz**. We call that a **SAME CALL**. Both calls are left. We know that about 85 percent of the time the offense will run the ball to the tight-end side. Un-

less they automatic, 80 percent of the plays are going to be runs. That comes from a 25-year study conducted at UCLA.

The 7 technique end gets more heads up. The 3 technique tackle widens his alignment. The nose tackle moves to the shade on the center. The open-side end gets a tighter alignment on the offensive tackle. All the linebackers cheat toward the tight end. We do that because 85 percent of the plays run will be toward the tight end.

We spend time with our lineman reading splits and weigh distribution in the stance of the offensive lineman. If the weight is forward, it generally is a run. If it is back it is pass. When the defensive linemen see a tendency in the offensive linemen's stance they communicate it up and down the line. If the nose tackle is reading a pull stance and the 3 technique is reading hard run, the play is going to be a power play with a double team on the 3 technique with the backside guard pulling. Our defensive linemen are calling that out so everyone can hear. The nose is calling "YELLOW, YELLOW," and the 3 technique is calling "RED, RED." If both tackles were calling Red, the play would be isolation. If both are calling Yellow, it is pass. You can do that in high school ball also.

The worst thing you can do to a defensive lineman is to treat him like a dumb quack. He has to have the same knowledge as the linebackers. They need to know what fullback off set strong and weak are. They need to know what the I formation is. They need to know all the tendencies of the offense. They can see if the right guard takes a wide split and the off guard has a tight split, it is going to be a trap. This does not take a rocket scientist to see that. This is not clinic talk. It happens. All you have to do is give them basic instructions. The reason we played such good defense late in the season was because we knew the play before the ball was snapped.

If you want to be good pass rushers, you have to practice the pass rush. Kids love to pass rush. In an offense, 50 percent of the plays are passes and

50 percent are runs. If that is the case, half of our practice time should be spent on the pass and half on the run. You can't slight one over the other. If you want to rush the passer you have to work at it.

I believe that 80 percent of a play is over before the ball is snapped. If you scout and look at film you can defeat 80 percent of that play before the ball is snapped. If you play the game one play at a time, you have to understand the call. This is where a defensive team breaks down the most. You have to be sure your player understand the call. They have to understand the call and recognize the offensive formation. You spend hours putting together a scouting report. What good is your time if your players don't understand it? One thing I learned at UCLA, I'll pass on to you. You better scout and understand you opponents. But you can't understand your opponents better than you coach you own football team. You win games because of what your players know, not what you know.

Scouting reports should be very simple. They should be legible to where your kids can read them. You have to personalize them. Put them in a folder with your player's name and number on it. Give it to your player and now it is his. You make him accountable for it.

The last thing to do in preparation to play the play is to get lined up properly. All of your kids are different. We've got a guy playing 3 technique now, who could line up inside the guard and the guard still could not reach him. When we got here, if we didn't want our 3 technique reached we had to line him up on the tackle. Different players adjust their alignments to get done what you want done. They are not all alike and you can't coach them alike.

For the guy to play the play he has to understand the call, recognize the formation, and take the correct alignment. The next thing he looks for is his key. Make them consistent and don't change keys. If you keep the technique and key consistent, your team will get better. The next thing to playing the play, is for him to do his job. That is his job, not his buddy's job, but his. If we have 11 guys doing their

job, then we've got MAD DOG. We have 11 playing as one. When that play is over, he gets his butt back to the huddle and we play the next play the same way.

When you are in an eight-man front you have to understand **TWINS**. The offense goes to twins to get you to move the eighth man out of the box into coverage. In this set the pass strength is left and the run strength is right. The call now is **OPPO-SITE**. Our basic adjustment to twins is what we call **STACK**. Statistics tell us that 75 percent of the time the I-formation team runs isolation to the split-end side. They are not going to run to the tight-end side. There are too many defenders over there. The apex guy on the defense is our safety. When he hears the opposite call he knows it is weak-side isolation. The nose tackle plays more heads up. The 3 technique tackle plays slower. The 7 technique plays more inside, so he can play the cut-back and not get cut off. We want the Sam linebacker to force the ball to the strong safety. If he stays inside he bounces the ball outside to the strong safety. Or he can move outside, kick the end down, and force it out that way.

TWINS

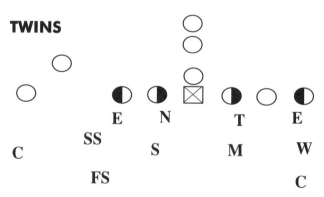

We don't have great football players at Pitt. But we have been able to put up some good numbers in the Big East Conference. We were third in rushing defense and total defense. I think in three years that is a step in the right direction. Three years ago we were 108th in the nation.

The second defense we are going to teach is the **BEAR FRONT**, which we call **TUFF**. It is very simple to teach. Stemming is a huge part of our defense. We move from Base to Tuff, and from Tuff to Base.

That gives the illusion we have more defenses than we have. If we want to end up in Tuff defense, we make the call **STRONG**. That means everyone is aligned to the passing strength of the formation. I don't think you can play a 2 gap nose tackle. A lot of people do in this defense, but I think you are going to get your butt cut up by the cut back run.

In our Tuff defense we kick the defensive line over. The nose tackle moves to a strong shade on the center. The 3 technique moves to a 4 or 4I technique. We do that to take away zone-type plays. The end moves into a 3 technique and the Will linebacker drops down to the 5 technique. Our Sam linebacker is standing over the tight end and the defensive end is outside the tight end. We bring our strong safety inside in the linebacker position. We have all gaps covered so he is a flow player and doesn't have to take on any isolation-type blocks. Our Mike linebacker is one of the better linebackers in the Big East. He is tough, big, and will knock your butt off, but he couldn't cover me on a pass route. We don't ever want him involved in pass coverage.

TUFF FRONT

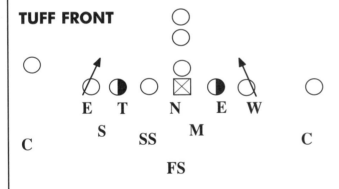

People that see this defense are going to throw the ball. We move the safety one side or the other. If we *Tango*, he is moving toward the tight end. If we call *Sally*, he is going toward the split end. If we get the Sally call to the split-end side the safety has the pitch on the option.

Let's look at the defense versus the Twins Set. We kick the front toward the tight end. The strong safety goes out on the Twins Set. The backside corner comes inside and plays linebacker like the strong safety on the other adjustment.

TUFF VS. TWINS

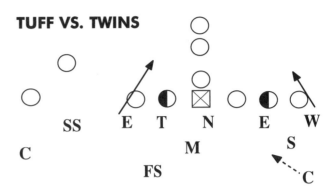

When we jump to the Tuff defense we feel we have to force the ball inside. On the base we want to force it outside. We are bringing our ends in a hip charge and coming under everything and bouncing it wide. We are trying to run everything down from the back side. If we stem to Tuff it is to stop the inside run. In the pass rush we gain one more man and increase our ability to rush the passer. For the last 10 years I've been a coach, this has been the number 1 statistical defense we've run. This defense holds people to 2 yards a carry. We are trying to increase the amount of time we spend in this defense.

Remember what people are going to do. They are going to run the option or throw the quick passing game. If the corners are up they are going to fade. If the corners are back they are going to run the hitch or quick out. Just listen to the automatics and play the play. Red 18 is the option. Green 380 is the pass. Get the jump on the offense.

In college and high school we have a great deal with the hash marks. The hash mark is the 12th man on your defense. People are going to try to

AFC-MIKE VS. TRIPS = BASE

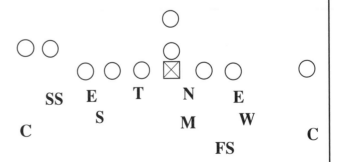

get you out of your eight-man front. We call AFC "MIKE" if the offense came out with three guys to the wide side of the field. All of our guys passed math and they can count to three. The three-man wide equals base defense. The AFC call means we are in automatic field coverage. It over rides all other calls.

If the offense came out with two men into the wide field, that equaled Tuff-Mike. What you have done is given yourself numbers leverage against either set. We can get the six-man rush from this front. We move the Mike linebacker to the outside of the end. The Mike and end knife to the inside and the 3 technique comes to the outside for contain. The Sam linebacker has the tight end and the corner to that side has second receiver coming weak. To the Twins side the strong safety and free safety can combo the slot receiver, while the corner has the number 1 receiver.

AFC-MIKE VS. TWINS = TUFF

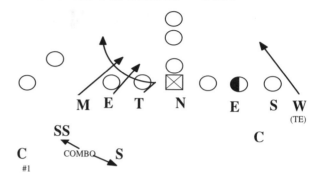

When we make the movements on our stem calls we use **READY MOVE**. We are trying to get people to jump offside. Five times last year we got the offense to move. Twenty-five yards are good when you are a coach. Take what you can get. The referee has yet to call us for illegal movement. It is like them refusing to call holding.

Guys I appreciate your time. It's been an honor to be here.

BASIC RUN-AND-SHOOT ATTACK

GEORGETOWN COLLEGE

First I want to thank the Nike Staff for giving me the opportunity to speak here tonight. It is a real honor for me and our staff and our school. Personally it is great to be selected as the Louisville Clinic "COACH OF THE YEAR." That award in not only for me, but it is for all of my staff as well.

I can remember, and it does not seem to be that long ago, when I was sitting right here in this room in that seat up front, listing to speakers here in 1978. I could just see myself up on this stage giving a lecture someday. WOW! Here I am. I think this goes to show you what dreaming and visualizing can do for you. We ask our players to do this all of the time.

I also want to say thanks to the high school coaches here. I especially want to thank the Louisville and Cincinnati area high school coaches. We get so many great kids from you guys. I know the job the high school coaches do. I know about the bus duties, the lunchroom duties, the weight programs, and all of the other things that go on. To do all of these things and coach football can be a big chore.

We had a tremendous year this past season. It was a tremendous experience for us. We were ranked #1 in the nation for 13 weeks in NAIA polls. Going into the year we did not think we would be very good. We did not have a quarterback and several key positions were questionable. Our players went home for the summer and came back and were ready to go and then got better very quickly.

We flew to California to play the defending National Champions and we beat Luther Pacific. What an experience. Our team had never been on a flight for a game at Georgetown College. To take 75 plus

players on the flight out there was great. To go out there and pull off a win was a great experience for us. We probably got too high after the win. It was like as Bowl Game for us.

We came back from California and had a chance to play for the NAIA National Championship down in Tennessee. We were undefeated until the last game. A lot of people are uncertain about NAIA football. Let me tell you, it is great. It is getting stronger all of the time. There is great competition at this level. Our kids had a lot of fun even though we lost the game in the finals.

This past year we were called the Most Prolific Offense in the History of the NAIA. I guess that means we were pretty good. We did put up some numbers. We averaged 583 yards per game. That is a lot of yards. We had over 8,175 total yards for the season which was a NAIA Record. We scored 710 points for the season. This is the second time our school has scored over 700 points. Our 1991 team did that when Kevin Donley was the coach. We had 97 TD's from 15 different players. If it were not for the NAIA rules where we were limited to the number of players we could play in a game.

The question comes up as to how we were able to score over 700 points in a season a second time. In 1990 we brought the Run-and-Shoot to Georgetown College. At that time we were an Option Team running the Veer mainly. We were making the playoffs but we were getting beat in the playoffs because we were so one dimensional. We brought in Coach Red Faught, who is the guru of the Run-and-Shoot. He is the greatest offensive coach I have been around. We just picked up as much as we could from him. We combined our option football and our power football with his finesse football of throwing the ball. What a difference it has made. In 1991 we won the National Championship of the NAIA with this offense. In 1992 our old staff broke up and moved to other schools. A new staff came in and made a lot of changes as most staffs would.

In 1997 they asked me to come back to Georgetown College. The first thing I did when I took the Head Coach position was to talk to the players. As I listened to the players all I heard was negative comments. They discussed things such as the 4-5 record, no fun anymore, and lack of communication with coaches. Some of the players said they want to quit because they did not like football anymore. In addition to those problems we had some budget problems.

I asked the players to look at the Positive at Georgetown. We were a good school, we had great people and we had great tradition. If you have been around our school lately you know that we have a new stadium. I was fortunate to tell the school officials when they interviewed me for the job that if they would build the new stadium I would take the job. So they built this beautiful 15 million dollar stadium. What a piece of work! If you have not been there you should come down and look at the stadium. So in our first meetings we talked about the new stadium and the positive things about our program. We talked about having fun again. In our first team meeting we sat down and talked with the team about how things were at Georgetown in 1991. We talked about the offense and how we scored so many points. We assured them we were going to do it again. I think that is one of the big things that made a difference for us. We convinced them "It Is More Fun To Score."

At this time I want to concentrate on what we call our TEN STEPS TO SCORE. We have done a good job of scoring.

STEP ONE: WE MUST HAVE COACHES WHO BE-LIEVE IN OUR SYSTEM. I do not care if you run the Run-and-Shoot, the Single Wing, or the Wishbone, and it does not matter what you run, but every coach on your staff must believe in what you are

doing. They have to believe in that offense. All of our coaches believe in what we are doing on offense. You must surround yourself with good people and they must show a genuine interest. You must have an offensive and defensive commitment.

STEP TWO: BRAINWASH YOUR PLAYERS WITH YOUR PHILOSOPHY. The way we did it with our team in 1997 was to sit down with our team and show them a film of the 1991 team and what we did on offense. We showed them highlights of the season. Also, we brought speakers in to talk with them about our offense. They talked about how much fun it was to play in our type of offense. We did everything we could to convince our kids that it WILL happen, not it can be done. Our kids bought this idea.

STEP THREE: YOU HAVE TO PRACTICE SCORING. In our individual drills we demand that they score. If you are going to score 50 points per game you have to practice scoring. In every drill we do we want to score. It does not matter where we are on the field we draw a line to indicate the goal line. We want them to score every time. If they catch a pass we want them to tuck the ball, turn up field and score. We constantly preach – Score, Score, Score. In our team drills we want to score. We have a drill for our backs that we call the "Dream Run." We get them back about 40 yards and have them run through cones, and dummies, and make all kind of moves. Then we have them dive into the end zone. Now they can do their dance in the end zone. We even get our linemen involved. We want everyone to score. They have to visualize scoring in a ball game. This is how we brainwash our players with our philosophy. We brainwash them to the point where they think "One On One" is as good as "One On None." Our players are convinced anytime we get a One On One situation we are going to win.

STEP FOUR: WE MUST PLAY GOOD, SOUND DE-FENSIVE FOOTBALL. You have to play good defense regardless of the offense you run. If you have a defense that is sound then you can take chances on offense once in awhile. You have to communicate this to your players. That is our plan and our players know this. We are a high risk offense. We can gamble a little if we know the defense can play sound. This past year we went for it on 4th Down 42 times. That is a lot of times. I hate to punt. When we get the ball out to our 40 yard line, chances are we are going to go for it on 4th Down. Field position makes the percentage of our offensive success go up.

STEP FIVE: USE A TOOL BOX APPROACH. We have a specific tool that we are going to use for whatever you will give us on defense. If you give us the outside blitz we have certain things that we are going to run on offense. We have the tools in our box to take care of anything you give us on defense. We believe in the Tool Box Approach. You do not go to fix a sink with a hammer when you need a wrench. It is the same idea in this offense.

Another thing that we do well in this area is our communication on the sideline. We have a sideline system for calling plays. I have one coach up in the box watching the far side of the field. I am on the sideline and I am watching the near sideline. The two of us are communicating back and forth. On my left side I have my offensive line coach. He is always looking in the Box area. We consider the Box from the inside shoulder of the Wingback to the inside shoulder of the opposite Wingback. He is always looking for the Trap, Draw, Screen, and anything we can attack in the Box. My other coaches are looking at personnel. Anytime they see a mismatch in personnel they will tell me. I do not want any of our coaches telling me "What the defense is doing." I only want them to tell me a play that they think will work. "Give me a play." If the assistants will do that it takes all of the talking out of the game. At halftime we can talk about what the defense is doing.

STEP SIX: EXECUTION IS THE KEY! KNOW OUR CONVERSION DOWN LETTER PERFECT! The key to any offense is execution. You have to practice a play 1000 times because 999 in not enough. The kids may get bored of watching the same old stuff over and over. This is where execution comes into

play. You must have a routine to your practices. You have to practice your third down plays. Anyone can call the first and second down plays. My line coach can call those plays. The players have to understand what is going to happen on third down. We constantly practice third downs. We have a list of what we are going to call on third down situations and we stick by those plays. When we go into a game we know what we are going to do on third and 3 to go, or third and long. I think this is very important.

STEP SEVEN: HAVE A PLAN AND PRACTICE ALL SITUATIONS. I know that most of you do this. This builds the players confidence and puts them at ease. I have written down a few situations that we feel are important to spend time on.

2-Point Conversion
2-Minute Offense
Backed Up
Last 4 Minutes of a Game
Last 3 Plays
Special Situations
TD NOW
Overtime
Safety

If you are going to score at will you must be ready for all situations. If you have not talked about what you will do in overtime it will be difficult to get the players to do what you want. If you have covered what you plan to do in overtime with them before it happens it will make things a lot easier to communicate to them what you want to do. Do not put any doubt in their minds as to what you want to do. We practice the 2-point conversion. We have two or three plays each week that we are going to use each week. If we use one of the plays this week we may not use it the next week. It all depends on the defense. There are only two or three plays that we are going to look at for a 2 point conversion. We practice these plays more than just one day a week. We think our offense is basically a 2 Minute Offense all of the time. However, we must still practice with the clock stopped, when it starts up, and how to get the ball out of bounds. We must practice when we have no timeouts left. We work on these things every day. We get into a 2-minute offense at least twice a week. We think we have become pretty good at it.

How many of you practice being backed up on your goal line? We were backed up 5 times this past year. We scored twice. A lot of teams will run the straight dive when backed up. Not us. We are going to throw the ball. We will throw the ball deep and we have a couple of other plays we like to run when backed up. We are going to get rid of the ball quickly. The point I am making is the fact that you have to practice these plays. In practice put your team in certain situations and make sure your players know what you are going to do in those situations.

In the last 4 minutes of a game, how many of you practice what to do when you are ahead? Then how many of you practice when you are behind in the last 4 minutes? What plays are you going to call. We know this and we script it daily.

What are you going to do on the last 3 plays of a game. Everyone has a Hail Mary in their offense. But most teams only practice that play one time per year. When they need it, there is doubt if you have not worked on it.

We never go into a game with out having one or two special plays. We always have something special that we want to use and we work on it during the week. How many of you work on the TD NOW situation when you get to the 25 yard line? If is the last play of the game and you must have a TD NOW. The clock is running out and you must have a TD Now. We have plays we chose from.

A couple of years ago I really feared going into overtime. But I sat down with Red Faught and talked it over about what to do in overtime. We sat down and came up with two pages of things that our players needed to know about the overtime situations. Now we have team meeting and go over all of these situations. We allow players to ask questions about the overtime. When we get into overtime our players will be prepared for it and they will respond.

How many times have we seen a safety beat us in a game? We cover all of the situations involved in a safety.

STEP EIGHT: RECOGNIZE PLAYERS WEEKLY. This is one of the things I really appreciate from my coaches. They do a great job of sitting down and picking the player of the week, and other awards. When we sit down and go over our film as a team it is almost like our team banquet. We make a big deal out of the film. We give out a little Tiger Paw for rewards. The players love those paws. We make it a special thing each week on our awards.

Any time one of our players is selected as Player of the Week by our Conference or gains National recognition, we stop practice and we are going to talk about it with the team. Anytime a teacher stops me and tells me one of the players is doing a good job in the classroom I will get the team together on the field and let them know about this. I want to tell the players about as many good things as I can. Their self esteem rises and this can make them better football players.

STEP NINE: EXPECT EVERYONE TO COACH AND COACH UP! You can see faster development when you are able to do this. We expect everyone to coach. We feel we have 100 plus coaches on our team. When a player is standing in line for a drill or running a play, we expect the man in line to coach the player in the drill or the player in front of them. Coaches only have so many eyes. They can see only so many things. From day one we expect our players to coach the player in front of them. This is a good learning tool. It is amazing how many more reps a player can get if they will watch the player in front of them. We tell them to visualize themselves in that position. There are just so many reps you can get during a day during a practice, but you can get a lot of reps mentally. We ask them to go home and visualize their assignments. It is amazing how fast they can learn from this.

STEP TEN: STRESS THE DEFENSE. We stress the opponents defense in several ways. We want the defensive coordinator of the other team to be throwing his head set down, and pulling his hair out, and yelling and screaming over on the sideline. One way we cause this stress is to have a Quick Huddle. We ask our team to huddle up 3 yards from the ball. Their backs are to the ball. The quarterback faces the defense. As soon as the quarterback breaks the huddle they turn and get to the line. They do not just loaf up there. They get up there are get ready to go. We do not hurry too much, but we want them to get there quick. Everyone gets ready to go. We do not have to snap the ball as soon as we get ready. But, what that does to the defense is to speed up their process of getting ready. They have to call their play quicker and they have to break their huddle quicker. We like to stress them.

Another way we like to stress the defense is to use the No Huddle. We may call two plays in a row. I do not go to the No Huddle every series of plays. We may call two plays in the huddle and after they run one play they come back to the line and run the second play.

Another way we cause stress to the defense is by huddling on the sideline. Most of the time we come on the field on first down and line up and run the play with out a huddle on the field. If the defense is not ready we will go on the quick count. We have a couple of plays we like to use in that situations and we have been successful in doing this.

We use motion, alignments, and formations to cause the defense stress. We throw to all receivers. We spread the ball around. We throw Screens to everyone. We like to throw the ball 5 yards and have them run 70 yards. We had 13 different screens in our package last year. We use many different looks on our screens.

Next I want to talk about Ten Essentials To Offense. These are things we want to go into a game with.

TEN ESSENTIALS TO OUR OFFENSE

First is the Option Game. You will see us run Triple Option, Double Option, and the Speed Option. It all depends on our quarterback and what his talents are as to how many of those options we are going to use. Ideally, we would like to run the Triple Option.

Secondly, we run Counter Motion. We do not want to go into a game with out Counter Motion. We can run Long Motion or Deep Motion.

We like the Toss Sweep. We like to get the ball outside. We turn and toss the ball and we are heading full speed outside. They get the corner quick and they go.
We run the Draw. It is probably our best offensive play.

We like the Trap. We are going to trap you to keep you honest on defense.

Our Gangster Passing Game is our 3 Step Drop Passing Game. We expect the ball to be out of our quarterbacks hand in 1.9 seconds. It is going to be gone quickly. The key is for the quarterback to know his keys before he sets up to pass. If he sets up to pass and then makes his read he is too late. Plus, he will probably get sacked.

Next is our Third Down Conversion Tools. We are going to have four or five things that we work on every day for our third down plays. We practice them every day. I can't emphasize this enough.

We are going to throw every kind of Screen Pass we can. There are many different ways to throw the screen pass.

We are not going into a game with out a Dash Play. The Dash for us is where we sprint or roll our quarterback out as quick as we can. We have the receiver run a 20- to 22-yard route. It is one of the highest percentage passes we have. When the defense brings the Blitz we are going to get outside and run the Dash on you.

We are going to run our Specials. I mentioned earlier that we will have two or three different Special Plays we will run against you. We like to do this mainly because it is fun for the kids. They love our Specials. You do not have to wait until Thursday night to do the Special Plays. You can work on them every day.

Next I want to talk about our offense. This is our Base Formation. This is the Run-and-Shoot Attack. We have four receivers wide.

BASE FORMATION

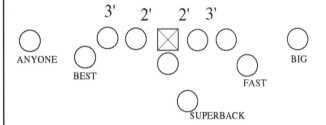

The Wingback on the left side is our best athlete. He is the man we want to get the ball too as often as we can. The wingback on the right side is our speed man. He can run. The wideout on the left side, anyone can play out there. If I put a player out wide someone on defense will come outside to defend him. It does not matter who we put out there, they will send someone out to guard him. The better the athlete out there, the more we can do with our offense. The same is true for the wideout on the other side. Now, we do want that wideout to be big enough to come inside and play tight end for us later.

The Deep Back is our Super Back. We are going to ask him to do a lot of different things. We ask him to catch the ball. We ask him to run the Dive straight ahead. We are going to ask him to block, and we are going to ask him to have some finesse when he takes the pitch and runs the Toss. We are going to do a lot of things with him as so we call him our Super Back.

Our line splits are 2 foot and 3 foot. The split for the guard is 2 feet, and the split for the tackle is 3 feet. We tell them if the defense will go wider, take them out. At times we get our tackles out four or

five feet. Until they come down inside on us, we will continue to go out side. This has helped our protection a great deal.

We are going to give you a lot of motion. We motion Flat and we motion Deep. The wingback goes across the line on the Flat motion and behind the fullback on Deep motion.

MOTION – FLAT OR DEEP

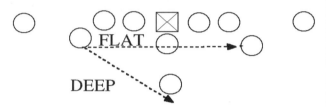

We can snap the ball when the motion man gets to a certain point. We can snap it at a lot of different places on the motion. In our system where we snap the ball is based on the play we are running. The kids know this by what the play is. We may take the wingback on the left and move him over to the right outside the other wingback. This gives us a Trips look. We can line him up outside the split end and give you a wider look. We can take our fullback and line him up anywhere back here. Once we get a few rules on moving the players around we can let the players do their own thing. They can be creative with this. The important thing is to get to the right place when the ball is snapped. We do not care where they line up as long as they are in the right place when the ball is snapped. That is our Run-and-Shoot.

The two plays we run up the middle are our Trap and Draw. We do run the Belly Series once in a while. Outside we are going to run the Toss. We may run the Option outside. We do run the Belly inside and outside at the tackle. That is it. From week to week it does not change.

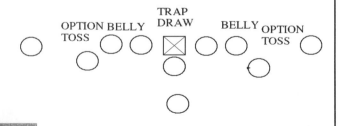

Now, we may run the Speed Option one week and the next week we may run the Dive Option. The next week it may be the Triple Option. We only Toss the ball one way. We may toss it to a wingback, or the fullback. We may go in long motion and toss it, and we may go from Trips and toss it. It is all a different look. To the defense it looks like we are doing a lot of different things. We do not do a lot in our Running Game. From week to week it is the same old stuff. On our practice plan we write it up on the board; SOS – SAME OLD STUFF. That enables us to get into our Passing Game and do some extra things.

On the Goal Line we like to go to our Unbalanced Formation by bringing our big end inside on the short side. We move the tackle over to the strong side. We still have our split end to the strong side. All of this counters all of the things I just showed you. We went from a wide open offense to an unbalanced line.

GOAL LINE FORMATION

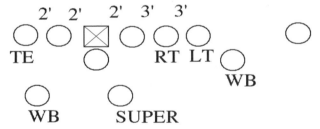

Now, we can send in a sub for the Tight End on the short side if he is not big enough to do the job blocking. We are getting the type of ends that we can keep in the game and still do the job. They can play the wide out or tight end. Remember the wingback on the left side. Now he is now our tailback. He is the best athlete on the team.

We can motion two different ways back toward the short side of the formation. By doing that we can give you three receivers on the short side. By doing this we feel it limits the defense to what they can do on the backside.

Someone asked me how we scored 50 per game. Well the Run-and-Shoot is just window dressing.

We run the heck out of the Unbalanced Formation. The thing that helped us so much this year was the fact that our strong side was very physical. We could run the ball to that side. They could come off the ball. We run the same basic plays that we run when we go Run-and-Shoot. We run the Toss, and we run the Power up inside a couple of different ways. We run a quick hand sweep to the strong side. We do run the Option outside and that is it. You do not have to do a lot of different things if you do what you do well. Again, we use the Tool Box approach. This is what we are all about. If has been successful for us.

I know you came for more than this. I am going to let our Offensive Coordinator come up and give you our Goal Line Offense.

COACH CRAIG MULLINS

I want to get into the X's and O's. This is a very important formation for us. Some teams think we are a slap happy passing offense. We are going to throw the ball first to win. We call this our scoring formation. When do we like to us this? We like to use it from the 25- to 20-yard line going in. We also like to use it coming out. Then, as a change of pace we will use it in the open field.

When I think of the Tight End I think of it as a condition instead of a position. It is really important in this particular set. It is nice if you have an in between type player. (Twiner) Hopefully he will be a little larger and a little more physical, so they can't hold him on the line of scrimmage. We want to be able to bring him inside from the Run-and-Shoot Formation.

We call this our Guards East Set. This is what I am going to be talking about. You can call it whatever you want. If you want to use numbers you can adapt it real easy. The base play is a Sweep to our Quick or short side. We call the Strong side on the side of the two tackles. Our Running Plays are *numbered* and our Pass Plays are called with *words*.

This play is our Goal Line – 39 Play. Our Cadence is: Set – Number – Go. When the wingback hears the Number he goes in motion as fast as he can. I mean as fast as he can. He has his outside foot planted and he is gone as fast as he can. You will see why he does that in just a minute. His aiming point is at the feet of the fullback who is set at 4 yards deep. If the wingback is slow we can cheat him up, if he is fast you can cheat him back a little. That is his aiming point.

The job of the Tight End is to hold the last man on the line of scrimmage. He steps with the left foot first, and makes contact, and keep him from making any type of penetration. Our left halfback's job is to block the next man outside our tight end. He will run a straight line and try to block his man. It has to be an aggressive block. We can cut them in college, but I know the high school rule is that you have to stay up. He does not have to seal the man inside. He can kick him outside and we can run inside. Our fullback gets some penetration toward the line and then comes outside to block the corner. This is a wide play. We want to stretch the play as wide as we can. Up front all we are doing is zone blocking.

GOAL LINE – 39

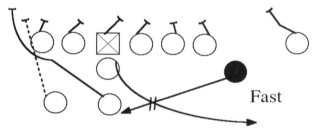

Fast

There is nothing really fancy about our running game out of our overbalanced formation. We try to use as simple of blocking schemes as possible because we don't want to have to spend a great deal of time working on it. We are going to spend most of our time on the important stuff...throwing the football! In our Run-and-Shoot it Is the threat of the pass that opens up the running game. In running the Guards East it is important to have the threat of the Hand Sweep.

Remember the wingback going in motion is getting the football going full speed right at our fullback.

When the quarterback comes out we want him to take a big step and then we want his arms extended to get the ball to the wingback. We do not want to wait on the wingback. That disrupts the timing of the play.

We also run 33 from this formation. We try to keep it simple. This is not a Wing-T offense. This is not a Wing-T Set. That is not knocking the Wing-T. We do not have the time to work on the blocking principles of the Wing-T. On our 33 we have the same type of action. The quarterback starts the wingback in motion just like he would on 39.

GOAL LINE 33

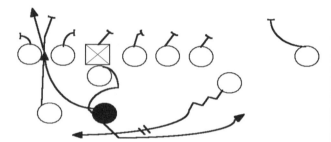

Now I have a cut up on film that I want to show. You will see these plays in game condition.

Let me talk about Guards East. Again, it all starts with the right halfback or wingback. We want him to sell play 39. If 39 is not any good then Guards East is not going to be any good either. When we run 39 we end up getting rotation in the secondary toward the motion. We drag the tight end across and he goes to the flat. The left half reads the safety. If he is dropping we want him to stop on his route. If the safety is even - he is leaving. He is going big. We use this concept a lot in our offense. The fullback replaces the tight end on the protection.

The quarterback takes the same action. We are going to run 39, but we are going to get a short bootleg to the inside tackle on the strong side.

We run a passing tree off the Guards East. If we want to alter the routes we "TAG" them. Another "TAG" we can use off the Guards East is "Trail." It is more of a short yardage or two point conversion tool. The basic reads to the play are the same as any other play within the series. You can see the pass plays on the film.

I know Coach Cronin has a few points to make before we wrap this up. If I can help you with any of this feel free to contact me. This offense is a lot of fun.

Thank you Craig. He was the quarterback when we first put this offense in. He is a great asset to our staff.

I know some of your are sitting back there saying, "we can't do all of those things in high school." I do not believe this. I did the same things when I coached high school. This is just a segment of what we do. We only practice for one hour and a half, and two hours maximum at the high school level. We were decent. You can run this offense if you have a good routine to your practices. The other thing you may be saying is that you do not have a quarterback like we have. Our quarterback last year was a paraplegic and Coach Mullins made him into the Player Of The Year. He is a great coach. Our quarterback is a great player but he is not a super star.

One of the best things I have done in coaching was to start keeping a Checklist. When I first started coaching I was at Carmel Junior High School. I would go over to watch Carmel High School practices. Dick Dullaghan was the head coach. Keith Fiedler was on the staff and he is the head coach now. I would visit with Keith and he would come in after practice and check off the things they worked on in practice that day. I thought that was very neat. Each day he would check off the drills that they ran in practice. That is what we do now. The offensive line has a Checklist. They write down all of the drills they use. He

labels the drills. Drills that he uses every day he labels A. Drills that he uses every other day he may label B. Drills that he uses only one or two times he labels C. But he keeps a Checklist. The other coaches do the same thing. We all have a Checklist. We want to make sure we are developing the skills and techniques. We get into a habit or just running plays. We keep a list of everything we do. It helps your practice plan a great deal.

I went to the AFCA Convention this past year. If you have never attended that Convention you should go. It is a neat experience. Next year it is down in Atlanta. *It is a very professional type meeting.* One of the things emphasized this year was this. WIN WITH HONOR! Win with Honor, not only on the field, but off the field as well.

There is just one quick point I want to get across tonight. You can open the newspaper and read every day where teams are breaking rules and they are put on probation or suspended. Most every day you hear about some team breaking the rules. That was the point they were trying to get across at the Convention. We all should take it on our shoulders to Win With Honor. This is on the field and off the field. If we can do this kids will be better off down the road. Many of us get so tied up in winning and feel it is so important. Expect more from your players than just a win. I just want to put my two cents in on this matter. I think you guys do a great job. You are here tonight because you want to do a better job. This is what it is all about.

If we can ever help you at Georgetown College feel free to pick up the phone and call us. We have no secrets. This is the basic of what we do. We have a camp during the summer. You have supported us on our camps and I hope you continue to do that. I appreciate this opportunity.

DEVELOPING DEFENSIVE LINEMEN

UNIVERSITY OF MIAMI

I admire you for being here today. A few years ago Nike asked coaches to go around and speak at clinics like this. I had the pleasure of going to New Jersey to do one. It happened to be on a Friday night. It was a small group of myself and 11 coaches. Eight of them were single or divorced and the other two guys couldn't get a date. We had a great time and I think they came away with something they could use. That is the purpose of these clinics.

In the introduction you got to hear about some of the places I've been and some of the things I've done. Probably the most valuable thing in my entire coaching career is the six years I spent as a high school coach. My father was a high school football coach in Oklahoma for 30 years. I spent a lot of time traveling around with him.

When I got to be a high school coach, I went to all the clinics I could. I went to the state conventions, Texas clinics, college clinics, and listened to coaches talk about football. I always felt when you went to a clinic two things usually happened. Hopefully this will happen today with you guys. The first thing is that you will be able to find one or two things that you will be able to use in your program that will help you be a better coach. The second thing is my talk will validate a lot of the things you are already doing.

A lot of times you wonder if you are teaching things the right way. The primary thing I am going to talk about today is "developing defensive linemen." However, I'm going to hit a lot of things about organizational skills and defense. If you have questions raise your hand and let's talk about them. Don't be intimidated to ask the questions you want answered. Hopefully we can leave here with a different understanding and appreciation about defensive linemen.

In 1983 I was intimidated from the standpoint that I had only coached the quarterback, wide receivers, and tight ends as a college coach. Jimmy Johnson had taken the job at the University of Miami right after they had won the national championship against Nebraska in the Orange Bowl. He asked me to go along with him. But he wanted me to change sides of the ball and coach the defensive line. Obviously, there was some apprehension leaving Oklahoma State and going to Miami. But to add to all that I had to coach something I had never coached at the college level.

I pestered everybody I could find for about five months that had ever worked with or coached the defensive line. I called back to Arkansas, where I had played. I talked to Moe Stewart, who had coached the Miami Dolphins and Baltimore Colts defensive line under Don Shula for the better part of 25 years. He was an elderly coach. He was 67 years old. He had forgotten more football then I probably will ever know. Those guys were kind enough to share a lot of the things they knew about defensive line play. They shaped my career as a young defensive line coach.

The things I'm going to share with you today are things you can implement. One of the most frustrating things to a coach is for someone to come in here and talk about how to win games with players you may never coach. I remember listening to a defensive coordinator from the University of Oklahoma when I was coaching high school football. All he did was tell stories about Lee Roy, Lucius, and Dewey Selmon. His most important job was to make sure nobody missed the bus. At the end of the clinic I didn't have a Lee Roy, Lucius, or Dewey, and didn't know how to get better.

The University of Miami has a long list of defensive linemen. They have 23 defensive linemen in the NFL still playing. There have been 12 to 15 first-round draft choices in the last 16 to 18 years. One of the ironies about this group of players is that very few of them were defensive linemen in high school. From 1984-89 I was the defensive line coach at Miami. We had 15 players make it to the NFL. Only two of them were defensive linemen in high school. The other 13 players were fullbacks, tight ends, and linebackers, and we even had one who was a wide receiver. At Miami we were never able to recruit the superstar defensive linemen. There aren't enough of those kinds of guys around. What we started looking for were kids with great athleticism and speed. That became the trend.

That is what Miami became noted for in the late '80s and early '90s. We have always had defenses with the ability to run. We looked for the 6-2 to 6-5 kid who was 205 to 210 pounds. From there we would grow our own defensive linemen. The one great trade-off that we found out was the ability to play with our hands. That is tremendously important when you try to develop defensive linemen. Years ago everyone tried to play with the forearm shiver. Linebackers in high school had learned how to take on blockers with their hands. That carried over when we put them down in a four-point stance.

We had kids who were athletes, fast, and played well with their hands. We developed schemes in the defense to take advantage of these skills. Now their liabilities weren't things that were going to keep us from having success.

If you are going to coach defensive linemen today, you have to have a process with which to develop them. You have to have a fundamental way of teaching. You have to know what you are going to ask them to do and how they are going to do it. I have listed 10 things in the progression of teaching defensive linemen. Of these 10 things, six of them every kid can do. I don't care if he runs 5.5 or 4.5. Every single kid should be able to do the majority of these things.

The first part of teaching is the KNOWLEDGE part. In that phase is **stance, alignment,** and **assignment.** There are a lot of conflicts about what type of stance to use. I have always believed that the players on the left side of the football should be in a right-handed stance, and the players on the right side of the football in a left-handed stance. Only one player in my 15 years of coaching didn't do that. I was smart enough not to screw him up. When I was with the Cowboys we traded for a guy named Charles Haley. He had been to the Pro Bowl for five or six years and he knew what he needed to do. We tried to do it for awhile, but it didn't work out. You have to get your kids into comfortable stances where you can maximize their initial explosion and their ability to get off with the football. I'm not trying to change the things you are doing, but these are the things I have learned over the past years. The pass rush moves, blocking scheme moves, and scheme recognition, ties in perfectly with the right- and left-handed stances, regardless of the shade on defense that you play.

The next two things are alignment and assignment. Every kid on your team has to know where he is going to line up and what he is expected to do from that point. They have to know their assignment and responsibility. That is a large part of your coaching.

The next big phase is TECHNIQUE. In the technique phase is **key progress and pre-snap reads, get off, hands-hips-feet,** and **separation.**

The first thing in the technique phase has a lot to do with coaching. In the key progress and pre-snap reads there are an endless amount of things you have to teach him. The better coach you are and the more things you find will help your players tremendously. It will help your players to watch film and try to find things that tip or give away what the offense is going to do. We coach them to look at line splits. Are the offensive linemen getting closer together for a reason? Is a lineman backed up off the ball so he can pull? We key the near back. We have to recognize the formation. We are looking at the pressure on the knuckles of the offensive linemen. We look at the heels of the offensive linemen. If they are up, they generally come out in a running play. If they are down, it is generally a pass.

I'm going to share some stories with you that are great illustrations for these types of things. In my third year of coaching with the Dallas Cowboys, we were getting ready to play the Phoenix Cardinals. Jim Jeffcoat played in our defense and had the pleasure of playing with Randy White in the Tom Landry era. Randy White was one of the greatest players to ever play that position, but he was undersized for a defensive tackle. He was an obsessive film watcher and had taught Jim Jeffcoat to do the same thing. The idea was there was one guy on the offense that will tell you the play, if you will just look. While we were game planning, Jim would be in the film room looking for keys. He came into my office one day and told me he had found something. The thing he found was hard to believe. This was a professional football team where the starting left offensive guard got into a right-handed stance for a run and a left-handed stance for pass. How stupid does that sound?

If you watch the quarterback's feet, he might get into a right-footed or left-footed stagger depending on the direction he is going. One of the things which are clearly evident in professional football is how sloppy the fundamentals are. Players and coaches get so caught up in the schemes and the X's and O's part of the game, that they forget to coach the fundamentals. Players get into bad habits and start cheating. Look for those things and you will find someone to tell you the play.

The next thing is what separates the good from the great and the average from the good defensive linemen. If I were asked the number 1 intangible that all great defensive linemen share it would be the **first step and initial explosion**. All the great ones have it. Warren Sapp and Reggie White are two that come to mind immediately. They can get off on the ball and explode. They can gain ground on the line of scrimmage. That should be what you are looking for. We run a drill in our off-season which

is a pass rush drill. We set up cones 5 yards deep on the side of the ball. One cone is set 3 yards back, which marks the outside hip of the set point of the offensive tackle. The other cone is set 7 yards deep in the middle, which is the set point of the quarterback.

Take the football and move it. Time them from their initial reaction to the set point of the quarterback. Then do it again and let them move when they want to. Look at the difference between their ability to get off on the ball and their ability to just run the drill. You will be amazed at what you see. The best player I ever had run this drill was Marco Coleman. He could run the drill in 1.28 seconds on his movement and 1.31 seconds on the ball. There was only .03 seconds difference. There were guys I coached who were great players. Their times would be 1.42 seconds and 1.69 seconds. That is almost two tenths of a second difference.

The next thing is what we call **hands-hips-feet**. This teaches kids exactly how you want them to play. We teach hand placement in what we call *clash ear holes*. That is a point of contact. No matter what the blocking scheme is, we want to clash ear holes. We want the facemask to hit the Vee of the neck, with the ear holes clashed, their hands inside, and them looking right over the shoulder pads of the blocker. We film every drill we do in practice. We watch the film and let the kids tell us what they did wrong. I want them to understand the coaching. I want them to know when they took a false step or got their hips turned. I want them to be able to tell me what went wrong.

Playing with the forearm shiver went out the window many years ago. The reason for it was defensive players couldn't get **separation** because they were too close to the offense. A lot of coaches think the guys who get the separation are the 400- to 500-pound bench-pressers. That is not always true. Having the ability to separate because you are strong in the upper body is only a portion of the technique. I would rather have guys who are strong in the hips and upper thigh. The initial get-off with the explosive power will rock and stop most offensive linemen. If a guy can't get off the ball, he could bench 500 pounds and still get the hell blocked out of him.

The last phase to the 10 steps is EFFORT. Within the effort phase is **escape, pursuit, and tackle.** In this phase there is absolutely no compromise. You have to be able to teach them to escape. Everyone wants defensive linemen that are playmakers. This year we did a study and *Sporting News* put this study out. Miami was number 3 in the country this past year with the number of negative plays we gave an opponent. We had 41 sacks, 43 turnovers, and 59 tackles behind the line of scrimmage. When you add those things together, it amounts to one out of every nine times the ball was snapped we gave the other team a bad play. Our defensive linemen were involved in 42 percent of those plays.

We are not a two-gap team. We don't try to tie up blockers to keep the linebackers free. We give our defensive linemen the opportunity to make plays.

The pursuit part of our play is nothing more than effort. It is fanatical, unbelievable effort. If you came to our practice and watched us, the one thing you would come away with would be an appreciation for our pursuit. We get after our kids about hustle and finish. We want them flying to the ball. One guy doesn't make the tackle at our place.

You will never see a practice at the University of Miami, as long as I'm coaching there, where we don't work on tackling. We tackle every single day. All through spring practice, training camp, and throughout the week we work on tackling. We may tackle each other at three-quarter speed, tackle the sled for form and technique, or full-speed tackle scout team running backs. But we are going to do some kind of tackling every day.

We did a study when I was with the Cowboys. Think about this as you coach your own football team. In the NFL 65 percent of the long runs occur in the last six games of the season. In the first month of the season next year there won't be but five or six runs over 25 to 50 yards. But what do you think happens

with most pro teams? They take the pads off and go in sweats. They implement very detailed game plans and let the fundamentals go. When you come out of training camps you are tackling every day trying to make the team. In September everybody is a great tackler. In October they are okay, but by November they are starting to get worse. In November, if the team is not in the playoff picture or the coaching staff doesn't think too much about tackling, those 5-yard runs become 25-yard runs. We did the study of all the teams in our division and found that all the long runs came in the second half of the season. So make sure you think about your tackling and don't back off. You don't have to beat them into the ground but don't back off.

If you come and watch us in practice, here are some of the things you will see in a typical practice day. As a coach you have 2 to 2½ hours to decide what you are going to practice. Some of the time is involved in prepractice, installation of the game plan, flexing and stretching, and some conditioning at the end. The other part of the practice is what you are going to teach and put in for that week. You are going to get 15 to 35 minutes during the entire practice for you individual work. How are you going to maximize that individual time to make sure your kids are ready to play on Saturday?

A certain part of your practice schedule has to be the continuation of the development of **athletic improvement**. Don't ignore the face that your kids have to continually get better athletically. This includes agilities, bags, footwork, flexible hips and torso, quickness, change of direction, body control, and burst explosion. We do 2-4 minutes every day with our positional groups doing things that allow transition, movement, quickness, and change of direction.

The next thing you will see is **individual teaching with an emphasis on fundamentals**. We did this with the Cowboys, and we are doing it here at Miami. We are going to continue to coach the little things. We are not going to lose games because we get sloppy at doing the little things. If we have to cut out something we think is important, we do it to teach these fundamentals. During this time we teach stance, explosion, contact points and hand placement, separation and escape drills, tackling, and creating turnovers.

I visited a lot of college practices when I was with the Cowboys. I like to watch how guys actually teach individual and combination blocking schemes. One of the things I saw a lot were guys trying to cover too many things. They were trying to make kids masters at playing blocking schemes. Take the time to make your practice specific to the team you are going to play this week. If the team you are playing is a one-back, two-tight-ends, zone team, don't spend time working on playing traps or spilling counters. Tailor your individual blocking schemes practice to what you are going to see this week. During this period work on the types of blocks you are going to see.

The next part is **pass rush skill development**. As you start to teach kids there are two things I want you to keep in mind. The first thing is, don't try to make a kid a master at a lot of pass rush moves. My first year with the Cowboys was Ed "Too-Tall" Jones's last year. I asked him how many pass rush moves he had. He told me he used three moves. He was a master at one of them and did the other two pretty good. He only used his best move maybe three or four times a game. He used it when the team had to have a sack or hurry. The rest of the time he set up the big move.

The other thing is, stop trying to teach pass rush moves to kids that can't do them because of their statue. Ed Jones at 6-9 and Russell Maryland at 6-2 can't learn the same pass rush moves. It would be foolish to work quick arm-over moves with Russell. We tailor a pass rush plan for each and every one of our kids. We fashion the things they do with the things they are capable of doing. If a kid is not strong enough to bull rush, we don't teach him to bull rush. But during this period they work on their moves. We work on stance, contact points, techniques in the rip / arm-over, as well as the counters, hand drills, combination moves, attacking offensive linemen, closing on the quarterback, and 1-on-1 (Vs) offensive line.

The remainder of practice is broken down into group or team drills. If you come watch us practice you will notice one thing. Our coaches constantly talk and coach to **finish the play**. If a defensive lineman rushes the passer, when the ball is thrown, he turns and bursts to the ball. We want our linemen to make plays outside their area of responsibility. The major emphasis in this part of practice is applying, refining skills, effort, and finishing.

The last part of our practice is **conditioning.** This part of the game has come full cycle. I truly believe that one of the fundamentally important things with defensive linemen is they have to be in great shape. They have to be in better condition than anyone on your football team. Think about what it is like for 75 plays every ball game. There is going to be contact on every snap. They are going to hit somebody in the mouth or get hit in the mouth every play. There is no backpedaling like a defensive back, or running over trash like a linebacker. They are hitting someone, getting off blocks, and pursuing. They have to rush the passer, get off the blocker, turn and trace, and retreat. Conditioning is the only thing in the world that gives them a chance to be great defensive linemen. If you want your linemen to be productive in the third and fourth quarters, you better have them in great condition.

I learned from Charles Haley a thing that we implemented back in 1992. We did pass rush games. We did it at the end of practice when everyone was dead tired. We got the guys on the line and had them run all the pass rush games they had. We did the two-man, three-man, and four-man pass rush stunts as hard as we could do them. We used them as aerobic conditioning. We did a two-minute no-huddle drill. The defense would run their stunts on air. The coach took the ball, snapped it, and walked 5 or 6 yards. We put the ball down, made a no-huddle call, and ran the stunts again. Sometimes he threw the ball somewhere and the defense had to chase it. The conditioning became a position metabolic drill.

Every good coach has a chart that he keeps in his office to track what he is doing in practice each week. If you are not careful you will fall into a rut, where you are doing the same drills every day. The players will get bored with the drills and so will you. My chart has the days across the top, Sunday through Saturday. Down the left hand side of the chart are listed the drills grouped by categories. Under *Agility* I have bags, hoops, and vertical bags, get off, and retrace. Under *Tackling* I have string out, angle, cutback, reach, shed, Okie drill, and quarterback strip. The next group is *Lockout/Escape*. The drills under that are fitted lockout, fitted push/pull, fitted slingshot, knees lockout, 6-point Sled, 3-point Sled, sled progression, and sumo lockout. Next is *Run Reads*. The drills are step reads, 5-man sled, half-line reads, 1-on-1 reads, block reads, base, reach, highwall, fold, back/down, veer-spill, double, slip, scoop, and draw sets.

From there I go to *Pass Rush*. We use chase progression, corner/cloth/hips, big bags, 1-on-1, 9-on-9, and mirror dodge. Finally there is *Pass Rush Moves*. Under that we have speed, power, fakes, counters, hands, and game progression. The chart is lined so I can keep track of what drill was done on what day. It is simple to keep.

When I was at Dallas we added another category to this sheet. We added a turnover section to it with the drills we were going to do. That let us check off what drills we were doing to help with our turnover ratio. We did a different drill each day and it paid off in the Super Bowl. We won it that year. In the playoff games we created 29 turnovers and our offense only turned the ball over three times.

It is important for all coaches to **Evaluate and Reward** your players. If you are a player, you want to know where you stand. You need to **Set Expectations** for practice and games. You need to grade your players. We grade on **Technique, Assignment, and Effort.** We give them three grades. We give them a **Participation Grade**. A participation grade is a standard of performance for the position they play. It says if you play this position you should make a certain number of plays in a game. The cutoff point for the defensive line is one out of every six plays. If they are not making a play one out of every six, we are going to find someone else to play.

What is a play? To us a play amounts to tackles, assists, fumbles recovered or caused, quarterback hits, pressures, sacks, or ball batted down. All those things are participation grades. If a player played 40 plays and made 10 plays, it is simple math to find out if he is making the grade. We want our linebackers to make one in five plays. The corners are one in 12 plays, and the safeties are one in eight plays We have been doing this since 1985. We did it with the Cowboys. You can't do this evaluating as a one-game tool. The kinds of teams you play will effect the grade of certain people. But over the course of several games it is a great indicator of who is making plays for you. We post the grades each week so the guys can see them. On the downside to this, we subtract from their plays for mental mistakes. You can't play with dumb players.

The second half to this is the **Reward phase**. I think coaches miss the boat by not giving kids enough incentive. There are two kinds of incentives: **Peer Recognition** and **Recognition where you physically give them something.** At Dallas the year we were trying to create turnovers, we decided to give our defensive players $5 for every turnover they caused in practice. This will tell you something about pro football players. Friday was payday. We would come in after practice and go over the game plan. After that I had a stack of about $300 in 5-dollar bills. We would go down the list and pay off. When I got to Charles Haley, I said he had made $25. He jumped up and said he had $30 coming. Here was a man making $2 million a year and arguing about $5. He knew how much money he had coming because it became important to him.

We put up a board in our locker room for guys who were making plays to win games. It was a play-making goal board. We went to the sports information director and got 3 X 5 pictures of the guys and put them on the board with a description of what they had done. That became a big deal with them to be recognized for the contributions they were making to the team. Find things and ways to reward the things that you want done. You have to make football **Fun** and you have to do it **Enthusiastically**.

Next I want to put on this video tape and show some of the things I have been talking about. What I'm going to show to some extent is what a typical day at one of our practices would be like. We video all our practices. You will see a cone at the end of each drill. That is placed there to give finish to the drill. After we come over the bags we sprint past the cones to finish the drill with a burst.

In a defensive drill, never run a drill on cadence. Always use the ball to get off. Make everyone aware of the movement of the ball. Cadence and sound should mean nothing to a defensive player.

To work on your escape drill, use a fit-up drill. Put guys in a position where they have been reached in a fitted-up position. Then let them work their technique to rip or go cross face, or whatever technique you use. This eliminates a lot of injuries and gives the defenders good work.

Every single week, once a week at Miami, we do the Okie Drill. We take our best offensive linemen against our best defensive linemen and do this drill. We do it for five minutes. We are going to hit each other in the mouth, come off, and tackle guys live, full speed, to the ground. The entire defense is going to be doing this. We have linebackers going against tight ends and linemen. If the lines get too long, and defensive backs going against wide receivers.

Everyone has sleds, chutes, and cages. Find something to use them for. Teach explosion, shed, and escape on them. Use boards to keep their feet apart in a good base. However, the most important thing is to shoot the hands inside.

A great drill we do for our defensive linemen is the Close Drill. We put the ball down, back the offensive lineman up 3 yards. Move the ball and have the offensive lineman retreat backward. The drill is over when the defensive lineman's hands touch the offensive blockers shoulder. It makes the defensive lineman close hard on the man that is going to block him.

Running the hoops is one of the things a defensive lineman has to do well. It doesn't matter how fast a guy is in a straight line. If he can't lean in and maintain his speed, he won't be a good player. The lineman has to be able to dip his shoulder, get under people, and run in circles. This is a great drill to do for conditioning when practice is over. Make it competitive. Start guys at different places on the hoop and tell them if they can catch the other guy, they don't have to go again.

Everyone gets caught up with teaching pass rush moves. You have to remember that only one out of every 10 pass rush moves works. What you have to teach is the counter move when the first move doesn't work. They work these moves on the hoops and it teaches them that pass rush is not a straight-line rush. I like to teach the spin move as a counter. We only teach about three moves. We teach the speed, rip, and bull rushes.

My time is up. Thank you for your attention.

THE SYRACUSE OPTION PACKAGE

UNIVERSITY OF SYRACUSE

I've spoken at clinics all over the country, and I really like coming back to this clinic. When you can get this many high school coaches to a clinic like this, that is something.

I want to talk about the Syracuse option game. That will include the different options we run. We will talk about how they fit into our scheme, how we teach them, and what our practice organization is. I will go into specific details we coach all our options and why. At Syracuse we run the option, drop-back passing game, power runs in the I formation, play-action pass from the I, no backs, and a five-wide scheme. We run it all. This is a multiple offense and our quarterbacks have to do a lot of things.

I have been blessed with my tenure at Syracuse. We have been to five bowl games in a row. The 13 years I've been at Syracuse, we've had 13 winning seasons. We have been to 11 bowl games and won eight of them. I have been blessed. I have had great quarterbacks. The thing that has made Syracuse the team we are is option football.

We are unique in what we do. That has been a plus for us. I am here to give you something. It is my obligation to give back to this game. I have learned a lot from a lot of coaches. It is my obligation today to give you whatever I got.

Reasons we run option football:
1) The option is the best way to get the ball into the perimeter. It makes the defense defend the width of the field. If you are a power run team, the defense has to defend from tackle to tackle. In our style of offense, they have to defend from sideline to sideline.
2) It neutralizes physical dominance of an opponent. Since I've been here we have only had four offensive linemen drafted into the pros. And we have beaten some big teams during that 13 years.
3) It forces the defense to defend the option. They have to spend practice time on defending the option.
4) It is an excellent way to handle safeties in today's football. It doesn't matter what level you are on, high school, college, or Pros, everyone has their safeties in run support like linebackers. There are nine people in the box.
5) This offense is a great play-action passing game. It puts the defense in a tremendous *Pass-Run-Bind*. If the safety comes too quick or too fast we are going to throw a post over his head or a dump to the tight end.
6) The option game is unique. People don't see it much anymore.
7) If you have a good quarterback, the option puts the ball in his hands every play. We have run this offense with all kinds of quarterbacks. We have run this offense with quarterbacks who ran 4.9 for the 40.

The next thing is the philosophy of the option game.
1) We want to run multiple options. If the defense takes one option away, we can go to another one. There are ways to take away certain option games, but you can't take them all away.
2) We run options from multiple formations, shifts, and motion to create "soft" perimeters.
3) We want the defense to constrict on the fullback. That is a great thing about midline options. The defense sucks in and constricts. If you don't have an option that makes the defense constrict, I think you are wasting your time.
4) You must have a play-action pass off of every option you run. If you run three or four different styles of option, you must have a play action off each one of them.

5) You must commit practice time as a staff to option football. If you can't do that don't run the option.

We practice a little differently because we have a multiple offense. On Monday we practice goal line, two-point play, short yardage, back to the wall, and blitz protection. That is what we install for our game plan on Monday. We are in full pads. The quarterback only gets that segment of the game plan on Monday. Our kids get one segment of the game plan at a time. On Monday I don't know what pass routes I am going to run, but I do know what protections I am going to use.

On Tuesday, we add the game plan on inside runs, outside runs, options, and play-action passes. We don't give the quarterback all his drop-back reads on Tuesday. We are not even talking about drop-back passes on Tuesday. He is working entirely on the option game.

On Wednesday, we install the drop-back passes, inside-the-20 running game, inside-the-20 passing game, screens, and draws.

Let me show you a time breakdown of our practice on Tuesday and Wednesday. We have five minutes of half-line inside veer drill. That is a triple option drill. We have two groups right next to one another running plays at the same time. One group is running the inside veer. The other group is running the midline triple option. The right group runs their play, and than the left group goes. While the other group is running, we reset the defense and

HALF-LINE DRILL

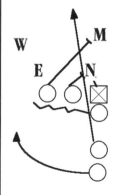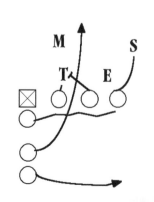

get the other offense ready to go. We get 25 plays run in a 5 minute period. It is rapid fire.

The next period is a 10-minute option teaching period. It is a 10-minute team period. We have two huddles going against one scout team. During that period we give the quarterbacks every option check. We call *Freeze Option-Check With Me*. We call all our option checks with two huddles running it. The team gets confident hearing the checks. If you can't check an option play, you can't run this offense. If the defense has six people on the right side, we want to go left. If the defense is balanced, we want to go to the field. We have to do this in team period so all our guys began to anticipate when a check is going to be run. If the guard sees a nose guard shift to the tight end, he should anticipate the check. The thought process for an offensive lineman takes more time to get ready. He has to anticipate the call to give himself more time to think.

After that we go to a 10-minute perimeter drill. We have to have this drill where the receivers block defensive backs on Tuesdays and Wednesdays. At the same time we are running a medium run drill, which is an inside run drill. We are running the same exact plays that are being run in the perimeter drill.

From there we go to a 7-on-7 drill. We run five plays of option pass in our 7-on-7 drill. In our team period we run five option pass plays. These are two five-minute periods. For 35 minutes on two days we are working exclusively on the option. That is a commitment to practice time. That's how we do it.

I want to show you some formations. If you watch us on TV, people will say this is our number 1 set. It looks like a three-wide-receiver set. What we like about this, is the slot to the two-receiver side or the single receiver could be a tight end. Why would we put tight ends in those positions? I'm going to give you the reason for that. When we count the guys to our formation side, we find six guys. We know we are going to run the option to the single-receiver side. If that split end is a 255-pound tight end, he is going to block on the corner. We call this set *Twins-Open*. That means our tight end is away from the Twins set and Open tells him to split out

BASE FORMATION

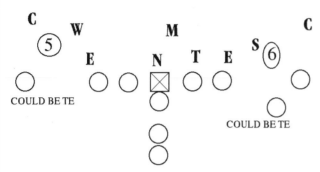

This next formation has been excellent for us with our option game. It is the *Unbalanced Twins* Set. The tight end is ineligible because the flanker is covering him up. We motion into this set. The split end comes in motion to unbalance the set. What this does is gives us another blocker into the perimeter. It gives you the additional blocker to block three defensive backs in the perimeter. We can get there by trading the tight end over. This is going to be in our game plan every week. We'll motion or trade into it.

UNBALANCED TWINS

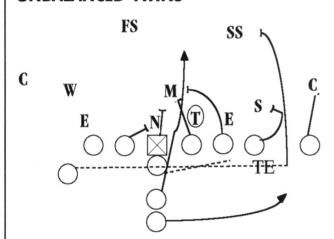

Our twins set has been real good for us. Miami is a 4-3 team and they go to squat coverage. They play three guys over our two receivers to take them

away. That creates no problem for us. We ran the play weak. The decision on what we are going to do is made on Monday night when we game plan as a staff. We study how our opponents play against formations. Then we decide what perimeters we can attack the best.

TWINS

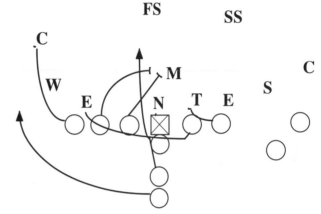

We like to take our best running receiver and put him in a 2-yards wide by 2-yards deep slot outside our tackle. We can run the midline option away from the slot and use the slot as the pitch man or run it toward the slot and use the tailback as the pitch man. We also run power I formation plays from this set.

TIGHT SLOT

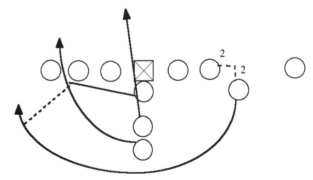

I want to talk about the midline options. I want to show you the agenda of options we have in our package every week. We are famous for the Freeze Option. We are going to run the counter freeze option, trap, midline triple, and play-action passes off each of those plays. Next we are going to run the belly G fullback play and the belly G option. Then we are going to run a series of zone options. The number 1 thing we do is run options with zone blocking schemes. We are going to run the same blocking on our inside and outside zone plays as we do on the option from them. From there we run a zone dive option, speed option, zone option from two tight ends and two flankers, speed option from four wide receivers, and a zone option pass. We are going to talk about in the next.

There are some misconceptions about the *Freeze Option*. The Freeze Option is not a triple option. It is a predetermined give to the fullback or a predetermined option. Air Force and Army run a true triple option from the Freeze Option. The intention of the Freeze Option is not a read. The fullback's hand is 5 yards from the front tip of the ball. That is deep. His toes are 6½ yards deep. He has to be that deep because the pulling guard has to go first and we want the ball riding from the back hip to the front hip of the fullback in the fake. That is not too far, but that one foot of ride stresses the linebacker. If you don't have time to spend drilling the quarterback on this play, don't think about putting it in.

On the snap of the ball the tailback freezes. The tailback does not go into the pitch phase until the quarterback's foot hits the ground in his second step. He wants to be 4 yards in front and 4 yards deep in his pitch relationship. That is the tailback's responsibility.

Let's talk about running the Freeze Option to a shade and 5 technique. The call-side tackle releases for the Mike linebacker. That is a kill shot for him. The guard blocks down on the shade technique. The center blocks back on the 3 technique. The pulling guard pulls into the line of scrimmage and logs the 5 technique. The thing about Miami's defensive ends was the way they played a down block. They wrong-armed everything. They closed hard from the outside and spilled everything outside. That is what we want. The outside linebacker is our pitch key. The backside tackle comes down and collisions the 3 technique, looks for the run through coming in that gap, and then turns back on the end.

The fullback runs the midline. Our definition of midline is the fullback's nose right up the center's rump. It is not the gap or foot of the center. It is straight up the center's butt. If the secondary is in quarter coverage, you have a receiver to block two defenders. He blocks the support and we make 5 yards.

FREEZE MIDLINE TO THE 5 TECHNIQUE

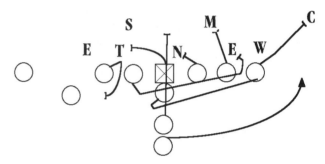

If the defensive end in the 5 technique slants inside, the frontside tackle takes him and the guard pulls up for the Mike linebacker.

FREEZE MIDLINE VS. END SLANT

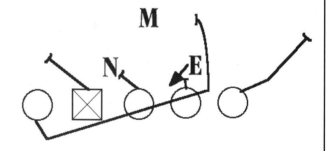

Now lets look at it to the 3 technique into the Eagle Front. The tackle comes off for the Will linebacker. The guard rips through the 3 technique and goes back side for the Mike linebacker. The center blocks the shade nose guard. The pulling guard pulls and logs the 3 technique tackle. The backside tackle and tight end step inside to stop the run-through stunt. If no one comes, they hinge back like a pass-blocking technique to protect the quarterback from getting hit in the back by someone chasing down the line. The split end blocks the hard corner and we option the 5 technique end. We are running the play into the sideline, and will make 4 yards at the least. That is a sound gain for an offensive play.

If the 5 technique gets upfield and the pulling guard has to kick him out, the quarterback has to be aware of what is happening. He can't pitch the ball. He has to jump up inside. What play should we be running against that type of technique, the option or the trap? The answer is obvious.

Like I said before, this is a predetermined play. We don't run the fullback early in the game, because the linebackers are coached to stop the fullback. They will do it early. But the first three or four times they hit him and he doesn't have the ball, they will ignore him later.

We also have a Freeze Option Counter we use when the linebackers start to read the Freeze Option and slide to that side. We come back with the counter. It is the same blocking. The only difference is the fake by the quarterback. He is stepping away from the direction he is going.

Let's move on to the Belly-G Option. This was made famous by Nebraska. It has been a good option for us. In the Freeze Option the speed of the quarterback is not important. In this option your quarterback had better be able to run. This is a formula to whether you can run this play based on the speed of your quarterback. If the quarterback is faster than the Sam linebacker, you can run this play. If the Sam is 5.0, your quarterback has to be 4.9. If the Sam is 4.6, your quarterback better be 4.5.

This is a tremendous play. It is great against a 4-3 defense like Miami runs. It is the best series against this defense there is. This is the Belly-G Option. The tight end takes an inside release, gets his shoulders square, and blocks the Mike linebacker. The tackle downblocks on the 3 technique. The call-side guard pulls and logs the 9 technique end. Remember Miami's ends are coming down and wrong-arming everything. That makes it easy for us. If the nose is on the backside shade of the center, the center and backside guard will zone the shade to the backside Will linebacker. The backside tackle zones the gap to his inside. If the nose tackle is over our backside guard in the G-position, the guard

cuts him and the center goes strong side and will VICE the 3 technique with the call side tackle. That is to prevent penetration.

The fullback is the key to the play. He takes a lead step at a 45-degree angle at the inside leg of the call-side tackle. The quarterback reverses out and rolls deep. He flashes the ball to the fullback's hip. The fullback will flatten out and block the first linebacker in the box. The Z-Back or flanker blocks the corner. We are going to pitch the ball off the strong safety or number 4 man in the defensive scheme.

BELLY-G OPTION

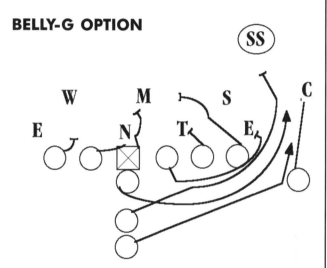

You can draw all the plays you want, but if you don't have the techniques it won't work. If the 3 technique is a Warren Sapp, the tackle will have trouble keeping him from penetrating. We use the VICE call. The center steps behind the pulling guard and gets into the 3 technique and squeezes him in the Vice to stops the penetration. The problem is when the center has a backside shade on him. He can't run a Vice call because sometimes Warren

VICE CALL

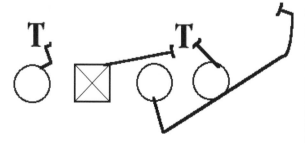

Sapp is playing the other tackle and you can't afford to turn that tackle loose. The call-side tackle is now on his own with the down block.

If you use your formations this play can be a killer play. When we go to the three-wide set and get a walkout alignment from the Sam linebacker, he is too wide to log, so he becomes the pitch key. We are two-on-two in the secondary and the fullback comes through and logs the Mike linebacker. They can't stop this play from that formation.

BELLY-G OPTION FROM TWINS-OPEN

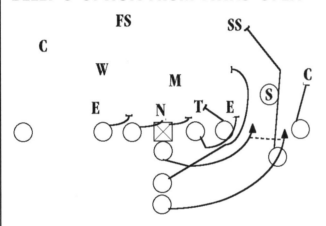

When you block the Eagle Defense, it all comes down to your personnel as to how you choose to block it. If you have a great tight end and a weaker center, we will block it like this. The tight end blocks

BELLY-G VS. EAGLE

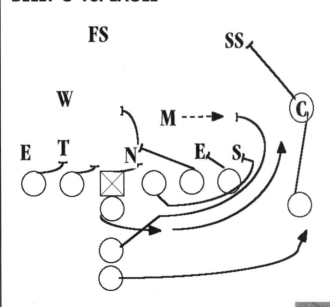

down on the 5 technique end. The center reaches the shade nose tackle. The call-side tackle comes down and chips the nose tackle on the way to the Will linebacker. The guard pulls and logs the Sam linebacker. We zone the Will linebacker run through to the back side with the backside guard and tackle. The fullback does the same thing, but the first linebacker in the box is the Mike linebacker. We have a one-on-two in the secondary. If the corner is support, the flanker bypasses him and blocks the safety. The corner becomes the pitch key.

If the tight end can't handle the down block by himself, we adjust the blocking. We double-team the defensive end with the tackle and tight end. Someone has to come off that block and go to the Will linebacker. The center has to chop cut the nose tackle. Everything else is the same.

BELLY-G DOUBLE-TEAM

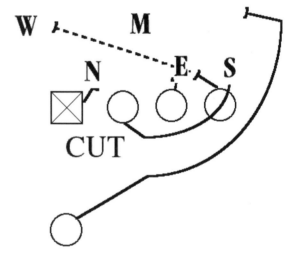

I can't tell you how to do it. Those are the two options you have. You have to consider your personnel. We teach them both. Everything with the pitch relationship is still the same.

The Belly-G to the fullback puts the 4-3 defense in a tremendous conflict. The tight end takes and inside releases but he keeps his shoulders square. Don't let him run to the Mike linebacker. The Mike linebacker will come to him. He keeps his shoulders square at that plane and works up the field underneath the Mike linebacker. If you let the tight end go inside, his shoulders get turned and the Mike linebacker will cross the tight end's face and he is finished. The tackle down-blocks on the 3 technique. The guard pulls and kicks out the end man. We zone the back side and Vice with the center if he is uncovered. The fullback leads at the tackle's inside leg. The quarterback hands the ball to the fullback and makes a great fake on the option to hold the safety. In the Belly-G option the Sam linebacker is blocked by the fullback. When he sees the play he is running outside to beat the block of the fullback. About the third or fourth time of running the G-option, we give it to the fullback on the Belly-G. The Sam linebacker is 7 yards outside and the fullback is 10 yards down the field. They can't stop both plays. Always run the option before you run the fullback.

BELLY-G FULLBACK

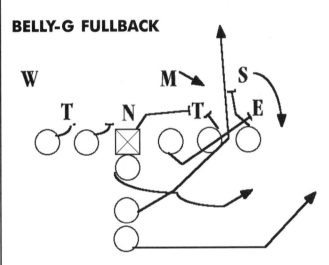

This is just like the other play. You can single block the 5 technique with the tight end or double-team him with the tackle. Someone comes off for the Will linebacker. The center uses a lead crossover step and chops the nose tackle, the guard pulls, and kicks out the Sam linebacker. We hand the ball to the fullback, and he runs past the Mike linebacker.

BELLY-G FULLBACK VS. TECHNIQUE

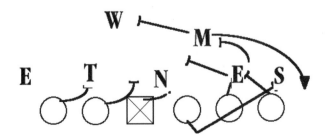

Let's move on to the Zone Option. Zone blocking is a cure-all for everything. It doesn't matter what defense, front, blitz, or scheme the opponent uses. That's why it is so popular today. In the NFL 99 percent of the running game is zone blocking. It is simple, sound, and they can spend more time on the passing game. We have utilized the zone-blocking scheme in option football. We have probably 10-12 plays in our offense with the same exact blocking scheme up front. The linemen get better at running the same scheme, but we are running 10 to 12 different things behind it. Our inside and outside zone, belly plays, stretch plays, zone dives, and seven different options, all have the same blocking scheme. That is how we can run multiple plays and offenses, because the linemen are doing the same thing over and over again. The only guys you have to worry about in a multiple offense are the linemen.

We want to run a zone option play at a 3 and 7 technique. We can run it against anything, but we would rather run it against a 3 and 7 technique. The tight end steps at the 7 technique with his first step. His second step is right up the field. The tackle comes on the 7 technique and double-teams him to the inside Mike linebacker. The tight end and tackle zone the 7 technique to the first inside linebacker. The guard and center zone the 3 technique to the backside linebacker. The backside guard cuts the 2 technique, and the backside tackle zones his inside gap. The flanker blocks the corner. The fullback almost repeats his Belly-G path. If the B-Gap defender is coming up the field, he cuts him right

ZONE OPTION VS. 8-MAN FRONT

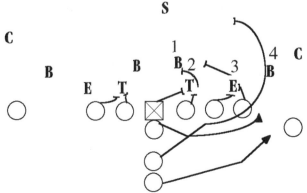

there. If that gap is secured, he flattens out and blocks the safety. The quarterback flash fakes the fullback, comes out on the option, and pitches off the #4 defender. He pitches off #4 on a zone or load option.

The technique of the double-team is critical. The tight end has to get off the double-team quickly to get the Mike linebacker. The tight end steps with his inside foot toward the defensive end but he keeps his shoulders square. On his second step, he is stepping straight upfield and getting square. The tackle takes a bucket step on his first step. That gets him off the line and in line with the block. On his second step he is on top of the block and can control the defensive end.

I tell our quarterbacks in the zone option, they open and walk off the ball. The defense reads the play as a dive to the fullback. There is no mesh. The ball is flashed by the quarterback. The fullback bounces around and goes for the safety. If your quarterback is faster than their inside linebackers they can't stop this play. The outside linebacker takes the pitch and the safety is the alley runner. But the fullback is going to block the safety. That means the inside linebacker has to make the play on the quarterback.

That is one zone option. But watch this one. Remember the zone-blocking scheme. We come out in two tight ends and two flankers. With two tight ends, we are probably going to get two 7 techniques by the defense. They can't stop this play with two 7 techniques. Run the same exact blocking scheme as the first zone option. Take the quarterback, reverse pivot, and option the outside line-

backer to the right. To the defense we have presented an entirely different formation and play. To the offense it is the same play.

This time you motion the left flanker to the right and block the outside linebacker. The rest of the play is the same as far as the line blocking is concerned. But now the quarterback and fullback run the stretch play. It is the same blocking scheme that we ran on the two previous plays. The linemen are working on the same techniques over and over again. We have run three different plays with the same exact blocking scheme.

STRETCH PLAY

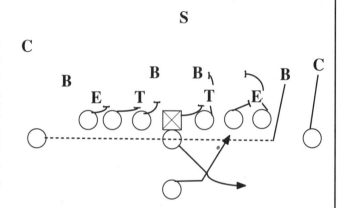

I want to go back to this play for a second. We have done this play a little different every year. We have done it with the quarterback pivoting out and running the speed option. If the play was going right, we've had the quarterback kick back with his left foot, square his shoulders, and run the speed option. I believe the counter action holds the line-

SPEED OPTION

COUNTER SPEED

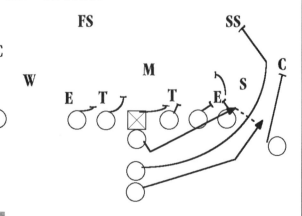

backers longer. They are coached when they see the speed option to run like crazy. There is no fake to the fullback and nothing to hold the linebackers. Every split second that you can hold the linebacker means something. This play is good because you can get a hat on the safety.

We can run it to the split side also. We still get the fullback up on the safety and pitch off the end.

You have been a great audience. I appreciate your attention for three hours. I have a great obligation to the coaching profession. I want you to know that. I have had a great career and have been to some great places. I have an obligation when I speak to you to give you everything I can. I want to tell you this from a personal experience. It may help you as a coach and a professional.

I had a great career at Syracuse and I went to the NFL. I always thought I wanted to go to the NFL and coach. I had a chance to go with the San Diego Chargers. When I got there I found out a lot of things. I found out in that league at times there are guys who don't like football. There are guys that don't like to practice football. There are guys that are looking for the next team and could care less about your team.

I tried my ass off and coached as hard as I could, the way I had always coached. On Friday nights my son played high school football. He played for Torrey Pines High School in San Diego. That is a big-time high school program. I watched them play on Friday nights. I would sit in the stands and watch those coaches coach. I said to myself, "These guys are coaching." I looked at my own situation and thought I wasn't sure what I was

doing. I was a manager. I wasn't coaching. I watch the coaches coaching and watched what the game of football meant to my son, being coached by those coaches.

At the end of the season I walked in to the head coach and general manager and told them I didn't belong there. I didn't have a job but I had confidence I could find one. What I am trying to say to you is this. I made more money than I've ever made in coaching. But I missed the intensity and enthusiasm of working with kids. I miss what you guys had every single day. But you don't realize it sometimes.

The ability to go down into that weight room and be around those kids is what makes it worthwhile. And to be around that kid when he says, "Coach, my girlfriend's pregnant." "Coach, I got in trouble." You don't understand what impact you have on young kids. Think back to when you got started in this business. That's why you are coaches. That is why I got into the profession. I didn't get into the business to have a big contract and make a lot of money. I got into it to coach. Sometimes when you look at other situations, the grass is always greener on the other side of the fence. I'm telling you it's not.

In today's day and age if you have a job coaching kids, you are damn lucky. You are the best man in your building. You do more for those kids than anybody does. If I can do anything for you let me know. I have great respect for everyone in this room who is a coach. You should wear that like a badge of honor. You're a coach. Don't ever forget it. If I can help you at any time don't hesitate to call on me. Thank you very much.

DEFENSIVE DRILLS THAT MAKE A DIFFERENCE

WESTERN MICHIGAN UNIVERSITY

First let me start by saying my experience here in Michigan has been wonderful. This is particularly true of my association with the high school coaches of this area. I am amazed at how willing coaches of this state are to learn. You give of your own time to go to different clinics. I am grateful to you for the time you take with us when we visit your school. I know it takes a lot of your time to get the transcripts of players sent out and it takes time to get the films mailed to us. You have been wonderful in that respect and you all deserve a round of applause for all of this. It is apparent that coaches of this state are interested in their players and they are interested in coaching good football.

My topic today is "Defensive Drills That Make A Difference." It is an interesting topic and one that got me to start thinking about drills. A lot of coaches will just go out and run drills. They run the drills because some other coaches have been doing them forever, and they ran those drills when they played. I went back and looked at the drills that we run and it got me to thinking. I actually saw some drills that I thought perhaps did not make a difference. We had been doing the drills for a long time but they needed to be upgraded.

I had my GA go over the overhead material that I am going to use today. I did not run the spell check on them. I hope he did. Hopefully you will not find any misspelled words. Forgive me if you do find any misspelled words. I was at Ole Miss and left there to be the defensive coordinator at Cornell University. The head coach at Cornell was a Cornell graduate. I made up our playbook and gave it to the head coach to review. I was expecting him to give it back to me with comments about the defenses he wanted to use and the ones that he would prefer not to use. Instead he handed me back the playbook with all of the misspelled words circled.

Also, he had corrected the grammar in the book. He was actually giving me a hard time about it. I told him that he had hired me to be a football coach and not an English teacher. It really helped me because now I can write something and hand it out to the kids and they do not think I am a dumb ass.

The format that I will use today will follow this script. First I want to talk about "What Makes A Great Drill?", then I want to get into three categories of drills. We all know there are a lot of different kinds of drills. The first part of the drills will be what we call Warm-Up or Evaluation Drills. These are drills we are going to do when we first come on the field. We are trying to get our players' muscles warmed up. They are drills we are going to do in spring practice or in fall camp. We use these drills to evaluate players to see how flexible their hips are. We want to know what kind of feet they have. We want to know what kind of explosion they have.

These drills are also drills that we do in the off-season. We are doing them at this time in what we call our Champs Program. This program is run early in the morning. But they are drills that we can evaluate and they are good drills to get players warmed up.

The next area I will cover will be defensive position drills. I have some defensive line drills that we will look at. I have some game film to show how the drills carry over in the games. I have a couple of linebacker drills and defensive back drills. After that I will go into what we call Circuit Drills. At one time I did not use these drills, but the way we practice at Western Michigan now we do not have a lot of individual time. We do a lot of work against each other. It may be an Inside Drill or a Skeleton Drill. Our individual drills are very short. We will combine some individual work with the Circuit Drill. For example we will do a Tackling Drill, or we will do a

Pass Rush Drill in the Circuit. We may do a Blitz Drill, and we do a Take-Away Drill in the Circuit. It is a real fast drill with emphasis placed on the particular things we are working on, and everyone gets in the drill. We may run the Pass Rush Drill in the Circuit and the defensive backs will be in the drill. They learn some pass-rush techniques so they will know what to do when they run a blitz and run into some blockers. I will go through these drills and then I have film on these drills as well.

I started out by asking myself this question What are the things that make a great drill? We all know we are running drills for a purpose. We are trying to teach our players how to play football. That has to be understood. It has to be a learning process.

I can remember my first coaching job back in 1976. I went to Kansas State to coach. We had an old grumpy line coach and I was working with him with the tight ends. On the first day of practice we were working on stance and he told me to make sure the players heels were up off the ground. I was going around checking the players when the old coach came over to me and said, "Do you see that young player over there with his heels flat on the ground?" I said, yes I do. He replied, "Do you want to know how to teach him how to get his heels up off the ground?" I assured him I did. He walked over to the player and kicked him in the ankle as hard as he could. The player went to the ground grabbing his ankle and screaming for dear life. The coach looked at me and said, "He will never have his heels flat on the ground again." I thought to myself that there had to be a better way to teach football. Football has certainly changed, and certainly for the better.

WHAT MAKES A GREAT DRILL?

First, we feel that any drill used should be football-related. I learned this from John Majors when I was the defensive coordinator at the University of Pittsburgh. Coach Majors was a great fundamentalist and a great football coach. He wanted everything to be football-related. For example, when I fist started coaching there we would run our drills by calling out "Ready, Ready" and then we would make

the tackle. When we called "Ready, Ready" the players would start chipping their feet. Coach Majors came up to me one day and asked me why I had the players chopping their feet before they made their initial contact. I told him that was the way I was taught to do it and had been doing it that way. He asked me to tell him when a player chopped his feet in a game before he made contact. "Never!" I understood his point. There is no sense in a player standing there chopping his feet and then running the shuffle drills. Now we let him start from the base that he is going to start from. We want no unnecessary movements in our drills.

As coaches we think of ourselves as teachers. Drills always have to progress. For example, when we teach tackling we are going to with two players in the locked-up position. We are going to get around behind them and teach them where the hands fit, where the shoulder fits, and how the body position should be. Then we will separate them a little and then have them come together. Then we will move them back to a yard apart and run the drill. After that we may turn that into a Sideline Drill. Now the players are covering 15 yards doing those things. Once again, these drills are football-related.

Why are you running a drill? We want to have a *Specific Purpose* when we run a drill. The things that are always important to us are these points. One, we want to teach body position. We want to teach the players to bend their bodies. We want to see them bend their knees and ankles. Too many of the players will bend at the waist when you tell them to get into a position. We want them to bend at the ankles and knees so we can obtain leverage. In any drill that we are doing we are going to demand some type of body positioning.

We are looking for some type of reaction. This is what defense is all about. It is the reaction side of the game. You must react to what you see. We all have our little sayings such as, "Don't Guess, React To What You See!"

We always want to react to a snap of the ball on our drills. We want to simulate the snap of the ball.

We do not go up to a line and call out "GO". We always go on some type of ball movement.

We are always trying to create some type of explosion on our drills. It is a contact game and we need to learn to have explosion. We have specific purposes on our techniques. What are the techniques that you are teaching in a drill? One specific purpose could be toughness. I feel you need to do some toughness drills. It may be a mental drill. It may just be an alignment drill. And certainly we want to include discipline to the list. If we are having a drill and we tell them we want their foot behind the line, that is what we want. We are not going to say it and then have them come up and have their foot on the line. We are always going to demand discipline.

The next area we look at in a drill is *Creativity*. By that I mean change up. Make the drills interesting. Don't run the same drill all of the time. Don't always do the same tackling drill. Have them come off the ground and tackle. Create some type of competition on the drills. Kids love drills that are competitive.

Tempo is another area we stress in selecting drills. You must have repetitions in drills. You do not want a drill where you have 20 players standing in line to catch one football. Have reps for them by setting up three or four lines. Make sure the lines have a good flow. Do not have one line going slow and the other line fast. Those are the things that keep the tempo of your drills going. On most of the drills we are going to have some type of "look" team. We have another player on the other side of the ball simulation what we want. It is important to coach those guys up on effort and technique. We are striving to get reps.

It is important on finishing the drill. We want them to finish a tackle when they come off a block. When they come out of the chutes what are you going to have them do? We always try to create some type of finish. It may be as simple as this. As we are running through the bags we want them to drop the shoulders and accelerate, and show a burst of speed. Then we will have a cone in front of them

and they have to sprint through that cone. Carl Nystrom, who coaches our linebackers and will help me with the demos later, has his linebackers simulate a tackle when they come out of a drill. They will dip the hips, put their arms in the holster position, and they will club through the tackle. You will see this on the film later. We may just have the players finish by running to a line. On another drill we may have them scoop up a fumble and score.

One of the first things I should have said about drills is this. You do not want to get your players hurt on drills. You have to make sure the area is not cluttered with equipment that does not need to be there. Make sure you are not getting ready to run them into the blocking sled. You do not want to do a backpedal drill while the receivers are running a takeoff drill. You do not want two players running together in two different drills.

Along those same lines you do not want to beat your players up in a drill. You do not need to have tackling drills where they line up 10 yards from each other and go at it head to head. Keep it close quarters.

Now I want to move to the *Drills Categories*. We are running these drills to get the blood to the muscles. We use them to get flexibility. We are working on foot quickness, reaction, and transition.

First is our *Warm-up and Evaluation Drills*. We do this drill early in the morning. It is the drill that most of you have. It is the Bags Drill. I go to a lot of NFL camps and the pros use this drill. Why do we run it? We are doing it for body position to teach a player to be able to run through the bags, through an obstacle in a good, strong football position. If we are running straight through the bags, or if we are turning the shoulders to the side over the bags, we are teaching good body position. You always hear about hand-eye coordination; we are looking for eye-foot coordination. We are looking for guys that can play without looking at the ground.

It is a good warm-up drill. It is a good drill to use to evaluate players. It is good drill to evaluate the players' foot movements. We usually work with one line on the drill. We are going to run in a straight line to start off. Then we work similar drills that include the following: Two In The Hole, Shuffle, Sideways Run, Low Hands, and Weave. At the end of the drill we have our finish. First we tell them to *Burst* through the cone. After that we may have them simulate a tackle. We may have them come through the bags sideways and then come downhill to simulate a tackle. There will always be some type of finish on the drills. Let me show the drills to you on film.

BAG DRILL

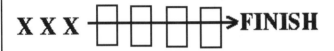

The next drills are drills that our head coach Gary Darnell, who was a defensive coordinator most of his career, strongly believes in. We call it Run-and-Shuffle.

The purpose of the drill is used to teach body position and to keep the eyes focused upfield. We are trying to teach players to run full speed with their shoulders turned up the field. We do not want to see a linebacker turning and running with his shoulders turned to the sideline. Once a player goes through his shuffle we want him to go through the progression on the cutback. Once he is in a pursuit angle we want him to be able to run with the shoulders pointed upfield and still be able to take care of the cutbacks. They must be able to square up and shuffle. That is what this drill simulates.

We use plastic DOTS on this drill. We put them down instead of cones. We have two lines of players facing each other. They start on the coaches' command at the first dot. They start in the shuffle. When they get to the next dot they turn and sprint full speed. They are keeping their shoulders square to each other. When they reach the next dot they go back into the shuffle. It is not a mirror drill. We are competing against each other. We want the players to work as fast as they can.

RUN AND SHUFFLE

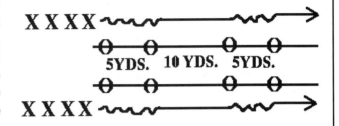

The next drill is a must for any defensive scheme you will ever run. We call the drill *Change of Direction*. For short you can call it COD or Reaction Drill. The purpose of the drill and why we run the drill is because it is a great evaluator. It is the first thing we do when we get our freshmen in camp. Also, at our special camps that we do, the first drill I am going to use with all defensive players is this drill. It will take about three reps for me to tell if that player has the defensive capabilities we are looking for.

CHANGE OF DIRECTION

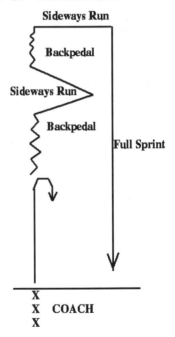

It is a great drill to evaluate the players. It teaches body position. It teaches reaction, which we all know is what you have to do on defense. It teaches transition from one direction to another. It is an excellent footwork drill. It is an excellent warm-up drill. It is the first drill I use with outside linebackers every single day of practice. It is a great way to measure effort.

I stand on a line next to the players. They run out 10 yards away from me. I give them the "Ready – Ready" and they sprint downfield 10 yards and turn around. They get in their normal stance and then I point in one direction or the other. I will point to their right, left, straight back, or I am going to bring them back toward me. It is a full-speed-run drill. It is not a shuffle drill. When I point in a direction they plant the outside foot and turn and run. We stress staying low on the drill. When I point the other way and they plant off the outside foot and sprint back the other way. At the end we have them sprint back to the starting line full speed.

We may run them four or five times on this drill. I may send them right and then straight back. I do not want them to guess where I am going to move them. We mix them up so they are reacting to our directions. We want them running full speed until I change directions. If they start to slow down or start guessing, I will start the drill all over again.

I want to put that part of the film on. You can see it is an excellent drill. (FILM)

We went through the warm-up and evaluation drills. These are drills you can do in your off-season and early in fall camp. I do the Change of Direction every day.

Next are *Defensive Line Drills*. We do a tremendous amount of Chute work. What is the purpose of the Chute drills? The number 1 thing we are looking to do is to teach body position. We want our linemen to play down low with leverage. Our defensive ends are not very big. One end weighed 235 pounds, and the other one weighed 225 pounds. Our 3 technique weighed 270 pounds, and our nose guard weighed 270 pounds. That is not very big. We have to teach our players to play down low and to play with leverage.

We are looking for body position and footwork. Then we teach a specific skill with the chute. We will teach a stunt technique under the chute. We teach what we call the ricochet under the chute. This is where we run a stunt and then we have to redi-

rect. We try to teach low hands. We teach leg drive under the chute. Anytime they are under that chute they should feel the burn in the thighs, because they are working very low.

CHUTE DRILL

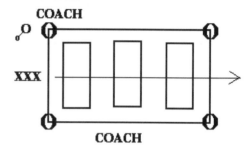

This is the progression we go through in the chute. The first thing we go through is the *Power Step*. You can put bags under the chute on the drills. To start the drill we do not have the bags under there. We want them going under the bags down low with the chest on the thighs and over the knees. They just power step their way through the chute. They have to stay down low or they will hit their head on the top of the chute. They will turn the knees outside if you let them. Make them keep the knees straight up the field.

The next drill is the *Shuffle*. We are gong sideways on this drill. We start out without bags and add them later. Again the chest is to the knees.

Then we do a low-hand drill, a stunt technique, and a ricochet drill. Then we do a 1-on-1 drill under the chute.

We get back to what makes a great drill and it is the finish. We always finish with something. Our coaches are very creative. You will see on the film the different things we do on the drill to finish. We have them go a certain direction. We have them scoop the ball on the fumble and score. We strip the quarterback on the finish. We get the hands up high to tip the pass against the quarterback. We combine whatever we can with the drill that we are stressing that day. We have to do this because we do not have all that much time to spend on individual drills. (FILM)

The next drills we run with our defensive line are the *Pipes*. I am going to go fast on this because you need to see the drills on film to see what we are getting out of it. We can take a baseball bat and cut the end off and use that instead or the pipes. Or we can take a piece of wood and use it. We put two players facing each other. They take the pipe, or bat, or piece of wood and place their hands on the side facing them. They bring the pipe up to eyes level. They start down the line pushing the pipe with the palms of their hands. They are both on defense and they are learning to play the reach block with leverage. We are working on good body position, footwork and leverage.

PIPE DRILLS

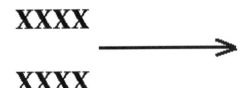

We work down to the end of the line and then we work back the other way. We work on flat back, wrist under the pipe, with the pipe at eye level and we work our leverage hand.

Now we go to our *Two-on-One Drill*. The purpose is to understand the proper fit to zone schemes and double-team blocks. We learn to Read and React to these blocks.

We must learn to read these blocks. I will go over a couple of them here. Today there is so much zone and double-team blocking. We line our players up on the inside shade of the blocker to his left.

TWO-ON-ONE DRILL

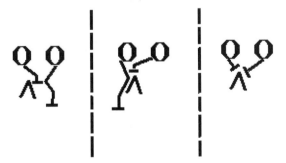

Then we switch them over and have them work on the inside shade of the blocker on his right.

TWO-ON-ONE DRILL

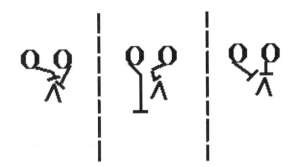

We have to teach the linemen the difference in the double team and the scoop block. We see the zone block and the double-team. On the double-team we teach them to play the first man to make contact as a base block on the double team. When we feel the pressure of the second man coming into us, we throw the hip into him and we try to run our feet in that direction. We do not want to hit the ground. Hitting the ground is a last effort thing to keep from being driven down the field. I feel you have to do the Two-on-One Drill all of the time. (FILM)

I have two linebacker drills. First is the *Strike Drill*. We do this with our linebacker, defensive backs, and the defensive linemen. It is a good drill to teach body position, blow delivery, leverage, timing, and toughness. It is a little like the old Bull-in-the-Ring Drill. The defender knows where the blocker is coming from.

We take three players, two blockers, and one linebacker. We use the other linebackers as blockers in the drill most of the time. The blockers are 1 yard apart. The linebacker is 2½ yards from the blockers. The coach will initiate the drill. The defensive player knows which player is coming first. For example he will know that he is going to take the first blocker on that is on his left with his left shoulder. Then he takes on the right block. He gets a Hit, Hit, and then the three players rotate. They get two hits and then they rotate.

STRIKE DRIVE

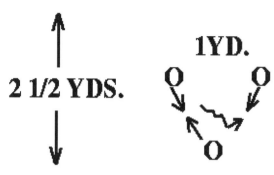

If we want them to go for a couple of reps we can. It is a quick-hitting drill. We have an *Inside Strike* and a *Cross-Face Strike*. On the Inside Strike we put the pads in the front and absorb the blow of the blocker. We want the blockers inside ear in the V of my neck. We want the pads under the blockers' pads. We are looking for leverage. We progress from that block to the Cross Face. Now we want the hat across the blocker. We do not teach hitting with the helmet. We use the hands and shoulder pads. We take on the first blocker, recoil, and take on the second blocker. Then we rotate the players.

The next drill is a combination of the Strike Drill but it had a couple of other things combined in it. Once again it is better to see this drill on tape.

It is called *Packer Drill*. Again we are trying to teach body position. We are working on block protection, escapes, and form tackling. We all talk about our players being able to get off a block.

We have the defensive linebacker facing the four offensive players. We have #1, #2, and #3 as blockers. The #4 man is the ball carrier. The coach starts the drill. The linebacker knows the #1 man is coming to block him. He will form a strike on that #1 man. As he sheds the #1 man the #2 man comes out low and the linebacker has to use a low-hands block on him. We want to make sure we get good bend at the knees and ankles again. We talk to our players about being able to defeat low blocks with the wrist below the knees. We want our hand on the blockers helmet. As the linebacker comes off the Cut block he faces a high, straight-ahead block

by #3. We want to get good body position on him and work our release. We can use what we call a punch and shrug, where we are trying to jolt him and them shrug off and go make the tackle. We can use a rip, a swim, or some type or release there. (FILM)

PACKER DRILL

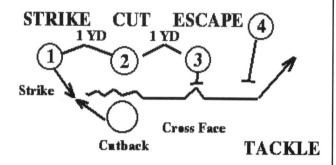

Next are our *Defensive Secondary Drills*. First is the Straight-Line Turn - 45 Degrees Drill. If I were in the pros the first drill I would run would be this drill. It is a very important drill for any player but especially for defensive backs. This drill teaches them to flip the hips. It helps develop hip flexibility. It is a warm-up drill. It is a drill that you do early in practice. We use it to evaluate players. It is great to teach change of directions and footwork.

The first drill is the *Straight Line*. We start the drill with a backpedal. He is lined up opposite the coach or the quarterback. I give him a direction. As he backpedals I will point in one direction or the other. They will turn and run full speed in the direction I point. When I flip back they flip their hips and turn and go. I finish the drill and the take off in a dead sprint.

STRAIGHT LINE

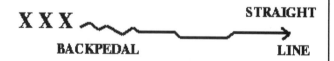

Next we do a *Speed Turn*. We start in the backpedal and then when the receiver beats us we have to turn and run at the angle the receiver is in. We call that a Speed Turn. Then we have them backpedal and have them turn and run full speed at a 45-degree angle. We use this when a receiver starts to run a Post and then runs a Corner and beats the back. He has to turn his head around and find the angle the receiver left and meet up with him. We have them turn two or three ways to each side.

SPEED TURN – TURN 45 DEGREES

This drill is a good drill to get warmed up. It is a good drill to evaluate players. If I am a high school coach I am going to take all of my incoming freshmen and give them this drill. This is the first drill I am going to give them. I can determine who can turn flip their hips and who can't.

Next is the *Angle Strip Drill*. It teaches what we call the Interception Angle. It teaches timing and hand placement. The defender is back 15 yards from the coach. The offensive receiver makes his cut to the ball 10 yards from the coach and 5 yards in front of the defensive back. The coach makes the throw and the defensive back must break at the proper angle to make the breakup or the interception. If he does not make the interception we want him to work on the strip. We will work the club out, punch under, or something along those lines. It is a drill our defensive backs coach does at least once a week. Sometimes we will put this drill into our Take-Away Circuit.

ANGLE STRIP

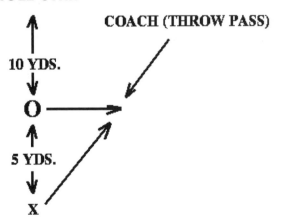

Our next drill is called *Defend the Break*. The purpose is to teach footwork, angle, and timing. It is a reaction drill as well. As the two players back up neither one knows which will be on defense until the coach points to one of them. After the ball is completed we want to work on the strip again.

The two start out in a backpedal. When the coach points one way or the other they start to weave that way. We are working on the backpedal, and the weave. The coach will throw the ball to the front man and the back man becomes the defender. He must play the ball and take the proper angle on the pass.

DEFEND-THE-BREAK DRILL

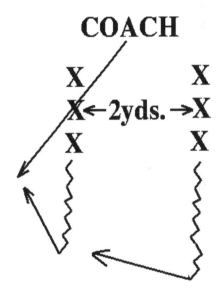

After we complete one side we start the other way. Now we work on the Out Route. We can start them on the backpedal and then weave and run the Curl back inside. They really do not know until the end which one of them is going to be on offense or defense.

We stress for them to be in a good stance down low. You can certainly teach them to play the Out and Up Route if we are playing Zone or Man Coverage. If they are in Man Coverage they must keep their eyes on the man. If they are in Zone Coverage they can start the break when the coach pumps the ball.

Going back to what makes a great drill is creativity. The coach only has a few minutes to run this drill so he has to get a lot done with it. We want to get a couple of things out of the drill. We are getting backpedal, transition, and angle fit, strip, and take away techniques. All of it has to come in one drill for us to be successful. We are limited in the amount of time we can practice. (FILM)

When we watch our game films and see the different drills that come into play we stop the film and let the players see the play so they will know why we do the drills. This will make them work a little harder in the drills.

The next segment that I am going into is what we call our *Circuit Training*. The first Circuit I am going to talk about is the *Takeaway Circuit*. We have a 10-minute period to run the drill. We will set up three or four stations. Most of what I am going to do from here on will be on film because it is better to see it that way.

What is the purpose of the drill? We want a Unit Emphasis on creating takeaways. When we go to this drill, as coaches we try to be enthusiastic in the drill. "Takeaway Circuit, Let's Go." We run to the drill because our guys know where they are going. We are working on proper techniques. We have three stations and we want to get them all in within the 10 minute period.

The first station we have is our *Fumble Recovery Drill*. We put our players down on all fours. We put a football out in front of them. We have them dive out and recover the fumble. We teach them to catch the ball in their hands just as a wide receiver would catch the ball. Too many times we have seen the defender go after a fumble and dive on the ball and it hits his hip and squirts out of there. We want them to see the ball with their eyes, grab it with their hand, and bring the ball into the midsection. Then we want them to get on their side and bring the knees up. We want to wrap both hands around the ball and be in good position on the ball. We do not want someone taking the ball away from us underneath.

Next we put them down in a stance and put a football 4 or 5 yards out in front of them. The coach will give a signal and they will run out and scoop the ball up and score. We just call it *Scoop-and-Score Drill*. We want them to bend at the knees when they dip to pick up the fumble.

A change-up is to put four offensive players out in front of the ball. Now we want him to recover the ball. We do not want to Scoop-and-Score in traffic. However, we do not want a player to jump on a fumble out in the open where he could pick it up and score.

After three minutes we go to the *Strip Station*. We put them into position and give the man the football. We have the defensive man come over the top on the overhand strip. Sometimes we will put the ball under the receiver's underarm and have our defenders reach in and pull the ball out of the receivers hands. We do the same thing with the punch trying to get the ball out.

We will fit the ball up under the offensive man's arm and have one put his hat on the ball. The second man will come in and drive the elbow up off the man with the ball. The first defender will form tackle to knock the ball loose, and the second man to drive the elbow up high. Most offensive coaches teach their backs and receivers to keep the elbow down. Once the elbow goes up, and I do not care who it is, that ball is coming out.

The next part is what we do with the defensive line. We line up in a base block and do a three-step drill. We hit into the offensive player in a bull rush. We want to get the hands up high to tip the ball with a quarterback throwing the ball. For the defensive backs and linebackers we have them work on the intercept. They run the drill 10 yards apart. They start on the backpedal and the coach throws the ball and they make the interception at the highest point.

During the fall practice we run this two days a week. In the season we run this a least once a week. I will go through the other Circuits and then show the film.

Next is the *Pass Rush Circuit*. We use this for our defensive line and outside linebackers and sometimes our defensive backs will go through it. We have had a lot of sacks over the last few years. A couple of years ago we had 41 sacks that ranked us in the top five in the NCAA.

What is the purpose of the drill? We place emphasis on technique. We can work on technique in small groups. We are not going to have 12 men in a pass-rush line. We break up into small groups.

First is the *Speed Rush*. It is for takeoff. We simulate the snap of the ball. We put several cones down for the line of scrimmage and then we put one back 5 yards deep behind the offensive tackle area. We run to the cone and try to get around it, and we always have something to simulate the quarterback. We always time the drill. We want them to know their best time on the drill. We encourage them to try to beat their best time.

The next drill is the *Sled Drill*. It is a tackling sled and we simulate the Bull Rush. We are working on the sled on takeoff, hands, hips, and feet. We work on explosion. We drive the sled and get the elbows inside. Then we want to clear the sled. We want to clear the sled with our hips, headed in the direction of the quarterback.

The third station may be the most important. This is the technique aspect of the drill. We work on hands in the drill. We run the rip, and the rip and spin. Whatever techniques you use, this is where you can work on them.

The fourth station is where we work on the Club. We work against the big stand up dummies. We work on takeoff, and we work our feet and our hips. We really want to accelerate on the play on the snap of the ball.

Next is our *Tackling Circuit*. Our purpose is unit emphasis. We teach technique in these stations. The first station is Hit and Release. We work on blow delivery and separation. We stress toughness. We work on head and hand placement and leg drive.

We start with two players close to each other. They do a strike drill and hit into each other. Then the defender comes around the block and a makes a shoulder tackle. They come back and do the opposite shoulder. After that they switch around and the other player becomes the defensive man.

Next is the *Popsicle Drill*. We work on releases on the drill. Again, we are working on explosion and leg drive.

We go to the *Skate Drill* next. We line up and work against low blocks. We come off the ground and make the tackle.

Our last station in this circuit is our *Sled Drill*. The defensive backs do a backpedal, and then go into a heavier sled. It is just like a stalk block. They jam it and then release, and then make the tackle. Again, if we are showing the film and we see the technique that we taught in the drill we point it out.

We do a couple of other things that I want to go over very quickly. We do the *Odd Man Out Drill*. We put four defenders on the sled. We put three big dummies on one side and three on the other side. We deliver a blow and the coach indicates the direction he wants them to go. The four defenders must sprint to the three dummies and take them out. There are three dummies and four defenders. They can do whatever they want to get to those three dummies. They can prevent the other guys from getting to the dummies. It is a good drill for building toughness, effort, and enthusiasm.

Another thing that Coach Darnell has added to our practice has really been great. At the end of practice or after every workout our players come together. He tells them to grab a hand of one of their teammates. Our players get together and shake hands. They slap each other on the back and tell each other "Good job, way to work." If a player had a problem with someone in practice they go over and tell them they understand that they were just trying to give a good effort.

My time is up. I appreciate your attention.

DEVELOPING THE WINNING EDGE

BEN DAVIS HIGH SCHOOL, INDIANA

I really appreciate this opportunity. The Coach of the Year Clinic staff runs a class operation. They have always done so. The Coach of the Year Clinic is always the highlight for football coaches in the winter.

I want to talk about what I know best, what I believe in, and what I feel from my heart. When I speak I always say that I have to talk from the heart because that is the only thing that really matters. When you talk from the heart and you speak with emotion it gets you going. I believe our job is a very, very big job. It is a very, very special job.

I started thinking about the subject to talk about here today. I asked myself this question. "Coach Dullaghan, what do you do best?" My response was that the best thing I do is to develop players. That is what I am going to talk about. The Winning Edge is the development of players. Most all of you here are high school coaches. In high school we do not have the luxury of recruiting athletes. We have to play with what God sends us. We all have the same amount of time to work on it, and we all have the same amount of time to develop those players. So what I am going to talk about is this. Develop the players, don't just coach the team. If my X's are better than your O's you are in a world of hurt. You know that and I know that. You have been beaten a lot of times, and as most of my opponents will say; "They are just too fast. They are too quick. They are just too tough. They play with such heart. They are everywhere. They swarm, and they play with great emotions." My opponents say we have the best players in the state of Indiana. It may or may not be true. But I know one thing. We have a player development plan and a player development program that I feel is second to none. That is what I am going to talk about today.

I have a staff of 10 assistants. That includes an equipment coach and a certified strength specialist. We have a great strength program. I can't say enough for the job all of the assistants do.

Here are the philosophical considerations that cause me to believe the way I believe. The older I get the more I realize that your philosophy shapes your program. My program is shaped so the players are the most important part. If a player wants to see me he comes before the assistants. On occasions my wife will come before my players. But, my players come first. If they walk into my office I usually stop everything I am doing and take care of my players. I believe in that.

PLAYER DEVELOPMENT IS THE KEY

Players are made in the OFF-season. Teams are made IN-season. It is the coaches' job to make both. Motivational skills are essential.

What you do with the players from one season to the next determines what kind of player they will be. Players become players in the Off-Season. He really does not become a player In-Season. In terms of athleticism and in terms of intrinsic motivation about how hard he will play is determined in the Off-Season. It comes from the demands you put upon him, and from the desire he creates and then by his refusal to surrender. This is because he has invested so much time in it. So we work very hard to develop players in the Off-Season.

My job as the coach is to make the TEAM after I have a group of players. You develop the players in the off-season and then you try to get the chemistry that is necessary and create that team chemistry during the season. It is the job of all of our coaches to develop that team chemistry.

The motivational skills of the people you have on your staff are very important. I have the ability to put my arm around my players and love them. I think you have to care for the players. Before you can give love away you have to have love. If you do not care about the people you are working with I do not think you can develop them. I make sure they know that I care about what happens to them when they leave me.

TO GET RESPECT, YOU MUST FIRST "GIVE IT."

I went to the American Football Coaches Association convention last year in 1999 in Nashville. I am going to suggest a book to you. The name of the book is *Daddy is Home at Last* by Mike Singletary. He spoke at the AFCA convention. When I heard his lecture I decided what would be our theme for the 1999 football season. We all have heard kids say that someone is "dis-en me." They mean that someone is being disrespectful to them. That is the vernacular of a teenager today. Mike Singletary said, "In order to get respect you have to give it." Saying "Yes Sir, and No Sir," and offering your hand for a handshake. In the AFCA Journal that came out in June last year contains Mike's entire speech. I think you would get a lot out of his speech.

After I want home last year after the AFCA convention I started telling my players that respect was a big word in our program. Respect the tradition. "Our tradition is of winning. You are going to respect that tradition by not doing anything to disgrace Ben Davis High School. Your heart will be in it because you care about Ben Davis football."

I believe the MAN UPSTAIRS helps me a lot. I believe in God and I believe he helps and guides many of my actions.

I was reading in a magazine where this auto had bumper stickers on it. The sticker said, "THE BEST IS YET TO COME." I said to myself, this may be what I am looking for. I would like to think the best is yet to come. In 1991 we were national champions. We have won six state championships. We have some great teams, and I was curious how the best is yet to come could be. I did not think we could ever duplicate some of those teams. I did not think we were going to be that good this year. We lost a lot of good players the past year. We did feel this would be a good year, but not a great year.

I hit on the theme "The Best Is Yet To Come," and we used that along with the word RESPECT. We are going to give respect in order to get respect. We were going to respect Ben Davis High School tradition. That is how we started out.

A few years ago I heard Chris Geesman speak. Chris won 89 games in a row at Penn High School in northern Indian. Chris said, "One Good Coach Is Worth 4 or 5 Good Players." I am very fortunate in hiring coaches. When we lose an assistant coach for whatever reason, the principal will come to me and ask me who do I want to hire. He will help me to find another coach. I have a commitment from the top. They want to win. They appreciate the fact that I will not hire anyone that is not a good teacher. I screen the coaches we hire and I make sure they are good teachers. I do not think you can be a good coach if you are not a good teacher. I think one good coach will make you four or five good players. So, put getting good coaches at the top of your priority list.

What is the job of the head coach? He must coach the coaches. His job is to delegate and to motivate the coaches and then let them coach. We evaluate their coaching ability. We have a list of Expectations for every coach. We give him a job description. We tell him what we expect out of him. We sit down with all of the coaches and go over his evaluation at the end of the year. We are interested in what is going to happen with that coach. What are his goals? Does he want to be a head coach someday? In what direction does he want to go?

We want to reward our assistant coaches the best we can. We try to do as much as we can for our assistant coaches. The essence of all coaching is the correction of errors. As coaches we look at film on Saturday morning and we correct errors.

On the practice field we are constantly correcting errors. The easiest way to learn how to make those corrections, in my opinion, is to work at summer football camps. All of our assistants work at least one summer camp. This is written into their job description. In the summer camps you see all of the errors that are made. There are a lot of errors made right in front of you and it is a technique drill. You want them to be sound in techniques and you want them to be able to correct errors. You want them to know how to correct errors. They must see the errors and they must see them corrected. They go to the camps to observe other people make those corrections.

The second-best thing to going to camp is going to early spring football practice. That is when they zero in on technique. They can see the college coaches correct the errors. The problem with that is the fact that college players do not make as many errors. High school kids make more errors. So that is why working with kids in summer camps is so important.

The time commitment of the assistant coaches is crucial. It is tough to work for me, and I will say that. It is tough to work for me because it is very demanding. Some families have trouble with this. Some assistants have left our program for that reason. But I know the time spent with the players is beneficial. I think it is very important and I do not think you can get the job done if you do not insist on the assistants spending the time needed.

We all have heard the statement that "Offense Wins Games, Defense Wins Championships." We start out by putting our best athletes on defense. A lot of coaches will say that and then not do it. We do it! The only exceptions to this include the quarterback, the tailback, and occasionally a receiver. We may include a center in that group, but not very often. The best players go on defense.

Creating turnovers can be coached. We work on this constantly. We do fumble recovery drills. We do not try to fall on it, we try to pick it up. There are situations when you want to pick it up and try

to score. We coach this in practice. They set goals for practice. They will say they are going to get three turnovers in practice on a certain day. If the defense does not get three turnovers for that day they have to do some type of extra conditioning after practice. They do that on a daily basis. They coach the creation of turnovers. We were plus 20 in the turnover ratio for the season. Our quarterback threw 24 TD passes and only one interception for the season. But our defense harps on turnovers in all of our defensive drills. We returned five fumbles for touchdowns.

We put a great amount of emphasis on Special Teams. We practice individual kicking a minimum of 10 minutes three times per week. This includes the individual phase of the kicking game. It is catching punts, kickoffs, punts, and so on. We work on team special teams 15 minutes every day. On Thursday we work on kicking for 40 minutes before we start practice. We feel a special emphasis on special teams is important. We do not do a lot on special teams. We do one kickoff return and do it well. We do one kickoff coverage and we do it well. We do one punt return and we do that well. We keep it simple and we practice the same thing over and over.

I work very hard on the development of kickers. I send all kickers to camp. I send all punters to camp if possible. We want quality punters, place kickers, and return guys We had 174 yards on punt returns in the state championship game. We send them to camp because we know they are going to develop.

Let me get to Ben Davis High School player development. First of all, when I first came to Ben Davis I started a Cadet Football League for grades 2 to 6. We started a traveling team called the Ben Davis Junior Giants. They are made up of fifth- and sixth-graders. We travel to other areas of the state to play games.

We put limitations on the offense and defense in our in-house league. We have the travel team and then we have a league of 14 teams. This league is made up of grades 2, 3, and 4 in one league, and grades 5 and 6 in another league. We have about eight teams in each league. We told them what defense they could run. One reason the football talent is going down today is because kids do not know who to block. They never know who to block because they never know where the defense is going to line up. You have Vince Lombardi IV coaching them and he has seven players running a blitz from one side. Those guys want to run 40 different defenses. In our program I finally got it where I want it. They only run one defense and they stay in that defense and they can't blitz. The players learn where they are supposed to line up. Then they get a chance to block on plays. They do not have a silly coach screaming at them because they did not block the right man. We want to get some standardization. I want them to have fun and to like football. They can't like football if they do not know what to do. You just can't yell at kids that age.

We council all of our coaches and the little league coaches on teaching values. You take this with you if you don't get anything else out of this lecture. We tell all of our coaches this. "The measure of your success is how many of your players are still playing football the following year." The measure of your success and weather you are doing the job is how many of your players still love the game the following year. That is what I believe. That is how I evaluate coaches. "Do their players love the game? Do their players want to stay with them."

We are in a battle for kids. Football is being eroded from the bottom. We need help. We need to make it fun. Those coaches need to realize they need to put their arm around the kids. They have to praise them and get them emotional. I wish you could see my assistant coaches get emotional with the players on the sideline as they come off the field. I want my coaches to be that way. I believe that is necessary today. We want our coaches to think before they scream and holler. Anyone can scream and holler. We want them to teach and to correct the mistakes.

All of our kids from the second grade on up go to some type of summer football camp. We have our own camp that we run at our school. It is called the Ben Davis Technique School. We try to get all Cadets in the camp. We have grades 2 to 5 from 8 to 10 a.m. and grades 5 through 8 from 10 a.m. to noon. Grades 9 through 12 are in the same week for four days from 5 to 8 p.m. We have the camp just to work on techniques. They go to learn to play the game better.

We preach to our kids about playing other sports. We are the last sport. We are the guys with the white hat. We are the good guys. We are the last sport that is preaching this. All of the other sports want the kids. They want our guys. They want to own them. That is wrong. That is criminal. That forces kids to choose the wrong sport too early. Where do they really belong at that age, and how do you know? They get them in the sixth grade and make them go to camps all summer. Then they play AAU ball all spring. They make them wrestle all year round. They make them play tennis all year round. That is wrong.

That is not what a kid needs. A kid needs choices and an opportunity. We encourage them to play as many sports as they can and then make that final decision when they have reached their full body growth. How many kids should have been football players but are not football players but never reached their potential? In Indiana we are the kings of that. Everyone in Indiana wants to bounce the ball. Why? Because it is easy. Anyone can run around in their underwear. MEN PLAY FOOTBALL. Gentlemen, we have to keep them in the program. We tell the kids to play as many sports as they can. Let the soccer people teach them how to run and how to kick and then let them come and kick for us. Let them come and play a man's sport. I mean this sincerely. We are the only sport that is preaching this. Other football coaches should be preaching it at their school. Everywhere I go I preach this. I do not want my players in that weight room all year round after school. To me that is boring. I would like to see our kids play another sport. Let him play where he can get discipline. Let him have some fun.

I waited until I found out that I was going to be offered the job at Ben Davis and then I started with my plan. I told them I had one additional thing that I wanted in the program. I knew they wanted me and so I asked for one additional thing. I told them I wanted one additional junior high coach at each level. They told me it would take them a couple of days to get approval for this to happen. Guess what? I got it! When I got it I knew they really wanted to win in football. When you take a new job you need to find out if they want to win. Don't find out there is a fly in the ointment later. There had been no fly in the ointment at Ben Davis. The rest is history. They had 10 winning seasons in 40 years before I got there. Now we have had 15 out of 16 winning seasons. We have won five state championships. We have done nothing but win because there is a commitment from the top. They want to win and I am going to show them how to do it.

Try to get the junior highs to run your system. If you do not have control of them you can't fire them. So you are not going to get rid of them. Try to get them to run your system. We have six coaches at the freshman level. Next year we will have three junior high teams that will be combined into one team. There will be six coaches at the ninth-grade level next fall.

We encourage our junior high kids to go to a technique school. We have our Junior High Technique School for one week two hours daily.

Our advanced physical education is second to none. I invite you to come and see it. We have a certified strength specialist instructor. He is excellent. He is totally organized. Our kids lift four days per week all year round except for the summer. In the summer they lift three days per week. They take advanced PE for their sophomore, junior, and senior years. They are in the program and they lift regardless of what sports they are in. The key to weight lifting, as you know, is consistency. They lift two days on the upper body and two days on the lower body each week.

If they are not involved in another sport they lift after school again. That is after they lifted that morning. They lift with the same body part. They work on auxiliary lifts. They work on lifts that are not in our Core Program. If you want to talk with our strength coach you can call him at school or drop him a note. We do recommend Creatine, but we never recommend anything else. We do not recommend any supplement. He would never recommend anything that is bad.

Over the Christmas break I bring the kids in for a conference one at a time. I spend about 20 minutes with each kid. I see about three kids per hour. We sit down and talk about a lot of things. When they come in I want them to have this three-page questionnaire filled out. The questionnaire asks questions about our program. It asks questions about the coaches. I ask for their input. I want them to tell me how we can make our program better. They do not have to sign the form. It is a good thing because it tells the coaches what the kids think. This is an evaluation of the program by the kids.

BEN DAVIS FOOTBALL EVALUATION
(Circle One) 12 – 11 – 10
(Circle One) Varsity/Both/Reserve
  1. What 3 things impressed you most this season? (this could be a player, coach opponent, event, game meeting, or something that was said of done.)
  2. If you were the head coach, what would you do differently?
  3. What things did you dislike about this season?
  4. Did you feel that our team was mentally ready to play every game? If not – why not? (What could we do differently?)
  5. Evaluate the coaches that you worked with. (What could they do to be more effective in their coaching?)
Coach A
Coach B
Coach C (list all of the coaches)

  6. What could we do to improve attendance in the: off season lifting, summer lifting, co-captains workouts?
  7. How could we make the Advanced PE class better?

8. Comment on the care and treatment of injuries.
9. Do we have any training rule problems that the coaches are not aware of? If yes, what could the coaches do to address the problem?
10. What needs to be changed in our Junior High Football Program?

The past test results are reviewed with each player. We look at all of these areas. Bench, squat, clean, big three, body weight, vertical jump, and 40-yard run. We keep these records from the time they come into our program until they leave. We also look at the clubs they made in our weight lifting.

After we review the chart we set goals for lifting and speed improvement. We get a Commitment Contract with them. We talk about position changes. For example we may move a player from fullback to linebacker. We will talk about personal problems if home life is a problem.

We have a yearly Speed Development Clinic in February. We have five hours of participation on Sunday. We work on the 40-yard dash and the starts. We work on flexibility and running form instruction.

We have an Inter-School Lift Contest in early March. We bring in 15 schools to compete as teams. We give trophies for the bench, squat, clean, and the 40-yard dash.

We test our lifts five times a year. We test in July, October, December, March, and May. We keep test result sheets on every player. We use Clubs to motivate players to lift. This is what it takes to get into the clubs.

200 Bench – 10 Reps = 200 CLUB
300 Bench – 1 Rep. = 300 CLUB
400 Squat 1 Rep. = 400 CLUB
235 Power Clean 1 Rep = 235 CLUB
935 Club (Total of Bench, Squat, and Clean - = POWER CLUB

We tell them the total number of club members will equal the number of victories. We have our goal boards and recognition boards in our weight room.

We have co-captains' preseason conditioning that our strength coach directs. It begins three weeks before our first fall practice. Our co-captains and seniors are taught how to lead. We have 12 workouts. We work four nights per week for three weeks. We go from 6 to 8 p.m. nightly. We stress discipline, leadership, and development. This gives the players a chance to meet new players. We give them a T-shirt for their attendance. The program is extremely intense and it is a demanding workout.

We two platoon our entire practice and staff. Every play is scripted. We have the Studs go against the Pups every day. They must learn to run with the Big Dogs or stay on the porch. We videotape practice and show it to players on Thursday in Advanced PE.

We pick a scout team Player of the Week. We pick one for each side of the ball for the first four games. We pick two from each side of the ball the last five games. We pick three from each side of the ball during playoffs. If a player is chosen three times he earns a varsity letter.

We dress everyone who deserves to dress. They dress for home and away games. If playoff games are a problem as far as dressing is concerned, we will take them on the bus to the game.

Another thing we do to inspire energy and effort everyday is with our Hatchet Club. It is our Consistent Performance Award. If you make the Hatchet Club this is what you get. They get their name on the board in team meeting room. They get a helmet decal each week they make the club. A player gets a plaque at the banquet if he is a member of the club for 80 percent of the games played. The position coach decides who makes the club.

I got this idea from Jim Young when I was at Purdue with him. I was an assistant at Purdue for three years. Jim got the idea from the University of Michigan when he was there. At Michigan they called it the Victors' Club. At Purdue we called it the Hammer Club. At Ben Davis it is called the Hatchet Club. The reason for that is because our idiot mascot, the Ben Davis Giant, carries around a hatchet in his hand. That is why we call it the Hatchet Club. It is a great motivator. They will get their names in the football newsletter, *Giant Footprint*.

What is the Hatchet Club? It means they played consistent for the whole game. The position coach decides who make the Hatchet Club.

The players will kill to get on the Hatchet Club. The know their position coach is deciding who is going to make the club. They have to practice hard and play the game well. Other teams want to know how we get our kids to play so hard. We tell them the Hatchet Club is a big part. They want to get that plaque at the end of the year. I make a big deal of the Hatchet Club at the banquet.

Admission to the club is decided on winning effort in practices and games. Knowing all assignments, being hard-nosed at all times in practice and in games. Willingness to come out early or stay after practice to work for individual improvement.

Week-to-week admission is based on all of the above. Also, be personally responsible for a key play leading to a victory. Being a member of the offensive unit that scores 30 points or more, or being part of the defense that holds an opponent to seven points or less. Outstanding all-around game. Offense-Defense must play 15 plays and kick specialist must play eight plays.

They can lose membership in the club. Being responsible for fumble, pass interception, penalty, missed tackle which is the turning point of a game. Lack of winning effort in practice or a game. Loss of temper or unsportsmanlike conduct. Missing a game or three days of practice the week of a game. Poor performance for a game.

We select a Player of the Week. We give awards for all of the following:
Offensive Lineman
Offensive Back
Kick Specialist
Offensive Scout
Defensive Lineman
Defensive Back
Defensive Scout

Each player selected gets a sandwich certificate. They get their name and picture on the bulletin board. We select Player of the Year in each category and they receiver picture plaques at the end-of-the-year banquet.

I have a pin on my lapel today. It is a small Tie-Tac Pin. On the Pin we have the letters P-R-I-D-E down the pin. This is what P-R-I-D-E stands for.

Personal
Responsibility
In
Daily
Effort.

It is a small Tie-Tac pin that only costs about a dollar. They are nominated by the position on Thursday. I meet with the coaches for about 15 minutes before we go out to practice. "Who are you nominating for the Pride Pin?" Each coach goes down his list of players. It is the player that has busted his butt all week. If he has a discipline problem in another class he does not get the pin. If he has been late for practice or had any negative reports that week he does not get the pin. I keep records of the number of times each player is nominated. They usually have to be nominated three times before the pin is given. Only one pin is given to each player.

We are trying to get perfect practice and maximum effort all week in practice. If we get that we will not get beat. We are talking about personal responsibility in daily effort. That is what energy and effort in practice are all about. We are trying to give the players a reason to give that energy and effort that we all talk about.

The last point I want to make reference to relates to our newsletter. It is called *The Giant Footprint*. We have a former player that writes the newsletter for us. It is a House-Organ type newspaper. Kids love to see their name in print. The newsletter is a summary of the game. We also include a summary of the JV game. We list the Hatchet Club members for the week. We also include the Players of the Week. Then we include some motivational message. On the last page we have one of our seniors write something for each week. One of our players wrote a short story and called it "Friday Night."

This may seem like it is not a big deal. I want you to know the players love it. They can not wait to get the *Footprint* each week. It is ready for them on Thursday. Most of it is written on Monday night. I get it to the computer people on Tuesday and they get it back on Wednesday. We get it run off and have it ready for practice on Thursday. We do this every week.

I put the *Footprint* in their game packet. We exchange our game packet with our opponent. We include our starting lineups and our depth chart. We exchange with our opponents a dress list. I exchange this with our opponents and I give it to the press, and I send it to administrators. I send it to everyone. We run off 800 copies of the *Footprint*. We put it in the game program. The Mothers Club just sticks it in the program.

Our Mothers Club does a great job. They feed all of our players on Thursday night during the playoffs. We have an emotional time there.

In closing I want to leave you with a few points that I believe in very strongly. You have to give of yourself in order for your players to give you 100 percent. We want that emotional response. I heard Coach Tony Mason speak several years ago. He was a great motivator. I remember what he said, "You are trying to deliver an emotional response from your players each game." How do you get that emotional response from your players? As Tony said, "If you do not build it throughout the year, if you don't work on it all year, you are not going to get it." You have to build it all year. What Tony was really saying was this: You have to put your heart in coaching. You have to put your heart in them for them to play hard for you.

I believe kids will give you whatever you demand. They will give you 100 percent more when they know you care. Last fall we had 42 former players playing college football. We are from a disadvantaged area. One year we have 24 seniors on our team and 17 of them went on to play college football. I was very proud of them. In our school only 42 percent of our students go on to higher education. We are not an affluent school at all. Many of our kids that do go to college are the first person in their family to have gone to college.

We are pushing them to develop themselves. We are doing everything we can to get our players to strive to be all they can be.

Guys, whatever you do put your heart into your program. Put your heart into your kids. Don't be afraid to hug them. When they do something good hug them and squeeze them. They do not get the attention they need at home. It is not like I was raised. I was the oldest of nine kids. My mother was there for me every day. My mother never worked while the kids were young. I believe that giving love and putting your heart into the kids will give it back to you 100 fold.

I am the luckiest guy in the world. I have a great job, home, and business. I have everything going for me and I love it. I love what I do every day. I think you get out of life what you put in it. There is another side to that. I do not do anything else. All I do is coach. I do not cut grass, and I don't fix things. There is not a tool that fits my hand. I do not care about any of that. I coach football and occasionally play a little golf in the summer.

Football is the greatest game in the world. Football is IT. There is nothing else that even comes close to what we learn and what we can impart to young people about being a team player. Everyone in business wants to hire the former players because they know they will be a team player. We have the greatest sport in the world. Preach it! Preach play every sport. Preach to your kids how they have to put their heart into their job. Develop the players all the way up through your program. They will give you back 100 fold.

KEEP THE DEFENSE SIMPLE

MISSISSIPPI STATE UNIVERSITY

Thank you. It is a pleasure to be here. I'm going to give you some of my philosophy on football. As you can see I've been at a lot of different places. I've been fired at some places. Hopefully Mississippi State will keep me around for awhile.

I have changed through the years. I've been fortunate to work for some people that would let me do what I wanted to do. I'm at a point in my life now where I don't think football rules everything. I've got three little kids and they come first for me. I don't plan everything around football. I have a schedule during the football season, the head coach approves. When we finish practice in the afternoon, I'm going home. I don't work at night. I'm going home and see my kids before they go to bed.

I get up in the morning real early and come to work to get everything I need to do done. I like to do it that way and Coach Sherrill approves it and doesn't have a problem with it.

Our philosophy on defense has changed a lot as far as I'm concerned. The philosophy we had a long time ago was that defense won games. That has changed. Now we believe that defense keeps you in the game. Because of the rules in college football, you have to have some offense. The thing we have to do on defense now is to keep us in the ballgame until the offense can win it. You can't let the game get out of hand. You can't give up 21 or 28 points in a hurry. You have to keep the game close. That is basically what we try to do.

We go out and try to shut everybody out every game. But the big thing is not to let the game get out of hand. We have been fortunate enough to do that more times than not. If we get behind by a lot, we are not going to win the football game. The passing game has become so prominent. When

Coach Spurrier and Coach Mummy came into the league it brought a new kind of football into the SEC. If you can't stop the pass, you are not going to win any SEC championships. It is not whether you can stop the run in the SEC anymore, because the SEC has become one of those leagues that airs the ball out. If you can't stop the pass, people are going to kill you. That is something we work on and pride ourselves on. We basically try to stop the pass first instead of the run. We have been first in the conference the last two years in pass defense.

The first year I was at Mississippi State in 1996, about the middle of the season I was trying to figure out what I was coaching. People were going up and down the field throwing the ball and we couldn't stop anybody. We couldn't even slow them down. We have basically changed because the rules have changed. They have basically legalized holding in college football. It is a rarity that you will ever see holding called in a football game. The offensive linemen have to almost rape the defender before there is a holding penalty. But you have to change with the times.

What we have done defensively to keep up with things is play five defensive backs. We have played every single down of football in the last three and half years with five defensive backs. That goes for the goal lines and everywhere. We don't change. I don't like to substitute unless we have a situation like we had this past season. The offenses have changed and made us put in five defensive backs. I don't like to bring someone out of the box to cover somebody. We cover everybody with a defensive back.

We have been fortunate enough to have five good defensive backs. It helps us because it gets more speed on the field. We are a better football team by playing five defensive backs the way we do it. In 1992 when I was at Mississippi we had 11 guys that played every snap in a football game. We didn't substitute anybody. They played all 85 plays in a game. This past season in our last football game, in the Peach Bowl, we played 105 defensive plays and rotated 19 players. The only two guys that didn't come out of the game were the two cornerbacks. We only had two cover corners. The guys behind them can't play, so I don't put them in the game.

It was fortunate we had that many people because 105 snaps in one game are a lot. Most of those 19 guys played about 45 snaps. The way the season worked out was kind of the way we planned it, but we didn't know it was going to work out that way. Recruiting is an educated guess. You don't know whether those guys can play until you get them in, get the pads on them, and see how they react with the top people you have. We had a bunch of guys who came to school in the fall. As it turned out we were able to play and rotate two units. We have a front six and a back five. The back five played most of the time and the front six rotated every series. One group was basically seniors and the other group was underclassmen. By the end of the year the underclassmen were probably better than the seniors.

I run the defense, folks. Don't nobody mess with the defense but me. I have complete control of it. I decide who plays. The position coaches don't do that. I am fortunate that I don't have to coach a position. I have four other coaches that do that. I have a linebackers coach, a secondary coach, a defensive end coach, and a defensive line coach. We have not had a problem with that situation, because they all understand who is running the show. I wouldn't take a job if it wasn't that way. They are going to run me off if the job doesn't get done, not the position coaches.

I don't have to meet with my coaches because we already know what we are going to do. That has always puzzled me about head coaches. They always want to go some place in August as a staff

and bond. Hell, you are going to be with those guys from September through December. Why would you want to go off and sequester yourself with those same guys.

We do something kind of special and different in the spring. During spring we run a 5-2 defense. The old angle-slant defense that Michigan ran back in 1973. In 1973 I got to go to Michigan and visit with them. A lot of the things we do today go back to that Michigan staff. Down through the years we have added to it. We don't play the five defensive backs in the spring.

What I'm going to do now is go over a few things I think make us pretty good on defense. It has nothing to do with football. It has to do with conditioning. I am in charge of conditioning for the defense. In fall camp we have a 15-minute period in the middle of practice. Fifteen minutes before our first break we run a pursuit drill. We do it for 15 minutes every single day of two-a-day practices. Our defense plays left and right. We don't flip-flop most of the time. We call our strong safety, the DOG safety. We are the Bulldogs, therefore he is the Dog safety. Since we don't flip-flop, if the formation were the other way the other safety would be the Dog safety. We teach those guys the same position. The safeties can play dog and free safety. The corners are playing left and right. We have a tight side end and an open side end and those positions are taught to both sides. We have a tight-side and an open-side linebacker.

It seems like it is better for us to play left and right rather than flip-flop. It is easier to find people to play on just one side. I measure everything in 40 yards. We run 20 40's every Monday during the season, plus one for every point we give up. That is basically all we do on Mondays. Each position has a low test guy. He has to run five extra 40's for making the low score. If he had a 15-yard penalty in the ballgame he has to run 15 extra 40's. We don't do anything until we get through with the 40's. I've been at places where we have had to run a hell of a lot of 40's on Monday. Two years ago we got beat 40 something to nothing. We had to run 60 some odd 40's to start with. But if the team buys into what your package is, they want to run the 40's. They know they screwed up.

In the pursuit drill we have the teams on the sideline. They run onto the field and huddle. We always run the pursuit drill against the dive option. Not many people run the option anymore, but it is something you always have to keep in the back of your mind. We have the goal line 40 yards from the drill with two coaches down there. We call 52 right. That gives the defensive line their slant direction.

We have a slant right for the line. We run a dive option left. The tight-side end knows he has the quarterback on the option. The left tackle slants inside and takes the dive. The nose guard slants right and pursuits down the line and up through the center-guard gap on the left side. The loop tackle steps outside and pursuits through the guard-tackle gap to his side. The open-side end checks inside and pursuits down field. The open-side linebacker checks his gap and pursuits downfield. The dog safety runs to the pitch man and the free safety runs into the alley. The tight-side linebacker fills his responsibility. The corners are running in place. All the guys that are running in place will run to specific coaches on my signal. I give the signal and they all run to their specific coach, circle around him, break down, and chop their feet. When I blow the whistle they hit the ground, get up, and run off the field.

PURSUIT DRILL

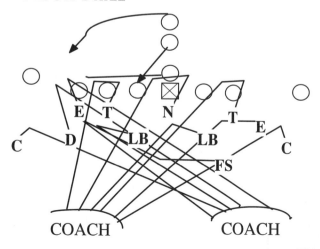

We do this every single day during two-a-day practices. While they are running for the coaches, I'll blow the whistle three or four times. They have to hit the ground, get up, and keep going. We do this with three or four groups. I have found over the years that blowing a whistle, making the guys hit the ground, and get up, is probably the closest thing to a football play that you can find.

In our morning practices during two-a-day practices we do something I call **Packer Day**. Our periods are five minutes in length. We take the last three periods and do 15 minutes of up-downs. I am the guy who blows the whistle. We start off by doing two and a half minutes of up-downs and two and a half minutes of 40's. Each day I increase the up-downs 15-20 seconds. This is something we do the last three periods of the morning practice. If you can do 15 minutes of up-downs, with me blowing the whistle, you are pretty good. They have gotten proud of themselves for being able to do it. It is an interesting thing to see, especially those big 300-pound kids. They hate it.

The other thing we do in the afternoon practice is called **Fourth Quarter**. We have four stations set up. It takes 20 minutes to run this drill. We run 40's, do bag drills, push-ups and sit-ups, and a cone drill at our four stations. We have four groups and they alternate where they start each day. They spend five minutes at each station. We have done this everywhere I've been.

I started the **Packer Day** back in 1976 at Chattanooga. It has been really good. I think it really helps us. I have been fortunate in that all the football teams I've coached over the years played hard. That is the one thing you really like people to tell you about your football team. If they hustle and play hard they have a chance of winning.

We have a big board in our defensive meeting room. Kids like to see all this stuff. We have defensive goals on it. Normally if you can accomplish seven or eight of the goals, you have a chance to win the game. They look at this board every week when they go into the room for a meeting.

We have a tackle chart with all the players' names on the chart. We record the tackles they make in the games. We also record their missed tackles. That is a big thing. That usually shows whether or not you played good.

Let me get into what we do. Everybody thinks we do more than we do. We play very few coverages in the secondary. We only play three coverages. We play a **3-Deep Zone**, **Man**, and **Man Free Coverage**. We don't do anything else. If you look at our films, it looks like we are doing more. Players sometimes get out of position. When you see us in something else, it is a mistake or a misalignment.

Up front we do a whole lot. I don't think you can be super-multiple in the secondary and up front. To keep it simple, the only people that are moved around a lot are the front folks. Our front six will get into a lot of different looks. In the secondary we try to make you think we are playing man when we are in zone, and vice versa. They have the freedom to be in a lot of places, but when the ball is snapped they better be in a place where they can take care of their job.

We don't give our people freedom to change the call. When I call the defense from the sideline, that is what they are going to run. We do not put it on their shoulders to change plays. That is not the way it works.

We play our three down linemen in a head-up position. They are going inside or outside. We have a tight-side and open-side end and linebacker. Since I've been at State we have never had two linebackers, that made you feel real good about them. That is why I use the fifth defensive back.

BASE 52 DEFENSE

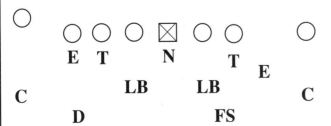

The stunts we run are **Tight**, **Open**, **Left**, and **Right**. The tight and open mean we are going to the tight end or open side. The direction of the tight end is the only call our linebackers make. They call tight left or right. We have tried to eliminate a lot of thinking. If we want our tackle to slant inside, we call *Pinch*. If we want them to slant outside, we call *Loop*. That call is made if we want them both to do the same thing. When those things are called the nose guard knows he is stuffing.

PINCH AND LOOP

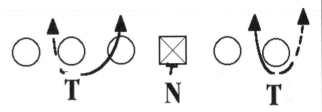

If we want to add the ends onto the tackle, we call *Bullet*. That brings the end on a pinch. You can't do that, however, with a loop call.

From there we go to one side or the other. If we wanted to make a tight side bullet charge we would call *Thunder*. If we wanted to do an open side bullet charge we would call *Lightning*.

Next we teach **Mad** and **Bad**. This came about when we left Chattanooga to go to New Mexico. At Chattanooga we used a strong safety blitz. We ran it to death. We want to do that stunt but leave four defensive backs in the secondary. We came up with this and probably do it more than anything else. We are using defensive backs now. Here is what it would look like in the spring. The defensive ends would be on the same side. That gives you an over load look. To the tight end side it is called MAD. To the split end side it is called BAD. Everyone slants away from the call.

MAD

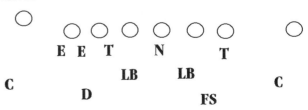

We came up with BAD because people began to trade the tight end to the other side. We didn't want to run two guys over with the tight end. We ran BAD. All that did was change our dog safety to free and our free safety to dog. The ends in our scheme now have been replaced with defensive back. They can get to the play pretty darn quick.

BAD

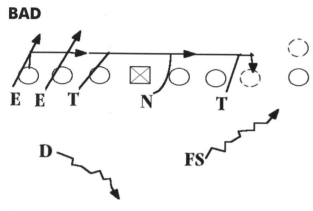

You guys need to make up your own blitzes. If you make them up you know what you want your people to do. I don't think you need to copy blitzes from everybody else. You better not call a blitz unless you know everything about it. You have to know where the weakness is.

In the spring we teach a **5I Look**. It is a defensive look and it is just what it says. We take one of our linebackers and put him in the dog safety position. If we want to stunt from this alignment, we tell the adjustment linebacker where to go. We can bring him from the tight or open side. Now we have a Mad or Bad stunt with another guy running the stunt. We run this defense in the spring to see if the linebackers and defensive ends can do what we want them to do.

51 LOOK

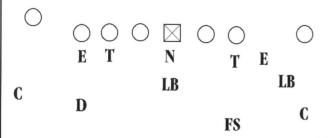

The next thing we teach them is what I call the **Stack Look**. This is a 4-3 look, but we call it stack. We have run the stack a lot in the past, but we haven't done it lately because of the five defensive backs.

STACK LOOK

The next thing I'm going to show you is what we

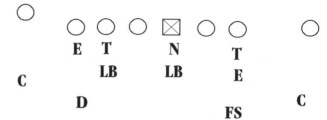

have been playing for the last couple of years. This is how we teach it in the spring. This is called **33**. We run this defense about 75 percent of the time. There is an enormous world of things you can do from this. You can run all kinds of blitzes or coverages from it. In the spring we stack the tight-side end and the linebackers behind the tackles and nose guard. The dog safety and open-side end are in the same position basically. We wouldn't put an open-side end in man coverage against anyone, but we play some zone concept with him.

33

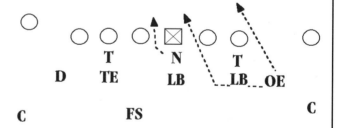

We played this defense the whole game against Southern Cal, when I was at Memphis in 1991. I went out to watch their spring game in 1990, because we had them on the schedule. I stood down on the field as they were coming into the Coliseum. You talk about big. These guys were very big. We didn't have that many big guys at Memphis and I was trying to figure out how many points they are going to score against us. I went up in the stands and watched the game. There wasn't a soul there. I was watching the game by myself. They had the stands filled with paper people, because they were going to do a movie shoot in the stadium that night. I stayed around and watched about half the spring game. I decided watching was not going to make it better. I drove across town to Santa Anita to the races. There were 55,000 people at the race track. That made me believe football was not as important out there as it is in the South.

We went out and played them on Labor Day and beat them. That was Larry Smith's last year there. We were fortunate and things went our way. We played 33 the whole game.

You can rush three and drop eight if you want. We can do a lot of little things from this defense. We can let the open-side end move up and blitz inside or outside the stack to his side. We can move the nose guard off the center into the gap. We try to make the offensive linemen think.

From the 33 we run the Mad and the Bad. The official call is **Mad Slam**. We bring the Dog safety on a blitz to the outside. The tight side end comes off the inside shoulder of the tight end. The TNT people slant away from the call. If we called **Bad Slam**. It would be the same thing coming from the other side with different personnel. We play man and man free behind the stunt.

33 MAD SLAM

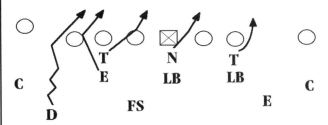

All the odd looks we run come from the 5-3 defense. When I was at South Carolina we played 53 defense all the time. People had two backs in the backfield all the time. The 53 defense is near impossible to run on. All the things we are doing now come from the 53 look. The passing game has really made things change.

We go from our odd front defense to an even front defense. The secondary doesn't change when we

go to this defense. What we get is a split look defense. There are a number of blitzes that go into this package. The thing I like to do from this defense is to blitz both linebackers into the A-Gaps. I like to do it early in a game to find out if the offense has done their homework. That is probably the most difficult thing to block. If they can't handle it, I may run it every snap.

SPLIT LOOK

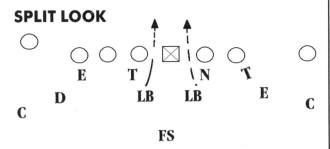

The next look is called **Split 1**. This leaves us with one inside linebacker and we put the other linebacker on the outside as an outside rusher. We have an overload coming from the outside and still have five defensive backs in our coverage. At times we take the linebacker out and replace him with a defensive back and let him do the blitzing. That gives you a faster guy off the corner. The guys we use at those positions are supposed to be speed guys.

SPLIT 1

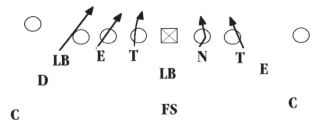

The calling of the defenses is the same as it was in 1973 when I started all this stuff. We do a multitude of things with our fronts. If we find people like to run the football against our 33 we'll most the tight side tackle into a 3 technique. We put our tight side end back up on the line and stack behind our 3 technique tackle with our linebacker. We call that a **42**. Again, the front six are moving and the back five remain the same. When we move the tackle down that is what we call **Hawk**. If we have some guys that can't pinch, we call the Hawk, which is a prepinch. To the split-end side we call **Eagle**. If we want them both down we call **Double Eagle**.

42 HAWK / EAGLE

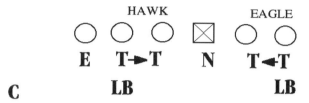

There are a lot of things I do specifically for one game. We try to create things that will help us. There is not a hell of a lot of secrets to the defense. If you are going to be good defensively you have to be sure the people that play for you can tackle. If your defense can't tackle, you can't win the game. That is the number 1 thing we look for in recruiting a defensive player. If he can't tackle in high school, he damn sure won't be able to tackle in college. The level of competition changes when you get up to college. Don't let your ego get in the way where you think you can teach him to tackle. The number two thing we look for is a guy that can run. Folks will find out who can't tackle. They will run at them like there was no tomorrow. For you to get on the field and play for us, you have to demonstrate to us that you can tackle in practice.

In the secondary we are going to play man coverage and a three-deep zone. Sometimes we have a free safety and sometimes we won't. We are going to play three-deep zone. We had a problems a few years ago with four vertical patterns. We have figured out how to play it now and the head coach is not mad at us all the time.

You can talk offenses out of throwing those stretch routes. All you have to do is holler, "Watch the Stretch Routes!" The offense will check out of them if they think you are watching for them.

The number 1 thing we do from the 52 blitz package is called **52 Go - 5 Free**. The linebacker to the tight end blitzes the B-Gap. The linebacker to the open side exchanges responsibility with the nose

guard. He blitzes the strong-side A-Gap. The nose guard goes into the open side A-Gap. This is a five-man rush. If we want to get to a six-man rush we call **Full Go**. That puts the open-side end into the blitz package in the open-side B-Gap. The coverage changes to cover 5. The free safety has to take the back out to the side the end vacated. The Go call means we are going to the tight-end side. If we wanted to go the opposite way, we would call **52 Away**. That would mean we are going to the open side with the same stunt

52 GO / FULL GO

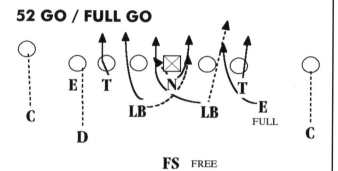

If we get into the 33 look, we can get the same stunt. We simple call **33 Trips** and we have the same stunt. The secondary coverage is the same. If we have a six-man rush we have to play cover 5.

The other stunt that has been good out of the 52 look comes from a **52-Eagle**. We call **52-Eagle/Fly**. The open side end comes up on the line. The tackle gets into the eagle alignment. The open side linebacker stacks behind him and blitzes the A-Gap. You have to play cover 5 even though it is a five-man rush. There is no one to cover the back out to the open side and the free safety has to take him.

52-EAGLE/FLY

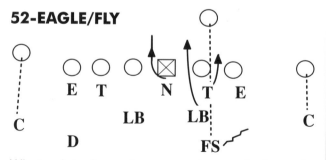

What a lot of people are starting to do from the even look is what Vanderbilt is doing. They are getting into a double eagle look and blitzing both

A-gaps with their linebackers. Then bring the free safety right over the center on a blitz. We tried to do that, but we don't do it anymore. We don't have anything where our free safety blitzes. We want to do it. But we've never been successful at doing it.

When we play teams that have a five out attack, we are going to rush the hell out of the quarterback. They still think they are prima donnas and don't like to get hit. By the time the fourth quarter rolls around he is not going to be near as good.

We react to all slip screens. We throw a lot of pursuit screen drills. Some days that drill replaces our pursuit drill in the middle of practice. We work hard and mentally prepare them for that play. We get caught occasionally but we play it pretty good most of the time. If you run it enough, sometimes it hits just right and is successful. In fact the play that beat us two years ago at Kentucky was a slip screen. We had a lot of guys there, we just didn't make the play. I don't know why. I guess it was because that little bitty guy that caught it could run like hell. Sometimes you just get overmatched. It happens that way in football.

When a football game is over, I don't watch the film but twice. I go into the office at about 3 a.m. and watch it by myself. When the rest of the staff comes in about 7 o'clock that morning we break the film down. After that I don't watch it again.

That game is over and I'm preparing for the next week. It is a rarity that I watch any film in the off-season. I don't dwell on the past.

In this business you can't worry about what happened yesterday. Even if you were a hero yesterday, you can be an ass tomorrow. That is the nature of the business and you can't worry about it. Go about doing your business and job and don't worry about what people think. If you are confident in what you are doing, don't worry about it. Just do it. The worst thing in the world is for people to talk you into changing things. All that does is screw you up.

Gentlemen, do you have any questions? The question was, what do you do if the offense is picking on one man in your man coverage? The only things I can tell you is get someone else in the game. You can't hide a weak defensive back by moving him somewhere else in the defense. They will find him. If you can't defend from man coverage, go to a zone. That may help.

Against a trip set we will be man-to-man. If we are going to attack the quarterback we are going to come from the side where there is a blocking back with more people than the offense can block. The reason we come from that side is to control the back. If he releases we can cover him.

It has been a pleasure and thank you for your time.

THE SHORT PASSING GAME

OREGON STATE UNIVERSITY

Thank you. It is a pleasure to be here on Sunday morning. I have spoken Sunday mornings before at a lot of different places. I am real proud of you people who have gotten up to hear this lecture. You know what it's like to be tough. I was around last night, and I know a lot of you thought you were tough. But you are here and I really appreciate that.

I want to talk about some of the things we have done over the years. I listened to Hal Mumme last night I have been to a lot of clinics over the years. I think a lot of the things we started doing back in 1980 with the short passing game have hung on in football. I was with Jack Elway at San Diego State then. A lot of people now use those things and ideas.

When I went to the University of Idaho in 1982, we put more of it in. When I was at Idaho, we were one of maybe two teams that were in the one-back set. We expanded on it and continued to get better. When I was at Washington State in 1987, there were probably five teams using the one-back set. If you look at it now there are not many teams that don't use the one-back set.

I think it is interesting about how the one-back set evolved. We are doing some of the things a little bit differently, and some of those things we are doing better. I have been to a lot of clinics. People hide a lot of things. We have nothing to hide.

When I went to Seattle I got caught up with some of the things you are supposed to do in the NFL. I regret that. We didn't run the one-back set as much as I thought we should have. The one-back set does some things that create a lot of problems for the defense.

The quick passing game is where it all starts for us. It enables you to do a lot of different things. If you look at what we do with our formations, we try to spread you out. We try to stretch the defense. Our number 1 formation is what we call **Doubles**. It is a pro set with the tailback or H-back sitting in the tight slot to the split end. People have to make a decision on what they are going to do against that set.

DOUBLES

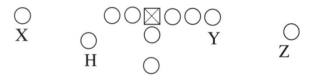

When you put three receivers to one side that constitutes a **Trips** set. We are in a Trips set if we have a tight end.

TRIPS

The best formation for us which we are using more and more is called **Trey**. It is a form of a Trips set, but we have a tight end and double flanker to the one side. We do a lot of things from this set. We are probably in this set about 60 percent of the time.

TREY

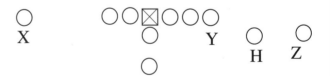

We get into another set similar to the Trey is called **Trio**. This is almost like the Trey except you have a split end and double slot to that side and a split end away.

TRIO

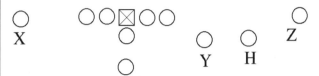

Another set we run is called **Duo**. It has two split ends and two slots.

DUO

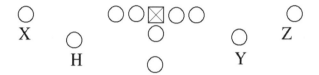

We are going to be involved more this spring in the **Deuce** set. That set has two tight ends and two flankers. I still believe you have to be able to run the football. In this set we like to run the ball.

DEUCE

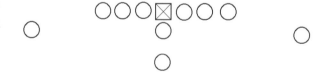

That is all one-back stuff. You can do anything with it you want to. You can motion and create a lot of the same sets you see all the time.

What I am going to do is put in a passing game with all these formations. We are going to throw the three-step passing game. If you put 7 in the box we are going to throw the ball. If you put 6 in the box, we are going to run the ball. That is the philosophy a lot of people use. I think it is the philosophy we started many, many, year ago.

We have done one thing a little bit different. We can do this with different personnel. We call it **Spread**. I started this thing at the University of Idaho. We set a trips set to the left, motion the H-back out of the backfield right, and throw a pass called

93-Y-UP-H-Option. We used the motion to determine where to throw the football. What has happened over the years is as soon as you motion people start blitzing. What we did my last year at Miami, was to just line up in a Spread. The reason we lined up in the set was to see if they were going to blitz us.

SPREAD H-OPTION

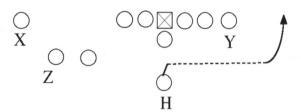

We don't motion into the empty set much any more. We just line up in it. The great thing about these formations is, you can do it with any personnel. What happens to you a lot of times, is the defense substitute with you. In the NFL, as soon as you put four wide receivers in a game, the defense put five defensive backs in the game. The thing that surprised me at Oregon State was, when we went with four wide receivers, the defense stayed the same. If you went to five wide receivers, they might bring in extra defensive backs.

We think, if we can spread people out and go with a one-back set, it becomes difficult to disguise blitzes. If they are going to blitz, the defense has to get people over all the receivers so they can play man coverage. When you spread people it is difficult to drop a defensive end and bring a linebacker. It kind of eliminates the zone blitz. You can see what is happening as far as the quarterback is concerned. If he comes to the line of scrimmage and he has the offense all spread out, he has a pretty good idea what the defense is doing.

I think the 90 game works the defensive linemen. They pass rush up the football field and the ball is gone. That wears out the defensive linemen, which not only enables you to throw the football but to run it. It frustrates the linemen because in three steps the pass is gone. They can't get to the quarterback and get tired of pass rushing.

Matchups are the reason we ran this offense to start with. If we go to a double set and the defense leaves the weak-side linebacker in a stack behind the defensive end, it is hard for us to block him. That is a mismatch to have to block him. It is also a mismatch for that guy to get out and cover a wide receiver. The mismatch aspect of this offense is a real key. The pass is going to be a 7- or 8-yard pass. We are going to catch the ball and maybe make a bunch of yards.

The quarterback in this offense doesn't have to have a big arm to make this offense go. As I talk about the things we do, I think anyone can do them. It doesn't make any difference whether it is high school, junior high, or little league. The routes are simple and you don't have to have a great arm to complete the throw. To throw a 6-yard out across the hash mark, you have to have a good arm. We don't throw that route. Everything we try to do is inside option routes. If your quarterback is smart and accurate, he can get the ball to the receiver.

You have to look at the protection for the quarterback. When you go empty in the backfield you obviously have some problems with protection. But when you keep the tight end and put the back one way or the other you have very solid protection. When we throw our 90 series, we don't go out and cut guys. When you go out and cut guys, and the defense starts bringing linebackers inside, you are venerable to them coming free. What we try to do is pack everything from tackle-to-tackle inside. We are not firing out but we are not retreating. We are blocking right on the line of scrimmage. We want to be solid inside. If anything comes free it will be from the outside. If that happens, we can get the football off.

This is a big-play offense. We are going to throw the football first. All of a sudden the defense starts to play cover 2 or 8 and everyone starts to move outside, we run the ball. I'm not going to get into the running game, but that is a real key.

The motion package causes a lot of problems. Over the years I know the first thing we talk about is,

who adjusts with any motion the offense has. The great thing about motion is it lets you know what the defense is doing. When you motion a guy across your formation, and watch who goes with him, you have a real good idea what that secondary is doing.

I want to talk to you a little bit about the technique as far as the quarterback is concerned. I'm not talking about his throwing, but his drops. We went back and forth on this thing. We throw the 90 game from underneath the center or from the shotgun. But if we empty the backfield, we like to put him back in the shotgun. I always wondered if you could throw short from the shotgun. Because of the timing in the routes, I wasn't sure about that. I didn't run the shotgun for a long period of time because of that. Basically we teach it from underneath the center.

Our quarterback is short. He has trouble finding lanes to throw. But a 6-3 quarterback has the same problem because the linemen are so big. What I did at Idaho and other places I've been, in the three-step drop, we want him coming straight back. If we don't do that, the quarterback, when he throws to the left, will start to drift. That messes up your protection when the quarterback is drifting around in the pocket. When the quarterback takes his right, left, right steps as he backs out, he doesn't drift.

I want to show you a couple of routes. Everyone knows our 90 route is the 6-yard hitch and the 91 route is the 6-yard out. There are some combinations routes that I think are really good. The one I'll start off with is called "94." We can throw it out of a number of different formations. I start out from the double set. It is a slant on both sides. It is a double slant on the split receiver's side and a flat-slant to the tight end side. We think the slant is an effective route because it is more timing than anything.

We teach the pattern so that the receiver breaks at 6 yards on his inside foot. If the receiver has someone bumping him or up in his face the pattern may not be 6 yards. It would be whenever he can get to a certain point at a certain time. That may be 4 or

5 yards, depending on what the defense is doing to him. We tell our quarterback if he comes to the line and reads a 2 deep or 4 deep, he is probably going to the double-slant side. What he is looking for is one safety or two.

We tell our inside receiver to the split end side to go to 6 yards, press the outside, and break inside. He is trying to beat the linebacker. We tell our split end, which we call X, the same thing. He runs his pattern at 6 yards and breaks inside under control. The tight end is running a flat route. It is a width for depth route. That is something that is difficult to teach sometimes. We want to make sure as they release, they get flat but up the football field. The flanker runs the 6-yard slant. If it is a cover 2, the quarterback goes to the two-receiver side. We are putting the outside linebacker in a bind. The quarterback keys the linebacker. As the inside receiver drives inside him, if he goes with him, we throw the ball behind him to the split end. If he widens we hit the inside slot on the slant.

94 VS. TWO SAFETIES

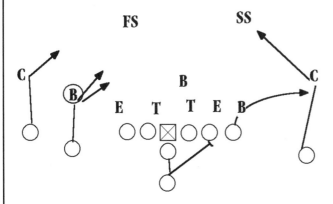

We don't like to go the other way because we know the corner is rolling up into the flat. That is why we go to the double-slant side.

If there is a 3 deep coverage, we want him to go back to the tight-end side. We get the 3 deep zone or some kind of a man situation. If there is one safety in the middle he is going to the flat-slant side. It gives the quarterback some options depending on coverage. You can do that with every formation.

94 VS. ONE SAFETY

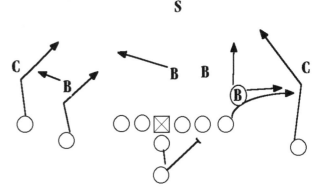

You can do the same thing with the Deuce Set. People think you get in that set to run the ball, but we can run the 94 easily.

The Trey set is one of our favorite formations. When we run the 94 from this set it is a little bit different. We run the double slant by the outside receivers in the Trey. The tight end releases if he can on the inside linebacker. On the one-receiver side, anytime we run Trey, we run a hitch at 6 yards. He is driving up the football field. At 6 yards he does his inside hitch and rolls away from the corner outside. We tell our quarterback, if the corner is playing off, hit the one receiver. If we get the two-safety look, we run the route off the outside linebacker to the two-receiver side. The tight end seals the inside linebacker who covers him. It is a simple pattern and easy throw.

TREY 94

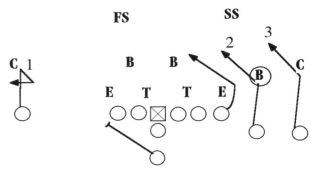

In our six-man protection, we try to get the back to go away from our double slant. That influences the linebackers to that side.

I really like this play from the Spread set. To the three-receiver side we are running the double slant, with the wide receiver going over the top. On the two-man side we are running the flat-slant. The read is the same for the quarterback. If the defense is in a 2 or 4 deep coverage, we go to the double-slant side. If they are in a 3 deep or man cover, we go flat-slant.

The point is we run this from every formation we have and have an option on both sides. Your quarterback has a pretty good chance to succeed every time. Any questions on 94? The key to the slant is to be patient in the route. If the receiver comes to the line and the defensive backs is playing him inside, he can panic. If he tries to get inside, the defensive backs will flat him out and the route is over. He has to make the defensive backs think he is running the fade, hitch, or out. Most of the defensive backs are impatient because for the defender to stop the outside route, he has to get on top or underneath. Either way, it gives the receiver a chance to get inside. We got better at doing that as the season went on. It is a difficult technique to learn and run.

I think this is the best route to throw. It is easy to throw and you can run it against any defense. We probably didn't run this play as much as we should.

The other play is 92. This pattern has the same principle. It is the slant-flat route to both sides. I don't like this as well as the 94 because you don't have an option. What we are looking for on this pattern is an inside technique on the inside receiver. If there is an outside technique on the inside receiver, we really don't have anything. The key to this route is the slant receiver. He has to get up the field to 6 yards.

92

As he slants inside, he has to get himself under control. He doesn't want to run away from the corner into someone else's zone. The key to the flat is to get up the football field as he gains width.

Unless your quarterback understands what you want, you are not going to succeed. You have to keep it very simple for him. Make him go to a side and make a decision where he going to throw the ball. Give him a place to throw the football.

Another thing I want to talk about real quick is our 95. This is a great route that can be thrown at any level. Basically what you have to do is get three receivers to one side and a split end to the other. All this stuff you can do with motion. The split receiver to the three-receiver side runs a streak. The slot receiver is running a flat for width and depth. You can use motion to do this if you like. The tight end is running a 5-yard outside route. The split end weak, keys the outside linebacker. He comes inside. If he can get inside the linebacker he sets down. If he can't get inside, he goes back outside. We tell our quarterback the progression is flat, tight end to backside split end. He takes the flat first. If the linebacker jumps the flat and runs with it, he takes the tight end running away from the inside linebacker. If he can get back side that is the third option.

95

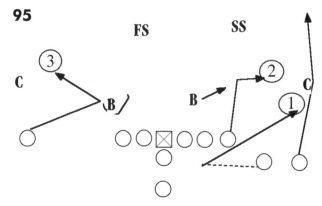

We can do it out of Doubles also. We have to get the third receiver to the right. We can motion the left slot back or empty out the formation with the fullback. If we empty out the split end on the left runs streak and the inside slot runs the backside pattern.

95 FROM DOUBLE

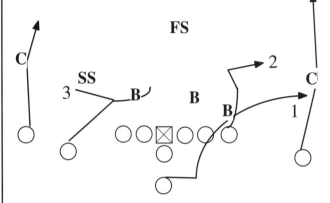

From the Spread set we motion the inside slot for the flat route. The slot to the right runs the tight end outside route. The slot receiver to the back side runs the backside route and both wide receivers run streaks. The read is the same for the quarterback.

95 FROM SPREAD

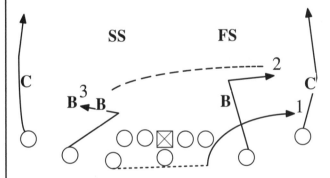

Again the thing that is great is, it is very simple for the quarterback to see. If you want to run this offense the quarterback has to know what he is doing. The quarterback has to know his progression and where he is going with the ball.

All this stuff is just that. If you don't have the ability to run the ball when the defense gives it to you, you're going to get beat. You better make them tough and they better be able to get off the football. You can do different things in the passing game to soften things up. All the things we did from the one-back set we did to soften the defense up so we could kick the crap out of them. That is what it is all about.

If you look at the PAC 10 it is different than it was in 1988. Parity has arrived. The Big Ten is one of those conferences that still say, "We are going to kick your butt, and come after you." To me, that's what football is all about. Next year at Oregon State we may be able to do that. I was a lot better coach at Miami than I was anywhere else. The reason was, I had a tremendous amount of talent.

I never had as much fun coaching as I did at Oregon State this year. They hadn't won much, and the smiles returned to their faces this year. It was a thrill for me and hopefully we can keep it going. Thanks for having me. It was a pleasure to be here.

KEYS FOR A CHAMPIONSHIP PROGRAM

ST. XAVIER HIGH SCHOOL, KENTUCKY

The big thing about coming to a clinic is to try to get something that will help you in your program. I am not going to stand up here and just talk about St. Xavier football. I am going to tell you what we do in our program. I am going to tell you one or two things that we do that you can put into your program.

My topic is "Keys for a Championship Program." I am not sure I can cover everything that happened to us this past year because it was a wild ride. I will cover a couple of things that I feel could be helpful to you.

Basically, they go back to our philosophy. When I started as head coach at St. Xavier. We do not use the pronoun I in our program. When we started we said we wanted to have a championship program every year. That is the key we strive for. We do not just want to win the championship one year and not be a contender the next year. We want to be near the top every year. In the last 18 years we have been in the final four in the state 12 of those years. In the '90s, we were state runner-up in 1991, and we won the state championship in 1992, 1995, 1997, and 1999. A lot of this is by design. After each season we look at our team and ask this question. "Can we win the championship next year?" We will usually agree that we have a chance.

If we do feel we have a chance to make it to the finals the next year we try to plan our season so we make sure we are at our peak toward the end of the season. Our juniors and seniors have to be a year older by the time we get to the playoffs. That is the way we do it.

I am going to give you three keys to our success.
1) Develop a *Philosophy*.
2) Develop a strong *Off-Season Program*.
3) Point toward the *Playoffs*.

I will go into detail on each of these areas later in the lecture.

To be a championship program you have to develop a philosophy. I feel that is a key ingredient that a lot of young coaches overlook. I do not want anyone telling me that we cannot win. We feel we can win any game if we approach our program in a championship manner. We feel it is a must to develop a philosophy.

We win championships in the off-season. We do not win them during the season. I will promise you this is true. We usually lose our first game of the season. That gets everyone off our tail and stops everyone from pointing to you.

The last point I will cover to win a championship is that you must point toward the playoffs. This is true with everything you do toward your offense, defense, and kicking game. It is also true in the way you develop the kids and their thinking. I believe high school football is about developing the players' minds more so than their body. That is where our success has been. We have not won just because we had talent. We have had some talent, but most of the times we have won because we have numbers, and we have won because we have players that believe in what we are trying to do. They think like we think and that is in a championship fashion.

Why build a championship program? After we won that first championship in 1986 I went to a parents meeting. I got up and thanked all of the parents for all they had done for us in the past year. I went on to tell them how much I appreciated all of the warm things they had said about our team and our coaches. I went on to say that I just hoped they would love me the next year if we went 0-10 or 1-

9. An older man in the back of the room raised his hand and spoke out. "Coach, we will still love you if you go 0-10 or 1-9, *BUT WE WILL SURE MISS YOU.*" So I found out real fast that people expect championships and want us to stay at the top of the game. The bottom line is that you need to build a top-notch program and keep on top. They will love you but they will miss you. They will not keep you around too long if you do not have the program at the top level. That is what kids want.

Let me go back and talk about our philosophy. You must have a plan and work the plan. We have a plan and we do not get off the plan. Last year we were 14-1. We lost the first game of the season. We did not panic and we did not change our plans.

I am going to give you our philosophy in a nutshell. First is defense. We are going to play an Eight-Man Front. We are going to jump fronts. We are going to have some different coverages in the secondary, but we are going to keep it simple. The one thing we are going to do each week is to find out what our opponents do best on offense. If we can find out what you do best we are going to do everything in our power to take that away from you. If it is your wide receiver we will do everything we can to contain him. If he is your go-to guy we will do everything we can to take him away from you. If your quarterback is the big dog, we are going to unload on him. We will put roadblocks up for him. We will have our guys chopping at the bits to get to him.

If you are a running team we are going to force you to beat us throwing the football. If you are a passing team you will have to run to beat us. We are a team defense in everything we do defensively.

On offense we are going to be simple. We are going to be multiple. We will run the Inside and Outside Veer. We run the Sweep and a few other basic plays. We are going to run the football so we can set up the pass. We love to throw the ball. We throw the ball 15 times per game but we will throw it 25 times a game if the defense allows us. But we are going to run the football so we can be able to throw the ball. We want to get the ball to different parts of the field.

The big thing we do on offense is to find a weak link in the defense. We will pick the weak link and go at him several ways. If you play us and you have a weak link you better have a plan to hide him. You better move him from side to side. We are going to find him. If one of your starters gets injured in a game and he goes out of the game we are going to test that sub. In our final game in the state we ran almost every play to our right side. In another big game this past year we ran to our left side 95 percent of the time. We were running at what we considered weak links in the defense. If we are throwing the ball we are going to pick one defender and pick on him.

Another big part of our philosophy is that offense must be a fast-break-type offense. We are going to be a get-after-them and go, go, go offense. We are going to try to get you winded. We will start a lot of series without a huddle. We will take four plays and work on them all week. When we come on the sideline ready to go on the field on offense we call "PRESS." That means we are going to run those four plays without a huddle. If it becomes third-and-long we may change the play. You may hear this talked about at clinics, but we work on it and we run it.

We feel we have an outstanding punter coming up next year. I think we have a Division I prospect in our place kicker. He had 10 field goals this past year. He has a strong leg and he works on it all year. We make sure our kickers are working hard all the time. The kicking game is going to be one third of our practice. If I am lying I am dying. It is going to be one third of our practice. We work on it every day.

WE and *US* are a *MUST* in our program. Every year during two-a-days we give our players a T-shirt that has the word *TEAM* on it. Last year the T-shirt had this slogan on it. **ONE TEAM – ONE GOAL.** Next year we will give them another T-shirt. It will have this on it. **NEW TEAM – SAME GOAL.**

I let the kids decide if they think they have a chance to win the whole thing. When they assured me they thought they could win it all we told them it would take a team effort. We preach *TEAM* all of the time. We do not build stars. In our indoor program we have a sign. "12-4-99" That was the date for the state finals. This year the sign will read "12-2-2000." WE and US are a must: TEAM.

The next part of our philosophy is our *Indoor Program*. That is basically what I will cover the rest of the time. The Indoor Program is not negotiable. I will show you our Indoor Program on film. We feel this is the most important ingredient to our success. We feel we can build a state championship team each year with our Indoor Program. If we are fortunate enough to win the state championship it will be because of Indoor Program.

When you are writing down your philosophy you should think a long time about the Indoor Program. I will tell you how strong we feel about our program. Before we had spring football I felt our Indoor Program gave us an edged. Now that we can have spring football some of the other teams can close the gap. We feel so strong about our program that we have to stick with it even with spring football. We go for eight weeks in January and February. We had to give up something if we did that so we are giving up spring practice. Last year we worked with our young quarterback and receivers. It helped us because a junior became our starter. This coming year we probably will just take our linemen out in the spring. We will take them out for six or seven days. But basically we are going to be doing agilities and lifting weights instead of going out in the spring as a team.

Here are the things we look at in our eight-week Indoor Program. None of our assistant coaches is here today. They are working out our players in the Indoor Program. They will be here later. We do not miss our Indoor Program for any reason. If we get out early they still have to stay for the Indoor Program.

We work for three days a week for seven or eight weeks. We make each day in the Indoor a Game Day. They come into the weight room and they will start chanting, "Game Day, Game Day." I talk to them about Friday being a Game Day.

Do you want to see something corny? If you have been there you have to do some corny things. Look at these. These are my work gloves. We tell them we are going to work when we go to the weight room. We try to teach them that work is a good thing. If the players come to the weight room and do not want to go to work we tell them not to come. We tell them to give it up if they do not want to work. We tell them that Barney Fife is on at 3:30 p.m. in Louisville. They can go watch Andy and Mayberry. We talk to them about going to work. Those gloves are the first thing I show them when we start our Indoor Program each year. These are nice wool gloves in green and gold. Those are our school colors. We have "GO TO WORK" written on the gloves. I take the gloves to the weight room and let them wear them for a while. We talk about going to work and they believe in what we are doing.

This year we are going to work our Indoor Program for seven weeks. We go three days per week. We treat each day as a Game Day. The first half is conditioning. The second half is weight lifting. We do not use anything to gain weight. We do not use Creatine. We do not want to put anything in their body that we do not know a lot about. We take them as they are. We never want them to think we do not want them as they are. We are just like a jockey in the Kentucky Derby. The coach is the jockey and we are going to ride the player and we are going to ride his behind but we are going to ride what we have. We can't switch horses after we have taken them into our program. Next year we do not have near the same amount of athletes as we had this year. But, we are going to get on what we have and we are going to ride them and we are going to have a chance to win at the end of the season.

We make each workout a Game Day. Each half is 48 minutes. That is four quarters. It is just like a game for us. Each segment is broken up into 15 minutes. We tell them it's 12-minute segments when we break the program down where we have 48 minutes in conditioning and 48 minutes in the weight room. We have two groups going at the same time. We have one group in the weight room and one group working on conditioning. We break our conditioning program down where we have four groups going at the same time.

Why do we have the Indoor Program? It sets the tone for the entire year. It is the first phase of our season and it is the most important phase. We break down into four groups. They go for 48 minutes. Both groups are going to do four things. They have a first, second, third, and fourth quarter in conditioning and in the weight room. One of the best things we do is to add a fifth quarter for our conditioning.

I want to stress this point again about the mind game. We have beaten teams that we should not have beaten because we believed we could win. We stress the things that we feel are necessary to bring about a victory without being a star. So we start in January and February training their minds. We use this theme: **"YOU ARE WHO YOU ARE."**

How do you get the weight and heights for your players? We measure our players stripped down and barefooted in the first week of the summer workouts. That is "Who They Are." We stress this in the Indoor Program. If they are 5'7" then they are 5'7". If they are 6'5", they are 6'5". If you ask them how tall they are they will always tell you they are a little taller. I have a tape measure in my office. If they come into my office I will ask them how tall they are. Then I ask them to take their shoes off and stand against the door jam. I get the tape out and check their height. We want them to accept who they are and to build themselves into players. That's what we think our Indoor Program does for us.

When we start the Indoor Program we give them a piece of paper to hang on the front of their locker. After the program is over we will give them something else.

INDOOR 2000
"BUILD YOURSELF INTO A PLAYER"

Attitude and effort count. *We* and *Us* are must words. Push hard to be quicker. Finish hard – "Finish What You Start." Learn to run low. Develop hip flexibility: low hips. Learn to run in a "LINE." See what you tackle and wrap your arms. Punish the bag! Make a Commitment to outwork everyone that you play.

"TAKE OUR EFFORT AND PERFORMANCE TO ANOTHER LEVEL IN 2000!"

We played five playoff games and we were behind in all five of them but we won. We played 15 games total and we were behind in nine of them. In the first game we got behind and lost that game. But we came back and won all of the rest. I think one of the reasons we came back to win those games was because of our Indoor Program. We developed their mind and they "Refused to Lose."

First I want to cover our Conditioning Phase. The first quarter is our Mats. You will see us do a lot of things in the film. We do these drills:

MATS
Grass Drills
Recover & Roll:
    Running
    Front To
    Front Away
    Back To
    Back Away
Seat Roll
Tiger Roll
Combative Drills

We end up on the mats. We wrestle. We work on Switches on the Mat. We only go for a short time. The rule is this: "Get your butt up." They can do anything they want to get off the bottom. We are not teaching toughness. We are interested in them going as hard as they can as quick as they can. That first quarter is 12 minutes and then we take a little break. I bring them together and call "Ready –

Ready – Break." I will tell them they just lost that first quarter of the game. I tell them we have to pick it up the second quarter.

We have four groups going at the same time. We change stations. The Mat group goes to Running, The Running group goes to Skills, and the Skills group goes to Agility.

Our second station is what we call our Running Station. We are not very fast. We do not have very many skilled people. We are going to beat you with linemen and with numbers, and not with skilled players most of the time.

This is what we do in the Running Station.

RUNNING
Stride
Form Run
Carioca
Backpedal Turn And Run
Sprints

ROPE JUMPING
Two Feet
Run With It
Alternate Feet
Speed Jumps (30 Sec./60 Sec.)

A 60-SECOND TEST!

We can make the drills geared to the different positions. For the linemen we may do more short, quick moves, and the defensive backs do more backpedal.

We work on the Ropes. I can't stand fat offensive linemen. I can't stand linemen that cannot go through the Running Ropes, and can't jump rope. We are fooling ourselves as coaches if we just let those big, fat guys come out and just waddle around. They may not end up as being the quickest players, but we can teach them some pride. Teach them to be thin. You can get a girlfriend if you are thin. I do not know of any lineman that takes pride in being fat. I do not know of anyone that takes pride in calling himself a HOG. They better be able

to move. Our fat guys can move pretty quick. We are not going to play with slow players.

We have a 60-second Rope Jumping Contest each month. This is something we test them on to let them see how much they have improved.

The third quarter is Skills. This is what we work on.

SKILLS
Form Tackle On Air
Form Tackle Bags
Hips And Hold
Hips And Go
6-Point Explosion (RT/LT)

Hip Rotation and placement of the head and tail are the goal. "Butt Down – Head and eyes up. Low Man Wins!" This is what they hear from us all of the time.

The fourth station is our fourth quarter. It is our Agility program. We are working on them changing directions. We want them to be able to stop and go. These drills can be made position specific. Here the drills we do with the bags.

BAGS
1 Touch Stride
2 Touch Stride
Lateral Bags
Figure Eight
Shuffle Slide
5 Touch
2-Foot Bounce

LINE DRILLS
Pro Agility (RT/LT Hand)
Carioca Touch
RT/LT Foot Hop

Here is what you need to remember. The bottom line is this. We have four quarters, 12 minutes each quarter. We have no rest in between. When the players move from one station to the next we blow a whistle. We blow a whistle and they break down.

The coach calls out "Ready." The group responds in unison "TEAM." Then the coach calls out "Ready – Ready, Break HARD!" On everything that we do we break the huddle. We break just like we would if we were going to the line of scrimmage to knock someone on their butt. The bottom line is that we want to be more physical than our opponents. If we are more physical we feel good about what we have done. If we are not more physical we probably lost the game.

We respect our opponents by the way we feel on Saturday morning after a game. When they come into our training room it is filled. We do not let them hang out there. They must go out and run or walk. No one stays in our training room while our team is doing their 12-minute run. If they are on crutches they come on out. If they must have the foot propped up that is different. We let them stay home. If they are the walking wounded they walk on our track while the other guys run. If they go to the weight room they can take their ice bag with them.

How many of you let your team have a workout and you let another player go to the training room? If a player has a problem with his shoulder we have him work with his legs. If we let one player out of the workout to go to the training room or let him work on something that is not team-oriented it will hurt you. I do not think a star system will win for you. The stars can win for you and we love to have good athletes come to our school. But the star system will not win games for you.

We have taken our Indoor Program one step beyond the four quarters. Now we have an Overtime Session. It is made up of pushups and sit-ups. We do them on cadence. We do them for mental toughness. We do them as a team. We do not allow them to make mistakes on them. If they do we make them do them over again. Our defensive coordinator gives the cadence and he makes the drill tough for them.

We can make them start over again on any of the drills we have covered. We even do this with practice during the regular season. The distance from our dressing room to the practice field is about 150 yards. I have called the team up after about 15 or 20 minutes of practice and given them a real butt chewing. I tell them to get inside and to get dressed and go to our meeting room. I tell them they have 20 minutes to be in that room. After 20 minutes I blow the whistle and tell them to get dressed and to get back on the practice field in 20 minutes. I have only done that a couple of times but it has been real effective when I have done it.

Why do we call this period the Overtime Period. We play a lot of overtime games. We won the state finals in overtime. In our last two games we won on the last offensive play of the game in both games. We feel you must prepare for this.

During the break before the overtime our players knew what to do. They were all excited because we had worked on this. They all wanted to run the ball over their hole. We were smart enough to run the ball to our right side because we had a lot of success there.

After the last conditioning period we switch with the weight room group. Coaches can do what you want in the weight room. Most coaches are going to do what you know. I do not have any secrets for the weight room. This is what we do in the weight room

CORE LIFTS
Bench
Squat
Clean
Incline

AUXILIARY LIFTS

We have four periods with 15 minutes in each of those periods. We vary the lifts and the workout. We stress form and technique. Those are the goals this time of the year.

I am going to show the film on the Indoor Program at the end. I want to cover a few more points before the film.

We break our season down into phases. We are going to build into the program what to do if we lose a game. Do not let one loss devastate your football team. A loss can be the best thing that ever happens to you if you know how to handle it.

This is how we break our season down. We start with the first five games. During this time, from the start of practice in the fall until our first five games we are going to establish the fundamentals. We are going to block and tackle and we are going in full gear. We are going to work them until they can't move anymore. We put in our base offense and defense. We have to play Madison Central High School next year in our first game. I do not know how we can win because we will not have all of our secondary coverages in our package. You may ask why we would not put them in if we know we are going to face a real strong passing team. If we do put them in at that time they will be mediocre by the fifth game of the season. We are going to put in our base offense and defense and we are going to win with our toughness and our intensity. If we lose that game it does not mean anything in all reality.

Coach Jerry Claiborne taught me this. He used to say, "Remember November!" We lost the first game this year and the other team went bananas. They were throwing helmets in the air and turning cartwheels. I called the team together and told them that our opponent had just won their state championship – *Ours Is Down The Road In December*. You have to point that out to them.

Have a plan and work the plan. You must have courage to do anything right. You must have your own convictions and stick by them.

In the first five games we are going to find our football team. We play Trinity High School in our fifth game of the year. We tell our players they had better buckle their chinstraps on for that game. We know it is going to be a tough, hard-nosed game. In the last 18 years when we have made a quarterback change it has been after that game. We are going to find our football team in those first five games. We will experiment with payers at different positions up until that fifth game.

In game 6 we set the starting lineup. The Trinity game is the first week we set our two-deep list. After that game we make any adjustments to the depth chart. After that our starters are not going to change unless they hit the skids.

From that point we are in Phase Two of our season. Now we are going to work on developing depth. We start working on the offense and defense we are going to use in the playoffs. We practice every day on the things we will use in the playoffs. We practice our X Screen to our tight end. We work on the Sprint Left Throwback to the flanker who we brought back inside. We put an athlete in that position and we get him the ball. That play has averaged 45 yards per game for us. We only use it four or five times a year but we use it when we need it.

You see some teams running up the score on weak teams They run reverses and all of their trick plays and run up the score on those weak teams. Do you know what we are going to do against the weak teams? NOTHING! We are going to develop toughness and we are going to work on fundamentals. We are not going out to impress everyone on how well we did this or that. We are going to save our best for the playoffs.

We practice those plays all of the time. The players will come up to me and ask me when we are going to run some of those plays. Everything we do during the season is going to be very vanilla.

Or last phase is the playoffs. We play five playoff games if we get to the finals. We hope we can make it to the championship game.

Remember our KEYS. Take a look at your *Philosophy*. Build a strong *Off-Season Program*. Play for the *Playoffs*. No one really cares what you did during the regular season. You can be 1-9 if you make it to the playoffs. If that one win will get you in the playoffs they are only going to remember what you did in the playoffs.

QUARTER COVERAGES AND TECHNIQUES

BALTIMORE RAVENS

I was with a group of guys last night and I told them I would find out who the real troopers were this morning. You guys are special for getting up on Sunday morning to hear someone talk on football.

I am going to go pretty fast and I have a habit of moving around. If you have a question raise your hand and we will try to answer it. I would like to make part of this a Question-and-Answer session. Basically I am going to talk about Secondary Techniques. I am going to talk about Quarter Coverage and how it applies to the high school level. Some people call this look Cover 4 and some teams call it Cover 8. Basically, what it really is is Four Across – Man. The Corners are locked up on the wideouts in a pro set. The Safeties are locked up on the number 2 receivers. If the offense does not break the set the backside safety is free.

How can this defense apply to the high school level? First, it creates a simple teaching environment. In high school you do not have a lot of time to teach a lot of different coverages. Everyone can understand Man-to-Man Coverage. So this eliminated teaching several techniques. It enables players to play fast. We are playing man-to-man. The corners always have the wideouts. Our philosophy is to be able to double any two receivers once the ball is snapped. The safeties always have the tight end and open back. The linebackers play the tight end and the 2 or 3 backs on coverages. They have the deep backs to back them up.

This defense eliminates certain offensive schemes. When we break the offense down for the defense we start with alignment and eye progression. We talk about keys, stance, and all of those things. My question to you is this: When we talk about keys what do they do? Is it a Free Snap Read or is it a Hard Read? Where do the eyes go once the ball is snapped. The defensive man's eyes go on his man, period.

Let me talk about the alignment for the Corner. If I were coaching this in high school I would align them 10 by 1. It would be 10 yards vertical and 1 yard outside the receiver. Our corners are going 8 by 1 on our alignment. The inside foot is going to be back. It is easier to tell them to move back than it is to tell them to move forward.

The first thing we want them to read is the Three-Step Drop of the quarterback. The corner forms a triangle from the receiver to the quarterback. He can read the quarterback on the Three-Step Drop out of the corner of his eyes. The thing you want to do with the cornerbacks is to start training their eyes. I want them to learn to put the outside eye on the receiver and the inside eye on the quarterback. We do the same thing over on the other side. I run a simple drill to help them on this. I line up a receiver, as soon as he moves they start backing up. If the quarterback moves the corner should be moving. Again, start training the corners to use their eyes. We are going to read the three steps of the quarterback.

From the Three-Step Drop the eyes go to the belt buckle of the receiver. In the NFL if you stay on the quarterback too long, the receiver is gone. That receiver will be on top of you. When the corner gets his eyes trained he will be able to pick up the Hitch real quick.

From the belt buckle we want the corner to look at the hip pocket of the receiver. His hips will tell you the route he is running.

One of the big mistakes I see with linebackers is that they keep their eyes on the quarterback too long. They drop back in coverage and pick up their man but they keep their eyes on the quarterback too long. The quicker you can correct that the better off you will be if you are going to play Man Coverage.

As the quarterback releases the ball we want our eyes to go through the ball. This will enable the corner to pick the ball off on the interception.

The safeties alignment is 10 by 2 off of the end man on the line of scrimmage. The key the triangle. The Free Safety keys the offensive tackle if the end is split. If the tackle pops up he knows it is a pass. If the tackle keeps his head down he can expect run. If the tackle pops up it should be pass. If he goes down with his head it should be run. It is easy for them to distinguish the difference in run and pass. When they have a hard time is when the offense runs the Draw.

Let me talk about getting the deep defenders to understanding the techniques and what they need. I think this is critical for the Corners and Safeties. First or all they can't take away everything. We tell the corner he has two routes he has to cover. Those routes are the 8 and 9 routes. The 8 is a Post and the 9 route is a Streak. We will be okay on everything else. If we tell them they only have to take care of those two routes they play better. If you start telling them they have the Hitch, Curl, Post, and the Streak they do not play as well.

The Safeties are next. It is critical for the safeties to eliminate the vertical move by number 2 first, and then double number 1. Once they eliminate number 2 vertical then they can go to number 1. As long as the offense has two men in the backfield we are going to double cover the number 1 receiver.

The Strong Safety is playing 10 yards deep and 2 yards wide of the end man on the line of scrimmage. He is visualizing the triangle. He is going to be able to see it all. Once the receiver starts vertically he counts two counts and gets out of there. If the safeties see the high hat they are slow to get out of their area. The receiver is going to declare

within 5 yards where he is going to go. In three to four seconds, which is 5 yards for you, he is going to declare where he is going. If his hat is high, where is he going? I will guarantee you he is going somewhere down the field. He is looking for an area. If he goes inside after those 5 yards I can go double on the number 1 receiver.

What does the corner have? He has to take away the 8 and 9 routes. Now, the 4 route is the Curl, and the 6 is the Dig route. Who is going to help the corner? The safety is going to help. Now, here is the problem with that when I say that. On the two-receiver side that corner on that side has to be thinking of nothing but Man Coverage. He is not going to get help. On the back side with the split end and two backs in the backfield, the corner on that side should know that he is going to get help.

The next questions we want to answer are these. How do alignments and techniques effect an offensive scheme? This first thing is that the defense has nine men in the box. The offense is outnumbered. We have better numbers on offense.

INTERIOR BOX

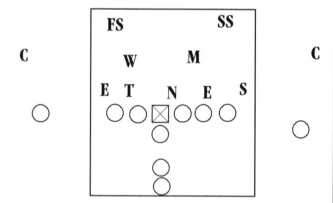

We can eliminate certain plays by adjusting our defense. If we move the safeties by moving the Strong Safety up in the alley on the tight-end side and move the Free Safety over the center we have eliminated the Option and Toss Sweep.

After we have moved the Safeties what does the quarterback do? He has been taught all week that the two safeties will be sitting back 10 yards deep in the middle. Then we make our moves and what does he do? Now he has to check out of the play and call something else. We have eliminated the "Coach in the Box." We force the quarterback to make the calls. We want to make the quarterback beats us. We do not want to let the coach beat us.

We can create the Eight-Man Fronts and Nine-Man Fronts. We already have the Nine-Man Front. How do you get that done? The first thing you must do is to make sure the front and the coverages are coordinated. You must have a support. The best way to do that, in my opinion, is to always have an edge on both sides. I do not care if it is a linebacker in an Over-and-Under, or a 4-3 with the linebacker, or the end to the tight end. He has to know right away if he is going to pursue or if he is going to force. He is going to spill the play or he is going to force it. On the other side you have to know who is going to do the same thing.

The first thing he has to do is to play the run. If we have nine in the box we can't let them run the ball. If they can run the ball with seven men against our nine we have the wrong lineup in the game. We want that edge on the corner. We must consider Down and Distance, personnel in the game, and Field Position.

A coach asked me last night what was the most important thing for a defensive back to know? To me it is the alignment on the formation of the offense. If he can't visualize what a pro set is he can't line up and he can't play. The next most important things to know are the splits. He must recognize splits from the receivers. He must be able to adjust to those splits. The third thing for me is communication.

The thing that is important is to think after the offense breaks the huddle. The offenses have tendencies and you must be able to recognize them in a game. They have to know Down and Distance. The reason I say that is because it is critical to whatever coverage we are playing. We want to make sure we are aware of the offensive personnel in the huddle. You have to know who is on the field. There are two

things that scare the heck out of the defensive backs. One is when he does not know the coverage. The other is when he does not know who is in the game. If you are a defensive back and you do not know the coverage you are in trouble.

We going to talk about field position. We will talk about the ball being on the hash mark and in the middle of the field. First let me talk about the coverages we can play from the 4 Deep look.

COVER 1 = 2 MAN FREE
COVER 2 = 2 DEEP
COVER 3 = 3 DEEP
COVER 4 = (1/4)
COVER 6 = 1/4, 1/4, 1/2

I think we can play all of those coverages. We can play 2 Man Free from our Quarter look. We can play 2 Deep from the Quarter look. We can play Cover 3. As a secondary coach, if you can eliminate what you have the linebackers do as far as alignment and where you want them to drop, the better off you are going to be against the passing game. All I need to know is how the outside linebacker is going to play. Once we determine that, we can play. If we are playing Cover 3 and the Sam is dropping 10 yards then I know someone has to cover the area behind the linebacker. If we start playing Cover 3, 6, or 7 different ways we have players getting lost.

Cover 6 for us is Quarter, Quarter, Halves. It is real simple. We can call Buzz X or Buzz Z. That is a form of 3 Deep Coverage. That means we are going to bring a safety down to double the X receiver or the Z receiver.

Let me talk about the techniques we must teach the secondary. We must teach them the splits of the receivers. You have to teach them how to play the Crack, and the Crack and Go. He has to know the difference between the two. He has to know the Squirm technique If number 1 and number 2 are eliminated the safety has to Squirm. They have to know how to Force Angles. They have to know how to push the ball inside. They must know the Cutback Angle.

Let me talk about playing the Coverages. I have these on tape and I will show them to you at the end. The first Coverage is our Cover 1. That is Man Free. We line them up in a 4-3 look. The corners know they are locked on number 1. They play Man-to-Man no matter where the receivers go.

If you want to bring a linebacker you can. Here we are bringing the Sam linebacker. This is out of a 4 Deep look.

MAN FREE

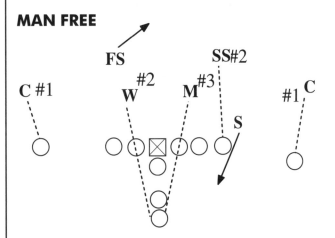

Let's take it a step further. If they come out with two tight ends you have to declare which tight end you want to declare to. We declare to the Field or the Tight End. For us, against two tight ends we are going to declare to the Stud end. Most of the time in college we went to the Field. If you have one back or two backs you always have to declare to the broken set. It does not matter if you call it Tight or Weak, it is a lot easier when you determine the set for the Safety.

MAN FREE TWO TIGHT ENDS

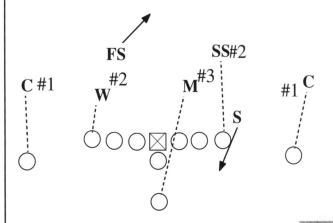

If the offense splits the end to the wide side of the field and puts the tight end to the weak side how do we play it? We have to move the Sam outside. Now, do you want Sam covering the slot man or do you want the Safety covering him? We want the Safety. We can still bring Sam on the rush from the outside.

MAN FREE SLOT TO FIELD

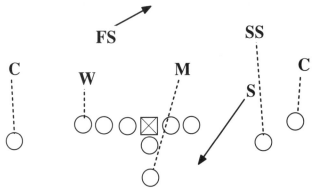

Now with this front, as a secondary coach I need to know from the linebacker coach, what he is going to do with the outside linebacker on the tight end on a vertical route. That is all I want to know. Now, when I know that it will help me out to the strong side. I want to know if the Sam is going to run with the tight end or not. If he is going to run with him, that is great. If he runs with the tight end, I know the ball has to go over the top. On the strong side the strong safety is going to play a tight one half. If the wide receiver and the tight end run a vertical route, the safety is going to play a tight one half to the number 2 man. On the weak side if the safety reads an outside release he has to go to the inside flat.

Now, let's talk about what we are going to tell the corners. This is where it becomes critical. You have to stay on top of your corners about this. I was brought up in the old school where we would jam the crap out of the wide receivers on Cover 2. But this is what happens. If the receiver starts to widen I lose the ability to jam him anyway. You can move him up to 3 yards deep and funnel him that way. If they are lined up 6 or 7 yards deep it is not going to happen. That receiver will start widening real fast.

On the tight-end side the safety is going to read the tight end and number 1. He is only concerned with number 2 when he goes on a vertical route. If number 2 receiver goes on a vertical route, that makes the corner a squat corner. He is going to reroute the wide receiver with his feet. If he can cut him off with his feet it does not matter if he gets his hands on him. If he misses him with his feet, he is dead. The Safety is not giving the corner any help what so ever. Over on the back side it is no problem because the corner only has one possible vertical receiver. That is Cover 2.

COVER 2

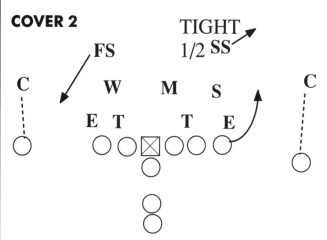

If we get a Trips look we are going to play 4 Deep. They have four possible vertical receivers. Anytime they have four verticals I want Cover 4. This is against a One-Back Set. The strong safety knows he has number 2 vertical. The free safety knows he has to take number 3 strong.

FOUR DEEP VS. ONE BACK

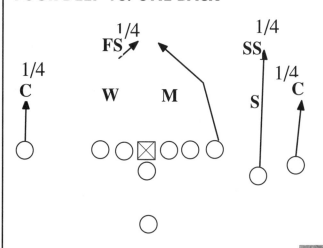

Let's move to Cover 3. Against the One Back we are going to be in the Eagle look. We have to bump someone down. If we get the slot on the back side we can play it two ways. We can key on the One Back. If he goes to the slot this is how we can cover it. We can bring the safety down inside of the Will linebacker. Everyone in the secondary is reading the One-Back Set. It gives us a chance to double a receiver again.

COVER THREE VS. ONE BACK

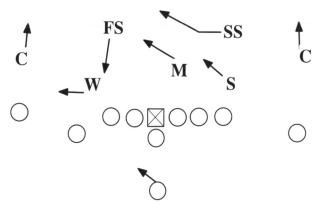

Here is the other way you can do the same thing. Anytime we get the One-Back Set with four wideouts this is what we tell our guys to do. We can bring the safety to the corner on the weak side and slide the linebackers to the tight-end side. That is our regular 3 Deep with 4 Underneath Coverage. But, the corners have to read number 2 to number 1 Read Corners.

COVER 3 VS. ONE-BACK SET

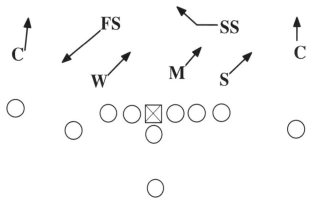

If you can eliminate them from being number 2 to number 1 Read Corners you are better off in my opinion.

If we get Motion we can bump with the Backers or rock and roll with the Safeties. We can handle it either way. If you do not want to bump the linebackers you rock and roll with the safeties. If you want to bump the linebackers you do not have to roll the safeties.

Cover #6 is next. That is Quarter – Quarter – One Half. On the two-receiver side we are playing force. On the one-receiver side we are playing One Half. On the two-receiver side we are playing Quarters. The corner has number 1 and the safety has number 2. The three linebackers are going to play off the two remaining backs. On the one receiver side we are playing flat and One Half. That is Cover #6.

COVER #6 QUARTER – QUARTER – HALF

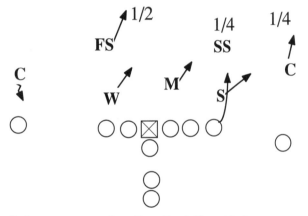

If they come out in a One-Back Set this is my question to you? Who is the most dangerous receiver? It is the wide receiver. On that side we play Quarters. On the tight-end side we play One Half.

COVER #6 QUARTER – QUARTER – HALF

We like to go to the two-receiver side that is the most dangerous. Another way you can go is to the Field. If the ball is on the Hash you can go Quarters on the Field side. If you do that you are going to give them one technique to do. The strong safety is always going to the two-receiver side. If you decide to do that and the offense breaks the huddle and sends two receivers to the wide side of the field your strong safety knows he is going to that side and he is playing Quarter Coverage. On Cover #4 he is always to the tight-end side anyway. That is what he does. He plays Quarters all of the time.

BUZZ, Buzz, buzz. Let's talk about Buzz. The critical thing about this is the linebackers must know which way you are coming to double. They have to bump opposite of the safety that is running the Buzz. We are getting the eighth man in the Box now. We have nine in the Box before and now we are running the Buzz and we are putting eight men in the Box. Here is our Buzz Z. This is just another form of Cover #3.

BUZZ Z

Here is the Buzz X. Again, the linebacker bump in the opposite direction of the call. We have eight in the Box. It is another way to get to Cover #3 and to bring another man in the Box. That is all we do.

BUZZ X

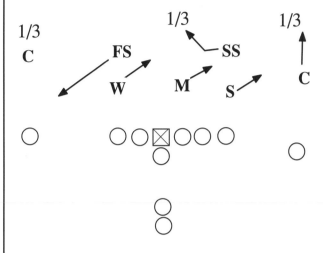

This may seem like a lot to different coverages but really it isn't.

In the time I have left I want to talk about understanding splits. This is how we start teaching our secondary people from the top. There are two things they must recognize immediately. Where is the ball? The ball is placed on the left hash mark and we have a corner on that side. He wants to know where is the tight end or where is number 1. If they put the formation into the boundary, you have to know where the wideout is lined up. Three things come into play here. He must determine if it is a tight split, a wide split, or a normal split. Those are the three things that must go through him mind. It is the same over on the other side.

If I am the corner on the boundary side and they come out with a receiver 4 yards from the sideline, he needs to know what type of split that is. Is it a tight split, a wide split, or a normal split? That is a normal split to us because we have a safety that is aligned 10 by 2 on the tight end. So, if the wide receiver is within 4 yards of the sideline that is a normal split.

For the corner a normal split puts him in a head up to an inside shade on the wide receiver. The ball is into the boundary. If we put the corner outside of the man we have lost our advantage.

NORMAL SPLIT

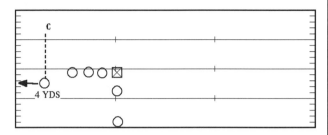

Let's go to the wide side of the field. The ball is still on the other hash mark. If they line up a receiver and line him up on the numbers, that is 9 yards from the sideline. He is lined up 5 yards from the far hash mark. What kind of split is it to the corner now? Go through the progression. Is it tight, wide, or normal? You better tell me it is a tight split. If he goes to a normal split where would he line up? He is going to be head up to inside. Well, look how much of the field is open. There is 17 yards from the hash mark. He wants to cut the split down and play tight.

TIGHT SPLIT

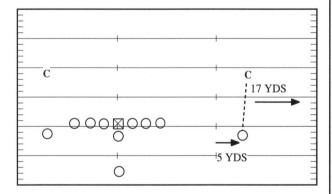

As the receivers start moving their alignment inside toward the formation we consider that alignment tight. Now we want the leverage to be on the outside. We still have the safety on the inside.

If we take the receiver and put him outside by the numbers about 9 yards from the sideline, hello! Which split is it? We know it is not tight. What do we have to take away with the corner? He has to take away the 8 and 9 routes. Now he comes back to head up, to slightly inside.

As they split outside the numbers we can move outside. They must know what they are looking for. They must understand what we mean by normal, tight, and wide splits. You must have something concrete about it. Personally I like to go with the numbers and the hash mark. Whenever in doubt if they start to condense the formation, what are they trying to do? They are trying to expand the routes.

Some of you run the Bunch crap. Teams bring the wide receiver in motion inside and run the underneath routes. They bring the man inside to expand the coverage. They are hoping that someone will get caught outside. We know the motion man is bringing the corner inside for a reason. Hello! They are expanding the routes on us. Stop! Stay outside and play the back out of the backfield.

BUNCH ROUTE

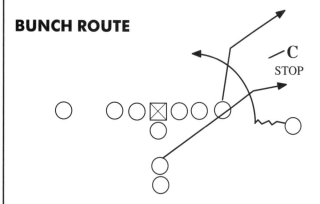

Next is the Crack and Crack and Go. Why is that important? How do you determine if it is a Crack by the wide receiver? How does the corner know if the Crack block on the safety is coming or if the Crack and Go is on? If the offense is in the I Set and they toss the ball to the tailback that receiver is going to crack on the safety. You have to have someone to replace the safety and it has to be the corner. How does the corner know if it is Crack or Crack and Go? How does he know? Here is how he knows. Remember when I said where his head goes the butt will follow? Yes or No?

The first thing that must happen is that the safety must get into the alley right now. It is a perimeter run. That safety must run hard to get to the alley. He wants to flatten and make the wide receiver turn toward him. If the receiver is going to block on the safety his shoulders must turn parallel to the line of scrimmage.

As long as the receiver is running toward that safety and his numbers are facing the safety, he better play pass. If he doesn't, what will they do to him? They will start him down toward the safety and break deep.

That corner must know if it is Crack or Crack and Go. Who is going to determine this? Number 1, the safety is. That safety must clear it up right now. If the safety sits back and lollygags that man is going to block two men. The corner does not know if it is an 8 route or not. It looks like a Post so he better get on top of it. What is the key point? That safety must get his butt within 4 yards of the line of scrimmage right now. Once he gets to that area the receiver must turn his shoulders to block him. Once the corner sees the receiver block on the safety he comes to play the outside.

If you are going to play Quarters you better learn how to play the Crack and Crack and Go. I will tell you right now, you will see it in the game.

Question? On the Crack and the Crack and Go, and the Post, the corner is working inside and on top of #1 inside out? Right! If it is a wide split the corner is inside. If he comes inside he is thinking Post. The safety has to clean up the play on the outside.

I am going to put my address on the overhead. If you want more information drop me a note. I usually charge $2 for this and I give it to one of my favorite charities.

DONNIE HENDERSON
BALTIMORE RAVENS
11001 OWNINGS MILL BLVD.
OWNINGS MILLS, MD 2117
AC 1-410-654-6290

In conclusion, playing Quarters is a very simple thing. It eliminates coaching several techniques. It enables the players to play fast. Also, it eliminates certain offensive schemes.

I am going to show the tape. Thanks for your attention.

THE OUTSIDE LINEBACKER IN THE 4-3 DEFENSE

UNIVERSITY OF MIAMI, OHIO

Thank you very much. It is truly an honor and privilege to be here. It is good to be back and be with people who understand what I do. After getting off the road from recruiting, I feel like a traveling salesman. Trying to sell your program and school to these recruits is a big job.

When you speak on a clinic, you want to come up with a topic that is applicable to a lot of people. We are a 4-3 defense and have been one for a long time. I can get tape out from 1992-93 and it would be almost what we do right now. We have not changed it very much.

I decided to talk about our **Outside Linebacker Play**. If you bring anyone off the edge in any form of defense, this talk is going to help you. That has been the key to our defense. A lot of people use our defense or some version of it. We have great success with the defense, but the key has been our outside linebacker play. We feature that guy. We have had the Defensive Player of the Year in our conference six of the last nine years and three in a row. Two years ago they picked two outside linebackers for all-league and we had them both.

We recruit that type of player. We try to get the guys who have the tools we want them to have to play that position. It is not only because they are great athletes that they are successful. Part of it has to be the plan they are put into. I tell our outside linebackers not to get too excited about themselves. We are giving them the opportunity to become great players. We are looking for guys that can run, are tough, but have good qualities. These guys are smart football players. I tell them I can get them aligned right, teach them the proper techniques, but when it comes to playing, they have to use the instincts they have. They've got to make plays.

Woody Hayes talked about the O.J. Simpson run in his book *Hotline to Victory*. He said there was the action, the reaction, and the re-reaction. That is what the special players have. We look for the same type guys. They are football players that can go beyond on their instincts. The most important thing to those guys is making the play.

Today I'm going to talk about what we do with our outside linebackers. I'm going to be pretty specific about it and concentrate on the split-side linebacker. That is where people try to attack us away from the tight end.

Our basic defense starts with a plan. Everybody has a plan. One of Bear Bryant's sayings was, *"Have a plan, Work the plan, and Plan for the unexpected."* We have a plan on defense. Our success as a defense will be determined by how well we accomplish our goals. To be the best defense in the MAC we must:

1. Stop the run consistently.
2. Be great in the Red Zone.
3. Eliminate SIWs. That means Self-Inflicted Wounds. (We led the league in penalties last year.)
4. Be an intimidating defense – both in our style of play by being physical and in our tactics by being multiple.
5. Be a smart defense. Know the game situation and what our opponent is likely to do in that situation.
6. Play with emotion and trust. Care greatly about the outcome and your performance and have faith in your teammates and coaches.

People try to spread us out. Therefore, we would like people to get into two backs a couple of times a series. If people play two backs against us, we will have something for you. We'll gang the line of scrimmage and get a lot of people there. We are not an eight-man front. Everyone says you have to get the eighth man into the box. We are a nine-man front. We have very aggressive safeties and outside linebackers.

Our goal is to give up only 16 points or less a game. We arrived at that number from some studies we have made. If we do that, we will be in the top 10 in scoring defense. Plus we will be in every game we play. In modern-day college football, that is hard to do.

One of the greatest compliments I've ever gotten came from an official. He turned to me on the sideline and said, "I've got to keep counting. It seems like you've got more guys out there then you are supposed to." We didn't but I liked the thought.

There is a challenge in today's football. For a guy to take personal responsibility for the outcome of the game, it is important to him. This is having pride in what they do on the field.

Let me show you how we line up real quickly. I don't want this to get into a lecture on 4-3 defense. Our defensive end to the tight end is in a 7 technique. We don't play much 9 technique with the defensive end. Our tackles are in a 3 and weak-side 0 shade techniques. The other end is in a 5 technique on the open side tackle. Our base coverage is Cover 4. That is a quarter coverage. Most of our defenses are tight end oriented. The Mike linebacker finds the tight end and makes a *Roger* or *Larry* call. That obviously means left or right. The one thing I like about this is, we can give you a lot of fronts, but we don't have great adjustments. Even if our opponents know what we do, it doesn't help them that much. You have to know what we are doing in that particular situation. We are going to show you one thing and give you something else. Our defense doesn't have to adjust to anyone much anymore. We dictate to the offense.

The key for our outside linebacker is what we call a *CAT*. People like to run at the bubbles in your defense. They like to attack the weak-side B-Gap,

strong-side A-Gap, and strong-side C-gap. Our defense crowds the line of scrimmage and comes as hard as we can. When we send one guy off the edge that is not a blitz to us. When we bring the outside linebacker off the edge, the end slants into the B-Gap, that is not a blitz. We don't have to play man to man behind that little stunt.

Part of the advantage is our Cover 4. It all starts with our quarter coverage. In reality the coverage is a 5 under and 2 deep coverage. This coverage allows us to be aggressive with our outside linebackers. The corners basically become the deep half defenders. The safeties become the robbers in the curl areas. Our outside linebackers are basically responsible for the flats. Our linebackers don't drop. When I first started coaching defense, I was really frustrated by that. I went back to my college coach and asked him, if I had two guys in my zone, who do I cover? He told me to cover the one they were going to throw to.

COVER 4

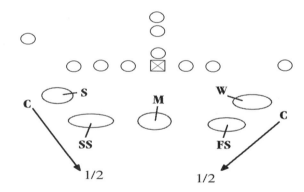

We play a matchup-type coverage. We don't drop our linebackers; we operate in a 5-yard line. If you run sprint draw at our linebacker, we step up. Someone else will worry about covering the curls and digs in the hole. As a linebacker I don't have to get back in coverage. That makes it tough to run screens and draws on us. People don't throw screens on us. We don't drop with our linebackers, so we don't have to react back up. We are already there. Our quarter coverage allows us to get nine guys into the box. If we send the outside linebacker on a Cat, the Free Safety has to move over and take number 2 weak.

WILL CAT BLITZ

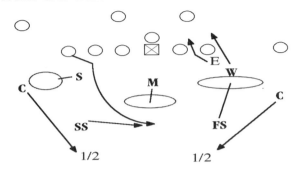

Let me show you our entire defense in our base set, so you can see it and know what I am talking about.

BASE DEFENSE

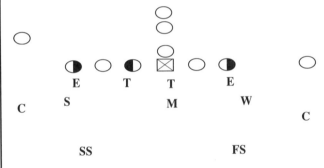

In 1994, when I took over at Miami as defensive coordinator, our leading tackler in the league was our free safety. If your free safety is your leading tackler, the defense must not be very good. We were first in the nation in pass defense and third in total defense. He was Defensive Player of the Year. At free safety, he ran by the linebackers who had to fight off blocks, and made the tackle.

Here's what *WILL-CAT* does for us. I'll give you an overview first and then get into specifics. We spend a disproportionate amount of time in practice preparing the outside linebacker to do what they have to do. We are going to ask him to come off the edge and do a bunch of things. An example would be the 5 technique coming under into the B-Gap and Will coming off the edge. One of the cat's rules is, don't let anyone cross your face. If a back flares and the Will linebacker continues to the quarterback, something bad is going to happen. The quar-

terback will throw over the Cat's head to the flaring back, who, with one block can run forever. In Cover 4 Will has to cover the number 2 receiver in the flat. The safety is taking #2 vertical, and the corners have bailed out to the deep responsibility. That gives you an idea of what we ask him to do.

What I want to do now is go through all the things we ask our outside linebackers to do on the run. As the head coach I don't have a position to coach. I really miss that, but they do let me run the *Cat Drill*. That is the drill he will be able to do in his sleep. We can call *Will-Cat* or *Sam Cat*, and bring one, or *Double-Cat* and bring them both. We have to adjust the coverage when we do that. We have to play man coverage when we bring both outside linebackers. What does he see?

They key the single back or tailback as they come. They have to know what he is doing. The first thing we do is to bring both backs toward the Will linebacker. He sees the tailback and the fullback running downhill at him. The play is a power slant at the Will linebacker. They are blocking down and kicking out the Will linebacker. The Will linebacker is responsible for containment. But contain is a word we don't use in our defense anymore. He has to make this play bounce to the sideline. An ideal running play for us is a play that goes to the sideline. We want to make the tackle for no gain at the sideline. We bounce the play outside and use our speed to run it down.

The Will linebacker wants to get inside the block of the fullback any way he can. We don't want him to sacrifice himself completely. We want him to be a player after the play bounces. But if he has to, he gives himself up and takes the fullback down, so that the tailback bounces outside. On the inside the defensive end is taking the B-gap inside. Hopefully he is protecting our Mike linebacker, who is 5 yards off the ball inside and keying on the tailback. He comes under and, as the ball bounces outside, he scrapes and makes the play. What I want the Will to do is get inside the block, pry up, and make the play. That is Saturday morning clinic talk. It is hard to do. But it is not impossible.

If the Will linebacker gets kicked out, the integrity of the defense is lost. The Mike linebacker is expecting the ball to bounce and it is running inside him.

That is half the drill. The other half is coming from the other side. This is one of my pet peeves. During the course of a year you see things that confirm and reconfirm some of your ideas. This is definitely one of them. We have been hurt on a play just like this. The backside Sam linebacker is coming and the tailback is going away. If he continues to sprint up field, he has a chance to make a play on the bootleg. It is a one-in-10 chance. If the linebacker runs upfield, he may as well go take a knee.

The Sam linebacker comes across the line of scrimmage and the play is going away from him. There are only a few things that can happen. We try to teach in series of three. I'm not sure they can handle more than three things. The first thing he has to do is find the football. Don't continue running upfield. Only two things can happen. The tailback will cut the ball back or the quarterback will bootleg the ball.

If the quarterback takes the ball, puts it on his hip, and gets outside the Sam linebacker, he had better wish he were born a girl. When I talk about these linebackers coming off the ball, they are not running as fast as they can to get to the spot. We make plays. When the opponents sees this coming they have second thoughts about running the bootleg. They don't want that negative play or the quarterback getting hit right in the mouth.

That is the first part of this drill. It could be run either way, because there is no tight end involved. We want our linebackers to see how tough the fullbacks are. How many tough fullbacks do you really play against? How many of those guys really want to do that kick-out block? They are mad because they don't get to play tailback. How many times are they willing to ROCK the linebacker? I tell our guys to ROCK them. When it comes to linemen, it is NO WAY. We don't fight with linemen; they are too big. With the fullback we want to know who is

going to win the battle. We challenge them. Who is going to win the war? It is going to happen sometime during the game. It might happen the first play of the game, so they have to be ready.

CAT DRILL VS. KICK OUT

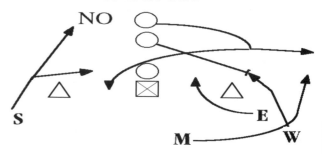

The second thing we work on in the Cat Drill is the option. I tell my quarterback, "Bag Pitch." He runs the dive play, pulls the ball, and runs option at them. The Will linebacker comes off the edge. We don't want him running up to the pitch man and creating this monster hole for the quarterback to run through. The linebacker has to put on the breaks. He stays on the line of scrimmage, works away, makes the quarterback pitch, and then he turns and makes the play. The trick is not to let the tailback get leverage on him. He is looking at the quarterback, but he has to be aware of the tailback, particularly if the quarterback pitches the ball quickly. We don't want to be chasing the tailback from the inside.

The back side is coming. He finds the football. Everything is going away. The quarterback, tailback, and fullback are going away. If the quarterback fakes or slows down, he can catch the quarterback from the back side. He is set up for the reverse, but I don't ask him to be responsible for that. I don't ask the backside Cat to check reverse.

CAT DRILL VS. OPTION

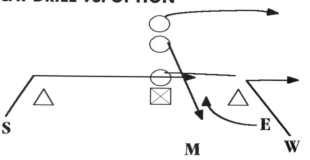

The next thing we do is drop-back pass with a flare by the tailback. The rule our linebacker has is *nothing crosses his face*. The Cat reads the drop-back pass and the back flare. If it is Double Cat someone has him man-to-man. We are not going to take a chance. If that back sees the linebacker coming and releases anyway, something is up. They intend to get the ball to the flare. We come off on the flare across our face. The other side continues his pass rush. We get more sacks from our Cats than anyone else. They are athletic, agile, and aggressive.

CAT DRILL VS. DROP-BACK PASS

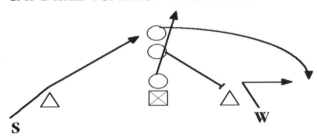

In our spring drills we can have 11-on-11 on just three days. Well, we take a 7-on-7 drill and make it live. This is completion. It is offense vs. defense. We use good judgment with the drill but it is live. We are not trying to get someone killed, but we want the completion. You find out a lot about your receivers in the spring.

We have a change-up to the Cat. Of course it is called *Dog*. That brings the end outside, and the outside linebackers in to the B- and C-Gaps. That is good and I like our ends, but it puts them outside doing things I want the outside linebackers doing. We ask the end in the Dog stunt to cover tailbacks if they flare. We do so much Cat, when the Dog does come it is usually pretty good.

DOG

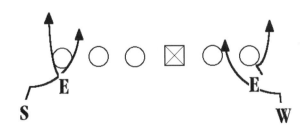

One of our favorite things to do is show the Cat and drop him into coverage. Remember he has no drop area. When the number 2 receiver comes to the flat, he jumps him and takes him away. If the second receiver goes vertical, the linebacker plays through him to number 1. We don't play curl to flat. We want to cover a man, not ground. If it is a one-back set and the back comes toward the linebacker he plays normal. If the back goes away, he squeezes the number 2 receiver and allows him no inside releases.

We have variations to our coverage, but if they learn those three things they can play the pass coverage. If the linebacker is showing Cat, and the tight end takes off to the flat, the linebacker jumps him in coverage.

The Mike linebacker has a simple pass rule. He has to find the number 3 receiver. He opens to number 3 and defends the tackle box. He doesn't drop. He covers the first receiver into the hook area. In the one back set, he keys the back, and opens to the side the back goes.

We took our fullback, and moved him to Mike linebacker. We had linebackers dropping like flies. In one week he started a game for us at Mike linebacker. Here is what we told him and how we coached him. We told him to play inside out on the ball. That is all we told him. We let him play instinctively. In pass coverage we told him to open to the side of the back and cover the guy they were going to throw it to. That was great coaching. The next week he played both ways. He played fullback and middle linebacker. I gave him the game ball. He had eight knockdown passes and a catch for 24 yards. He had seven tackles and the biggest hit we've had from a Mike linebacker in a long time. As of right now, Nick is a Mike linebacker.

With our Cat we also get into an *EAGLE DEFENSE*. This originated as a check for us and became a call. We call Eagle and stem to it. The 3 technique tackle stems to a 5 technique. The shade tackle changes his shade to the strong side. The backside end stems into the B-gap. Because we are a 4-3 team, when our end stems into that gap we call that the *ninja technique*. When he stems to that gap, the offensive lineman can't see him. He disappears. All he does is run into the backfield and make plays. The Will linebacker comes onto the line of scrimmage and is in his Cat technique. The Sam linebacker moves inside with the Mike linebacker. The only other thing we have to do is make the free safety aware that he has the number 2 receiver weak, because the Will linebacker is going.

EAGLE FRONT

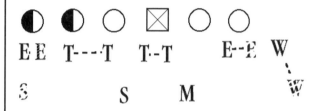

The other way we can get into the Eagle is by what we call *SLANT*. Our alignments are 5, 3, 0 shade, and 5 technique. The defensive end to the tight end stems to a 7 technique. On the snap of the ball he loops to a 9 technique. That gives the tight end one more thing to think about. The 3 technique tackle slants into a 4I position back up through the back of the offensive tackle. The shade 0 uses a dash or cross-face technique to get on the other side of the center. The 5 technique on the back side uses a gap technique to get inside into the B-Gap. The Will linebacker runs his Cat on the backside. We have the same defense as the Eagle, but we get it from slanting into it.

SLANT

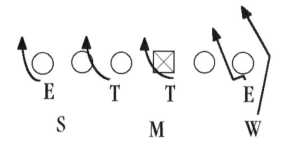

The technique played by the 7 technique end is good against a tight end run. When he loops outside, the Sam linebacker hangs back, doesn't get blocked, and plays the C-Gap.

The last thing we can do pretty easily is get into the *BEAR DEFENSE*. We don't call it that, but that is what it is. We slide the backside end down into a B-Gap technique. We bring in an additional defensive backs or linebackers and play. The Sam and Will linebackers move up and Cat.

BEAR DEFENSE

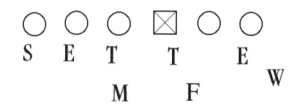

Gentlemen, let's watch this tape of the things I've been talking about. If we can every do anything for you at Miami don't hesitate to call. Thank you very much. I hope you guys enjoy the rest of the day.

THE WING-T PASSING GAME

ALLEGHENY COLLEGE

I am going to talk about the Three-Step Drop Passing Game from the Wing-T Formation. The things I am going to talk about are things others are not doing with the Wing-T.

We put the Three-Step Drop Passing Game in for several reasons. I played and coached under Denny Creehan. He did not like the Three-Step Game. He said if you ran it you would get a lot of teams that would roll up their corners on you. When that happened you ended up throwing a lot of Fade routes. So he made me do a study on the Three-Step Drop Passing Game. That study included a lot of passes. What do you think the number 1 pass was in the Three-Step Game in that study? The Fade Route was number 1. The Slant Route was number 2. What was the lowest percentage of completions route? It was the Fade. It was the most thrown and the lowest percentage of completions. What was the least-thrown route of the four routes? It was the Hitch Route. What was the highest percentage of completions? It was the Hitch. Everything was just in the reverse order. What we are doing with our Three-Step Drop is a way of negating those things.

First of all, the Three-Step Passing Game has a high percentage of completions. When you run the passing game like we do you complete passes and are effective.

Second, you can utilize run formations as well as passing formations. Again, as much as we run the ball, we need to be able to run the ball from the same formations.

We use combination routes to control defensive adjustments. Also, we limit the route adjustments versus different coverages.

We utilize Wing-T motions, shifts, and formations with our passing game and still run the same plays.

This system is simple to teach the quarterbacks. I will work with you for the next hour just like I am going to coach the quarterbacks. I will explain the entire package just like I would to our quarterbacks. It is simple to teach. When you are the quarterback running a play, you know you have a chance to be successful when you hand the ball off. What is the number 1 thing that hurts the passing game? It is quarterback reads. Out of 10 passes how many times does the quarterback throw the ball to the receiver you want him to throw the ball to? Some coaches respond with one, some will say five. If you only get the quarterback to throw to the receiver you want him to five out of 10 times you are not going to have much success. Now, out of the five throws to the man you want him to throw to, the pass has to be accurate and the receiver must catch the ball. We want to increase that number. How do we increase that number? We want to make our quarterback reads simple. We want him to throw to the right receiver nine out of 10 times.

The Three-Step Drop Passing Game is an excellent first-down play. You do not have to wait until third down to call pass plays like a lot of Wing-T coaches do.

As we begin, we call this the Allegheny College Attack Offense. About 60 percent of our offense is from NO HUDDLE. The biggest thing we mold our offense around is this: Whoever has the chalk last wins. We all have heard that phrase. In the game, who has the chalk last? The QUARTERBACK. When we get in a game I call the play and we line up on the line of scrimmage. I have put the chalk down, right. The defensive coordinator calls his defense, and he has dropped his chalk down. The two coordinators are done. Who has the chalk last? The quarterback goes underneath the center, he has the chalk last. In our offense I want to keep the chalk in our quarterback's hand as much as possible. I want to make sure he has that chalk last.

How do I make sure the quarterback has the chalk last? I have to provide him with the knowledge, and I have to empower him to use the knowledge. In everything we do we try to empower the quarterback to use that knowledge. He has the chalk last. He has to put us in the right situation at all times.

Our passing game is based on these Combination Routes. I will explain the routes and the combinations. I will show it to you in parts at first and then I will show you the formations. We use a lot of formations and a lot of shifts. We use a lot of motion.

COMBINATION ROUTES	GOOD VS.
Hitch Combo	Soft
Out Combo	Soft
Slant Combo	Any Zone
Flat Combo	Any Zone
Jet Combo	Man

On our Three-Step and Five-Step Game all of our routes are good against all coverages. The Hitch Combo is good against a soft corner. The Out Combo is good against soft coverage. The Slant Combo is good against any Zone Coverage. The Jet Combo is good against any Man Coverage. This is all the quarterback needs to know. If he knows this page we are going to be good. If he knows this page we are in business.

What do we mean by soft coverage? On the outside receivers are the Cornerbacks back off the receivers. SOFT! If he is up we say that is Squat or Hard Coverage. There are a lot of ways to determine Man coverages. We want to teach the quarterback the coverages.

The Slant Combo is good against anything, really. It is good against the Soft Coverage. Anytime we are talking about the passing game we are talking about time and distance. We draw up everything we do in the passing game. We feel you learn when you can visually see what we want you to do. I draw everything up on a graph. We want our players to see the routes. Every square on the graph is a square yard. It has 53 yards across the field. When I draw the plays up, the receivers sees where he is to line up. I do not have to tell him where to line up all of the time because he sees it. When we draw up a play our players know exactly where we want them to line up. Every time I draw up the plays it reinforces them.

HITCH COMBINATION - SOFT

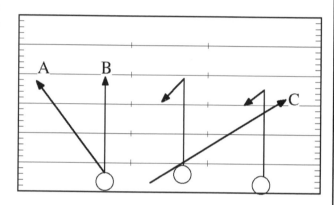

We read Inside Out. They are running 6-yard Hitch Routes. When we talk to wide receivers we talk to them about three techniques. First, I want ONE-STEP breaks. I do not want the receiver to chop his feet. Second, I want the receivers' arms INSIDE. We do not want the arms to stop. We want them to drive the arms. Third, I want the receivers' eyes UP. We talk about that all of the time. Eyes up, eyes up!

On the Three-Step Drop game the quarterback is reading Inside Out. Can you throw to the inside receiver? If you can't throw to the inside receiver you can throw to the outside receiver.

The Out Combination is good against the Soft Coverage. We run 5-yard Speed Cutouts. A Speed Cut is run off the outside foot. The outside receiver gains ground on the cut and the inside receiver gears down. The quarterback looks to throw inside first.

OUT COMBINATION - SOFT

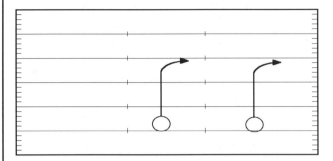

SLANT COMBINATION – ANY ZONE

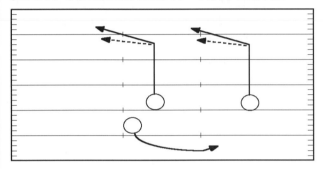

The outside receiver is going to run a Slant at 3 to 4 yards. Then he breaks inside at a 45-degree angle. The inside receiver is going to run a Slant at 4 to 5 yards and then break at a 45-degree angle. You see the dotted line with the receivers. I tell them whatever they do they must regain leverage. They must make the break that will allow them to regain the leverage. It may not be a break at 45 degrees. He may have to get under the defender to get leverage. What is leverage? It is when you are on an inside route you are inside the defender, and when you are on an outside route you are outside the defender.

We used to run a Slant Flat as our Base. We got away from that. We went to a Double Slant. Here is the reason why. We have changed the read for the quarterback. I want a simple, simple read for the quarterback on the Three-Step Drop so we can throw to the right receiver eight or nine times out of 10. We are still reading the Slant inside out. Can we throw the Inside Slant? Yes I can. Then throw it. If he can't complete it we want him to throw to the outside man.

Any time we run a Slant Combo and we have a tight end we are going to have a flare route with one of the backs. Here is the halfback that runs the flare.

Next is our Flat Combination against any Zone Coverage. We run this with a Wing. The tight end has the easiest release. He may release inside or outside. He releases for 5 yards and sits in the open area. He sits and gears down in the open area. If he has to keep running that is fine.

The wingback takes one step forward and climbs 4 to 6 yards in the flat. If the halfback is in a Dive Back alignment he runs a flare route.

FLAT COMBINATION – ANY ZONE

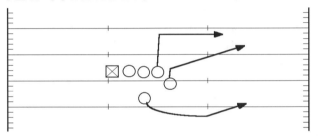

Our Jet Combination is good against any Man Coverage. The outside receivers run a GO Route. The inside receiver is running a four-step roll route. He goes 1, 2, 3, 4, and runs the rollover. It is a four-step Rollover. It is all about speed on this route.

JET COMBINATION – VS. MAN

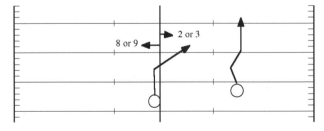

You see the line down the middle of the diagram. How many defenders does the defense have lined up to the left of the line? Right! Eight or nine. How many defenders are on the right side of the line? Right! They only have two defenders over on the right side. The quarterback reads inside out. If he can't complete the Rollover he throws the ball deep for the home run. When we throw the Jet Combo we are going to throw to the inside man eight out of 10 times. We will throw the ball to the wide receiver if the inside man is covered. If the outside man catches the ball, who is going to stop him? The man that is playing him Man. If he misses it is left up to the free safety to catch him and he is running away from him.

That is our Three-Step Game. Now we can put the plays together. Let me draw up some plays. I will start with one formation. This is the call: "Blue – 77 Hitch." The BLUE is a formation for us. The 70 is the Three-Step Drop, and the second 7 is the protection: 77. The Hitch is the route. We are running the 6-yard Hitch route. The wing is running the Flat route. Protection wise we slide the protection. The seven tells the tailback to go to the 7 hole. He comes outside the tackle and blocks the first thing that shows. He goes as hard as he can go. We can cut the defender in college. You can't cut in high school. The thing we tell that tailback is that he has a license to miss. That means he can go all out after the defender. He is going inside out. Everyone else has the gap. They all step opposite the tailback.

BLUE 77 HITCH

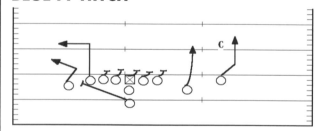

We ask our quarterback what is the coverage? It is soft coverage. Where is he going? We are going inside, outside, Hitch. The quarterback takes a three-step drop. The first step is a big step. The first step determines the speed of the drop. The second and third steps are little steps. We say big One, little Two. It is One, two, three, throw. He looks inside first. If he does not like it he looks outside. The quarterback sees soft coverage and he drops back and throws to the tight end.

The first thing we ask the quarterback is WHY did he throw a certain route? If you can get your quarterback to ask himself that question it will help him. Do you think he could become pretty good? I ask

him every single time. We ask him during two-a-days. You have to work on them all of the time.

Against Man Coverage we change the route to Jet. When I signal in the Jet I want the other two receivers to acknowledge that they got the Jet signal. They can tap their helmet, wave, or stick up their finger, as long as they acknowledge the Jet signal.

Remember when I put the five routes up for the quarterback? The Jet is good against the Man Coverage. That is all the quarterback has to know. What is the Hitch good against? The Hitch, right!

Next we go to "Blue – 77 Out." What are we running Out Routes on the wide side? What is the coverage? Soft! Where is the quarterback going with the throw? He goes inside out. Could he go back to the Flat Route? Yes he could.

BLUE – 77 – OUT

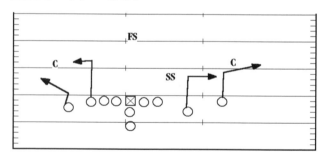

Next is Blue 77 Slant. What is the coverage? What is the Slant good against? Any Zone Coverage. When I ask the quarterback this question I do not want them to have any gray areas. I want him to make that decision before he goes back to set up on the pass. If he thinks it is a 2 Deep with a Hard Corner, I tell him fine. Then I tell him to look at the

BLUE – 77 SLANT

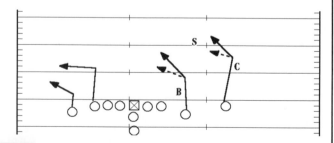

corner. That is the pre-snap read. Now lets look on the post-snap read. What does the corner do? He squats. I want them asking WHY all of the time.

If the quarterback cannot go inside he goes outside. If the inside is covered, the window will be there for the outside Slant.

Why do we want to read Inside to Outside? It is a shorter throw and we have a higher rate of completion. Shorter throw – higher rate of completion. Inside, Outside.

If we get Man Coverage, what is the quarterback going to do? He checks to Jet.

Next is M Blue, 77 Hitch. When you run Three-Step Motion, what percentage of the time are you running the ball toward the Three-Step Motion? We start the man in motion to the right. How many times out of 10 do you run the ball to the right when you send him in motion? Most teams will say seven or eight times out of 10. I would think it may be 80 to 90 percent of the time. What play do you run away from the motion? How many of you run a Counter Game? Not many. Some teams run the Waggle away. Not many teams run more than 20 percent of their offense away from the motion. Most of the time it is less than 10 percent of the time. How do most teams stop the Wing-T? They slant to the motion.

M – BLUE 77 HITCH

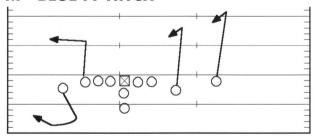

I am going to give you three legitimate ways to run plays that have nothing to do with the Three-Step Motion. I could give you a lot of our Counter plays, but I am not going to do that now. Our Base Plays for the Three-Step Drop are out of our Blue Formation with our Motion.

Now we are going to talk about Formation Variables. I believe in certain things. If I get on a player in practice and start asking him why he did something, what will he do? He starts telling me why he did something. He may say something like this. "I thought he was open." He may respond by saying, "I THOUGHT." How many of you have heard that? Now, how many of you have answered that comment with, "DON'T THINK." Many of you have said that.

It would be a good thing to get the defensive players to think, right? I promise you one thing, when they play us they are going to be thinking. Why? We will line up in Blue and then be unbalanced. I am going to line up unbalanced and then be in Blue. We are going to line up unbalanced and then be in Trips. We will line up in Double Slot and then end up in Wing. We are going to shift and we are going to go in motion.

When we line up in the Double Slot, what does the defensive coach tell his players? They are going to run the Option or they are going to throw the ball. We get them thinking one thing and we do something else. It is easy for the offense but hard for the defense.

Now we are going to talk about different formations. First is the Spread Formation. We call Spread – 177 Hitch. Is there anything different for the quarterback? NO! Is there anything different for the line? NO! Is there any change for the defense? YES!

SPREAD – 177 HITCH

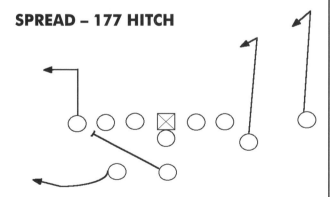

What do we run out of the spread? You run more counters, more bootlegs, and perhaps more counters, more bootlegs, and perhaps more option.

You may run more key passes from the front side. Now, you have a Three-Step Game. We have a Three-Step Game out of Blue, them with Motion, and now you have a Three-Step Game out of the Spread. The Dive back has to run the Flare. Everything else is the same.

Now we go to 77 Slant or we can call M – 977 Slant. We can put the Wing in motion. What is the defense thinking? They are looking for the Belly or the Belly Option.

M – 977 SLANT

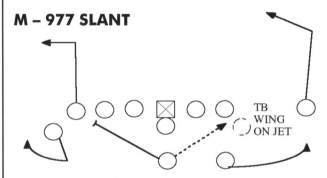

What happens if the defense goes to Man Coverage? We would call "Jet – Jet". Then the tailback goes to a Wing position and runs a Go route. We have run Blue, Blue M, Spread, and M 9. Can you get multiple? We still have not done anything different.

We can run 577 Slant or Loose 177 Slant. We run the Loose 177 Slant a lot more than we run the 577. If we have a two-back look the linebacker will stay tucked inside and we have a short throw into the boundary against soft coverage. We end up doing that a lot.

LOOSE - 177 SLANT

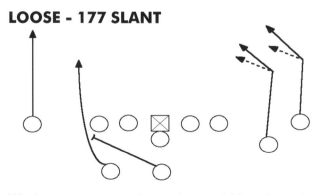

We have two more formation variables. Next is Loose 977 Slant. It is the same concept.

LOOSE – 977 SLANT

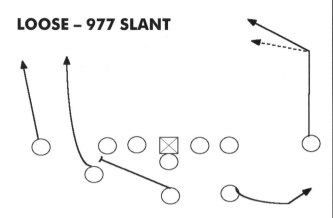

Next we go to Pro 177 Out. It is Pro 100 for us. We have a tight end, and the right halfback is out wide as a flanker. He lines up just like a wide receiver does. He is 4 yards outside the hash and he is back off the ball. The tailback is at left halfback. The other wide receiver is on the line on the left.

PRO - 177 OUT

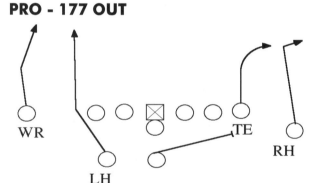

What is the down side of doing this? We have nothing for Hard Cover. If you are gong to run this you better be thinking you will get soft coverage. Otherwise I would not run this combo.

Now we go to Trips Formation. That is Orange for us. We have a left half at the X end position. We

ORANGE - 77 SLANT

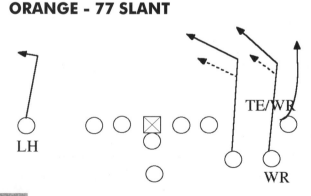

have our right half in the near slot. The second man in the slot is the wide receiver. The outside man on the line is our tight end or we may put in another wide receiver in that spot. It depends on our personnel.

We have covered Blue, Spread, 100, 500, 900, M Blue, and now we have Orange. The quarterback is going to know what we are going to do from each formation.

If the X end is a single receiver to the boundary he runs an out route. Against soft coverage it is an easy throw. Again, he is a halfback on the line of scrimmage. They are lined up three and one half to four yards from the offensive tackle. They are allowed one-half yard in any direction they want to get their job done. Everyone knows the Slant Combo.

This year we will run Orange 77 Jet against 3 Deep Coverage. The quarterback reads the strong safety. If he comes up to cover the inside man we throw to the second man. If he stays back we get the ball to the inside man.

ORANGE - 77 JET

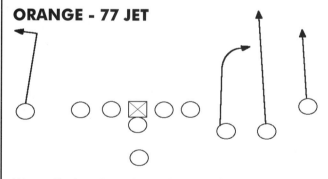

We call the deep back in our One-Back Set a TAILBACK. If I went to my stud back and told him he was going to play fullback he would probably be disappointed. But if I went to my stud back and told him he was going to play TAILBACK he would be excited. We call it Tailback for recruiting purposes for that simple reason. That man is our best runner.

Our line splits are 2, 3, and 3 on the line. Now, our tight end is going to be about 7 yards outside of the center. If the quarterback drops 5 yards on his set that means the defensive end has to cover more

than 10 yards to get to him. If the quarterback gets the ball away in 1.5 or 1.4. seconds, it means the end must run a 1.4 or 1.5 to get to him. If the defense is running a blitz we are going to be running the Jet Combo and he will get the ball away in 1.3 or less.

If we are going to run an option we have our front line split another foot. When we run the Mid Line we go to 3 feet with the guards and 4 feet with the tackles if we are running there as a general rule. We still need to work on our splits. We start out saying we are going to be two feet, three feet, and three feet. It does not take long to forget all about that because the blocker has forgotten who he was suppose to block. It all is good in clinic talk, but we need to continue to work on our splits. Our line coach carries around a yardstick. He will check the splits in practice. If they are not where they should be he will whack them on the butt. Just by carrying the yardstick around it serves as a reminder to our line.

I put together a film of our best plays. I hope you will be able to see what we have been talking about. I also brought a true game tape so you can see us in a real game.

I want to talk about being Multiple. I will go into the Five-Step Game with the time I have left. I am going to go over one route and show you how you can take a simple concept and become multiple. Again, you do not have to worry about coverage.

The first play is 559 L Cross. It is a 5- to 9-yard crossing route. The first thing the quarterback reads

559 - L CROSS

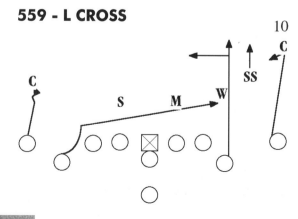

is the flat coverage. The flat coverage is the strong safety that has set down in the hole. If the flat is not open the quarterback hits the 10-yard hitch route.

The next man is the slot man. If the Will linebacker is low we throw high. If he is high we throw the Curl. We do not teach the third read. Why spend time on something he is not going to get done.

This is how you become Multiple. We are in our Blue Formation again. We call this play Blue 59 Y Cross. We just had the L run the Cross and now we have the Y run it. We do the same as we did on L Cross. The quarterback has the same reads. If he can hit the flat he takes it. If he can't hit the flat we high low the linebacker.

BLUE - 59 Y CROSS

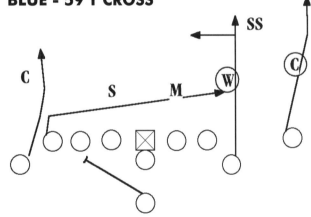

We are in a Double Slot with a tight end and Wing look. We had the halfback running the cross before and now we have the tight end running the cross. Our middle read is to see if that inside man can beat the underneath coverage. We run Orange 259 X Cross. We run the X end on the Cross. That is how we become multiple. If the flat is open we take it. If not we go to the Curl. If the Strong Safety has taken the flat and the Free Safety is dropping deep, the receiver goes as deep as he needs to in order to beat the linebacker.

ORANGE - 259 X CROSS

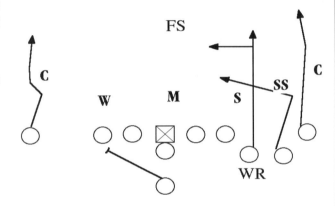

If you want to e-mail me my address is: blair@wing-t.com. You can send me questions if you want. My offensive coordinator and offensive line coach does a great job. We encourage questions. Thanks.

PUNTING, KICKING, SNAPPING, AND HOLDING TIPS

UNIVERSITY OF CINCINNATI

The first thing I want to do is to thank Coach Paul Bryant for the time he spent with me and for what he taught me about football. A guy by the name of Paul Davis taught me what I want to pass on to you. As coaches it is important to go back and give credit to the people you learned from.

I am going to break this talk down into three segments. I want to talk to you about the punter, the placekicker, the kickoffs, and the snapper. Along with the placement, I will talk about the holder. I have been in coaching 21 years and four of those years have been in high school. I think it is important for you to coach your punters and kickers. The best way to coach them is to find out all you can about those techniques.

I am not going to use the X's and O's much here. I am not going to get into schemes. You protect the punter the best way you know how. We are going to start with the mechanics of coaching the punter.

There are a couple of things you look for in a punter. First, you must look for a great athlete. If your quarterback is the best athlete on the team I would try to make him the punter. I would make his backup a punter. They are the types of players that are going to be able to handle the football. Handling the football is something the punter has to do consistently.

I am a firm believer in teaching the Two-Step Punt. I do not even talk three steps. It is the same with the placekicker. I teach him to kick the ball off the ground. I am not going to give a scholarship to a kid that kicks off a tee. First, it takes too long to change from the tee to the ground. Second, it gives him a chance to kick from a wider surface. And three, it gives him a chance to watch the techniques used on TV on Saturday and Sunday. If you have a two-inch block and you love it, I am not telling you to change. I am telling you what I like to do.

MECHANICS OF COACHING THE PUNTER
I. STANCE – BALANCE IS THE KEY!

For coaching a punter in the two-step method I will cover the Stance first. Balance is the key to punting. I have heard Coach Bryant and Coach Davis say that a thousand times. By balance I mean the same as if you were teaching a lineman or a linebacker. You must have balance. We want a little weight on the inside of our feet. We want the feet shoulders' width apart and squared up toward the snapper. I want to be squared up to the center. There is no need to do the angle snaps or the angle punts. You will get more out of the kicking game if you will let your center snap the ball straight and let the punter kick it straight. The hips are the key to punting as well as the stride. The stride should be normal. We want a slight bend at the knees. We want the shoulders over the toes. Many of you coach another position and you will tell your other players to get a slight bend in the knees.

We want a slight bend in the knees. The reason is for the high snap. That is the reason for the weight on the inside of your feet. That is so you can push up. By having your feet spread helps keep the balance. I do not like to see punters that have "ants in their pants." They are always wiggling. I do not like movement. It is a sign of anticipation of the snap. Watch film to see what happens. Watch your punter as much as you can to see what problems he has. A punter that is moving his feet or dangling his hands has a nervous twitch. Before he ever makes the catch of the snap that twitch is going to stop. He is going to come to balance. He is going to come to a pause. We do not want them to sit there and move around. We want no movement. Once they get their feet set, stay set.

I am going to teach the two-step punt. I have a left-footed kicker. I can't demonstrate for him very much. Everything has to be transferred back to him because he is left-footed. Some punters will stagger their feet. I like for them to be squared up, toe to toe. If I have a player that takes a false step I will have that player put more weight on the foot that he takes the false step with.

II. CATCH – FOCUS IS THE KEY!

We all use some kind of signals to let the snapper know that we are ready to go. The personal protector usually gives that signal. We may say SET or we may say READY. Someone tells the snapper and punter that we are ready when they are. We have to have some type of communication.

On the catch you want the punter to catch the front stripe of the football. It is no different than what it is for the receiver. The difference is the receiver catches the football going away from him. The punter has to catch the ball coming toward him. We want to see the front stripes of the ball from the center's release to the hands on the catch. We want him to focus in the area through the center's legs. He needs to extend and lock his elbows to get the football quicker. It is just like teaching the receiver to reach out and catch the football. You teach the punter the same thing. When the ball is coming he extends his arms. He does not have to lock them out completely, but he wants to be able to get to the ball faster. The quicker he gets the ball the better the punter is going to be. The get-off time from snap to punt for the punter is going to be 1.8 seconds to 1.7 or 1.9 at the most. You are still dealing with 2.2 seconds of operation time with a 14- to 15-yard snap.

We want the punter to get his pinky fingers touching together to form a cup. We do not want him in a situation where his hands are open. We want to firmly squeeze the ball with both hands. We talk about a Grip and a Control Hand. If I am a right-footed punter I catch the ball and immediately put the ball in the V of my right hand. I want the laces pointed north. I want to control the football with one hand. That firm grip is all I will need on the ball from the standpoint of going through the progression of my steps and dropping the ball on the punt. I want to stress getting the control hand up on the ball. The higher on the point of the ball you hold it the more problems you will have with the drop. You want the back elbow to be at a 35-degree angle in the bend. We want the shoulders in square. Keep the feet and hips square just like you were playing linebacker or end. Keep the control hand to make sure you keep pressure on the football to keep it on the ball in the V of the hand.

III. FOOTWORK - MAINTAINING AN UPRIGHT TORSO!

Again, let's talk two steps. If you have a three-step punter how do you get him to become a two-step punter? I tell him I am going to step on his foot so he can't take that first step. That first step is just a comfort step. Most three-step kickers take a first step with the off-foot first. They take the second step and then the third step and they punt the football if they are right-footed. The only way a player is a three-step punter is because we let him be.

The first step is a normal stride pattern. (Right) It is with the punt foot. That first step has to be a normal stride because I want to keep my torso erect. I want to stay tall. We love a tall punter. You do not have many of them. You love a tall punter because that is the guy that has the leverage on the football.

The second step will be slightly elongated. (Left) The second step is longer because the hips will have to come through to the football. The body will tell you what to do. It is okay to make the second step longer because the next step through is going to be your hip. It is going to be the strike step. The strike step is the contact point. It is the foot up in the air. The finish phase is the key to your distance.

Now you start talking about the drop. The more the punter pulls the ball into his body the harder it is going to be to get a good drop to his foot. He must keep the ball extended.

One thing you cannot do is to allow the punter to turn his toe toward the sky. You are talking about locking out the heel to point the toe straight. Don't let him point the toe upward, which punters like to do.

IV. BALL MANAGEMENT – USE BOTH HANDS UNTIL THE RELEASE POINT.

Grip the back one third of the ball and maintain the extension with the control hand. Kick the ball high and above the waist. We are not talking about high above the head. We are talking about high above the waist. As long as the ball is above the waist you will not run into a problem kicking on a windy day. The drop will not be a problem if it is consistent. Where you make contact with the strike is about hip high. Film the punter from the side and watch him.

The control-hand release is maintained until the last second. The drop should start above the waist and the ball needs to be tilted.

V. THE STRIKE AND FINISH - ALLOW HIPS AND SHOULDERS TO HELP YOU.

A 45-degree bend in our grip-hand elbow is a major factor. Keep your shoulders square throughout the entire process. Allow your balance foot to be naturally lifted off the ground. Learn to keep your hips and feet underneath you at all times. Keep the strike foot locked out throughout the entire time.

The bottom line of all of this is that it starts with balance. It is important to end up on a balanced stance.

I have a couple of film clips of a punter that I want to show. You are not going to see everything perfect. We were 12th in the NCAA in net punting and a lot of if was because of our punter. (Film)

I have a SPECIALIST TIPS sheet that I want to cover. It covers the phases of the Kicking Game. I did not

invent the Wheel but I really believe in these things. The first part is for PUNTERS.

PUNTER'S CREED

1. Have a balanced two-point stance with every step planned.

2. Total concentration on completing a perfect punt. (Every time)

3. Total confidence in your snapper and protections.

4. Keep eyes down on the ball after the catch and use good follow-through.

5. Be sure to use directional calls to alert the catch and use good follow-through.

6. Get in front of the bad snaps. (Handle it as a good shortstop would.)

7. Work on punting the bad-snap situations and when one occurs in practice take advantage of the experience it gives you. (Punt all snaps.) Remember to bring the tip of the ball into your view and get your hands in front of you as quickly as possible.

8. When punting on or near the end line (Always have at least one full step from it.) Know the situation so you can make the correct decision regarding an intentional safety.

9. Your most effective punts will take place in situations where you have a chance to use our Sky punt call. Remember, the best punters in football are those that display distance, height, and skills when punting the football in the + FIELD.

PUNTER'S WARM-UP

All punters will start 45 minutes before every practice time with the goal of being ready to go full speed when our specialty period starts. During this time you are responsible for jogging two full laps around the field (as a group with the other specialists) and for the stretching that you need (as a group with the other specialists) before you touch a football. This warm-up phase will be done every day of practice so you can get your timing down for our pregame procedures as well. Your warm-up with a football will consist of the following drills that should be done on a line.

1. PEDALS – Five minutes of one-legged pedaling to increase leg strength and balance.

2. REACH – 10 leg swings to insure that you reach your highest leg elevation with your foot pointed.

3. DROPS – Four times across the field on a line. (Done properly, ball should come back to you.)

4. PASS OFFS – 10 reps to insure that you see how the ball should come off your foot.

5. NO STEPS – 10 no-step punts to a partner 15 yards away.

6. 1 STEP – Eight one-step punts to a partner 25 yards away.

7. FULL STEPS – Eight full-step punts to a partner 40 yards away.

8. GOAL POST PUNTS – 10 reps from 10 yards away with a snapper to insure punts are reaching their highest elevation.

PUNTER'S INDIVIDUAL PRACTICES

As a punter you must make sure that the following schedule is done on a weekly basis for you to be a successful punter.

1. Stretch at least two times a day (four during two-a-days) and three days of distance running. (one mile a day.)

2. 30 minutes of balanced pedaling at least three time per week (M, W, and F).

3. 50 catches per week including the following snaps: Good, High, Low, Left, Right, and Wet Ball.

4. 75 drops per week. (Does not include teamwork.)

5. Two days of SET BACK with a partner. (Works your Sky punt technique.)

6. Two days of punting into the sideline NET.

7. 30 of the following punts on your own: Normal, Hashmark, Coming Out, Sky, Raw (No catches and no returns), and Corner.

8. Three days of HORSESHOES for at least five minutes that include the following punting situations: Hashmark, Coming Out, Sky, Raw (No catches and no returns), and Corner.

9. At least three PUNTS: AFTER A SAFETY or PENALTY, WET BALL and END LINE.

The next part of my lecture will cover Placekickers. This refers to the PAT's and Field Goals. I do not equate them with Kickoffs. We are talking about a person kicking for points. Again, it starts with the Stance.

I. STANCE – BALANCE AND SETTING THE 90 DEGREES ARE THE KEYS.

The feet should be shoulder's width apart with a slight stagger. The feet cannot be square. How many of you have had a straight-on kicker before. God bless them. The last one I had was in 1984. I loved him to death because he won two big games for me. We don't have those straight-on kickers anymore. Now we have the soccer-style kickers. They are going to have a stagger with their feet. It does not have to be elongated. They still need an erect torso. The knees are slightly bent and the shoulders are over the toes. The real bend comes in the front knee. I do not want the back leg locked out, either. We want them to keep the back heel flat on the ground and the left foot flat on the ground. The arms should hang to the side. We do not like for them to swing the arms. We do not like the kickers that have happy feet that keep moving their feet and arms.

II. FOCUS POINT – WE NEED SOME TYPE OF SIGNAL TO GET ALL 3 ON THE SAME PAGE.

How many of you use some type of signal for the center to snap the ball on the PAT's or Field Goals? Joe Paterno did it for years. I could give you our signal at UC but I would have to shoot you before we leave here tonight. Come to practice one day and watch us. We do have an indicator. The worst thing you can do to a high school kicker is not to tell him when to go. "When do I start the kick, Coach?" Give him an indicator. It could be the center saying "SET." It could be the holder saying the "Snap Count." It could be a little hand signal, or it may be something else. We want the center, holder, and kicker to all be on the same page. The kicker must see the big picture and then focus on the job.

The thing that hurts these three positions is when the coach cannot be with them. When they kick on their own in the summer, that is when bad habits are formed.

III. APPROACH – MAINTAINING AN UPRIGHT TORSO!

The first step sets the direction and he must do something with it. It should be a short step. Don't let him lift the first step and put it back down on the same spot. A lot of kickers will not use the left foot. They do not do anything with the front foot, provided they kick right-footed. That is okay. He is a natural two-step kicker. Don't change him. I tell the kicker he has the two outside rushers. I tell him I can't move him back in the cup if his operation time is bad. If it is slow, the man will block the kick from the corner.

The second step gets the tempo started. That is why I do not like bare-footed kickers. I do not like kickers with ballerina shoes. I like a kicker that has a cleat on his off foot and his kicking foot. The second step is going to get his momentum going.

The third step is the key to the ball's direction. (plant) That is the step that is going to take the ball through the goal post.

The strike must be consistent and it must come with force. In the Tips for Specialist you will see BUTT Kick. It has been around a long time. We still have them do it. We have them do the One-Step, the No-Step Kicks. But, the kick must come with force. The main point here is to be consistent. If he is not consistent, find out why his tempo is not the same.

IV. THE STRIKE AND THE FINISH – "CONTROL THE LEG – DON'T LET THE LEG CONTROL YOU."

The strike must come from the waist down. We want to get the foot through the ball as quickly as we can and then get it down as quickly as we can. Once a kicker plants his nonkicking foot, and meets the football, what does he become? He becomes a straight-on kicker. That is all he is. Once they get to the strike spot they become straight-on kickers. They do not believe it, but that is what they are.

They must contain a consistency with their width of the plant foot from the ball. They must learn to keep the weight equally distributed at all times. They must firmly stick the plant foot and control their torso. Film the plant foot. That is going to tell you what he is doing. It may be too close or too far away from the spot. He has to learn where that spot is and he must be consistent. As the plant foot becomes secured insure that your strike foot is pointed downward.

On contact allow the kicking leg to fully complete its swing. Try to avoid any pivoting or lateral sliding by the plant foot. After the strike learn to force yourself to walk through to the finish. Follow the kick.

The contact point is important. We chalk the toe to see where they are hitting the ball. That will let you know if they are hitting the ball in the sweet spot. The only two panels of the ball are the two on the bottom, and with the laces on top. You have to work like crazy with the holder to get the laces pointed up. The natural flight of the football is controlled by the laces. The more the laces are off from being straight toward the goal post, the more chances of missing the kick. Most long field goals missed are probably because the holder did not get the laces pointed toward the goal post. That is, if it is a solid kick. You kick the PAT and field goal the same way. You may back up a little more. Kick it firm with good tempo.

KICKER'S CREED

1. Have a balanced two-point stance with every step planned.

2. Total concentration on completing a perfect kick.

3. Total confidence in your ability to land kickoffs in the hit zone, and complete faith in your holder, snapper, and protection.

4. Keep your eyes focused on your strike spots and a good controlled follow-through.

5. Your most effective kickoffs will come in those kicks where height, distance, and accuracy are the objective; effective placement kicks will take place in situations where we are in the + field, so we must be accountable for every kick

KICKER'S WARM-UP

All kickers will start 45 minutes before every practice time with the goal of being ready to go full speed when our specialty period starts. During this time you are responsible for jogging two full laps around the field (as a group with the other Specialist) and for the stretching that you need (as a group with the other Specialist) before you touch a football. This warm-up phase will be done every day of practice so you can get your timing down for our pregame procedures as well. Your warm-up with a football will consist of the following.

1. BUTT KICKS – 4 times across the field, insure that every rep has a heel to butt emphasis.

2. REACH – 10 leg swings to insure that you reach your highest leg elevation with foot pointed. Insure that with every rep you maintain good body balance.

3. PUSH DRILL – 10 reps to insure that you see how the ball should come off your foot. Insure that with every rep you maintain good body balance.

4. NO STEPS – 10 no-step kicks that are done within 8 yards or less of the goal post.

5. 1 STEP – Eight one-step kicks that are done within 8 yards or less of the goal post.

6. FULL STEPS – Eight full-step kicks that are also done within 8 yards or less of the goal post.

7. GOAL POST KICKS - 10 reps from 10 yards away with a snapper to insure kicks are reaching their highest elevation.

KICKER'S INDIVIDUAL PRACTICES

As a kicker you must make sure that the following schedule is done on a weekly basis for you to be successful.

1. Stretching at least two times a day (four during two-a-days) and three days of distance running (one mile per day).

2. 30 minutes of balanced pedaling at least three times per week. (M, W, F)

3. 30 minutes of abductor work on the field for the inner and outer thigh. (two times per week.)

4. Two days of HURRY-up kicks with an emphasis on your accuracy and distance. (No timeouts.)

5. Two days of kicking into the sideline NET.

6. 20 of the following kicks on your own: PAT, +4-yard line from L, ML, MR, and R/L hashmarks.

7. Three days of HORSESHOES for at least five minutes that include the following kicking situations: NORMAL, LEFT and RIGHT, TACKLE OVER from the middle left and right, and from left and right hashmarks.

8. Two days of at least 10 kickoffs from following: M/M, M/L DEEP, M/R DEEP, HIGH FLORIDA'S, MUST ONSIDE, SURPRISE ONSIDE (lob).

9. 20 bag kickoffs – to reinforce your height and hand times.

10. At least five KICKOFFS: AFTER A SAFETY or PENALTY, and WET BALLS. (FG steps)

MECHANICS OF COACHING PLACEMENTS

My big thing with the snapper is to approach the football. Do not let them take the football from an up position and spot it on the ground. Make them approach the football every time they come up to snap the football. Make it realistic for them. It all starts with the feel. This is what we work on.

1. STANCE – WEIGHT NEEDS TO BE EQUALLY DISTRIBUTED.

The feet should be wider than your shoulders and squared up to the punter. The heels are slightly tilted inward and the knees turned outward. It is not an easy position to play the way we coach it. I want the center to be able to squat, and then hold it. They must get the knees out. They have to force the knees out.

2. HANDS AND BALL POSITIONS – HANDS SHOULD BE FIRM AND SECURE.

The ball should be in front of your nose and the grip hand should be able to control the ball. (Work the laces to the ground.) The guide hand should have a light touch on the ball. (Don't bear it!) You can use the weighted ball to develop the strength needed to snap. Use the Medicine Ball if you do not have a weighted ball. We do not want the ball extended too far out in front. I do not want the ball

turned up on the point. I want the ball flat. I want the ball pointed toward the holder or the holder's hip. If they get it up on the point, the next thing they do is to develop the forward hitch. Hold the ball flat. The thumbs should be up. They need to shoot the thumbs through on the snap.

3. FOCUS POINT – YOU NEED SOME TYPE OF SIGNAL TO GET ALL 3 PLAYERS ON THE SAME PAGE.

You must see the Big Picture and then FOCUS on the JOB. Go on the Indicator.

4. PULL AND RELEASE

As you snap the ball, start to rotate your hands to create a natural spiral that is caused by the rotation of your hands. Reach up and through your legs and allow full extension of the arms. As you release the ball allow momentum to pull you backward.

I want to talk about the holder. Let me talk about the laces. The same things apply for a holder on a field goal. I thought everyone snapped the ball with the hands on the laces. I had a kid at Tulane that did not put his hand on the laces to snap. It taught me something. He got the ball to the holder with the laces perfect every time. I left him alone. Coach Bryant said it best. "COACH THOSE THAT CAN'T PLAY – DON'T WORRY ABOUT THOSE THAT CAN."

For years Coach Bryant practiced the field-goal snap and the punt snap as the same. He said a punt snap was a PAT snap that went through the holder's hands. I do not use the same snapper on both anymore. I like a bigger snapper on the field goal for blocking.

SNAPPER'S CREED

1. Total concentration on placing the snap where it is needed.

2. Keep your eyes on the target and vary the rhythm that you use in your snapping so that the opponents will not be able to focus in on our snapping keys.

3. Always approach the ball separately each time you snap in practice situations. Do not stay in one spot and merely get in a groove. You want to provide yourself with as many game-like situations as possible. Remember to always take at least 10 minutes to warm up (heavy ball if possible) and never, ever snap without pads.

4. Have a balanced two-point stance with the following characteristics: The feet should be evenly positioned slightly wider than the shoulder width (no built-in staggers.) Make sure the legs are spread sufficiently to allow for proper follow-thorough of the elbows. Work on keeping your heels slightly tilted inward to help you on forming an apex with your lower body. (An example of this would be a man sitting on a horse.) Your butt should always stay nearly level with the shoulders. Weight needs to be distributed evenly. (Balance is key.)

5. Have a firm two-handed grip on the ball with the following characteristics. **GRIP HAND** should grip the ball with your dominant hand in the same manner as if you were going to throw the ball. (Fingers on the laces.) When spotting the ball you want to have the laces facing downward and the seam opposite the laces is facing your.

   The **GUIDE HAND** comes next. This hand needs to have your middle finger on or close to, or near the seam of the ball as it faces you. By placing your middle finger on the ball you have helped yourself increase the rotation and spiral of the snap. Also, at this time, on both the long and short snap, you can start to learn about cocking the wrist of your **GRIP HAND** more in an effort to start having your snap arrive to the Holder or Punter with the laces up.

6. Be consistent with your release and have good follow-through using the following guidelines. **BALL RELEASE** and **FOLLOW-THROUGH** is the next progression in the snapping phase. With the wrist properly cocked around the ball you should get a spiral when released with the correct fol-

low-through of the hands. As the ball is pulled through, rotate the palms outward with the thumbs pointing up at completion. The **OVER-HEAD RELEASE DRILL** is the best way to start practicing the **BALL RELEASE** and **FOLLOW-THROUGH** motion. In this drill you should spread your feet to the proper width of your stance and then grasp the ball with the correct grip placement. Bring the ball overhead. Then bring the fire arm forward and release the ball with the palms rotating outward and the thumbs pointing down on completion. Concentrate on developing a tight spiral through proper grip, release, and follow-through. Your target should stand 10 yards away. Try to keep the ball aimed and release at the partner's belly button.

7. Maintain good speed on the ball by using the following tips to aid in the hip flexion needed to get velocity on the ball:

   HIP FLEXION is where most of the velocity in the long snap comes from. It is a result of your hip and lower back flexion. To begin the motion of the snap, the hips are contracted moving the butt down and in slightly. Form this position the hips explode backward providing the immediate impetus to the ball. (This action must be instantaneous in order to keep the rushers from timing their takeoffs.) As the hips explode backward the arms should move simultaneously to coordinate the major muscle groups of the snap. The total explosive effort of snapping should then cause the Snapper to slide backward just slightly creating separation from the rushers. Our **HIP FLEXION DRILL** will help you get a more realistic practice progression going for this. Again, as in the **BALL RELEASE** and **FOLLOW-THROUGH DRILL** you should spread the feet to the proper width apart and grasp the ball correctly. Bend at the ankle and knees to get yourself in position to see the catcher and while suspending the ball in the air sight your target and execute the proper release and follow-through. (This drill forces the snapper to use his hip flexors and lower back muscles to propel the ball.)

SNAPPER'S WARM-UP

All Snappers should start 30 minutes before every practice time with their goal of being ready to go full speed when our specialty period starts. During this time YOU are responsible for jogging two full laps around the field (as a group with the other Specialist) and for stretching that you need (as a group with the other Specialist) before you touch a football. This warm-up phase will be done every day of practice so you can get your timing down for our pregame procedures as well. Your warm-up with a football will consist of the following:

1. 10 – 15 Overhead releases with a partner from 15 yards away using the Heavy Ball.

2. Five Overhead releases with a partner from 15 yards away using the Heavy Ball.

3. 8 – 12 Long Snaps with a partner from 10 yards away, using the Heavy Ball. (If only a Short Snapper, do it from 6 yards away.)

4. 10 – 15 positional snaps from regular depth (14 yards away if Long Snapper, and 6 yards and two feet if Short Snapper.)

SNAPPER'S INDIVIDUAL SEASONAL AND OFF-SEASON PRACTICE SCHEDULES.

As a Snapper you must make sure that the following schedule is done on a weekly basis for you to be a successful Snapper.

1. Stretch at least two times a day (four during two-a-days) and three days of distance running (one mile per day).

2. Squat drills at least three days a week for five minutes at a time to stress the importance of having flat heels and maintaining good balance.

3. Thrust drills for 15 yards at a time to insure the heels are being shot backwards. This is for you to have the lower body follow-through needed to help the ball have good velocity and to create the needed separation between you and the defenders. (Done on a line or hashmark at least eight times per practice day.)

4. Hand Slaps done to insure the feel of getting your hands through for good follow-through. Do at least eight sets of three per practice day.

5. Stadium steps run two days a week to help promote the ability to get your knees up.

6. Heavy ball to help in the development of your upper body strength and the reinforcement of your follow-through. You should always use the heavy ball in your warm-up phase. On those days when you do not wear shoulder pads you should only snap the heavy ball. NEVER DO MORE THAN 10 AT A TIME. START OUT 7 YARDS FROM THE CATCHER AND WORK BACK.

7. Also responsible for following specialized snaps per week:
   a. WET BALLS – Only if weather conditions warrant.
   b. TIGHT PUNT – We consider any snap from 5-yard line going into the end zone to be a tight punt snap.
   c. FLANK PUNT – Snaps that are 10 yards away.
   d. QUARTERBACK EXCHANGE – In case we use the FREEZE PLAY.
   e. MAN OVER ME – Snaps that occur when the center has a man over the ball.
   f. NONRHYTHMIC – Snaps that destroy our tendencies.
   g. SNAPPING – Working with the punters, kickers, and holders based on their schedules.

HOLDER'S CREED

All Holders should start 15 minutes before every practice time with their goal of being ready to go full speed when our specialty period starts. During this time YOU are responsible for jogging two full laps around the field (as a group with the other Specialist) and for the stretching that you need (as a group with the other Specialist) before you touch a football. This warm-up phase will be done every day of practice so you can get your timing down for our pregame procedures as well.

HOLDER'S WARM-UP

1. Three Sets of Finger Push-ups.

2. 15 up-to-spot practice holds on air (using your finger key).

3. 15-20 holds with Kicker without Snapper.

4. 10-15 holds - Kicker and Snapper before Specialties start.

HOLDER'S INDIVIDUAL PRACTICE SCHEDULE

As a Holder you must make sure that the following schedule is done on a weekly basis for you to be a successful Holder.

1. Catch work vs. high snaps, low snaps, inside snaps, outside snaps, and wet ball.

2. Fire passes; left and right.

3. Shuffle pass (WHOPPEE) work going left and right.

4. Blocking work for snaps that get into the kicker's hands

5. Coverage work from middle, left, and right.

The opt time is very big for us. We want the snap back to the punter in .75. The total opt time is 2.0. You have to develop a tempo. We use a lot of naked rushes with our field-goal people and our punter. If the snap and the hold are there you should get the kick off against the rush.

We do not tilt the ball on the hold. We want it straight up with the laces pointing toward the goal post.

Men, I am glad you came tonight. Most of the time when you start talking about the Kicking Game at a clinic a lot of coaches get up and leave. Did we have a good time? Good! I enjoyed it. Thank you, it has been my pleasure.

UNBALANCED LINE VS. EIGHT-MAN FRONTS

MOELLER HIGH SCHOOL, OHIO

I want to give you some thoughts on what we have done from our Unbalanced Formations versus the Eight-Man Fronts. Also, I want to discuss some of the reasons we have gone to the unbalanced attack. We have used this against the Seven-Man Front on occasions. What I am going to cover is not revolutionary.

I heard a lecture several years ago that stimulated my thought process on this subject. It got me interested in going out and looking for additional information on the subject. Then, when we started to see a lot of defenses playing a four-deep secondary on us with one player coming down toward the line real hard we ended up playing against a nine-man front. If our receiver was not physical and you did not have some things you could do against them you had a hard time blocking those support players at the off-tackle hole. The unbalanced formations made the defensive player that was coming down hard at the line of scrimmage go out and cover your wide receiver. This allowed us to put a blocker on that guy so the defense would not have as many support players at the line of scrimmage. This is basically how we started getting into the unbalanced formations. We wanted to block some half players that were very good and were very good run support players.

Basically we are a Pro I Formation team. North or South is I Pro for us. We can call splits backs or whatever we wanted the backs to do. This is the first formation we started with in the Unbalanced Formations. We just swapped the Tackle and Tight End. We put the Tight End on the short side and brought the tackle over on the strong side. In the old days we did this because our tight end was not a good blocker. If we did not want to run behind him at the point of attack we just switched the two. We called it Opposite. Those two players switched positions.

NORTH/SOUTH OPPOSITE

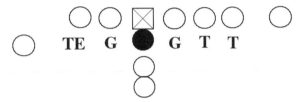

Against defensive teams that played a Cover 3 or a coverage with a Strong Safety alignment it put them in a bind as to where they wanted to put their strong safety. A lot of the times the safety would go to our strong side or our heavy side and support in that area. What we did was to run the short game out of the back side of the formation. We would bring both backs to that side and turned everyone else back inside. We ended up throwing to the Tight End. We threw the Slant, Hitch, and Seam Routes. We ran the Tight End up the Seam and the wideout ran a Slant, Hitch, or a Fade route. When we started running this our Tight End came off the line and most of the time he was free. So we started running the Slant, Hitch, and Fade routes on the back side. This kept the defense off balance and helped us a great deal. In the heat of the battle we would change it one time. We worked with our quarterback looking at the defense to see how they adjusted on the formation. We went back and forth depending on what you gave us on defense. We used this against the Seven-Man Front more than the Eight-Man Front. This formation against the Eight-Man Front is not very helpful. That is because the defense has four men to the weak side of the formation. If you get into this formation the defense will slant to the strong side. So, we got into this formation to give us a different wrinkle from game to game.

The next formation we got into was what we called our Elmer Set. This is just an End Over Formation. In this case the Tight End is not eligible for a pass.

We ran this to get the defense to unbalance their Eight-Man Front.

ELMER RIGHT

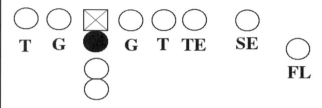

The point we are trying to make is that if you are a balanced Eight-Man Front then we want to unbalance you offensively if we can. You have that choice if you are going to adjust or not against our formation. Then our offense has to take advantage of what adjustments you make.

The one thing about running the unbalanced formations is that you do not know how the defense is going to adjust. You do not see that many teams that are unbalanced so you do not have a lot to go on. You have no idea how the defense will adjust. You go into the game blind in that sense. You do not see enough on film to know what people are going to do to adjust. The one thing I have noticed in the last few years is this. Teams have stopped kicking one man over on the line of scrimmage. On the defensive side of the ball that used to be the first thing everyone did. They would move everyone over a man on the line. They used the same keys but it was not the same because you were not lined up on the same players. Now, we see more secondary rotation where the defense is trying to balance their alignment. They keep the front the same but rotate the secondary. Now, that is what we expect when we go to this formation.

Another thing we started running was this. We had an Elmer Right and Elmer Left. Next we went to what

ELMER RIGHT – OPPOSITE

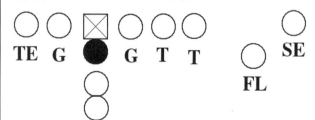

we called Elmer Right Opposite, or Elmer Left Opposite. Now we left our tight end on the back side.

We did that because we wanted a better blocker on the strong side. We could still run most of the plays from the Power I Formation. We like to run the Power I Off-Tackle play. We run some Inside and Outside Zone schemes as most normal I Formations teams run. At times the outside tackle for us was Michael Munoz. That was the player that we wanted to play on that edge. There was not anyone that he was not going to block. The bottom line is that we used that as an advantage.

Those are the three formations we have fooled around with the most. This past year we used the Elmer Right Opposite a great deal of the time.

I want to cover some of the things we ran out of the formations. Our first concern was how the defense was going to align out of the Eight-Man Front. There are two ways most teams align on this formation. They are going to take their Sam Linebacker and split the difference between the Split End and outside tackle. They will keep the Free Safety back. They will keep the Rover and backside Corner on the back side.

ELMER RIGHT OPPOSITE

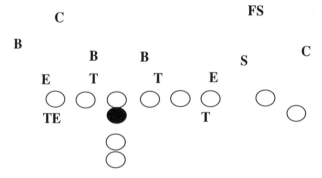

Most teams are very concerned about the back side. We do not see a lot of teams that brought the Rover over. If it were me I would bring the Rover over first. The bottom line is this. We are going to run to the strong side if you will let us. I would make the offense do something they do not want to do. The way we decide which way we are going to attack is a little old fashion. We just count the number of players on each side of the ball. We want to see if we have a numbers advantage. If you only have six players to our strong side and we have seven counting the two wideouts, the two tackles and guard, and the center and quarterback count one half each, and the two backs count one half each. That gives us seven to your six men. If the defense does not do something to change that number ratio we are going to run to that side or we are going to pass to that side.

Sometimes the defense will bring the Sam Linebacker up on the line and play Man with the Free Safety and Corner. We do see this at times. We usually get Man Coverage on this formation. Most teams do not want to kick the defense over.

A lot of the times we get the second receiver uncovered. If you do not cover the second receiver we will let him take his one step and come back to the ball. Hopefully he can make the catch and get 6 or 7 yards. If you do not cover the second receiver we are going to get him the ball. If they do not take it away from us we will throw it. If we can throw the Hitch nine times in a row we will throw it. A lot of teams have a lot of plays but only run each of the plays one or two times per game. If we have something that works we will run it until you stop us. We are going to do things until you stop us from doing them. If you do stop us I want to have one other thing that I can execute and do well that I can hurt you with when you do make the adjustments to stop one particular play.

We are going to do one thing or the other. We are not going to get fancy. If you do this we are going to do this. We may only have one or two plays and one pass play that we are going to use. But if you stop us on with the adjustment I want to be able to hurt the defense in another area. If you do not cover our second receiver we will throw the Hitch on the three-step drop. I like the three-step game out of the unbalanced line. We want to come off the ball hard and chop the defense. We want to force the defenders to get their hands down when we come off the ball low. We do not want them knocking the ball down on the three-step drop. So we like to get into the unbalanced game just to throw the three-step drop.

I have heard college coaches talk at clinics and they will tell you that the number of unbalanced plays has tripled in the last three years. Teams are getting into the unbalanced look because they are looking for an edge. They are looking for the number advantage.

If a team keeps throwing the Hitch route and keeps gaining 6 and 7 yards per try I would do something to stop that play. Most teams will bring the Rover over to cover the second receiver. I would move Rover over and make the offense prove to me that they can run off the back side and that they can hurt me to the back side.

ELMER RIGHT OPPOSITE

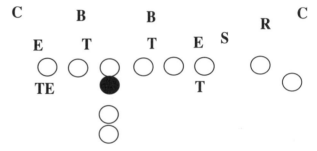

If we get the Rover over we will run or pass to the back side. You can run a play to the back side and do a good job. At this point it is a 4-on-4 situation. I believe you must run the option out to the back side. You need to have a way to option to the back side. We have not been forced to run to the back side very much because most teams do not bring the Rover over. If you run the package you must have the ability to run the option to the back side.

The first play we run out of this formation is our Outside Zone Play. A lot of teams will blitz the Sam Safety upfield into the seam on the snap of the ball. They feel we are going to run the ball in that area. We have been able to run the ball inside of the Safety and outside of him. It depends on how good the two backs are. If the fullback can log the Safety we can go outside. The problem the defense has is that the Safety is the contain man. The Corner and Free Safety are in Man Coverage on the two receivers. If we can bounce the ball in the gap we can gain 15 to 20 yards before they can find the ball.

ELMER RIGHT OPPOSITE/OUTSIDE ZONE

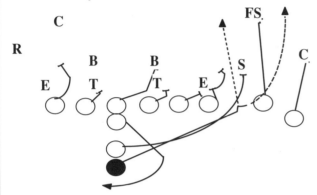

If the defense brings the Safety up hard and comes upfield to stop the Outside Zone, we have been fortunate to have a fullback that could kick the man outside and we have turned the play back inside. We go inside and back outside again. We have been very successful on this play. We run the play until you stop us.

If the defense brings the Rover over and we have an outstanding Tailback, we could run the Outside Zone to the back side. We just want to see if that Corner can make the play on our Tailback if we can't block him. We know a lot of the times their Corner is not their best run support player. He is a cover man. So we take a chance of going one-on-one with him on our Running Back.

ELMER RIGHT OPPOSITE/G-POWER

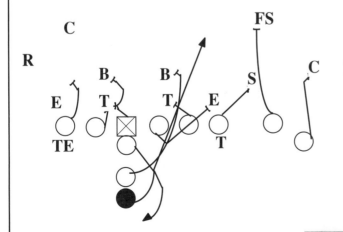

The Outside Zone play sets up our Elmer Right Opposite – G-Power Play. Because we have had success on the Outside Zone the defensive end in a 6 or 7 technique will play the outside play as soon as he sees our head turn in that direction. The defense thinks this is the Outside Zone. We run the Tailback back inside off-tackle. The Free Safety and Corner are in Man Coverage.

The next thing is what we called our Special Block Power. It is a special scheme. We like to run in the C Gap because we think that is the soft spot in the Eight-Man Front. I think a team has to be strong in that area to play that defense. We always have some type of combinations that we like to run off-tackle against this defense.

POWER WITH A SPECIAL SCHEME

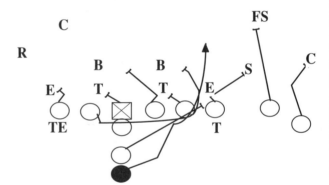

The other thing we like to run is our Power with a Base Scheme. We move the back outside where he has a better angle on the Safety. Now the outside tackle blocks the 6 or 7 technique end. The Running Back makes his cut off the tackle's block.

POWER BASE SCHEME

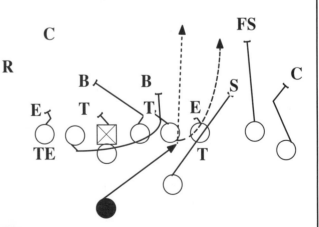

We have never been a big option team mainly because we never had a quarterback that could run it well. We are looking at some things in the off-season because we will have a quarterback that is more athletic. We are looking for ways to get our quarterback involved and being a threat. It was similar to what Nebraska did this year. The quarterback becomes another runner in their attack. So we are looking for the Lead Option. If you want to block the support and make it a quarterback sweep you can. If you want you can pitch the ball.

LEAD OPTION

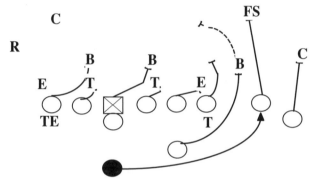

If the defense moves the Rover over to the strong side we go to the back side. We can run the Lead Option to the back side. We bring our fullback out to block 4. We will go ahead and pitch the ball. If you have the numbers to your advantage you have to run that play or some form of that play to the back side.

ROVER OVER – LEAD OPTION WEAK

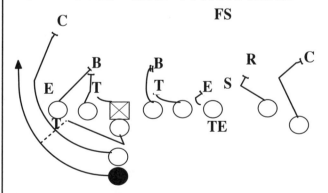

We also run the G-Option on the back side. A lot depends on the ability of our quarterback. If the defensive end logs upfield we do not try to log him.

We will go ahead and trap him outside. At that point the quarterback will follow the fullback inside. Hopefully, the Corner will cover the pitch because you have put some pressure on him. It ends up as a quarterback Iso-type play. If you have a quarterback that can run you can get him in the seam on the play and it can be a good play.

ROVER OVER – G-OPTION

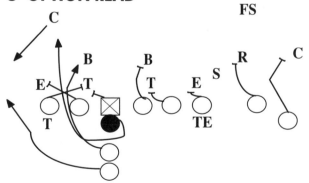

The way we pick our players for offense and defense is like this. We take our first pick and select a quarterback. The second pick is our tailback. We make take a third pick and choose a split end. Then the defense can pick all of the rest. What the defense does not take will come back to the offense. Our quarterback would have never been picked in the last several years. Our quarterback has been more of a thrower than he was a "true athlete." It was funny to us to make a pick because no one would take our quarterback for another position because he was not a good athlete. He has been a passer more than an athlete.

G-OPTION READ

This is another way we run the G Option. It is important to make the corner play the tailback on the pitch.

Off the G Option we run the Fullback Give. Now we pull our center and have him kick the end outside. This ends up as a good play because we can block the linebacker with the tackle. Now the corner has to decide if he is going to support outside. Nebraska will run the fullback inside and force the linebacker to scrape outside. We have done it that way also. If we really want to get the ball to the fullback this is the way we run it.

FULLBACK GIVE OFF G OPTION

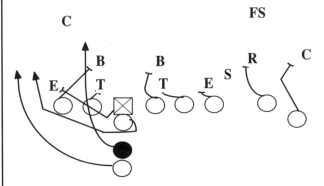

Those are three plays to the back side that we like. That is what we like to do if the defense moves the Rover over.

The last thing I am going to cover is on a pass that we use out of this formation. We have used the play out of Split Backs to get the near back into the seam. You can offset the back over to the short side if you want. However, I think that is too much of a tip, especially if you bring the Z Back in motion to the back side. The quarterback reads the corner to see which man he takes. The quarterback comes to the front side and stops at the inside leg of the tackle. What I like about the play is the fact that the strong safety is going to get blocked by the outside tackle. Our backside end is the hot receiver. If he can make the catch he will be hard to catch. The defense gets used to the tight end sitting back and blocking. Then we send him on the seam and it is a shock to the defense. You are not throwing the ball that much. Then all of a sudden you raise up and hit the tight end in the seam. It can be a big play. Over the last three or four years we have run the play 10 or 11 times and we have had six or seven TD's out of the play. It is not a play that you can do over and

over again, but it is a play that has a good chance to be successful. That is our 3 Up Panther Pass.

3 UP PANTHER PASS

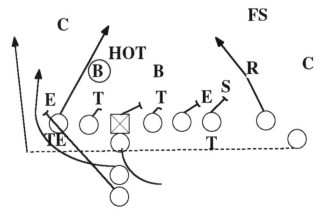

We have gone unbalanced and run our 5-Step Drop Passing Game. We still have our Twin Passing Attack whether we drop back, run play-action, or run the counter action. You can do a lot of different things out of this formation. You can force the defense to come outside and cover the two wideouts. Some teams will not do that. We have run the 5-Step Drop and the 3-Step Drop to the two-receiver side. We have run the Flat – Curl to the two-receiver side. We have run the Streak routes. We have done a lot of different things from this set.

If the defense keeps the Rover on the short side and brings him on the pass we have the tailback pick him up as he starts on his seam route. We will block the end with the fullback. We will still have the tight end down the middle. We feel we have everything covered if you do blitz us.

Just some food for thought. Most offenses run a lot of plays and a lot of formations. The unbalanced formation does not change any of our running plays. They are the same. The defense has to be aware of where the tight end is lined up. The unbalanced package is to give the defense something else to look at and to work against. I do feel this is a trend in offense. When we started running the unbalanced attack I want to make sure there was one thing we wanted to do and if you stopped that play we had another play that we could run. Also, we have a pass that will keep the defense honest.

THE BUBBLE SCREEN PASS

OREGON STATE UNIVERSITY

Thank you. It is a pleasure to be here representing Coach Dennis Erickson and Oregon State University. Today I would like to share some of our thoughts about the Bubble Screen, which has been real good for us. Let me start out with a little of our philosophy. When we get seven in the box, we want to throw the ball. We are going to throw the ball first and set up the run off the pass. People have started playing the outside linebacker to the open side in a position where he is not in the box, but at the same time he is not out of the box. It was this halfway spot that was creating a problem for us when we wanted to run the football. We had a big gap where the slot receiver had to get a piece of the outside linebacker.

We borrowed the play from Louisiana Tech and it became almost a complete offense for us when I was at Purdue. We used it a bunch of times at Oregon State last fall. We threw the play 10 times going to the right and 22 times going to the left. It averaged 6.2 yards going to the left and 4.2 yards going to the right. It is not a home-run play. It is more like a sweep play. It is a way to get the ball to the perimeter and attack the secondary with the play.

At Purdue we had a different type of personnel than we had at Oregon State. The kid we had at Oregon State in the slot ran about a 4.5 40. The kid we had a Purdue was a burner as a hundred-meter man. We were more explosive at Purdue simply because of the speed of the receiver.

Over the years a lot people have tried to run this play and have ended up struggling with it. The quarterback has to get rid of the ball extremely fast. It is a left-right step, open the hips, and cut the ball loose. The biggest problem with this play is the defensive end. He will try to take it away by a wide alignment and rush. The offensive tackle has to

understand, he has to go get the defensive end. He has to get into him low and get his hands down so he can't jump and block the ball.

The steps for the slot back are probably the most critical things in the whole play. The slot's alignment is 4 by 2. He is 4 yards outside and 2 yards back from the offensive tackle going into the wide side of the field. We don't run this into the short side of the field. His step is called a **J-Step.** He opens up so he loses about a yard, takes a cross-over step, and starts to run downhill. This now becomes a foot race between the outside linebacker and slot back. The linebacker is trying to cheat inside and play in the middle. The slot back wants to lose that yard to make the angle better for the throw and to make sure it is not a lateral. The blocking for this play is man-on-man chop blocking.

The throw of the quarterback is critical. If the receiver has to adjust to catch the ball, the play is dead. The ball has to be delivered so the slot back catches it in full stride. If he has to stop or turn to catch the ball, the play is dead. The quarterbacks have to drill the throw in their individual periods.

Let's go to the formations we use. The first one is called a 2 by 2 formation. That means we are in a double slot. We have two split ends and two slot backs. The guy the quarterback is keying is the le-

BUBBLE SCREEN FROM A 2 BY 2 SET

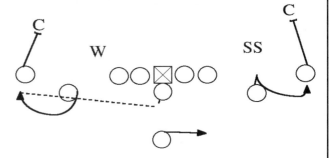

verage player on the slot back. If one of these outside linebackers is playing extremely hard inside one of our slot back, we will check to the play.

Another way we ran the screen from the 2 by 2, was to motion the tailback out of the backfield. He went in motion and his job was to hook the leverage defender on the slot. That became an effective way to get the pass secured.

If we got press coverage, but we really liked the match we were getting, we still ran the play. We would still swing the back away from the throw. We brought the slot from the other side in motion. He blocked the press coverage guy and we threw the screen to the call-side slot guy. Even if there was man coverage and the defender ran the hump trailing the motion we still had what we wanted. The defenders are still 4-5 yards off the receivers and we have what we want anyway. The motion man released through the outside knee of the press coverage and rolled him up. This meant we could run the play even against press coverage and the defense couldn't run us out of the play.

SCREEN / MOTION FROM 2 BY 2

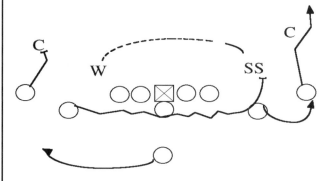

After we started having a lot of success off this, we decided we had better throw a pass off it. I'll show you what we did from the double slot set. We emptied our backfield with motion to the right. We snapped the ball and ran four verticals down the field. The right slot ran his screen route. We keyed the corner to the slot side. We pump faked the Bubble Screen and hit the split end behind the corner. We got a huge play against Fresno State this year. We pumped the screen and the corner

drove all over the screen. The split end ran right past him for the score. When we threw it against Fresno State, we didn't empty the backfield. This keeps people honest.

4 VERTICAL FROM FAKE

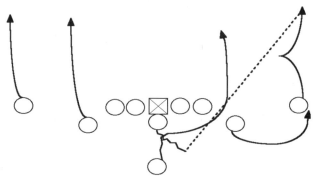

The best thing about that play was we did it in the second game of the year. That meant it sent a message about the deep ball and made people play honest. When we got into the 3 by 1, we always ran this to the three-receiver side. Nothing really changes. The split end comes off and stalks the corner. The second receiver came off and stalked the strong safety. The inside slot ran the screen as he did in the double slot set.

SCREEN FROM THE TRIPS SET

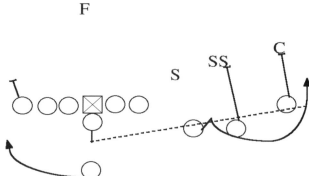

We really liked this play against a two-safety look. It gave us a natural crack on the man over the slot. We had to be careful on the rolled-up corner. We couldn't cut him, because every time we tried to do that, the corner would get off the ground and make the tackle. We concentrated on the stalk block. All the receivers want to run the play, but the blockers have to stay with their blocks or the play doesn't go.

We also used motion from the backfield or a flanker on the other side to run the play. If we read cover one or zero, man coverage, we would simply run off the defenders with our receivers and that was as good as a block.

To keep the defense honest we had a pattern we ran at them. The split end ran a skinny post. The outside slot ran a shallow dig route at about 7-8 yards over the middle. The inside slot ran the screen. The motion coming from the other side ran a rub to the flat. If the corner drove on the screen, we had the post behind him. All we did was read number 2 and throw the ball.

4 OUT PATTERN WITH MOTION

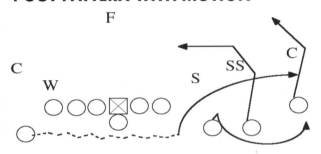

If you don't have a guy playing your inside slot who can run in the open field, this play is not going to be very good for you. If he can't beat linebackers and defensive backs this play is not going to work. The slot has to get his shoulders square, run downhill, split safeties, and hit seams. If you have a guy who wants to dance and make a lot of moves, this play will not work. This play is a race to the sideline. If he sees one little crease in the play that is what he is looking for. We want 4-5 yards from this play. But it can go all the way if someone makes a mistake. We didn't have a burner at Oregon State this year running this play. We did have a slasher who would hit seams and was physical running.

If we were in the 3 by 1 set and the defense came up and pressed all receivers, we checked out of the play. We generally checked to what we call 90. The split end ran a 7 yard hitch. The outside slot worked to the numbers on a streak pattern. He used the numbers for his landmark. The inside slot ran up the seam or hash mark. His pattern was a

yard or two outside the hash mark. We keyed the corner. If he sat down with the hitch we went to the outside slot or the inside slot. We felt if there was a true strong safety over the outside slot, that would be a good matchup.

CHECK 90

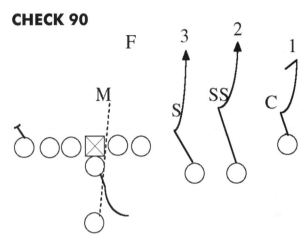

The only other way we could run the play other than checking out of it was to empty the backfield with motion to block the man over the inside slot.

Another pattern we ran from this set was the **clear out**. The split end blew the top off the coverage and cleared everything deep. The outside slot ran a 6-7-yard out pattern. The inside slot ran his fake screen to pull the coverage. The tailback coming out of the backfield ran a 13-15-yard sail route. That looked like a shallow flag route working for the sideline. We read the flat coverage and threw according to what the defense was giving us. The quarterback pumped the screen first.

CLEAR-SAIL

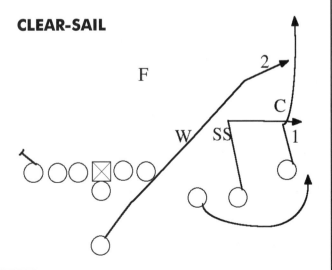

When we went to our **Spread Set**, which was our 5 wideout set, nothing changed on the three-receiver side. When we knew teams were going to cover us down regardless of where the set ended up, we took advantage of that. We would put our three-receiver side into the boundary and give the two-receiver side all the field to work with. That gave people problems. The slot ran as hard as he could for the boundary always looking for the crease or seem to cut up into.

BUBBLE SCREEN FROM SPREAD

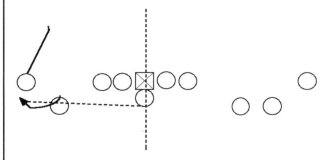

If the defense walked up in press coverage we could motion from the three-man side, block the press defender, and still run the screen.

Because we were having success to the two-receiver side out of the spread, we ran a pass off it. We motioned the inside slot from the three-receiver side and ran a flat-wheel type of pass. The slot to the two-man side ran the bubble screen. The motion man ran a wheel up the field. The split end ran a dig route to the inside. We threw the ball off the corner. If he drove on the dig route, we hit the wheel. If he stayed back on the wheel, we looked for the dig route on the inside.

SPREAD / FLAT-WHEEL

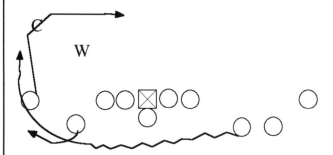

We were running a lot of screen to the two-receiver side. This was the answer to the defender driving on the screen and dig routes. These plays are not touchdown plays. They are plays designed to take advantage of defenses that don't cover your receiver. When the defense tries to get the outside linebackers into the box we use this play. We couldn't block the outside linebacker on our inside zone. We had to make him play wider and more heads up on the slot and this is how we did it. The results have been real good. Our quarterback was really inconsistent throwing the ball to the right. It looks simple but you have to work on it. When he went to his left he was a lot more accurate.

I just got back from Purdue, which runs this play. They run it from the shotgun and I wanted to see how they did it. When they run it from the shotgun, the slot is cheated back a little more. On the snap of the ball he took two quick sets up the field, pushed off the inside leg, and ran the same pattern. I don't know if we are going to do it, because it is a lot harder throw for the quarterback. The problem they were having was the defensive end getting too far upfield on them. Their tackle wasn't quick enough to get to the end before he jumped and batted the ball down. The thinking is right but you have to spend more time on the timing of the play.

When teams started to widen their defensive end to keep us from throwing the ball, we put in a Utah pass to the running back. It worked real well for us. That was our answer to the real wide defensive end.

I've got some film on all of these things. I'm running a little short of time, so let's get to the film. That's it fellows. It was a pleasure for me to be here. If we can do anything for you don't hesitate to call. I'll be around the rest of the evening if you would like to watch some more film. Thank you very much.

QUARTERBACK TECHNIQUES AND DRILLS

UNIVERSITY OF LOUISVILLE

What I am going to talk about today is quarterback techniques. Hopefully you will be able to get one or two points here that you will be able to use in your program. It does not matter if you run multiple formations and throw the ball 50 times a game or throw 10 times per game; it does not matter. Techniques are universal. They are things that are going to make your quarterbacks better and they are going to make your team better.

I played quarterback at the University of Idaho in the early 1980s. That was when the One-Back was coming into its own in college football. I had the pleasure of playing for the person that really started using the Spread Offense, and that was Dennis Erickson. He came to the University of Idaho in 1982. The program had been going in the wrong direction for years. They had one or two winning seasons in 20 to 30 years. In Coach Erickson's first year we went 9-2. We went to the quarterfinals in 1-AA. He turned the program around in that first year.

Being a part of that system, we continued to grow and won a lot of football games. We did that by putting the ball in the air. We had some quarterbacks that came into our program that were able to develop and play at the next level. I went on to coach at the University of Washington before I came to the University of Louisville. But, what I learned from the time I went to Idaho was how important it is that your quarterback be sound fundamentally. You cannot assume that a kid who has been successful in high school will be able to come into college football and play right away.

I am going to talk more about the fundamentals in the Passing Game. I will talk to you about some specific drills and some of the things we do. They are everyday-type drills. We are going to talk about Stance and Starts both from under Center and from

the Shotgun. I want to talk about the Center-Quarterback exchange drill that we do every day. I want to cover the benefits you will get from that drill. The next thing I will cover will be our Warm-up progression and throwing fundamentals. I have a 5-year-old son and I take him through these fundamentals every day. If you can start teaching them that young, then you can teach this in the Pop Warner Leagues or little leagues. You can develop those throwing mechanics.

Next, I will talk about our Drops and how we categorize our drops. Then we will move to some pocket movement and cover some things on how we evaluate our offense. I just want to give you an idea of what this lecture is all about.

After I graduated from the University of Idaho in 1986 I tried to continue to play at the next level. It did not take long to find out there were others a little better than I was. I sat out a year and I decided I wanted to get into college coaching. I went back to Idaho to coach in that system. Dennis Erickson had left Idaho and a second head coach by the name of Keith Gilbertson had been at Idaho for a couple of years, but moved on.

John L. Smith came in as head coach at Idaho after Keith Gilbertson left. The first thing he tried to do with me was to tell me not to get into coaching. I spent about three hours in his office and he told me I could make a lot more money in something else. He assured me it would be a while before I would make any money that would be worth anything. But, he was looking for a bunch of young, hard-working assistants that were willing to take as long as necessary to get it right.

As I grew under his leadership I was able to take some things that will always be with me. Everyone has a *drill book*. If you don't have one, you should make one. If you do not know how to make a drill book, get one from someone and learn. The thing that Coach Smith always harped on was a *Must List*. At first I did not get it, but later it made sense to me. Our drill book is what we call our MUST LIST. It is the things we must cover every day. It is like getting up in the morning to go to work. You have to shave before you go to work. You do that every day. The same is true working with a quarterback. We must cover these fundamentals every day to be successful. You cannot have a gray area in this. We must work on certain things every day. You know what offensive plays you have to perfect to win. My big concern is this; don't take anything for granite.

In our office we have a Must List within our position groups. We have listed the things we must cover and we do it every day.

What I do with the quarterbacks when we first meet in the spring and in the fall is to go over the Must List daily and weekly. When we get on the field we have to cover those things on the list. The reason I like it this way is this. If we write it down and keep it on the board it makes us more accountable. It is there and I read it every day and I am more accountable.

The daily *Musts* include *Huddle Procedure* and *Play Calling*. It is a fundamental thing but we have to work on what we are doing for each week. We may be running the No Huddle one week, we may be huddling on the line the next week, and we may be running in subs the next week. There may be something fundamentally different each week and the quarterback will be orchestrating all of this. You may be mixing your snap count and your audibles. Those are the things we talk about. Those are the things we work on every day and they are things we must cover.

Next is our *Warm-up Progression*. We are always early out on the field. If the quarterback does not get warmed up properly he is going to have arm problems. He is throwing a football that is 10 times heavier than a baseball. He has to learn to take care of that arm as well as working on his mechanics of throwing properly.

Then we work our *Center-Quarterback Exchange*. I will talk a little more about that later along with the Stance, work on our Drops, and Play-Action Passes. Then we work on timing with our backs. We work on *Pocket-Moving Drills*, and some *Progression Drills*. Then we work on ball handling drills and some leverage drills.

Each week our quarterbacks come in and watch film on their own. They watch things we do not have time to cover in our meetings. Sunday is their day off. On Monday we watch video. We have two game films for them to take home to watch the film on their own. The quarterback has to go the extra mile as far as watching film.

Another thing we do is to give out our *Goal Card* for the week. We do not want to wait until the end of the week to set our goals. We set our goals weekly. Sometimes we set them daily. Our Goal Cards go out on Monday. On the Goal Card are two or three things we have to do to make you better for that game, based on what you did the week before. Yes, these are short-term goals, but in the long run you can keep abreast of how each player has progressed. But this gives us immediate communication each week. This is not only for the starters, but for the backups as well. It is very important to sit down and spend some time with them and let them know what they have to do. While it is early in the week we write it down and make them accountable.

What we do on Thursday if it is an away game, and Friday if it is a home game is this. We call a short meeting of the offense. We talk about the theme of the game for a few minutes. Then all of our players put their individual goals in a lunch box that we have decorated and have a slogan on it. They all put their Goal Cards in the box. We feel this gives them a feeling of team unity.

On Tuesday we watch formation tapes. We go over the tapes and talk about our game plan. On Wednesday we have situational tapes in our meeting. On Thursday we have special situations in our meeting. Friday is a day where we are polishing up, having our walk-through, and doing the last-minute things. On Saturday we have a quick walk-through. We have a couple meetings and then we are ready to go.

Before you talk about drills and plays I think your philosophy as a head coach or as an offensive coordinator is to make sure we are accountable for our position. We write it down. "This is how I am going to make our quarterback better day-to-day and week-to-week." I really believe this makes you a better teacher, and it makes you a better coach.. You are all working in the same direction.

For every position, before we go to anything else, we all have a base *Stance and Starts Philosophy*. It is real important. It does not make any difference if it is the defensive backs coach, it all starts with the base Stance and Starts. It is the fundamental football position. The proper position for a quarterback, from under center and from the Shotgun is this. What we try to do when we get into our Stance is this. We teach the staggered start from underneath the center. Why do we do this? Because it gives the quarterback a little more room in the pocket, and it gives his pivot foot clearance from all of the traffic in front of him. It keeps him from getting stepped on. Our Stance and Start for the quarterback is a heel-to-toe stagger with the feet almost shoulders width, so they are not too wide. It is important for your quarterback to be able to see downfield. Don't have him looking down at his feet. We want a heel-to-toe stagger with an upper knee bend. If I am a right-handed quarterback my left foot is back. If you are left-handed you switch the feet. I am going to basically nail that foot in the ground with my knees comfortably bent. I am not going to bend at the waist. I sink my hips slightly. I am going to stay tall and erect. I want to keep my eyes down field where I can see the front and the secondary.

I am going to keep my right hand firm and straight and place it in the crack of the center's butt. I spread the fingers as wide as I can. I do not want the quarterback digging down for the ball. I want the center bringing the ball to the quarterback. The quarterback must raise his hand slightly so the center can feel the five fingers. The big mistake I see is where the center cannot feel the five fingers and we get

separation. The center needs to feel the wrist and the back of the hand and the fingers. Again, it is important to keep the right arm straight and firm. We do not want to see the elbow bent. The problem when he has the elbow bent is that he will have too much shock absorbed. The shock absorbed will come from the off-hand. When the center snaps the ball he wants to put the ball on the palm of that right hand. We put the off-hand one knuckle deep and roll the hand underneath. That will give him the shock absorber to take the blow. When the ball hits the center's hands we want to hear the POP! We want you to be able to hear it on the other side of the field.

It is important to teach Stance and Starts to a quarterback when he is young so he does not develop bad habits. His eyes are on the front; he has a bend at the waist. He wants to be able to see what is going on in the secondary. He wants to be able to stand tall so he can see the defense. He should be comfortable. Every drill starts with Stance and Starts.

When we get in the Shotgun we move them back where the back heel is 5 yards from the ball. The difference in our Stance and Starts from underneath the center and when he is in the Shotgun is where the quarterback is standing. We do not change the Stance and Starts. When the ball gets in the quarterback's hand we want him in the position, especially in the passing game, where he has the ball in his hands and is in the position where he would be if he took the five steps on his drop. We are not worried about getting stepped on now. So the stagger eliminated that.

In the Shotgun he has his knees bent, his eyes downfield. He has his hands down in a ready position to be able to take the snap. From here we go through the same techniques as we did under center. If you are going to start with Stance and Starts in the running game or the passing game it is very critical.

Every Stance and Start Drill must have an On-The-Ball Procedure. We have an On-The-Ball Procedure for Front Recognition and Coverage Recognition. The quarterback has to do it all. The receivers must recognize coverages. The tight end must recognize technique and coverages. The center must recognize technique and the front. When we get to the line of scrimmage, part of Stance and Start is Front and Coverage Recognition. The first thing we do is to rock from left to right with our eyes. We see the Front. Then we go from right to left to right to see the Secondary. We do that 100 percent of the time. When you do your Stance and Start Drills you have to see your quarterback doing that. That way you can check to see if he is looking at what you are teaching him.

Every quarterback must learn to recognize Fronts and Coverages. At times it is very basic in terminology what you are teaching. As they get to where they have a little more experience they can see that we may have the middle of the field open on a Two-Deep look, or that the middle of the field is closed on a Three Deep look. He must learn where to look to read on each coverage. They have to be able to come up to the line of scrimmage and say, "Front, Coverage." It may be on the Running Game. When they see the front they must know where the techniques are. We may have a "Check With Me" run called. He may have to go to the 1 technique. He must be able to see that and he must know where the 1 technique is. After he goes right to left and sees the secondary, he is supposed to make a throw to the boundary on a 3 Deep look, and to the field against a 2 Deep look. I must be able to look to see what I have. We try to keep it as simple as we can for them. But, we demand that from our quarterbacks 100 percent of the time. (Film)

I want to talk about the most important drill you can teach the quarterback. It does not matter what level you are on. It is the *Center-Quarterback Exchange Drill*. It is not just the Exchange. Obviously that is a big part of the game. You need to have 100 percent on the exchanges. But, the Center-Quarterback Exchange Drill is a direct carryover, in my opinion, from whatever you covered for the game plan or whatever you covered in the two-a-days to the practice field. What I mean by that is this.

We come out and get warmed up. Our quarterbacks have to stretch, but they do it early. During Stretch

our centers and quarterbacks work this drill. We are not going to give up this drill for any reason. The Center-Quarterback Exchange Drill goes basically like this.

We have talked about the quarterback's hand position under center. The key on the Quarterback-Center Exchange is this. The pressure applied by the quarterback on the center must be applied all the way until the snap. He must never lose contact with the center's behind, and the back of the hand and those five fingers. It is very important. Both hands must ride the center until he feels the exchange. You must make sure the center is moving. So, when you work the drill don't just let the center snap the ball. Make sure he is moving forward. When was the last time the center did not move in a game when he was making a snap? We make sure we have a play called every time we run this drill. This gives the center an assignment on the drill.

A key coaching point. When I get that ball from the center on the perfect snap the first thing I do is to bring the third hand and the ball into my stomach. That back tip of the ball is on my belly button on my first step. That is what we call "Third Hand" the ball. That is part of accountability. We talk about this all of the time with our ball carriers. They must maintain possession of the ball once they get the handoff. The quarterback is a ball handler 100 percent of the time. His job is to protect that football on his first step. The fumbles you see quarterbacks have will be when they do not have two hands on the ball in the pocket, or when they get run down from behind, but the most fumbles you will see occur between the Center and Quarterback. A lot of those fumbles can be avoided by the "Third Hand" technique. After I bring in the ball with my "Third Hand" I can do anything I want from that point.

The way you check this is when you are working on the exchange with the running backs. I will stand just behind the quarterback. When he takes the snap and steps back from center I take my hand and try to knock the ball out of his hand. This is just a check to make sure they are "Third Handing" the football.

During the drill we remind them if we had any problem with a fumbles the past week with as a result of the "Third Hand." We show them the film clip. That is the reason we do it. The guard may be pulling on the goal line and hit the ball. The quarterback may bobble the ball because he did not have the "Third Hand" on the ball. We always make them accountable for the ball.

Here is the Center-Quarterback Exchange Drill. We line our centers 5 yards apart opposite the way they would be going on the field. We want them on a line. We run the ball on the sideline. The reason we do it on the sideline is to stay off the middle of the field. We put the quarterbacks on a line. Why do we want them on a line? We deal with the CLOCK as most of you do in working with the quarterback on all of the techniques we do. We deal with the first step. We want our quarterback in a straight line when he is dropping back. We want him to step at 5 o'clock on a Zone to his right. He steps at 8 o'clock on the Outside Zone to his left. That is the way the quarterback can visually see his first step in the Center-Exchange Drill.

I stand out in front of the centers so the quarterback's eyes are on me. I go back and forth so I can see all of the quarterbacks. The quarterback has a straight line down the center of his legs. He is checking his first step. They are lined up 5 yards apart on one line.

CENTER-QUARTERBACK EXCHANGE DRILL

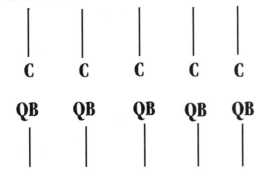

The offensive line coach will come over and do basically the same thing I am doing. He coaches the first step of the center on the exchange. I am coaching the first step of the quarterback in the exchange.

One quarterback calls the cadence. Why do we not have all of the quarterbacks calling the cadence? It is for obvious reasons. We rotate the quarterbacks from one line to the other. The quarterback in the same line is going to call the cadence. This helps you become consistent in your snap count. This allows you to work all of the quarterbacks on the cadence, and they all get to work with a different center. If you only have two centers, that is fine. You can get two other linemen that you think could be a center if you need them and start training them. Don't wait until you lose both centers and start looking for a center. "Oh man! Has anyone ever snapped before?" It could happen. You can start developing young players to snap.

As we go through the Exchange Drill now we are working on the exchange and our cadence. We are working on keeping our cadence consistent. We mix the count up. I talked to you about our "Must List." We talk about mixing up our snap count and working on our Audibles. It is a lot easier to teach a young quarterback all of this without a defense. I can see him execute it verbally and physically, without the defense going crazy and yelling in their positions.

On the quarterback snap the quarterback and Center will take the first step of the play called. We do not just line up and say, "go on this snap count." The first thing we do is to work on the run game. The first quarterback in the line will call out "32 ON HUT." We get into our Stance and Start, work the exchange, and snap the ball. The center takes his first step on the 32 play, which is our Inside Zone Play to our Running Back. The quarterback will reverse pivot at 6 o'clock to his right. He is working on that first step on "32." Once we start the drill; bang, we are gone.

We come back to the line of scrimmage. I do not care about the other 20 steps he has to take. I want the first step to be right and I want the ball to be "Third Handed." I want the ball secure and the first step is on his landmark.

The next quarterback steps up and taps the center. The reason we do that is to let the center know he is there. By doing that we do not get the false snap with all of the calls the defense makes. The quarterback calls the play; "32 on Set." We snap the ball and the quarterback steps at 6 o'clock and we go to the next quarterback. We are moving so they have to be thinking. They must know the first step on the play and they must execute the technique on that first step. It is a unique time to work on the quarterback. You only have the center and quarterbacks. You do not have anyone else to bother you. The most important position in any play is having the proper first step.

I want to show you the Center-Quarterback Exchange Drill so you can see how it works. I want you to see how fast it goes. You may say that this could take 20 to 25 minutes to run the drill. It takes us eight to 10 minutes. We get through our offense as far as techniques. We do not always run both 32 and 33, or 38 and 39. We may go one way and then switch it up each day. We get through all of the techniques the quarterback has to get through prior to practice. We can place emphasis on the plays that are new or the ones we may be having problems with. This is where we are going to work on the fundamentals that are going to win or lose a game. We work the run game first from under center. Then we back them up in the Shotgun. (Film)

When we work on the Drops we make sure the ball placement after the snap is proper. We like the placement anywhere from the hips to the shoulders on the passing arm side. The quarterback will tell the center where the snap was as he comes back up to the center. They communicate with each other about the snap. The specific coaching points for the center are covered in the drill. We are reinforcing the snaps by making any corrections as we go along.

This may sound like a very simple drill, and it is. You may say this is no big deal. Here is what I am saying: Make a commitment to work on the Center-Quarterback Exchange Drill, and approach it this way in practice.

Let them know we are going to be accountable for the football and we are going to have proper exchange on the center snap. We are going to be fundamentally correct on the exchange. We are going

to take proper steps on the first step. If you can get a chance to coach that phase of the game a little more, you are going to make extra points for the quarterback. If your quarterback is not making good decisions, you had better be running the ball every down. You had better be running the right play. It is another chance to hit them again with the fundamentals. It is a chance to take the mental game to another level.

Now I will cover the *Warm-Up Progression*. Hopefully, you will like some of the things we have done on this. On our Must List are the things the quarterback must do on his Warm-Up Progression. Does this mean it is coming out and getting warm? Yes, it is a part of getting warm. You can teach your quarterback as he is getting warm to throw the ball properly, transfer his weight properly, and to finish his throws properly. You get to coach the fundamental part of throwing that is going to help the quarterback to make the kind of throws you are going to ask him to make later.

I have always tried to keep it as simple as possible. I have seen a lot of drills on how to do this. The big thing on warm-up mechanics is to make sure they do it properly. Make sure they are managing their arm. Make sure they are not doing too much. When they are done, they are done. They get in the phase of practice when they are through with the drill. They are going to be throwing a lot. If you throw as much as we do they have to throw a lot in those drills. Make sure they do it right, and then they are out.

WARM-UP PROGRESSION

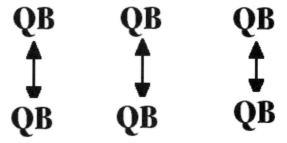

We come out and we pair up quarterbacks. I want them spread across the field. I want them to have room to work when we start our drill. If you do not watch, the first thing they are doing is standing close to each other shooting the breeze. If you have four quarterbacks make sure they are not too close to each other.

In the warm-up never throw more than 10 yards apart. They will say they are warm and start backing up. The key is this. We are getting warm and we are going to be accurate. Let them know we are still warming up. Make sure they are warm before you back them up.

I will tell you this about the grip. If a quarterback is struggling we make sure he is keeping his middle finger and ring finger on the laces of the football, or at least close to the laces. Those two fingers will control the football if they are on the laces. When you throw the football you throw it with the middle finger and the index finger. That is where the zip and the snap come from. If the ball is not coming off those two fingers last, there is a problem. If the ball comes off all three fingers there is a problem. We want the index finger to split the tip. Some players like to roll it back on the laces a little. As long as the ball is coming off the last two fingers I do not make a big deal out of it. The pinky finger is on the laces or slightly off the laces.

Some quarterbacks like to palm the ball. The big-hand quarterbacks can palm the ball a little. That is okay as long as there is a little air between the palm and the ball. When he throws he must lock out the wrist when he throws. To do that he must have a good grip on the ball.

One thing we do with our quarterbacks and our linemen is Towel Pull-Ups. If you have a quarterback with a weak wrist take a bunch of towels and hang them over a bar and make them do 30 Towel Pull-Ups after practice until he starts to develop a strong wrist. Our guys do it, but they hate it. I see a benefit in it because they get a stronger wrist. This will give them a little more snap with the wrist when they follow through.

The first drill is our Bullpen Pitch Drill. The one thing that upsets me is to see the quarterbacks come out and just start throwing without any purpose. They might as well not warm up. When we come out in Bullpen Pitch we are doing it with a purpose. We are concerned with our mechanics, but we are throwing for accuracy from the very get go. If I see a quarterback that is not throwing for a purpose I will tell them to get out of the drill. If they do not have two hands on the ball and are not throwing for a purpose they are wasting our time. Tell them to go play another position or to go play another sport.

The big key is this on mechanics. It is just like a pitcher in baseball coming out of the bullpen to pitch. I do not want to see a lot of wasted motion. I want the elbow high, and I want to see the ball carried high at all times. I want to see the shoulder rotation. I want the front shoulder on the target. I want to see a high release and finish. I will pull with my off-elbow, and I want a transfer from my back foot to my front foot. That is what I want to see. I do not want to see the ball drop down, or see the ball thrown off the back foot. I do not want the elbow to finish low, or across the body. Those are the things I am concerned with from the get go. I want them to finish at the target. It should be picture perfect every time.

Next we do a Feet Apart Drill. We spread the feet and face right, we face left, and we get on our knees. We work on a high release, we fade and throw, and we run the step-through drill. Don't sacrifice these fundamentals. Don't assume these fundamentals will be followed just because you have a polished quarterback. (Film)

Why do we spread the feet? We take the legs out of the throw. I want shoulder rotation and I want finish. I want to make sure everything is going down the middle of the body. When you take the legs out of it, you can see if they are throwing across the body and you can see if they are finishing properly. I tell them I want my shoulder at the target. I am working on flexibility. We always want the shoulder at the target. We want the ball high just as we talked about earlier. We have them reach down after the throw and grab a pinch of grass. This is to make sure they are finishing in the middle of their body. That is how we talk in terms of finishing down in the midline of our body. We do not want to see quarterbacks hurt throwing across their body. If they do that they will not get the spiral and spin of the ball.

Why do we run the Face Right and Face Left Drills? Now we want to start emphasizing the front shoulder. If I am right-handed it is going to be my left shoulder, and if I am left-handed it is going to be my right shoulder. I want to get the shoulder at my target. While we are warming up I stand there and call out, "Left Shoulder; Right Shoulder."

Then we get on the Knee Drill. We are taking the legs out of it. We are working on a quick release. We are working on proper mechanics. We are working on getting the arm high and we are working on arm accuracy. I may move them up a little if I feel they are not warmed up at this time. We work on accuracy. We move the ball around. We may tell them to throw the ball on the facemask, on the numbers, or on the shoulder. Again, we want to work on fundamentals. We want a tight spiral coming off the hand. I want to see all of the proper mechanics that we talked about.

Another drill we use is what we call "Find The Handle." It simulates a bad snap. They must pick the ball up from the ground and make a quick, accurate throw.

The next drill is what we call "High Release." We take all of the steps and mechanics out of it from the last step on the throw. It is the last part of the throw. It is the forearm with the wrist locked and the finish. We hold the pose as we let the ball go. I want to see the ball come off the last two fingers. I want to see a nice tight spiral.

Over the years we have found that about 50 percent of the throws the quarterback makes are on the move. We work on throwing and exchanging the weight on the move. I am not talking about throwing on the run like a sprint pass. I am talking about moving left or right to evade a rusher and throwing the ball while on the move. We have them move left or right out of the pocket and work on getting the ball up high and getting the shoulder turned to the target. A lot of the times the quarterback can't throw the ball off the front foot because they are getting hit. The mistake they make is keeping all of the weight on the back foot. Their accuracy goes out the door because they do not have their shoulders parallel to their hips. On our Fade Right and Fade Left Drills we want the shoulders over the hips and we want to throw downhill to the receiver. As we fade right we want a high release. We do not want to throw uphill with the elbow down low. I want as much accuracy as possible.

If you Sprint Out, or if you Bootleg, a lot of your quarterbacks will have to throw on the run. You have to coach how to throw on the run properly. Now we back them up to 15 yards instead of 10 yards and we throw on the run. I have them throw on steps. We have a Sprint Out where we throw on five steps. I like to work on their timing as part of the technique of throwing on the run. I tell them if they are right-handed the right foot comes out first. They go five steps and throw on the run. We are throwing our Step-Through Early Drill. What do I mean by Early?

Let's talk about the proper techniques of throwing on the run. We want two hands on the ball, we carry the ball high, with a high elbow. We want the weight out over the toes. We want to gain momentum on the throw. He starts our slow and speeds up as he throws. He wants the shoulder at the target. The chest is out and the weight is over the toes. If he is right-handed he starts his throw on his back foot. The weight transfer is from the back foot to the front foot. The big mistake quarterbacks make on throwing on the run is that they drag the back foot. When you are standing in the pocket throwing you transfer the weight from the back foot to the front foot on the throw if you are doing it properly. If I drag the back foot I am not transferring the weight. On the run what we do is step through early so we are transferring our weight on the throw. It feels awkward at first. Most of them want to drag the back foot. We want to be quick and fast and step early on the throw. I tell them to speed up their throw when they get through their steps.

The last coaching point on the run is this. I always follow the ball for three steps. I make them count it. They take 5 steps, then accelerate on the throw, and then it is "one, two, three." and they hold the pose and then they are finished. We still stress the same coaching points. Everything is throwing down a line.

If we have time we will jump into our Drop Steps. Most of the time I do not have enough time. If we do not get to work on them early we work on them at the end of practice, or I will do it for the first five minutes of our 90 Progression. I make it part of our drill.

The hardest throw to teach the quarterback to make is the second-level throw. It may be against a Zone Defense, or over a linebacker in a seam. He must put enough on the ball to get it there and to get it over the linebackers. That is the hardest throw to make. During this drill I want to see their rhythm, and I want to see the shoulders rocking back over the hips. I want to see them transfer their weight back to their front foot. I call this "In-Between Ball." He throws the ball with enough loft on it to get it over the linebacker and with enough zip on it to beat the secondary. That is our Warm Up Progression and we do it every day. It does not matter what day it is. We work the heck out of this.

I will get to the video to show you our Drops from under center and from the Shotgun. This will give you an idea of how we categorize our offense within our Drop-Back Passing Game. It is real critical that you categorize what you do offensively. Some of you may not run Shotgun. Some of you may not run the Three-Step Drop. Some of you may not run any Five-Step Drop. Some of you do not run any Sprint Out. But, whatever you do, categorize it so the timing works out with the quarterback's drop and the receivers' steps on their routes. If you do not know how to do it, ask someone. That is what we do. We categorize the plays so the timing works out for the quarterback and the receiver.

I will go through the drops very quickly. We have what we call the Two-Step Drop in our 90 game.

We have the Three-Step Drop in our 90 game. We have a Big Three-Step Drop. Our quarterback knows when I give him a 90 play that he has two steps. We use two steps for the Bubble Screen and plays like that. The three steps are our Quicks from under the center. We throw those on timing and reading off the Three-Step Drop in our 90 game. We have the Big Three-Step Drop. We have three or four of those per game. That is a 90 play that takes a little longer to develop. The techniques for the quarterback are a little slower and it takes a little longer in the drop. He can't take a Five-Step Drop or it will be too late. So, in our 90 Game we use our Two-Step, Three-Step, and we have a Big Three Step Drop.

In our Drop-Back Game from under center we categorize our offense this way. We have a Quick Five-Step Drop. That is five steps and no hitch step. It is all timing. It is intermediate routes thrown on time. Now, if the receiver is covered we are going to be hitching the ball. Also, in our Drop-Back Game we have a Five-Step and Hitch. Basically it is a Big Five and a Hitch. That is off maneuvering routes. All of our 90 Routes except for the Big Three are going to be timing routes. Let me take you through this on the film. (Film)

We do not teach a crossover step. The most important step in the drop is the first step away from the center. The next two steps are gather steps. We do not crossover. I tell them to click heels. They take the first step slightly past 6 o'clock. His heels are going to slightly click. And then his third step is his plant step. The key coaching point is to keep the shoulders over the hips on the throw.

I appreciate your time. Thanks.

THE 4-3 BLITZ PACKAGE

COLORADO STATE UNIVERSITY

Thank you very much. It is a pleasure to be in Louisville for this clinic. I coached at the University of Miami after Jimmy Johnson left. We continued to run the 4-3 defense for the four years we were there. We had some great players and won a lot of football games. We were probably one of the best defensive football teams in the country.

At Colorado State we have been pretty successful on defense. There are a few new wrinkles we are adding to the defense each year. But we are doing exactly the same thing. I want to give you an overview of the defense and go into as much detail as I can.

At Colorado State and Miami we were a basically a 4-3 and Eagle front. The coverage we played out of our defense was Cover 2, quarter-quarter, and what we called Cover 8. We call it Cover 8, but you guys may call it quarters all the way across. When you set up your defense, you should ask yourself two questions: 1) Is our defense the best thing for our conference? 2) What coverages are best suited for it?

At Colorado State we play the 4-3 defense with some slight movement. We play a Cover 2, which is five under and two deep. When we install our defense in spring football, we have four down linemen, three linebackers, and try to keep the coverages simple. This year we are going to change some things around. We usually have a right and left tackle. We are going to change our tackle play. We are going to have a 1 technique and 3 technique tackle. The 3 technique tackle is going to be a stud. Warren Sapp plays Tampa Bay's 3 technique tackle. The 1 technique tackle doesn't have to be as big or as physical and strong as the other tackle.

We have started going to visit the Tampa Bay Buccaneers and study their defense. We aligned the defensive down four in a 39 to the tight end and a 15 to the split end. That means the end and tackle to the tight-end side are in a 9 technique on the end and a 3 technique on the guard. To the split-end side we aligned the tackle in a backside shaded 1 technique on the center and a 5 technique on the tackle. The idea is to get the inside hand toward the ball down on the ground and the inside leg back. We want to come off the ball hard and fast aiming for the V in the offensive lineman's neck. We want to play in the outside half of the opposite player.

When I was at the University of Miami all four of the down linemen were drafted into the NFL. We also had two subs drafted. Russell Maryland was a first-round pick, and the worst of our players was a third-round pick. That made us good coaches. That is the way we coached these guys.

Now we are going to align our techniques on a foot-to-foot alignment. That means we will be a little wider in our alignment. The 3 technique's inside foot is on the outside foot of the offensive guard. A lot of the times we do not get a piece of the offensive lineman.

The Sam linebacker aligns in a hip position on the open side 5 technique. The Mac linebacker is 4 yards deep in the middle. He has the strong-side A-gap on flow to the tight end. If there is flow to the open side, he is in the B-gap. Our linebackers key through the backs. They never key linemen. That is what I have taught for 40 years. I guess it is a matter of preference. The Will linebacker aligns in the 50 alignment. If flow goes away from him he is the cutback player.

RAM FRONT

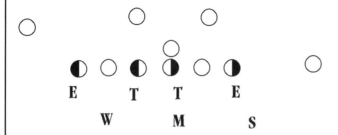

The keys on the three coverages I'm going to show you are all the same. We have a zone rule, which we probably follow 95 percent of the time. The eyes have to be on the football. Our corners are about 7 yards off the football. They are settling in the flat and trying to get a good jam on the receivers. They are trying to knock them to the inside. The safeties are 12 yards deep keying the quarterback and seeing the number 2 receiver to his side. The number I receivers are on the outside. The safeties have halves, and the corners are jam flat players. The Will linebacker has the curl area. The Mac linebacker is playing the middle hook area, and the Sam linebacker is playing the strong curl area.

COVER 2

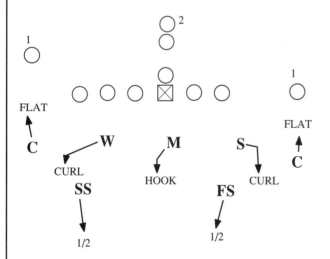

I don't know if you saw our bowl game with Southern Mississippi, but they had a good football team. They were ranked 10 or 11 in the country. We had a bunch of average guys. In our secondary the fastest guy was 4.7. We had a bunch of tough guys that played good technique and were smart. We

just had a staff meeting before I came out here. We were discussing what were the most important things for a defensive back to have. The number 1 thing he has to have is football smarts and he has to be tough. Speed and quickness are all secondary in my opinion. Get smart people on the field and they can take care of it.

When we go to work in spring practice, that first day I take half the secondary and the secondary coach takes the other half. All we work on is seeing the quarterback, feeling the number 1 receiver, and knowing what the number 2 receiver is doing. All the offensive coaches out there know how to attack Cover 2. They have three or four routes they work on to attack Cover 2. That is what we work on. We play the four verticals like a champion. We work on all those things, plus our run support. It doesn't matter which coverage we are playing, the keys are going to be the same.

In a passing situation we are going to be in Cover 2. That is our best pass coverage. Everything we do starts from this shell. But if we need to stop the pass, we will be in Cover 2. When we went down to play Southern Miss all we heard about were their two great receivers. They were NFL material. We didn't know if we could play any other coverage. We had to jam and double them. At the end of the game they had 85 yards of total receptions. When you play cover 2 you are hanging out on the run. You are weaker playing the run, when you are in Cover 2.

The next thing we go to in our scheme of things is Cover 4. This is our *quarter-quarter-half* coverage. Nothing in the defense changes as far as alignment and stance or the appearance of the defense. There is nothing new for the open side of the coverage. The corner is still jamming and playing flat. The free safety is playing half coverage. The major change is on the tight-end side. The strong safety tightens up to about 10-11 yards. The corner is taking the deep quarter of the field depending on what the tight end does. The strong safety has the other deep quarter to that side of the field. What we found out is, every time the ball is on the hash mark, 70 percent of the passes are thrown into the boundary side. Most quarterbacks don't have a strong enough arm to get the ball to the wide-side boundary. We don't have them in our league and you don't have them in your league.

The reason we are playing Cover 4 is for run support on the cutback play. The toughest play for us to play in the 4-3 defense is the weak-side lead play or the one-back zone play weak. We are fine to the boundary side of the defense. The 1 technique tackle is fighting to stay in the A-gap. The Mac linebacker is filling and blowing up the lead block to bounce the play outside to the Sam linebacker. The Will linebacker is fighting like hell to get into the backside A-gap. The problem comes when the ball comes back behind the double-teamed 3 technique. There is no one there.

When we play the Cover 4, we have a strong safety who is unblocked filling the cutback lane on the back side. If we are playing a team in an I formation, it better be third-and-long before we get into Cover 2. We'll be in Cover 4. The difference is with anything inside the box our safeties are thinking pass first. Any fake inside the box is treated like pass first. If they try to run the stretch zone play outside, our secondary is flying to the ball in run support. The strong safety is seeing the quarterback and is feeling the tight end. When the tight end blocks, the strong safety is now an unblocked cutback player. In this defense we can stop the cutback for a 4- or 5-yard gain.

If the number 2 receiver disappeared outside and the strong safety gets hung up a little, we still are alright. The corner is playing deep quarter, and his first rule is to protect the post. He would take the number 1 receiver over the top to the post and the strong safety can recover and help underneath.

In our scheme of things, 80 percent of the time when we think it is pass we are in Cover 2. If there is any doubt whether you are going to run or pass, we will be in Cover 4. The teaching is the same for the linebackers, except for the Sam linebacker. He has to go flat on Cover 4.

The next coverage is what we play on running downs. At Miami we used to call it *Cover 4 Funnel*. At Colorado State we call it *Cover 8*. The corners and safeties are playing quarters all the way across. We haven't changed anything up front with our four down people. On first-and 10 this is the defense we are in. We can get both safeties into the run scheme. If flow goes left, the free safety is the cutback player. If flow goes right the strong safety is the cutback player. The safeties are up at about 10 yards instead of 12 yards showing a Cover 2 look. On the snap of the ball we are not concerned with them retreating out of there. The keys are the same. They are looking at the quarterback and feeling the number 2 receivers.

COVER 4

COVER 8

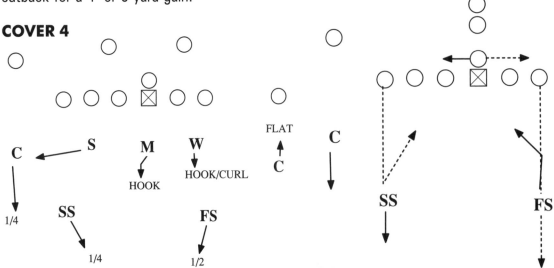

On any bootleg, the safeties are playing the crossing routes and the corners are playing halves. We tell the safeties to think and play like linebackers. The linebackers' look is the same. The weakness of this coverage is the hitch route. We hope to disguise it enough so the quarterback can't come up and read it. We tell our players to be patient on the hitches and short patterns. If the offense catches 10 hitches a game at 6 yards a catch, that is only 60 yards of offense. That will never beat us. What beats you is the 6 yard catch that goes 60 yards because of a missed tackle.

We play this coverage in first-and10, where we think you are going to run the ball or play-action pass. Everybody knows it, so we just practice it and get good at it.

Let me show you some of the adjustments we have to make to certain situations. If we call *Ram Cover 2*, the linebackers are the adjusters. If a team motions from a pro set across the formation into a slot set the linebackers bump over slightly. The corner comes with the motion to the area of the tight end and the linebacker bump over. The Sam linebacker moves outside into a wider position.

ADJUSTMENTS

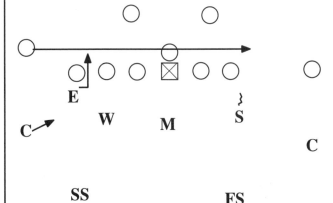

We do just the opposite if they start in a slot and motion into the pro set. The Will linebacker tightens up, the other linebackers bump over slightly, and the corner widens and gets a little depth.

We haven't done this next thing I'm going to talk about for a couple of years. We are starting to come

back to it. If we get the one back set to create a three-wide receivers set, we make a slight adjustment. We get an automatic *Gap Call* to the split-end side. The end to the split side slants into the B-gap. He becomes the cutback player. If they try to run something on us, we have all gaps covered. The ball has to bounce out to the Sam linebacker who is unblocked.

GAP CALL

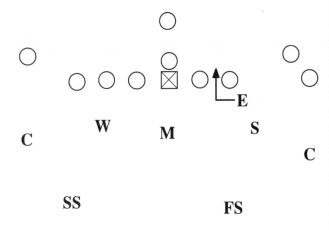

We can switch our linebacker if we want to. Our Sam linebacker is a little quicker and the Will linebacker is a little stronger. But it really doesn't matter. The linebacker tells the end he is gone, and moves out to the Deuce set.

We do the same thing on a Trips Set. Our outside linebacker bumps out into the Trips Set and gives the end a *Fullback Call*. It is the same thing as the Gap Call except it is to the tight-end side.

FB CALL

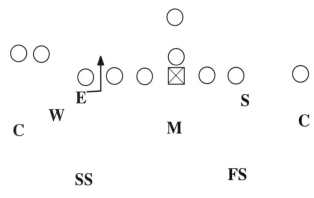

These calls have helped us 100 percent. Of course, the offense knows we do those things. If they start to run the bootleg and take advantage of the leverage, we have a call that overrides all automatics. If we are in our 4-3 with any kind of a long-yardage play, we call *Go*. If we call *Ram-Go Cover 2*, we disregard run all together. That tells our defensive line to GO straight up the field and play pass. It calls off the Gap or FB calls.

This is something we just fell into recently. If the tight end comes out to the left, we give our left call. If the tight end trades to the other side, we give a *Pirate Call*. The Sam linebacker moves up over the tight end. The Will linebacker adjusts inside. On the snap of the ball the end and tackle to the open side slant to the A and B gap on that side. The Will linebacker moves outside for the cutback. The beauty of this is, we have stunted into our Eagle Front.

PIRATE

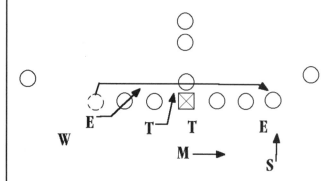

The Pirate stunt is a boundary-side stunt if we line up in our Eagle Front. Into the boundary we are in 3 and 5 techniques with our tackle and end. To the other side we are in 1 and 5 techniques. The Sam linebacker walks up over the tight end. The Mac linebacker is in a 30 alignment. The Will linebacker is in a 20 alignment away from the tight end. If we get the Pirate call, the boundary corner has to be alert for the bounce of the ball coming back side. Just telling the corner to be alert is the difference between him getting there for a 3-yard gain or no gain. This is against a two-back set in the backfield.

EAGLE / PIRATE

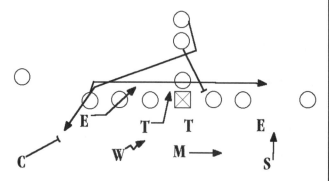

You have to have adjustment to any defense. The simpler they are the better they are. Sometimes the tight end doesn't trade, but continues in motion. If that happens, we call *Yukon*. We still run the Pirate to the back side, but everyone is alerted to what the tight end might do.

What I just showed you is our defense. That is all we do. That is all we will do in spring ball for 15 practices. That is all we will work on in the spring.

There are a couple of stunts built in which I want to show you. We can call the Gap Call against a two-back set, and we have a feeling they are going to run the ball. We can do the same thing with the FB call. It becomes a good short-yardage defense. We simply call *RAM-FB-GAP*. That brings our end inside and our linebackers scrap outside or come over the top.

I coached in high school for 10 years. I went to clinics on my own money. I used to jump in the car and travel. I've been to Nebraska, Arkansas, and a lot of places. I went down to Arkansas when Monte Kiffin was down there with Lou Holtz. I'm convinced on one thing. The sounder you are and the more repetitions you can get the better your player will feel about themselves. It has to be simple. I'm convinced you can win by doing that.

Let me show you some of our blitzing game. This first one is the one I like the best. We categories our blitzes as run or pass blitzes. This is a run blitz. I'll run this from the Eagle Front. This stunt is called *Under Snake Blitz*. It is a left formation so our right-side tackle and end are in 3 and cocked 5 techniques. To the tight-end side we are in a 1 and 5 technique with our tackle and end. The Mac is stacked behind the 1 technique. The Will linebacker is in a 20 to the open side and the Sam LB is in a 9 technique. We like to call this stunt when we think they are going to run the ball.

The hardest part of this stunt is the left end. He has to fight his ass off to get outside on the tight end. He runs what we call a *Stab* outside. The Mac linebacker goes first through the B-Gap. The Sam linebacker is playing nice and loose. He comes off the Mac linebacker blitz and blows up the strong-side A-gap. The 1 technique tackle gets across the center's face and into the backside A-gap. The backside tackle and end go upfield. In the secondary we are showing Cover 2, but we are in Cover 0, which is man-to-man coverage. The corners are on number 1 and the safeties are on number 2. The Will linebacker has the third receiver on a screen or out the back side. You may see us in Cover 0, six to eight times a game. If you can disguise this and they don't see it coming, it is something to see.

UNDER SNAKE BLITZ

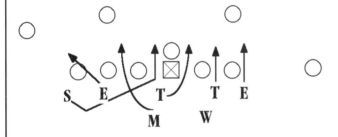

This next blitz is a run blitz, also. We can run it from our Ram or base front. We call it *Ram Blitz In*. We aligned in the Ram front. On the snap of the ball, the 6 technique end and 3 technique tackle run an FB and Spike stunt. The Spike stunt for the tackle is the same thing as the FB stunt for the end. On the other side the tackle uses a blitz charge through his gap and the end runs a Gap stunt. The Will and Sam linebacker blitz off the outside. The Mac linebacker is stacked in the weak-side A-gap and has the first back strong and second back weak man-to-man. The secondary is in Cover 0.

RAM BLITZ IN

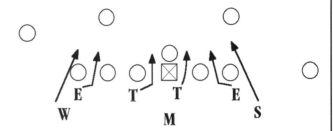

A stunt that helped us a lot was what we called *Fire*. We did this against I formation teams. We called *Ram-Fire*. The Fire meant the strong side or play side. We ran the strong-side part of the *In* stunt. Everyone else played normal. The Mac linebacker has the B-gap going both ways. We played Cover 2 behind this stunt. We broke the rules of coaching by doing that because we were one linebacker short in coverage and we give up his zone. We do this on occasion and when we are thinking run. We don't make a habit of doing that. If we have the term blitz on any of our stunts, we have to be in man-to-man coverage.

One of our best pass blitzes is called *Go Weak Blitz*. This stunt brings four men off the weak side. Make sure your ends know that on blitz they have to stay outside when they rush outside. They must contain. We get in our Ram alignment. The 1 technique tackle crosses the center's face and rushes through the A-gap. The ends are a go charge upfield. The Mac linebacker blows the B-gap and the Sam linebacker comes behind him through the A-gap. A coaching point to any blitz is the speed at which the blitzers come. They have to be able to redirect if it is a draw. If they get going so hard that the back runs right past them they haven't done us any good. They have to think pass but be ready to play the run.

RAM GO WEAK BLITZ

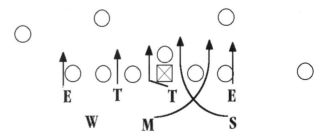

We have a blitz to the strong side called *Go Field Tim Blitz*. We bring four rusher to the field side. I'll show it to you. The ball has to be on the hash mark for us to call it. We like this blitz when a team is sprinting out to the field side. We call the blitz and don't know what type of set we are going to see. It could be a slot or pro set, but we still run it the same way. To the back side our end might get into a head-up position on the tight end, but he doesn't have to. If the offense runs the ball into the boundary, they probably are going to be able to. But we are calling this play on long yardage. The one thing they won't be able to do is get outside of us to the field side and that is the purpose of the stunt.

RAM GO FIELD TIM BLITZ

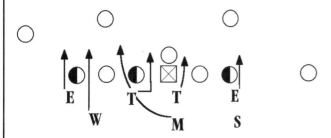

We are starting to get to a position that we have to stop the running game. I want to show you our Under or Eagle defense. To the strong side we are in a 1 and 5 technique for our tackle and end. The Sam linebacker is in a 9 technique. To the other side we are in the Eagle adjustment. The Mac is in a stack behind the 3 technique tackle. The Will linebacker is playing a 30 technique to the strong side. The secondary is showing Cover 2. This is the only thing new we've gotten in the last couple of years that has really helped us. This is called *Under 1 Free*. The free safety walks up to 7 yards deep over where an imaginary tight end would be lined up. The strong safety moves back and into the middle. The corners drop into deep thirds. We go from a seven-man front to a true eight-man front. When the Mac linebacker hears the 1 Free call, he knows he is the spill guy on runs. If an isolation comes at the Will linebacker, the Mac linebacker plays into that gap, also. They blow up that gap right now. If the ball cuts back the free safety is coming hard into the backside A-gap. He is playing like a linebacker.

If they throw the ball, we are in a 3 deep zone, and the free safety has the first back coming out the weak side.

UNDER 1 FREE

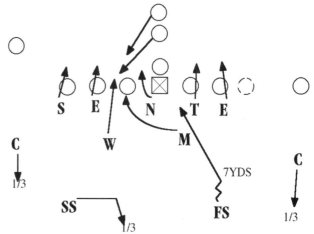

We ran this defense about 70 plays last year, which works out to about six to eight plays a game. This defense adjusts great to one-back sets or two-tight-end sets. What people will do is fake the isolation and run the bootleg. The free safety is aligned on the second tight end, which is his pass responsibility. If the ball is running outside he comes on and boxes it back inside. He is in position to take the cross coming from the other tight end and we have a three-deep coverage behind it. This defense kills a one-back offense. We have every gap covered and it takes care of the waggle.

If we are having trouble with the run out of our Ram front we can call *Ram Free*, and brings our strong safety up into the run support. It is just like the 1 Free out of the Under front. It allows us to get the eighth man into the box to stop the run. When we are in the Ram front the gap that is unprotected is the B-gap strong. On flows away, the Will linebacker has to fill the strong A-gap. The 3 technique tackle is really vulnerable to the double-team. The strong safety moves up to 7 yards over the tight end and fills that gap.

That is all the time I have. If you need anything or want to ask some more questions, come on up. Thank you for you attention. I appreciate it.

THE UK BLACK FLAG DEFENSE

UNIVERSITY OF KENTUCKY

I am excited to be here. The only time I was ever in Hawaii was when I was at UTEP with Coach Young. Hal Mumme was the offensive coordinator at the time. We used to come here to play the Rainbow Warriors and get our butts beat and go back home. This is a beautiful place. I envy each and every one of you that lives here. This is the first time I have been able to vacation here. It is a tremendous place. The people here are great. I went down to the beach today to watch the finals of the Bonsi Pipeline. Those folks can surf. I am putting that place on my recruiting list. I can assure you there are some guys there that will take on anything. They could play defense for me.

I have one little story I want to pass on. I was raised in Texas. In Texas we are spread out big time. My dad was in the oil business. I had a younger brother. We did not get to go to town very often. One day my dad came in the house and said, "Boys, tomorrow we are going to go to Tyler, Texas, and take mother shopping." I was about 5 years old and my younger brother was 3.

The next morning we loaded up in the car and drove to Tyler, Texas. As soon as I got there I saw some of the biggest buildings I had ever seen in my life. There was a three-story bank building, a J.C. Penny's, and a Sears building. We got out of the car and my mother said she was going shopping. My dad said, "Let's go down to see that big building, boys." We went down to this great big building. We went inside to the lobby. They had big leather couches and real leather chairs. There were real oil paintings on the wall. There was this box-looking thing over in the corner of the lobby. Over the box were big numbers: 1, 2, and 3.

We were sitting there trying to figure out what the box was for. We looked up and here came a big, heavy-set, well-built, not very good-looking woman, walking over toward the box. She pushed a button on the wall next to the box and the doors of that box opened. The lady walked in the box and soon the door shut. Over the door a red light came on. The light lit up indicating 1, then 2, and then 3. The light remained red for a few minutes. We sat there a few minutes just looking at the light. Then all of a sudden the light blinked again and it started coming down; 3, 2, 1. The doors opened and out stepped the most beautiful woman you have ever seen. My dad punched me and then he punched my little brother. He said, "Boys quick, go get mommy! We are going to run her through that thing once or twice before we go home." That is how far back I came from.

I am going to start out with a few things on philosophy. If you are interested in any of the things I am talking about I will be glad to mail anything to you if you will drop me a note. Send it to: Mike Major, University of Kentucky, Commonwealth Stadium, Lexington, KY 40505.

Hal Mumme and I have been coaching together since 1979 and we do not hide anything we do from anyone. We have coached on and off in high school and we love high school coaches because that is where are roots are from. We learned how to coach in high school. There is nothing better than good high school coaching because you have to coach everything. You see a different offense and defense each week. You have to be able to coach everything. Then you have a lot of other personal problems to deal with in working with the players. You have the weight program to deal with and a lot of other things that college coaches do not deal with. I have a great deal of respect for the high school coach.

I have coached at about every level. The higher up you go the less coaching you do. In the NFL you see the same offense every week. You just have to defense the personnel. In collegiate football you see almost the same offense every week. You just have to do a better job of recruiting. This is what I tell people about college coaching. You win championships by recruiting. You win games with defense. You sell tickets with the offense.

Our philosophy on defense is this. We do not want to stop plays, we want to "Make Plays." Kids love to do that. I was in here last night listing to Bob Wagner of Arizona talk on defense. I heard some great questions asked by the coaches in the audience. Those were great questions. Someone asked Coach Wagner if he thought they could run their defense in high school. Everything I am going to show you here today we have run in high school. That was a proving ground for our package. That was a part of our commitment to the things we were going to do.

I am a writer, and if I can't write it down we can't do it. These are the things we must do to be successful. We want to make sure we get all of this covered as a coaching staff.

We want to make sure we have a Philosophy. We want to make sure we have a playbook. We want to make sure we have playbook information.

We want to make sure we have Goals for the team. We call ourselves the **"BLACK FLAG DEFENSE."** If you have read much history you know that was the only way they could communicate. They had so many different languages and they could not communicate with anything except colors. If you wore a WHITE FLAG it meant you were going to Surrender. You would give quarter and you would take whatever came because you were not willing to continue the fight. But, if you raised the Black Flag, that meant you were going to fight until the very end. If you whipped those bastards you were not going to give them any quarters. They would become enslaved to you. We adopted that philosophy a long time ago and we say we are the "Black Flag Defense."

We made up a big Black Flag that hangs out at practice on our tower at the practice complex. We have the years at the top of the flag—1998, 1999, 2000. When we beat a team we take their logo emblem and sew it on the flag for that year. That flag hangs on the tower Wednesday and Thursday during practice. It is a big deal to our kids.

I do not want to get ahead of myself here. We say it takes 13 stops for a defense to win a football game. That means we must force the offense to punt, throw an interception, fumble, or turn the ball over 13 times in a game to win. If we can get 13 stops in a game we can win. I will give you two examples of that. This year we lost to Mississippi State in the last 20 seconds and the game was on ESPN on a Thursday night. They kicked a 48-yard field goal and beat us. We had 12 stops that game and got beat by one point.

We played Syracuse in the Music City Bowl this year. We had 12 stops and got beat. The score was 14-13 near the end of the game. They had the ball and were killing the clock. Coach Mumme came up to and said, "Mike, do you know what we have to do?" I said, "Yes I know what we have to do. WE HAVE TO LET THEM SCORE!" Hal said I do not think they will do that. I think they will take a knee and run the clock out. I said, "I don't think so." We called time out and I got the team over on the sideline. I told them we were going to line up and then as soon as the ball is snapped to back up and let them score. If we let them score we can go for two and tie the game and beat them in overtime. We let them score and got the ball back but we couldn't score. The clock ran out on us. We got beat 21-13. We had 12 stops in the game but needed 13 to win.

Our kids keep a ring of tape on their wrist. When they come off the field I have a graduate assistant mark the tape on the wrist if we stopped the offense. It is just like the notches on the old western guns. They can look at the number of stops and know how many more we need to get to 13 stops. I tell them if we can get six stops the first half it is a great game. Our kids can keep up with that and they can monitor that during the game.

The other thing we do is this. We say this team is an 85-play team. When we come off the field we tell them how many total plays the team has played after every series. They come off the field and we tell them they have run 57 plays. How many do they have left? They have 28 plays left.

Most offensive teams have patterns or trends. They may be a team that scores in the first quarter. Or they may be a team that scores in the second series. If you chart the film you can find out a lot about the opponent. You may find that they really gear it up and try to score on the first series. Or you may find that they may just be trying to find out what you are doing on defense that first series. You can chart these things by watching the films. There are some tangible things that you can teach that you learn from the film. That is what we do with goal boards for each game and for the season.

We only break down four films. We have enough film that you would not believe it. But if you get too much film it all starts running together and becomes the same. We pick four games our opponents played teams that ran a defense similar to our defense. We break those four films down and that is what we use. We try to stop the best four running plays. We try to stop the best three passing plays. That is all we work on. WE do not play "What If." I do not have enough time to do that. We are going to take away the bread-and-butter plays.

The way you get to their bread and butter is like this. "What do they like to run on third-and-medium?" Every offensive coach has a philosophy of what he is going to run on third-and-medium. We put all of those situations together on a video. We did this when we coached in high school Our kids could tell us that the opponents like to run off tackle on third-and-medium. They like to pull the guard and run the big fullback off-tackle on the Power O. Now we have the kids involved in the teaching process. They get in the game and they know what to do when that situation comes up. The more you can get them to play the game the better off you are.

In our off-season on Wednesday we have Competition Day. We feel kids must learn how to compete in the off-season. As the off-season comes to an end we start doing that on Saturday morning or afternoon because that is the time they have to compete in the season. This gets their juices flowing at that time. We are just teaching them how to play the game at that time. When Hal Mumme and I were coaching in high school we used to practice every Wednesday night under the lights because we played all of our games at night. We wanted our kids used to playing at night so we practice at night on Wednesday.

We all must understand the Scouting Report. We try to make our Scouting Report as much as we can an indication of what is going to happen in the game. The first thing we do is to give them the Game Plan. You may look at one of our Scouting Reports and ask how in the heck can we teach all of that. Everything is broken down. We break it down like this: Fronts, Stunts, Blitzes, and Coverages. We cannot get all of this in the report. So what we do is to put bands on all of our players. We do not huddle as a defense. I never have been able to find out how huddling helps you win a game. We feel every player needs to be the signal caller. If I am a defensive tackle and some linebacker calls the defense it does not mean he knows any more about the game than I do. We do not huddle anymore. That takes away the No Huddle people on offense. We have bands on all of the defensive players. We have the base calls on the bands on one side and the blitz calls on another section. We change those up. One week they will be odd numbers and the next they will be even numbers. I have a female manager that holds up our cards to indicate our defense. She may hold up a card to signal "42." It may align us in a bubble front, a twist stunt, and the coverage may be Red. For each of those cards we have three or four Hot Calls. If the offense comes out in a certain offensive formation we know right then it is a blitz call for us. All they have to do to play defense for us is to be able to read. If they can get in UK they should be able to read. If I were back coaching in high school that would be the only way I would call the defense.

You hear the statement that you want everyone on the same page. Well, I want them on the same page, paragraph, and same sentence, and the same work with me, and not just the same page.

We give them a schedule of practice for the week. We let them know what type of gear they will need to wear.

Next I am going to tell you about our off-season. These things keep coming to me as we go along here. Do you know how you find your best football players? I am going to tell you how you find your best players. Watch the kids in elementary school. You give John a team and Bob a team and then tell them to choose up. They will pick the best 22 players. They know the kids that will compete hard and kids that will do things. You have to trust the kids sometimes.

How many of you have had a player that could run, could lift, and he looked the part of a player? But, you put him out on the field and he could not compete. Those kids know this. The first 10 players those kids pick will usually be your best players.

Back to the Scouting Report. We break the opponent's offense down: Two-Back Offense, One-Back Offense, One-Back Set, No Backs, Adjustments, Receivers, and Tight Ends. Does the tight end flip-flop? We want to make sure we have all of this covered before we go out on the field. We have a book of this and that is in our report.

Next we go to our Game Plan Preparation. We want to check personnel. First we want to look at our own guys. We look at our opponents. If they put in an extra wide receiver we want to make sure we have our Nickel back in there. At UK we call him the JOKER. We want to make sure we have gone over all of the fronts and stunts we are going to use. We cover the adjustments and techniques. We review the linebacker Dogs and secondary blitzes. We go over our coverage and our short-yardage defense.

We review the goal-line defense. We only play the goal-line defense inside our 3-yard line. We go to the goal line if you get down to the 3-yard line. We do not work on it very much. If the offense gets the ball down that deep we need to stop them out on the field more. We only work on it on Wednesday and we are not in pads then. I do not have time to worry about the goal-line defense. We work on stopping them out in the field. We do not do much in that area.

We cover the Prevent Defense, the Victory Defense, and the two-point play. We work on the two-minute situations. We work on the last two minutes of a half if we are ahead and if we are behind. At the end of the game we work on the last two minutes if you are ahead or behind by 14 points or more. If we are less than 14 points behind we are playing our standard defense. We are not into that Prevent crap. If we are 14 ahead, yes, we will do some of that soft-cover drop-zone stuff if we have to. We do cover Automatics and Gadget Formations and Trick Plays.

Next we move to Game Day Preparations. First are our Pregame Meetings. I rehearse with all of my staff on what we are going to talk about that day. I have each coach go over his talk. For example, I have Coach Darrell Patterson who coaches the defensive ends, talk to the other coaches on what he is going to talk to his players about. It does not take long to do this. Instead of going into the meeting and shooting from the hip, you have something you can say and everyone is consistent on what they are doing.

We walk our players through our Pregame Warm-up. We do that twice a year. We do that before the first game and before we start our SEC schedule.

We talk about our Sideline Organization. I let them know where I want everyone on the sideline. I do not want players getting lost where I can't get them in a game. We do grouping on the sideline. We have our position coaches aligned on the sideline where we can make our substitutions. Coach Tim Keane is on one side and he is going to make all

Joker substitutions. Darrel Patterson is going to send in the defensive ends. Coach Tom Adams has the tackles. I am making all of the calls on defense. Also I make the linebacker substitutions.

We have two types of substitutions. If a player is really good we make him a GREEN Dot type player. For example it may be our fifth defensive back. He is usually pretty good. But, we may go to our sixth defensive back. I may not be too sure about him, especially if he has not played a lot. We label him as a YELLOW Dot type player. If a yellow dot type substitution gets ready to go in the game, I want to know about it. I will have to adjust my play calling if we have that player in the game. If I have all of my Green Dot players in the game I can do more. The kids do not know who is green and who is yellow. This is just for coaches. This is organization.

Let me go over our halftime procedures. We practice halftime. I want my kids to know we have something to do every second we are in that dressing room. We go in and the first thing we do is to take off the pads and put them down. If it is hot I want them to change T-shirts. I want them to get a clean, dry T-shirt for the second half. I tell them this will make them faster. It doesn't, but they think it does because it feels a little better. If it's real hot and their socks are wet I tell them to change them. Why do we do this? Instead of Joe, Bob, and Bill talking about what happened they are busy taking care of their business. This takes them about five minutes to do that.

This gives all of our assistant coaches time to meet and make our adjustments. Now we can go back and meet as a team. I want to make sure they drink a lot of water at that time. They have to get a drink and they have to change T-shirts and socks. We make all of our adjustments and talk about what we have to do. Then the head coach comes in and makes his rah-rah talk and BOOM, we are back on the field. We go through all of this every week.

Now, what happens if someone gets injured? What if it is your best linebacker? How is this going to effect the defense? You have to work through things

like that. I can put in a sub but he will not be the best player I have. My best linebacker is hurt. Now I must make sure I make the right call when that sub is in the game. I may have to adjust my play calling. It is not the kids that have to adjust all of the time.

Who is going to call timeouts? Who is going to call them? It is real easy at our place. Coach Mumme calls all timeouts. I do not have to worry much about that. But it is something you need to think about and develop a strategy for.

Now we move to After the Game. This includes how you are going to evaluate your game film. How are you going to grade the players? What do you expect out of your staff on the day off? What about the players? What we do about lifting weights and conditioning are covered.

How do you cover Film Evaluation with the players? I do not show all of the film to our players in our team meeting. We take the best 20 plays from the past game. We praise the hell out of them. "Man, that was a great HIT!" If we swarm to the ball like we are supposed to we tell them, "Great Pursuit Angle." Everything we can come up with we do right there. We clap, we cheer, and yell. Then we show them four plays, one from each quarter. The plays are types of plays where we were not so good. "Guys, if we had only done this or that, we would have had a perfect game." That is all we do with the film evaluation with the players. If the players choose to look at the entire game, and they will, they do that on their own. We are not going to put our players in an embarrassing situation in front of their peers. It is always going to be a pat on the back, and "That a boy" type of talk that we give them during that session.

That is what we are there for. I learned this a long time ago. I am an ole Texas guy. If Joe Bob is the best player I have, I am not going to evaluate Joe Bob as a 60 percent player and chew on his butt because Joe Bob is the best player I have. You better get Joe Bob ready to play and you better hope he is happy about playing for you. He can spit the bit and tell you to take it and stuff it. "Here is your Nike gear, and here is you Riddell helmet. The hell with this, I am going to go ride around with little Sally. That is more fun." You have to understand these guys and have a little give-and-take in dealing with them.

I want to talk about our Philosophy. We want to be simple and aggressive. We want to Attack the Offense. General Grant, a leader in the Civil War, did not have a very good Cavalry Army under him. His philosophy was this. "When you are surrounded by superior forces attack, Attack, ATTACK." That is what we are going to do. When we first got to UK we did not have very good players. We decided we were going to ATTACK! We were not going to take any quarters nor were we going to give any.

We are going to limit the techniques by position. This will allow you to increase reps against the offenses favorite two or three plays. We did stretch this out to four plays. We work on four run plays and three pass plays.

We have simple, consistent adjustment rules. If a receiver goes in motion the Rover will adjust. If there are two backs in the game and one of them goes out, the Rover will adjust. If the offense goes to an empty backfield set the Will linebacker will adjust. He adjusts to all empty sets. That is it. We can adjust to everything. Our kids are smart about that.

We teach as few exceptions as possible. We want to eliminate "What Ifs and Buts." I can't throw chicken bones on the field and tell them what they are going to do. But, I can watch the film and tell what coaches are going to do. I am going to trust that. We do not defend Ghost. Don't "What If" yourself.

We want to put speed on the field. We sacrifice size for speed. We are going to have the fastest guys we can put on the field at all times. In high school that is all we ever did. We may have a 180-pound defensive tackle. But I will guarantee you he could run. This is what I did when I coached in high

school I would put the defensive tackles in the jerseys with low numbers; 8, 9, 10. Those linemen look at those guys with those low numbers and start thinking. "I have to block this running back and he can fly. I don't know if I am fast enough to block him." We put a seed of doubt in their minds. When I would go to coaching meeting the other coaches would ask me why we played so many running backs at tackle? They were not running backs. They just had a running back number on their jersey. We were trying to get the psychological edge on them. Then our players start thinking if they have a low number they must be good or they would not have that number.

We are going to put dependable athletes on the field. We play players that believe that football is important. When I talk with kids in recruiting if football is not real important to them I probably will not recruit that kid. He will not do everything necessary to win the game. It is just like you that are here today. Good football coaches go to meeting and attend the sessions at clinics like this. There are a lot of coaches that could be here today that are not here. Football is not the most important thing to them. It is the guys that football is the most important thing to them that win football games.

When we went to UK we were 101st, 103rd, and 105th in the three defensive categories in the NCAA. They had not had a winning season in about eight years. We took that same bunch of athletes and won five game our first year. We finished in the top 50 in all categories on defense. That may not sound like a lot to you but it was to us. We have gotten better each year. We went to the Outback Bowl and played Penn State tough. We went to the Music City Bowl and played Syracuse tough. It was the first time UK had gone to Bowl Games back-to-back since 1980. We finished in the top 30 in all defensive categories this year. If football is important to you, you can do this.

We defend situations on the field. I never could remember if we were on the plus or minus side of the field when we had the ball or when we were on defense. So we broke the field down like this. We break the field up into six zones.

From the minus 1 to the minus 20-yard line is Zone 1. Most coaches like to grind it out in that area. If it is 5 or 6 yards to go we have to stop them. We have to expect some type of pass in that situation. Usually it will be on first down. They are trying to get the ball out toward the middle of the field.

Zone 2 is from the 20 to the 40. Most coaches are conservative. These are things I have found to be true over the years. They do not want to turn the ball over. They are going to run the ball in that area more than they are going to throw it. Now, that is unless you are playing a June Jones, Hal Mumme, or a Steve Spurrier team. They are going to throw the ball all of the time.

If you are going to win football games you have to play in the extremes. What do I mean by this? If you are a great throwing football team then you are going to throw the football. You know how to pick up every type of blitz. You know where the hot routes are. You know the routes that are easy to complete for your quarterback. You are going to have the edge. If you are playing Nebraska they are going to run the option against you. They are going to play in the extremes. They are going to keep the football. You have to understand that good coaches play in the extremes. That is true for the good defensive coaches. That is how you win.

Zone 3 is the favorite area. It is from the 40-yard line to the 40-yard line. You have to force the punt in this area. You have to be free-wheeling. On third down you have to bump it up and play great third-down coverage.

The fourth zone is where we apply more pressure. It is from the 40 to the 20-yard line. We are going to force the ball a little more. We are going to do more Man Blitzing here, and not as much Zone Blitzing, or Fire Blitzing. We want to break the rhythm of the offense.

Then we get into our Yellow Zone down here. It is from the 20 to the 5-yard line. This is where we want our players on the field that will say, "Run that ball straight at me. If you come at me I will stuff it right here."

The sixth zone is our Red Zone. That is inside the 5-yard line. For us it is actually inside the 3-yard line.

The next area is what we do on DOWN and DISTANCE. First-and-10 is normal yardage. Second-and-4, 5, or 6 are normal yardage. Expect a run then a pass. The play-action pass is very good here. Second-and-1, 2, or 3 are short yardage. That is a waste down. Second-and-8 or more is long yardage. Expect the long gainer, wide play, trap, pass, screen or draw. If it is an option team the quarterback is going to keep it or pitch it. They are not going to hand the ball to the first back on that situation too many times.

For us, third-and-4, 5 or 6 are normal yardage. Expect the run first then the pass. Play-action passes are good on the second or third time in this situation. Third-and-1, 2, and 3 are short yardage and clutch downs. We must not allow the first down. We want to force the punt. If it is a run look for the off-tackle power run in the bubble.

Third-and-7 or more is long yardage. This is a pass first and then the long gainer. Look for wide play, traps, draws, or screens. Again, if it is against an option look, we look for the quarterback to keep or pitch.

We do Down and Distance based on these things: According to field position; the Zone we are in; the score (ahead or behind); the time left to play; 1) Quarter – 2 minutes before a half, 2) 3rd Quarter, right after the half, 3) 4th Quarter, 2 minutes to go.

Now let's talk some defense. This is our Philosophy. The primary objective of defense is to obtain the football for the offense. The three fastest ways to obtain the football are the following:

OBTAINING THE FOOTBALL

Three Downs and out.
Interceptions.
Cause and recover fumbles.

PRIORITIES

1. Aggressive attacking defense.
2. take one play at a time.

PLAY THE NEXT PLAY.
3. Force turnovers.
4. Force teams to make mistakes.
5. Be a great tackling team.
6. Score on defense.

To accomplish the above we must do the following.

MUST

1. Be in excellent playing condition.
2. Eliminate mistakes – make daily improvement.
3. Great execution and second effort.
4. Maintain poise and confidence at all times.
5. Have love and respect for your teammates. *We Play For One Another.*

"Men Have Fought and Winners Have Won Because of Their Commitment to Each Other."

Let me start with our receivers' numbering and letting system. Most teams number the eligible receivers 1, 2, and 3 from the outside to the inside on the strong side of the formation and 1, 2, and 3 from the outside to the inside on the weak side of the formation. When we were coaching in high school we did not have a lot of assistant coaches and we needed to be able to communicate with those that we did have. So we number them from our strong side to the weak side. On the back side we have number 4 and number 5. We knew if we heard a 4 or 5 we were talking about the weak side. It was easier for us to communicate that way.

FLANKER = **Z**
TIGHT END = **Y**
SPLIT END = **X**
HALFBACK = **H**
FULLBACK = **F**

Our first defense is what we call Charger. We play a shade to the weakside and a lose 3 technique to the tight end side. Our ends are called Rush ends. We do not flip flop the R's. We play a 6 or 7 technique on the strong end side. The only people we flip are the tackle and the nose, and the Sam linebacker and the Will linebacker. We do flip the Free Safety and Rover when we have a check on them. Everyone else stays the same.

We turn our belly button to the ball with our Sam linebacker. The Mike linebacker is over the center and he is 5 yards deep. The Will linebacker is in a 40 technique and he is 5 yards deep. The depth will vary depending on down and distance situations. We have a low hole player and a high hole player on each side.

RECEIVERS NUMBERING AND LETTERING

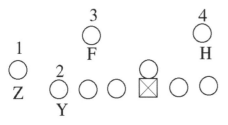

CHARGER

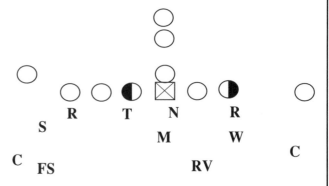

On the snap of the ball we want the front four to get their feet in the neutral zone. We are going to play with our hands and hat and play to the neutral zone.

We want them to come across and then look back inside. If he is on the tight end side the first man that can block the tackle is the strong side guard. If the guard does not block him he stays square and works inside. The next blocker that can get him is the fullback. He sets and takes on the fullback and tries to work all the way down to the B Gap. If the fullback comes at the tackle we want him to put his outside arm on his inside thigh board. We want to knock the hell out of him. After he spills the fullback we want him to wheel it straight up the field. That is the most important part of it. We are trying to make the tailback make a radical bounce on the Power O play outside. When the tailback bounces we want him to bounce East and West.

On the split-end side we want the nose to make life miserable for the center. If he can backdoor the play we want him to. If he can't he can work to the play and front door the play. Most of the time we want the nose to backdoor the play. We want the backside end to squeeze the play inside and stay square. He is responsible for everything coming back to his side. He has the reverse. We do not want him to turn his shoulders to the sideline. He must stay square and shuffle flat down inside.

We have a great player in that position. Dennis Johnson made All-American. He has started for us two years now. He started when he was a true freshman. He played for his father when he was in high school. This is a true story. He started playing high school football when he was in the third grade. I went up to him when he was a freshman and said, "Dennis, how does it feel to be starting as a freshman in the SEC." He replied, "Heck, coach, it is not as bad as when I played for my dad when I was in the third grade."

The Will linebacker is the cutback player. The Corner lines up on the inside of the split end. If the split end is split in a regular position we will play INK on him. To us the INK means inside. If the end is only split 3 to 4 yards we will play some Ork. Outside is ORK. Those are the adjustments on that side. We do not play any mirror, or head up. That is the hardest technique you can teach a corner.

Next is the Mike linebacker. If the Y comes out the Mike must get underneath him. He has Fire Flow. Mike must get underneath the Y end. He is the only man we can get to play the C Gap. If Mike goes over the top of Y the back can cut it back inside and there is a big hole inside. There is a crack inside. What do we tell our Kids? We tell them to put their hat in the crack. If we have a hat in every crack they can not run the football.

If we wanted to play Charger Strong we change the Rover and Sam linebacker. If we did not want our Sam linebacker outside we just switch the two and let Sam play head up and Rover is outside. The call on the wrist band will be Charger or Charger Strong.

CHARGE STRONG

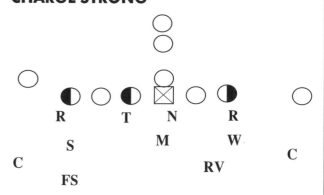

We line up with our front line with the inside hand down and the inside foot back. The reason we do that is because you have to play the option.

This year in the NCAA every team that averaged 300 yards throwing the ball won 50 percent of its games. In the NCAA this year every team that had a player with a 100-yard rushing average won 71 percent of its games. So we are going to stop the Run first. That is the reason we have nine men playing football inside the two wideouts. We have committed nine people to the run. This past year we gave up 89 + yards per game. We were still sixth in our conference. It is a tough conference. It is unbelievable.

We play the same coverage on both Charger and Charger Strong. We play Cover Blue.

Two years ago I went out to Washington State. They do a great job. We got their UP Package from them. If we want to put the Mike and Will up into the line of scrimmage we call it MOB. We could call Charger Strong Mob, Blue. That would be our 42 call on our bands. Everyone looks down at the band and they see 42 and they know what we are going to do.

Let me tell you what we have done with our video people. We do not watch the video together as a team very much. For our next opponent I will put their best plays on the video. We make up the videos and send it home with the kids. We give them a video every week. We know what happens. The girlfriends watch the video with them. If the girlfriend will watch it with them, they will take the time to watch it. We put a little music to the video and we jazz it up a little. We make it an entertainment-type package. My wife sits in the stands and she can hear some of the girlfriends and moms and dads talk about seeing the video. "Tom, Tom, that is the one we saw over at Anthony Wadja's house the other night." So we know the kids are watching the videos. This has been a big plus for us. It is a pain in the butt for the video staff and he hates me, but it is good. Our kids love it.

I hate those offensive coaches that are always trying to get the chalk last. They will shift and split people out all across the field. I can tell you how to beat the Horizontal Stretch. You beat it with Vertical Movement. If they split you wide on the line we walk our linebackers up in the line. I guarantee you they will cut the splits down. Now, as the defensive coach, you have the last domino. My grandfather raised me because my father died when I was in junior high school. My grandfather was the best domino player in the state of Texas. The reason he was so good was because he always held a Double Six and a Six-Five in his hand. Through hell and high water he was going to keep those two dominos. Those were the count dominos and he could always beat you. I tell my kids if they will keep Double Six and Six-Five in their hand they will never get beat.

If the offense oversplits we want to move up on the ball. We crowd the ball as much as possible. If I have a player that is not too fast I will not move him too close to the ball. Those are ability adjustments. You have to adjust to the ability of the kids you are playing. I call those Ability Adjustments.

We play what we call Read Coverage. We played this every snap in high school. In Read Coverage the Sam, Corner and Free Safety read the number 2 receiver. The Will, Corner, and Rover are reading number 4. The Mike is reading the number 3 receiver.

We have our linebackers heels at 5 yards. The corner is back at 7 yards. The first 5 yards off the line is what we call the Uncovered Zone. This is where we read everything they are going to do.

The first thing the Y can do is to come off vertical. If he comes off vertical that tells Sam he is to open and harass the Y, knowing he has help on the top. He becomes the underneath Sail player in case he breaks outside.

This tells the corner he is Man-to-Man on the number 1 receiver. He is playing inside out on number 1. If he is inside tight he can play on the outside on number 1. He uses INK or ORK alignment.

The next thing Y can do is to go away from Sam. If the number 2 receiver goes away we want Sam to drop to the Curl area and look for number 1. If the Curl is not there he looks back inside because something will be coming across to him. The Free Safety will Zone up and play One Half Coverage. He has post coverage.

The last thing Y can do is to go on what we call a Shoot Route. If that happens the Free safety is the Over-the-Top player. Sam is the Curl player. That takes care of everything on that side.

On the back side we just mirror it. The X receiver can go vertical. The Will is the Inside-Out player and the Corner is the Over-the-Top player and in Man-to-Man Coverage.

If the X receiver goes away the Will is going to Zone up. He is looking for the 5 receiver on the Curl. The Rover has One Half Coverage

If the X receiver goes Shoot, Will looks for 5 on the Curl. The Rover is the Over-the-Top player. The Corner has the Shoot route.

This year we finished fifth in the nation on turnovers. We had 17 interceptions and recovered 16 fumbles. We had 33 turnovers. Every time we give the offense the ball from a turnover that is a plus 35 yards for the offense. We figured it up to be 1065 yards that we gave the offense this past year. We have blocked 12 field goals, blocked three punts, and we returned two punts for touchdowns. All of this is a big deal to our defense. I coach the Special Teams and we are going to put the best 11 out there except the quarterback.

On our Blue Coverage we can call Trade. That means we are going to have the Rover take the number 4 receiver. That puts the Corner on the number 5 receiver outside. That Corner plays Ink technique on that outside man. He is walked up as tight on the receiver as he can get without being offside. If you run this defense the two corners will be offside more than anyone else. They are too lazy to look over to the official and ask him if he is line up ok. The offensive players look at the officials and they give them the signal if they are okay or not. They just stick out their arm. The defender can do the same thing. That official will stick out his arm for the defender as well. Ask the official if you are okay. That is what he is out there for.

We press the outside receivers as hard as we can. Why do we press them? In the NFL you can only bump them for the first 5 yards and they can only chuck them one time and then let them go. In college we can bump them until the ball is in the air. Why not press them! We want to beat the hell out of those guys all over the field. That destroys their rhythm. Those little receivers do not like that at all. If they did like it they would be inside with men in the line. We press the two outside receivers. The Corners know they have help on the Post. They do

not have help anywhere else. We are going to Ink or we can Ork. We can play inside or outside depending on the split. The Rover has number 4. We crowd him up to about 6 yards of the line of scrimmage. We walk the Safety down inside at about 7 yards deep. We can run MOB with the Will and Mike.

If we want to play Red Coverage we just flip it. The Free Safety is the low hole player, and the Rover is the High hole player. That is our Red Coverage.

We play our Even look 33 percent of the time. It is a great defense. We shade the R end on the 5 and 9 techniques. We want the nose and tackle head up with the guards. We flip-flop the nose. We run Go and Whip on this look. If we want them to go Strong it is a Go call. If we want them to move weak it is a Whip call. All we want them to do is to get to the gaps and flatten and get into the neutral zone. That is our Go and our Whip on the Even look.

EVEN

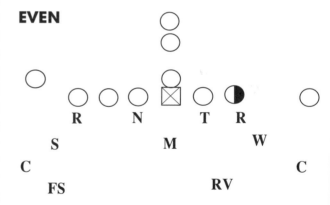

If we wanted to angle the nose and tackle to the gaps we call that Aim Strong and Aim Weak. You may thing that is not a big deal. But that big guard does not know what you are doing.

If we catch the offensive guards sitting back off the ball like all of those cheating guys do we run our DDD call. It is a delayed stunt. We go up the field and then we run the stunt.

Men, I will be around as long as you want to talk. I will be here tonight for the chalk talk. If there is anything we can do just drop me a note. I have enjoyed it. Thank you.

ONE-BACK ATTACK

UNIVERSITY OF UTAH

Eleven years ago when I took the job at the University of Utah I had made up my mind what the recruiting base was going to be. The Islands was one of our targets. We need some players that were excited to play the game. Since I have been at Utah we have had a good relationship with the Islands. I would like to thank the coaches here who have sent me many great players. We have had 53 players from the Islands on our roster from the time I started until now. They have all played extremely well for us. They have made a difference for us. The last 10 years has been the best 10 years of the history of Utah football. We have averaged 7.5 wins for the last 10 years. We have been in five bowl games in the last eight years. A lot of our success has to do with the kids from Hawaii.

I am going to talk about our One-Back Running Attack. It all starts out with our *Dive Play*. That is our first play. Tonight when we have the individual sessions where we go one-on-one, I will be glad to sit down and go through any part of the running game that you want to discuss. I will spend as much time with you as you want. We will go through the technique, the splits, and the thought process.

Our running backs are lined up 6 yards deep. We can run it against the odd front or the even front.

DIVE VS. ODD FRONT

DIVE VS. EVEN FRONT

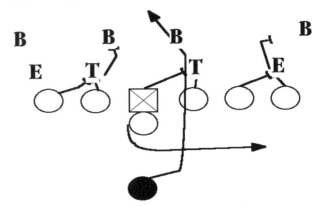

Our next play is our *Zone Play*. This is really our bread-and-butter play. Anyone that runs a lot of One-Back Offense, the Zone Play has to be a big play for you. It is the same concept except the running back is hitting off the outside of the hip of the right tackle. The tight end has a base block. The tackle and guard have a smash block. The inside people have smash blocking.

The technique between the on-side tackle and guard is an interesting combination. Every defensive team slants differently. Some teams slant and penetrate, and some teams cross over and slant. You have to be prepared for the slant or the loop when you come off on the combination block. We do not want to turn the foot outside because we lose our power. We want the tackle and guard to push the linemen as they come off the ball, then one of them will come off and pick up the linebacker. The linebacker could go inside or outside.

The coaching point for the block is this. The first step has to be correct. If you make a bad step on the first step you are in trouble. The first step must be a square step. If you look at your film and find that your blockers are taking rounded steps you have to take them and work against air. Force the players to take square steps. If you take an angle step you give the defender a chance to split the double-team. He can't split a double-team if the guard and tackle are square. The defender can dive under them but he can't split them.

It is just like a lineman pulling up through a hole. He has to be square as he comes through the hole. If you let them, they will round off the block. They will take the easy way out. You think you have them corrected and then all of a sudden they go back to the old habits. We like to run that square drill every day to make sure they keep square.

ZONE VS. ODD FRONT

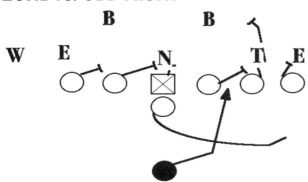

ZONE VS. EVEN FRONT

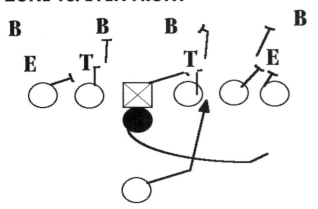

If we have the defense spread wide we use the bucket step. We want to use leverage on the block. As we come out of the bucket, if the defender is a man that penetrates, I am going to use my inside hand and knock him out of the lane. Then the back can cut outside. If the defender is a reader, when I bucket step, he will come into my face. Now I have to accelerate off the opposite foot, bring my hands up, and push and pull. The key is to keep the el-

bows down, and keep the thumbs up so you can push and pull on the defender. When the elbows get outside you lose all of your power. Your elbows have to be down and you have to be able to move in both directions.

Now let me talk about the base technique. Never overstep a base step. If you watch film of offensive linemen you see some of them taking a big giant step on their first step. The defender penetrates and goes by him. Anytime you are using the base block you must take a short first step. When you take a short step you can gather, and you can block against any movement. Most of the time the defenders are not going to sit there and let you knock them off the ball. They are going to give you some type of movement.

The *Zone Play* is the base of our offense. Everything we do comes off this play. We will run the Zone to the strong side and to the weak side. We are going to look for mismatches in the front. We want to know what you do on defense. Do you flip your linemen? We look for mismatches to run the play. We try to get our strength against your weakness. We know that play has to go for us. We must average 5 yards per carry on the play.

Our next play is our *Stretch Play*. Everyone runs the Stretch differently. The technique we use on the Stretch against a 50 look is what we call an Over Technique. The on-side tackle comes off hard and makes contact with the tackle. He is really trying to clear the tackle. He is not going to get too wide on me. The guard is sprinting to the block. He is going to make contact at the point of the tackle. We are sprinting hard and we are going at that area. We make contact and take what happens.

On the Reach Block we go a little wider. If the defense gives us a slant, blood, and a scrape technique, we have what we call a Triple Slip. Teams will slant the tackle and end and scrape the linebacker. When we see that the offense comes back and calls Triple Slip. We slip the tight end to the linebacker, the tackle takes the end, and the guard takes the tackle. The Smash Technique to the inside is a little wider. You are aiming wider on the inside of the tight end. You are trying to flatten out. So, the Over Block is a different combination.

STRETCH VS. ODD FRONT

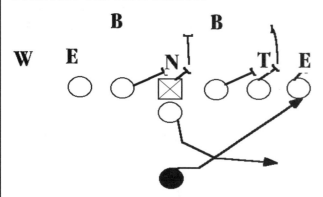

STRETCH VS. EVEN FRONT

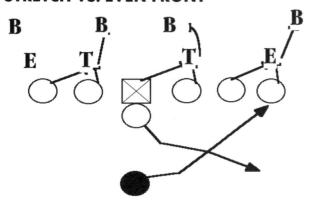

I can't tell you how important the execution of the offensive line is. They have to be able to execute the basic fundamentals in their sleep. They have to know it so well that everyone does it correctly. If you are coaching offensive linemen you have to be precise in what you have them do and how you have them do it. You cannot change the technique from day to day. You have to ask them for the same things every day if you want it to be efficient. You have to make them believe in your system and they must know how it works.

The Dive, Zone, and the Stretch all look the same. They all look the same to the defense. The block on the nose man is a hard block. Most defenses have a good nose guard in college football. You cannot let the nose guard knock you back. If he knocks you back it screws up your running game. You have to

make sure your center can block. You have to have a center that can use leverage. I do not like a tall center. I do not like a center that is 6'4" or 6'5". I like a center that is 6'1" or 6'2". I want a center that is real strong in the lower base. I want a man that has real explosive legs. If he has that he has leverage. I want a center that is strong in the legs so he can move that nose guard. Most of our centers are linebacker types. We may recruit them as linebackers and then move them to center. All of our centers played linebacker in high school. We are looking for guys that can escape, guys that can run, and for guys that have leverage. We are looking for guys that have a strong lower body. We want a man that can move at center. If you have a center that is slow, he will not be able to block any linebackers. If he is slow he will not be able to get off the combination blocks to get the linebacker. You have to have an active man to play center. You have to have a smart man to play center.

A Scoop Block is different than a Smash Block. On an Over Block you run your butt out of there. On a Scoop Block you are stepping. You want to get the nose guard to turn to the side facing the play. If you can do that you have him. You want to push as hard as you can, but don't overstep it. Push the defender's shoulders and try to come up square. The key on the Scoop is that the center has to clear. The center has to clear to get to the off linebacker. So when we say Scoop, the center has to clear the offside linebacker.

If we say Smash, we step and push, and come off the block late and pick up the man wherever he is. On the Scoop Block you want to get your butt out of there.

On the Stretch the back gets downhill and gets outside. We want him to get to the line of scrimmage and then we want him to get into the running lane.

Next is a misdirection play. The hardest play in football for a linebacker to diagnose is the Tackle Trap Play. Everyone can read the Guard Trap. We run what we call 20 and 21 Counter. The technique on this play is extremely important.

Here we talk about the Flash Technique of the left tackle. If I am the left tackle and they have a Whip linebacker sitting up there it means the defensive end is probably going to slant. There are a couple of ways to teach the blocking. If our tackle flashes, and the end slants we wash him. That means the trapping tackle is going to pick up the Whip or he is going to come around and turn up and take the linebacker. When you have a Whip and an end sitting there is more difficult to run.

COUNTER VS ODD FRONT

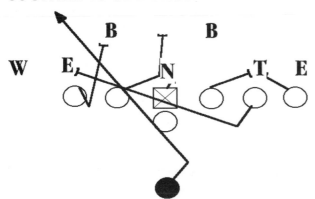

COUNTER VS. EVEN FRONT

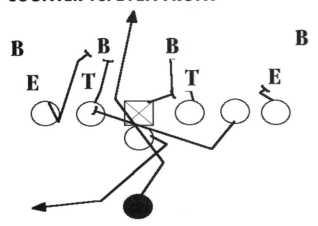

The key to the play is this. What kind of *Set* do you teach your left tackle? How do you determine this? You do this by what the defensive linemen are taught to do. In other words you watch a film of your opponent. You want to know how he gets up the field. What makes him come up the field the fastest? When you find that out, you give that set to your tackle. We will use anything from an arm over, to an arm under, to an arm through, to a deep

set. It all depends on what the defensive line coach teaches his linemen.

As an offensive line coach you study and you study the technique that is being taught. You know their techniques as well as they know it. In that way you become more efficient in what you are teaching.

The double-team inside on nose guard has to be square. On the stretch technique you must make sure your steps are correct. The tight end uses a Seal Block. He has to come down and seal for the pulling tackle. You have a seal block with the right guard and tight end.

We have the Flash Block at the left tackle. We have a Double-Team Block with the guard and center. The right guard and tight end Seal Block. The right tackle pulls and traps.

Now the running back starts downhill just like he does on the Zone Play. He takes that first step and he is running the Zone Play. Then, boom, he is turning back and running the Counter Play.

It is hard to key the trapping tackle. I started running the tackle trap 35 years ago. We were an I formation team at the time. In those days everyone played the 50 Front. Most teams trapped with the guard. You could read the Guard Trap. When we trapped with our tackle it was foreign to those people. We made a living off that out of the I formation.

On the Even Front the Press Technique is really KEY. The center and the right guard have to come out and press the defensive 3 or the 2 technique on the line. The guard cannot step too wide. They have to press, press, and press. They do not have to come to the linebacker until late. The backer is going to be sitting there. He will be there for you. Press, press, and press, and then boom — pop the linebacker.

On the Trap Technique we want to gain as much ground as we can. The influence is the same as the Flash. It depends on what the defensive line coach teaches as to the kind of influence we use. We use the best one to get him up field.

What we like to do in the running game is to tie one play together with another play. To the defense the plays look the same. We tie the G-Scheme together with the Sweep and another play and they all look the same to the defense. The blocking combinations and the running back action all look the same to the defense. You can't sit there and let the defense smash your butt. You have to have combinations.

On the G-Scheme Play we double with the tackle and end. We pull the near guard and kick out. The running back comes through the off-tackle hole. We double the nose man and we use the arrow technique with the backside tackle.

G-SCHEME VS EVEN FRONT

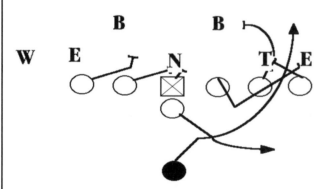

If the defensive end on the play side is lined up a little inside we have the tight end give a call to the guard. He tells him to be alert because he may have to come around two defenders instead of only one. If the tackle and end come inside then our tackle and end block them inside. The guard pulls around two men and turns up. Now, our running back will cut outside and get into the running lane. We crack back with our wide receiver.

We get a call from our tight end that tells us what to do. Now, I hate line calls. I always tell our coaches that I do not want line calls. How many times do you have some offensive lineman say, "I did not hear the line call."? How many times have you heard them say, "I just missed the call."? This is what I

say to him: "Really! Our running back just got his neck broken because you missed the call."

When I first started coaching I had calls everywhere. We were making calls everywhere. I thought I was a sophisticated offensive line coach. We did not block anyone. Now what we do is to take all of the thinking process away from them and let them play the game. *The game is still about blocking and tackling.*

On the G-Scheme the tight end has to get off the tray pretty fast. Arizona will scrape the near linebacker wide and have the offside linebacker cover the onside guard gap. They are real sound in what they are doing on defense. They have great defensive coaches. They are as good as you could have. They understand how to stop what you do. You have to be pretty good if you are going to get something done on offense with them.

The Toss is like the G-Scheme. We want to block the play the same way. We can pull the guard and tackle if the linebacker is coming outside.

TOSS SWEEP VS. EVEN FRONT

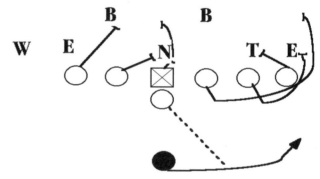

The last in the series is the *Stutter Play*. That is our weak-side *Counter Play*. If you allow penetration when you run this play you are done. You have to know the defense off the ball. Here is a good question. How do you Chip block? Here is how you chip block. If I am going to chip block I am going to drive my hand inside and then come back square. I am not going to round my steps. I punch inside as hard as I can and then square my shoulders. The chip is not an angle. It is a flat step. If you screw it up the nose man will nail your back for a 4 yard loss.

STUTTER (COUNTER) PLAY

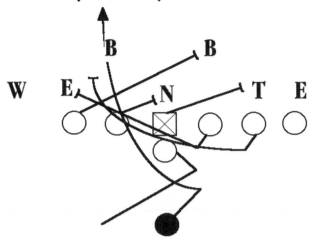

Off any kind of Stutter action you must have a good pass off it. On all of these plays you need to have good play-action passes. If you are running a Zone Play you must have a good play-action pass with it. A lot of teams will play you with an Eight-Man Front. They have a man sitting back as a safety. Then they cheat him up within 3 yards of the line of scrimmage. All of a sudden you are playing against an Eight-Man Front. You can run the Post Route behind the safety to keep him out of the hole and then you can make teams respect what you are doing.

The Stutter or Counter Play is the last part of our One-Back Attack We will run some Speed Option back to the split-end side. We have some other wrinkles that we use.

In going back and looking at this thing there are a couple of things you need to know. A lot of you see what some call the Bastard Fronts where the defense lines up in the gaps. They are running here and running there. What you do is to end up with one scheme. If you have teams that are trying to screw you up this is what we do. We line up and knock them off the ball. If we see that we just line up and we run the gaps. Each man on the line takes one gap—A, B, and C gaps. As soon as the ball is snapped we run into those gaps. We block forward. We are taking what you give us. It is the same for the backside people. We tell the back to take the first crease he sees. That takes all of the thought process away from it. If you play teams that give you a lot of gap looks you can run this. Just block A, B, and C gaps and let the back find the hole. But, you have to knock them off the ball.

If the rules do not hold up, we just Zone Block them. That is option football. You just come off the ball and run. You run until something shows and then you knock the heck out of them. Do not go chasing anyone outside.

I want to show the film of these plays. After the film you can ask questions. That is it. Thank you very much. (Film)

EFFECTIVE USE OF THE SCREEN PASS

SADDLEBACK COLLEGE

Today I'm going to talk about coaching the screen pass. I am going to talk about screen passes from a scheme point of view. I think you will walk away with some good ideas about the screen.

I coached at BYU in 1988 and '89. That is where I came up with the foundation for my offense. Just like other coaches we've drawn on napkins, talked to other coaches, and come up with some creative ideas that go into the formation of your offensive system.

The screen pass is the most underrated part of an offensive package. If a team is considered balanced or employs a strong passing attack, screen passes serve as a great complement to enhance offensive production. I'm going to talk about the how's and why's of the screen pass. I am going to give you seven of our best screen plays. I have nine screens in our scheme every single year.

Why do teams run screen passes? 1) Slow down the pass rush. 2) Warn defenses to blitz less or a big play could occur. 3) Complement the pass game. 4) To keep the defense guessing. 5) Big play potential with low risk.

I don't know about you, but I only have one good quarterback. I want the defense to know early in a game, if they blitz my quarterback, I will screen them. To me the screen pass is a long handoff.

When should you run screen passes? I like to run them early in the season. I run the screen a lot early in the first, second, and third games. When the opposing coaches and I swap films, I want them to see those screens. When they see us being successful throwing screens, it makes them think twice about pressuring the quarterback too hard. It will probably make them a little more conservatives when they compete against you.

I like to run the screen early in a game. That sends the message to watch out for the screen throughout the game. I like to screen against teams that are real aggressive. I like to screen against teams that like to hit, and really get after the quarterback.

When are running screens dangerous? Screens are dangerous against "Reading" defenders. If you play teams that read a lot it is difficult to run screens against them. Teams that have big and slow defenders are hard to screen against. Guys that are big and slow are not going to get after the passer. They are going to hang too close to the line of scrimmage. Late in the game when teams are beginning to fatigue is a bad time to run a screen. I run a no-huddle offense and we run about 25 percent more plays than other teams are used to seeing. Because of that, they become fatigued late in the game. When the offense is option and/or run-oriented, I don't like to screen. If the defense is playing option, they are more disciplined in their accounting for you personnel.

Establishing the screen can slow down the pass rush, keep defenses from blitzing often, and screens should simulate pass and run scheme actions. I don't particularly want to hit a screen pass for a 30-, 60-, or 70-yard gain. I just want to let the defense know I will screen. I run the screen to give my quarterback more time to throw the football on other passing plays.

I have cutups of my screens when they produced big gains and when they gained only 5 yards. I don't have the type of cutups that you guys have been seeing from the rest of these guys. I don't have a 50-foot tower or end-zone shots. I have tape just like you guys.

I'm going to show you seven of these screens. I'm going to tell you the history of the play or where it came from. I'll tell you how we practice them efficiently. I'll show you the techniques and responsibilities of each position. Than I'll talk about formation/motion variations and timing.

The screen passes I've drawn up are out of the single-back set. However, most of these screen passes came from two-back offenses. I also have them drawn up against a 4-2 look on defense. When I was at BYU, I was playing a little tennis for fun. There was a book called the *Inter-game of Tennis*. In the book, it explained how good players could hit the ball back so quickly. They would look at the seams of the ball and focus on it. I wondered how they could see the seams of the tennis ball when it was coming that fast at them. What they meant was this. Since they had focused their attention on the seams of the ball, the attention had focus clearly on the ball itself. As a result of that, the ball looked bigger. That was called **Intentional Narrow Focus**. I took that idea and transferred that to my receivers and running backs catching the football. I had them look at the stripes on the ball and later the cross hairs. Little did I know Steve Largent had been doing this for years. Give them the tools to concentrate, tell them to look at the seams on the football, it will make it look bigger.

Here are the screens, I'm going to cover. They are: Misdirection Screen, Stanford, Throwback Screen, Fake Throwback Screen, Middle Screen, WR Screen, and Middle Screen Special. Some of you probably run some of the screens already. But I'm going to show you some ideas that may help.

The first screen is a *Misdirection Screen*. Let me share something with you before we get into this screen. I went to Saddleback College this year and was hired so late that I didn't get a chance to recruit. We had eight ACL injuries this year. I had none in the previous eight years. My starting right tackle was recruited as a tight end. His coach said he had great hands but couldn't block a lick. I lost six running backs. We are so weak and small up front we had no running game in our goal-line of-

fense. The last game of the season we went with a no-back offensive set. It wasn't because it was a great idea. It was because we had no running backs. This screen scored eight touchdowns for us this year. All of them came inside the 10-yard line.

Here is the basic idea. If you have a right-handed quarterback, I would suggest only throwing this to the right. I would never throw it to the left. The center, right guard, and tackle are the only linemen that release. They are going to count ONE-THOUSAND-ONE, ONE-THOUSAND, and release. That is for one and a half counts. The right tackle quick pass sets, lets the defensive end go by, and comes out flat. He is coming on an inside out angle at the corner. If he comes out too high, he will end up clipping the back. The right guard comes out flat. He knows his guys is the Mike linebacker. He knows from the beginning that he is responsibility for him. If the Mike linebacker is in the gap and tight he will stay and block him. The center comes out and pick up anyone coming across the field. The backside guard and tackle are running normal pass protection.

We are in a double-wide slot set. The two receivers away from the play run a switch route and release downfield. The split end to the side of the screen is going to block the strong safety. If he is an aggressive hitter we don't worry about him. He will bypass him and go up on the free safety. If the strong safety backs off in coverage and hangs in the area, the split end has to seal him inside.

MISDIRECTION SCREEN

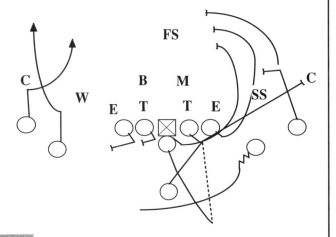

The right slot back is faking a reverse to the left. The quarterback comes out, gets depth, and fakes to the tailback on the inside zone play. The quarterback uses his hand to fake the running back and tucks the ball on his inside hip to hide it from the people on the edges. The slot receiver comes behind the quarterback and fakes the reverse. The quarterback doesn't put out the ball for the fake. The receiver makes the fake by rolling the shoulders and gets depth like he has the ball. As soon as the quarterback makes the reverse fake, he has to get his head around and continue to get depth. He will end up throwing the ball off his back foot and could get hit. But his momentum is going backward so he is not going to get hurt. The tailback catches the screen in the area of the right guard. If the quarterback tried to throw this play to the left, it would be really difficult for him to get his hips opened up to make the throw.

We got this screen from a little high school who hit it for 90 yards against us. I liked it so well I put it in our playbook. We practice screens by introducing the ideas during two-a-day practices. We have special teams periods during our practice organization where I take the quarterback, snapper, whoever is catching the screen, second-string quarterback, and work with them on the timing of the play for about 15 minutes. Our offensive line coach works with our screen package in individual periods at the beginning of the year. After that he doesn't do that much with them. The only time we work on the screen play is Tuesday. We have a screens and specials period where we work on our screens. We work the team against "air" for timing and conditioning. We run through all screen plays during this period. The kids run the screens, sprint 20 yards, and jog back 20 yards. They get in the huddle and get ready for the next play. We are working on timing and technique against "air." We do that for 15 minutes. During the team periods I will script in the screens we are going to use in the up coming game.

This next screen we got from Stanford in 1994, when Bill Walsh was there. They ran it out of a two-back set. Let me fill you in on some concepts

with this one. We use check with me on this play. This is a low-key screen. It is really easy. Against the 4-2 look, this play can go either way because the defense is balanced. I drew it up to go left. The inside slot on the back side runs a quick slant. The reason for that is to have an answer for the Mike linebacker blitzing. If he blitzes we throw hot to the inside slant. I have never had to throw hot on this play, and we have run it 60 times. But I want an answer in case it happens. The quarterback's first read is to check the Mike linebacker. The split end on the back side is an outlet man. If we have to throw the ball away or dump it, the split end retreats behind the line so we don't get a penalty for having linemen downfield.

The left tackle invites the defensive end up the field, and drives him outside. The play-side guard uses a short set and forces the defensive tackle inside. The uncovered lineman is going to pull. That is the center. He takes a quick pass set, stays flat, and comes out to seal the inside linebacker to his side. What generally happens is the center ends up going in front of the defensive tackle. The running back steps up, waits for the defensive end to get upfield, and moves out to take the pass slightly outside the tackle box. He is keying the inside and outside linebacker on his setup to decide which way to take the ball after the catch. Hopefully the center can seal the inside linebacker. If the outside linebacker flows outside, we are in great shape. As soon as the tailback catches the ball, he turns it up into the seam between the linebackers. If the outside linebacker hangs, the tailback may have to go outside of him.

STANFORD

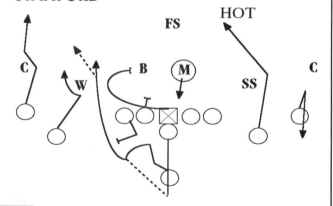

The Throwback Screen is one of my favorites. I learned this screen at BYU. We would run trips to the field and a single tight end into the boundary. We could throw the screen to the tight end into the boundary. You can throw this screen to anybody. This screen is drawn up with the quarterback in the shotgun, but you can run it from under the center. The play side receivers run some type of switch route and end up blocking downfield. When we sprint our quarterback out we bring someone in motion to help on the force man. The play-side tackle is blocking solid and controls his block at the line of scrimmage. He is not involved in the screen. The center, left guard and tackle, are involved in the screen blocking. They are going three full counts before they come out on the screen. Linemen, when you say a three count, they think that is one and a half. You have to get your coaches to really work on the rhythm and timing count before the movement. When linemen hear the work screen, they start thinking about leveling some pencil necked defensive back in the secondary. We tell our linemen in the open field, all we want him to do is play basketball with man-to-man defense. All we want him to do is get his base sound, move his feet, slide and get in front of the defensive backs. We don't want them to kill them. We want them in position to set a screen or pick on the defensive backs.

The outside receiver is 6 yards wide and bypasses the corner and goes to the free safety. If the outside linebacker blitzes off the back side we let him go. In fact, if we hit him, he could get involved in the play. The left tackle comes flat and probably will block the corner. The left guard has the inside linebacker. The center comes out and seals anything coming across the field. I don't want these guys to give up much ground. If they do they will be right in the middle of the throw. We pass set, are good actors, but don't let the defensive linemen beat us until three full counts. If someone wants to hang, we'll take our outside arm and shove him upfield.

The quarterback takes the ball in the shotgun and sprint right 5 yards and back 5 yards. He doesn't run straight back 5 yards and than over 5 yards, but he goes to that point. He looks, plants, turns, and throws. When we are teaching I put a cone at the spot he is to drop to. When we are in team periods, I stand at the spot he has to get to before he throws the ball. The back shows pass protection, than drifts backside outside the tackle box to catch the ball. Once the back catches the ball, we tell him the sideline is his friend. Don't cut the ball back. Run to the sideline because we are setting up a picket line.

THROWBACK SCREEN

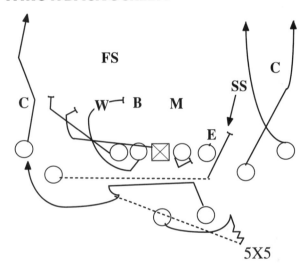

5X5

The throwback screen has been a really good screen. I don't throw it down inside the 10-yard line, but it has been a very successful screen for us.

We threw the throwback screen so many times, the Mike linebacker started to sit on the play. We ran a Fake Throwback Screen. We brought the slot in motion to help seal on the end. The center, left guard, and tackle, do exactly the same thing they did on the throwback screen. The only difference is they are coming out on a count of two rather than three seconds. The tailback shows the screen and prepares to catch the ball. The slot receiver and split end to the play side, are blocking the free safety and corner.

The quarterback takes the snap and retreats to a 3-by-3-yard spot. He looks at the back and does some play acting. He wants to look like he is in a panic. As he panics he gains depth. The play is all about getting the defense to believe what is going on. The H-back that we sent in motion, holds for three and a half counts, and turns around. He is outside the tackle box. The play-side tackle takes a 3 count and goes after the strong linebacker and kicks him out. The strong linebacker probably has widens because of the slot receiver's pattern. This screen takes some time to develop and it does take a little bit of guts. If something goes wrong, the quarterback just launches the ball out of bounds. I am not going to call this play in a third down situation. I am going to run it on a second and short or something like that.

THROWBACK FAKE SCREEN

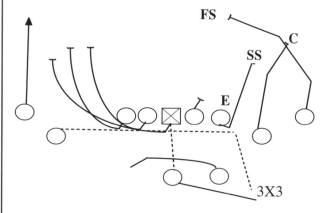

The next one is the Middle Screen. It seems like everyone runs this play. I'm just going to share a couple of things with you. You can run the middle screen to any receiver you want. In my opinion there are a couple key things to remember. The first thing is timing. For us we believe, the receiver needs to be thrown the ball so he catches it 4 yards outside the tackle. That is our aiming point. It doesn't matter whether I am in shotgun or under the center.

The right tackle drop steps, sets for a count, and takes the first man to the outside. The center and guards are taking the two inside linebackers. If there is a good linebacker inside, we may double team him with the center and the guard to that side. If we think we can handle them we will have the center go for the free safety if he is not covered. You have to coach your linemen to get away from the

thought of leveling people in the open field. We want them to get into position to shield them off to the outside.

The most important thing on this play is the timing. Choose the guys carefully that you want to throw the middle screen to.

MIDDLE SCREEN

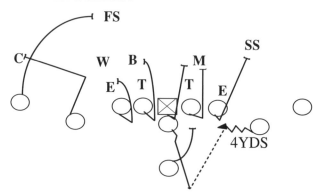

I can throw variations of this screen. Personally I don't like to throw middle screens out of a two-back set. I am trying to spread the defense and a two-back set doesn't do that. I like to throw it out of a one-back or an empty backfield.

The quick screen or Bubble Screen is the next screen I want to talk about. We do some things differently than other teams. I coached high school football and this throw is a problem. The quarterback takes one step and wings the ball to a receiver. The split end determines who is the problem in the throw. If the inside defender is too far off the receiver, the split end takes the corner. If he feels there is a problem with the inside defender, he cracks him. If inside receiver takes a belly step and flares toward

BUBBLE SCREEN

the sideline, that is a difficult throw for any quarterback. Here is what we do differently than other teams. As soon as the ball is snapped the receiver back paddles toward the sideline. We tell the quarterback to throw to the front shoulder of the receiver. By doing that, we eliminate the backward pass which could be a fumble if not caught. We could just as easy throw the ball the other way with the double slot set.

Let me show it to you from the Trips Set. If we split the Y, H, and R receivers into the trips set, we have particular rules for each man. We tell our Rip or R receiver he is cracking on the number 2 defender. The Y or Yoda receiver, is to block the man covering the H-receiver, unless he is of no consequence to the play. In that case he kicks out on the corner. Even if we don't block the corner, I am getting the ball to one of my best athletes, in an open space, and one on one with a defender.

BUBBLE SCREEN TRIPS

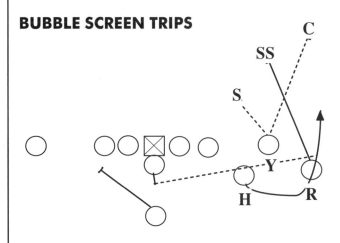

The next thing is a Fake Middle Screen. This has been a good play for us. Our outside receivers come down and start yelling, "SCREEN, SCREEN, SCREEN." Hopefully the defenders will bite and play the middle screen. The inside slot runs a corner route into the wide side of the field. We can throw it out of three or two wide receivers. But I think it is more effective from the three wide receiver set. If for some reason the corner backs off, the quarterback checks back side to the split end running what we call a PIN route. The PIN route is a post-in route similar to a dig pattern.

FAKE MIDDLE SCREEN

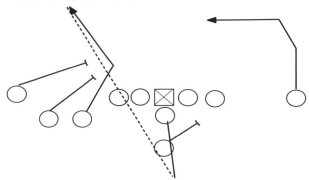

We also have variations on this play. Both wide receivers are faking the inside block. The inside slot is taking a path to kick out the corner. He by passes the corner and runs a flag route. The backside pattern is the same. We throw the ball high and outside just like you would on a corner route.

FAKE BUBBLE SCREEN

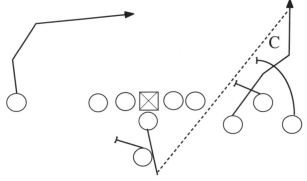

The last thing I want to share with you is this. I am the head football coach at a place called Saddleback Community College. We play in the Mission Conference in southern California. I know there are many athletes in Hawaii who don't get the opportunity to play Division I football. Our rules are I cannot contact any of them first. If you are interested, feel free to let me know. Once they have contacted me, I can start to communicate with them. We would love to have any of your young men come play for us. I want to say thank you to the Nike clinic for allowing me to come and share with you coaches. I think you live in one of the most beautiful places in the entire world. Thank you very much for letting me come and talk.

TIPS TO HELP ORGANIZE THE DEFENSE

GEORGIA TECH

Thank you. This is your clinic. If there are some things you want to talk about just sound off.

I've been coaching for 32 years. I left this morning to come up here. We've just got off the recruiting trail. My wife got me up this morning about 5:30 a.m. She looked at me and said, "George I believe you love football more than you love me." It's 5:30 in the morning, and I didn't know what to say. I probably said the wrong thing when I replied. I ask her if she was talking about pro or college football. I'm sure I won't have a warm welcome when I get home.

I've coached at all levels. I've coached in the pros, college, and high school. Things really don't change. When you get done with your season you have to evaluate what you have done and where you are coming from. In staff meetings the first things we may be looking for are the reasons we didn't play good defense.

I talk about *defensive errors*. The first things I look at are our adjustments. We go back to our base defense. On defense you are only as good as your base defense. The guys that don't play good defense try to change every week. We want to know if the *adjustments were correct*. The second thing has to do with the defensive coordinator. Was there a *poor call* made? We have a game plan. Were the calls made in the game plan, and was it what we practiced? These sessions are not fun sessions. I want some answers as to why things didn't go well.

The second thing I look at is *individual error*. Are they carrying out their responsibility? Are they playing poor techniques? Are they out of position or lined up wrong? That drives me crazy if they are lining up wrong, because that is the coaches' fault

if they are not aligned properly. That is the stuff the coaches are supposed to get done during the week.

The third thing we talk about is *lack of contact*. When I talk about lack of contact, we look at our front. After the ball is snapped, if they end up more than a yard from their original alignment I call that "K." That means he got knocked off the line of scrimmage. That is how I grade it. If he gets a "K" that means he is catching people instead of attacking them.

The other part of that is control of the line of scrimmage. If you can't control the line of scrimmage, that means you are going to lose.

The fourth area we talk about in our meetings is *missed tackles*. I don't worry about poor tackles. I worry about missed tackles. The thing I notice most is that they do not wrap up with the arms. Pro football is the worst example of that.

When you see on our grade sheets "G and G- (Minus)" that means how many times they were on the ground. If a player is on the ground he can't make plays. If you go back and look at your defense when you have given up a big play, I'll bet you money that seven of your 11 players were on the ground. They are going to get knocked down. But the most important thing you teach is getting up off the ground. If a player gets a "G" he got knocked down. If a player gets a "G-" that means he hit the ground and stayed there. Some of these guys look like they have been shot. If I see a guy hit the ground and he doesn't jump up or his head doesn't snap up that is a "G-." When he gets a "G-" he is going to run hard Monday night. When the head snaps up that means that guy is trying to get off the ground.

If a guy has too many "K's" and "G's" on his grade sheet, we move him to offense. He can't play defense. I am very critical in that staff meeting, but that is how you get better. I don't like *Yes Men*. I like guys that are going to sit down and make a point and argue. I don't want to be telling guys what to do. I want them thinking on their own. However, when we leave that meeting we are all on the same page. That is how you become good coaches.

The next things we talk about are our objectives. Basically if you *don't give up a long run or pass*, you will be in most games. Preventing the long run or pass equates to field position. *No missed assignments*. That is how you get beat. When I was with the San Diego Chargers, we lost our first four games. I counted up the defensive calls we had made in those four games. Counting coverage change-ups, line blitzes, and things like that, we had made 168 calls. We sat down and cut that back to 32 calls and we went 12-2 the rest of the season and won the AFC. It is not the amount of calls. It is what you are teaching that the kids can get done.

No foolish penalties. Jumping offside in a third-down situation is an example of that. That is concentration and poor coaching. All the great defenses I've been around have always played *great short-yardage defense*. That has to be one of your objectives because that is what gets you off the field. Those short-yardage battle are the ones you have to win. You have to win 75 percent of them.

We have to *stay focused on turnovers*. What I do every day in practice when we practice as a team, I put down **CPR**. That stands for *Club-Punch-Rip*. Those are take-away techniques. I like gadget words. When we say CPR our players know we are talking about take-aways.

Every team period we have in practice, I'm going to focus on CPR. In our script of plays I'll put CPR next to one or two of them. How many times have you been on the sideline and heard, "We need the ball back!"? You need to practice as a team at getting the ball back. We have all kinds of individual drills that teach those thing, but we don't do it in team drills. If there are 25 plays in that team period, two of those plays will be CPR plays. The defense knows which plays are CPR plays, but the offense doesn't. When those plays come up, the ball better come out on the run. If it doesn't, the defense will pay for it after practice.

There is nothing worse then saying you have to get the ball back and have never worked on it as a team. The first guy in secures the tackle. The next guys are clubbing, punching, or ripping, trying to make that damn ball come out. On those two plays the ball better come out. That is how you get better on takeaways.

That is basically the objectives of the defense. Philosophies of defenses don't change very much from pro to college. We are a *Put-the-Ball-Down Team*. I don't want to know about sudden change and all that stuff. When the offense fumbles the ball I don't know what to tell the defense. You see the defense huddled up. What is the coach telling them? Is he telling them the offense fumbled the ball? The defense shouldn't be playing any different than they were before the ball was fumbled. *Just put the ball down and let's play*. That is what I sell our defense on. Turnovers are going to happen on offense. I don't think you should make a big deal about it.

If we are on the field for more than three plays at a time, I want to know why. Was it our calls or their execution? That is where CPR comes into effect.

I'm not trying to tell you what to play defensively. But your package has to be flexible enough to defend the field, boundary, and formation. If you are going to set in the same defense all day, the guy you are playing is going to attack you into the boundary. When they do that, your defense better have an answer.

I don't think you need a lot of fronts and coverages. You need coverage change-ups. It is not important the scheme you choose as your deep coverage. What is important is what you are doing underneath the deep coverage. If you are not doing something underneath I will pick you apart. That goes for throwing as well as running.

Everything you put into your package must be sound. All the adjustments we make to motion and shifts have to be sound. If a coach wants to install something new, he has to go through 32 formation change-ups to add it. If there is one that doesn't work, I won't add it.

Let me talk about field position awareness. I took 10,000 plays and came up with these numbers. When the offense starts with the ball on the minus-10-yard line it has a 2.5 percent chance of scoring. That is a field goal or touchdown. When they start on the minus-40 it becomes 11 percent. When they start on the 50-yard line, they are going to score 25 percent of the time. That tells you to be aware of field position. Great defensive teams play good field position. That's why turnovers are so important. They establish field position.

Everyone grades their players. You may have a guy who grades out at 80 percent, but he hasn't done a thing. No one has run the ball at him. Take this down, this may help you. This is how we grade. We grade on a scale of 2-1-0. If he does everything right, with great technique and play-making, he gets a 2. If he makes a play, but it was because the offense made a mistake, or his technique was wrong, he gets a l. If he doesn't do anything correctly, he gets a 0. We take the total amount of plays he has and divide it into his points, the average should be about 1.5. The further a player is from the ball the higher his grade should be. The closer you are to the ball the lower the grade. That average grade is not important to me. His productivity grade is the thing that is important to me.

We won the national championship in 1990. These grades I'm going to show you were the productivity grades for that team. We were in the top three defenses in the country. Our nose tackle was involved in one out of every five plays. Our tackles were one out of seven. Our Sam and Will, and our

outside linebackers were one out of five. Our inside linebackers were one out of every three. The boundary corner and free safety were one out of seven. The field corner was one out of eight plays because he wasn't involved in a lot of support.

In 1989, Bobby Ross was the head coach at Georgia Tech. He thought this kid was playing well because he was grading out 1.8. I kept telling him the kid wasn't doing anything. He was grading out well because he wasn't making mistakes. But he wasn't making any plays. I went back and graded productivity.

I used these things to grade my players: 1) tackles, 2) cause fumbles, 3) recover fumbles, 4) interceptions, 5) tackles of loss, 6) pass breakups, 7) deflected passes or tips, 8) sacks, and 9) hurry (pressure), as the basis for play-making and productivity. If a guy played 50 plays and had 10 of those points, his productivity was one in five. You can win with productivity like that.

When I graded the guy who was averaging 1.8, his productivity grade was one in 13. Your defense needs to be productive. This type of grading made us better as a football team. This tells you the guys who are making plays.

That reminds me about the guy who came home and his wife was waiting for him. He walks in the door and she smacks him with a frying pan. He said, "What is that all about?" She said that she went to clean his pants and found a note in his pocket that said "Love Betty." He told her that was a racehorse he bet on and won $500. He gave her $100 and told her to go buy a dress. The next night he came home and there was his wife with the frying pan again. He said, "What is that all about?" She said, "Your horse called today."

The productivity grade made us a better team because it made the coaches more aware of who was playing good. It wasn't so much the players, but the coaches. Go back home and grade one film this way and you will be amazed. You will have guys who you think are playing well that are doing nothing. The reason they are grading well is because they are not doing anything wrong.

The next thing we do is like everyone else. We do the personnel categories so we know who is on the field. When we talk to the people in the press box and they tell me, the offense has **REGULAR PERSONNEL** on the field, I know what they are playing. We chart those personnel groupings:

	RB	TE	WR
REGULAR	2	1	2
PAIR	2	2	1
QUEEN	2	0	3
CLUB	1	1	3
FULL	3	2	0
EMPTY	0	2	3

The reason I want to know that is because of their tendencies. They are not going to change. Our people upstairs tell me they have Ace personnel on the field. Now I start to think about the bootleg, stretch game, and gut game. Code everything up so it cuts down on the time it takes to get the defenses in the game. If you are calling them you want to make sure you know what's on the field. Don't let those offensive coaches fool you. Make them show you what they can do. They don't do a lot. They spend most of their time in college looking for their next job. One place I was at, they had co-coordinators. They asked me if I had ever worked with two coordinators on offense. I told them I had once. When they asked me what happened, I told them they both got fired at the same time. One guy has to make decisions. That guy is the coordinator. He needs help from the rest of the assistants. You need to know what is on the field and you need to know quickly.

Let me show you something. People will tell you they play Cover 2. My first question to them is what type of Cover 2 do you play? Do your corners sink or do they play hard? As soon as they tell me how their corners play, I know how to attack them. Do the corners sink and play the 7 cut? Do your corners jump the 1 cut? If they do, all of a sudden teams are throwing the 7 cut on your safety. That is the decision you have to make. If you are going

to play it, you must have change-ups outside. The corners have got to be able to press and run. They have to be able to hit, come off at 7 yards, and catch it. They can sink and read number 1 or number 2. Don't be a constant Cover 2, where you do the same things every time. If the offense knows what the corners are doing, you are not going to win if they've got equal people.

You are either a zone drop team or a progression team. We do both, because I think you need to do both. If you come out in a pro set right with an open backfield, we call that Left Split. The left call is the two-receiver side. We number the receivers starting from the call side. The flanker is 1, tight end is 2, split back to the tight end is 3, split back to the split end is 4, and the split end is 5.

PROGRESSION NUMBERING

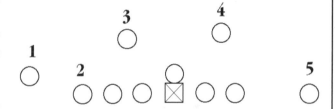

Our underneath coverage people know the numbering system. On every call someone is responsible for those progressions. This is man within a zone concept. We can spot drop, but I don't like to cover air. That is just killing grass. The strong corner knows he has a progression on number 1 to number 2. That is his progression. If number 1 disappears inside, he is looking for number 2. It is still in a zone concept, but we are looking for men. The Sam linebacker progression is 2 to 3. If 2 goes vertical and 3 comes out, the Mike linebacker should give him a release call. The Mike linebacker has a progression of 3 to 2. That is called progression pickup. The Will linebacker has 4 to 5 and the weak corner has 5 to 4.

In every coverage we play, we spot drop it and progression it. It all depends on what the offense is doing to attack us. The corners play cover 2 press, 2 catch, 1 by 7, 3 step jam, and 2 trap. On the 2 trap, I'm telling the corner, if number 1 makes an outside cut, he is going to sink at a depth of 17 yards. Our safeties are about 12 yards deep. I make our corners cover the number 1 receiver for 17 yards. At 17 yards the ball has to be launched. I expect my safeties to make plays from 21 yards to the end of the field. The corner has 17 yards of the 21. On 2 trap the corner carries the number 1 until he sees number 2 come to the flat. He jumps that move right now. The strong safety is keying number 2. As soon as he sees the break outside, he breaks like a son-of-a-gun on number 1. That is 2 trap.

2 TRAP

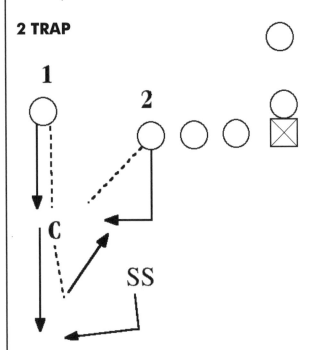

Everyone who wins consistently *can run the ball* and *stop the run*. You can throw the ball in your underwear, but you better be able to run it and stop it. I'm not saying you don't need to throw but when you look at history, the teams that win consistently do those two things.

Here are our change-ups in cover 2. The first one is **2 Bird Dog**. That means whoever has progression on number 2 has him man-to-man. That stops the crossing routes and things like that.

If they have a great receiver in the number 1 position, I'll call **2 Tag**. That tells the corner on number

1, he is in man coverage on number 1. It looks like Cover 2, but that corner has number 1 all over the field. Everyone else is playing cover 2 because it doesn't effect your support on the run. The same thing to the split-end side would be **2 Cinco**. That means the weak corner has the number 5 receiver all over the field man-to-man. That eliminates your progression and makes it easier for the underneath linebackers.

If I call **2 Poncho**, we are on number 1 and 5 receivers man-to-man. The linebackers are going to zone everything. I don't like true man coverage. When the offensive players see the linebackers in man coverage they start running crossing routes and the linebackers end up chasing fast backs around.

The next thing is **2 Jump**. I'm going to take 3, 4, and 5 out of the game with man coverage. We don't go into every game with all those change-ups. I want to see what you do on offense. We go into each game with a mini-package. That gives us certain things to take different guys out of the game. In high school a team my have one good receiver. They line him up all over the place. We would call **2 Jersey**. That means wherever he lines up, play him man-to-man. Whoever has that progression is man-to-man on him.

The key to good coverage is the ability to get to the quarterback. We play all the coverages. We play zone, man, and combination coverage. The key to all those coverages is *Pass Rush*. If you don't get a pass rush, those defensive backs are on an island and they are not good enough. I make no bones about getting after the quarterback. When I was in the pros, rushing the passer was the biggest thing they did. Some of those guys in the pros are making $160,000 a game and some are getting $2500 for every sack. If they pressured the guy, they get another $1000. That is the extra incentives in their contracts. That's why they jump up and demonstrate so much.

I know you can't pay people in college and high school, but you better get some real live *Jesse's* who don't like people. I tell our defense they can't sack the quarterback every time. But anytime the back of his head hits the ground, that is like a sack to me. We play through to the echo of the sound of the whistle. We want to hit the quarterback. Most teams are like the NFL; they have one good quarterback. The second quarterback has the best job in the NFL. However, as soon as the team has to play him, they cut him because he is not good enough.

If you are going to blitz and rush the passer you better know about protections. You have to think what you are doing when you blitz. If you are blitzing with six guys and they are blocking with seven, that's stupid. Study their protection. Most teams, when you line them up, are a 3-3 protection unit. They are blocking with five linemen and one back. They are generally free releasing one back. As soon as you know how they are protecting, you know how to rush and what type of game to use. If they are blocking five linemen and both backs, send eight on the rush. That is when you blitz smart.

We have six drop-back protections that we use. We have six so people can't get tendencies. We have two or three teams in our conference that only have two or three protections. If I can rush four to the weak side, I can get home almost every time against these guys. That is big because you are making them throw hot or make sight adjustments all the time. Know where the center is going on protection. Most of the time he is assigned to the Mike linebacker.

That is basically some of the thoughts on defense that we have. We are a seven-man front and play basically a 4-3 defense. There is no secret to coaching. It is what you can do and what your kids can do.

When I coached high school I was at a school that had 4800 kids. When I took over they weren't winning. They had two freshman teams and two JV teams, along with a varsity team. We had 14 coaches. It wasn't the kids fault they were losing, it was the coaches. After the first year I fired eight coaches. You are here tonight because you are trying to get better. I love coaching football. I think the high school coaches are the keys to America. Keep working at it. You are more than welcome down at Georgia Tech. Atlanta is a nice place to come into—especially if you are single.

That reminds me about this guy who wanted to get his wife something for their anniversary. He went into this sleep shop. He wanted to get his wife a nightgown. He asked how much the first one was and the clerk told him it was $50. He told her to give him the sheerest one they had. When he asked the cost he found out it was $500. He took it home, gave it to his wife, and told her to go up stairs and put it on. He laid down on the couch. She went up stairs. The nightgown was so sheer, that she decided to come down nude. The guy looked up and saw his wife. He said, "You would think for $500, they would iron the thing for you."

Fellows it has been a pleasure being here. Have a great clinic and enjoy yourself.

THOM PARK, PH.D.

LEADING THE MODERN FOOTBALL PROGRAM

FORMER COACH

In the recent epic film *Saving Private Ryan*, actor Tom Hanks portrays Army Captain John Miller. Seated on a bridgehead in northern France, a bullet through his breast and his life blood ebbing out of him, and he looks up at Private Ryan and says, "Earn this." This scene captured the hearts of American patriots everywhere because it represents the essence of those values that we as Americans cherish so dearly. Tom Hanks' character portrays not only admirable and cherished patriotism, but also communicates effective leadership that each of us as football coaches might seek to emulate. Leading the modern football organization is more challenging today than it has ever been. Understanding how to lead and how to communicate to your players and to your organization through your leadership style is a skill set that each coach critically needs today.

If we look at business, industry, education, the military, government, or the political environment, we know that the top 10 leadership and management concerns rank effective communication at the very top. Leaders must be effective communicators. Increasingly, it is clear the ability to interact with your subordinates, in the case of a coach with your players, and to move them to do what it is they must do toward the success of the team and the football program is the critical function of the head coach. The essence of this task is to communicate through a relationship, and assistant coaches must likewise relate to their subunits and players.

Coaching then, like leadership, is a specialized form of attempting to influence the behavior of others within the context of a football organization. Giving your subordinates feedback on their performance is an aspect of communication that is critical to the role of coaching and is one of the top leadership and management concerns across any context. It is clear that leadership style and leadership skill is one of the critical variables in moving a football organization toward success.

The call for leadership is greater than it has ever been before because sport, and football in particular, is a teaching medium of criticality in our culture and society. Just as we admire the sacrifices embodied in the movie *Saving Private Ryan*, sport is a mechanism that can preserve, protect, enhance, and continue the great values that have made our society and our culture what they are. This is why the role of the coach in transcending the winning and the losing of football, is so important because coaches are also great teachers of young people. The why of leadership can be asked at many levels and it is important in many ways. Optimizing and enhancing your leadership skills as a coach with your team is therefore extremely important. As a football coach, you are in a leverage position as the leader of your team as well as a role model and authority figure in your educational institutions. You are someone in the community and society at large who is looked to for leadership. The coaching process encompasses all of these elements where you can exercise your leadership skill. How you do so shapes the Private Ryan's of the future.

Scholars in modern times have studied significant motivation and leadership theories and models at great length. If we simply look at the past century, scientific management began at the beginning of the industrial revolution with Frederick Taylor and his scientific management theory in 1911. Through two world wars and a host of great scholars with their theories and models, the discipline has essentially arrived at a concept called "situationalism." Situationalism can be described by many models. It generally suggests that the optimal leader understands that the variables of his style interacting with the readiness or maturity of the subordinates' behavior. It calls for an interactive style that will optimize on communication and, hence, responsiveness to it in the form of enhanced performance behavior. The model which describes this in most relevant terms is the one conceived and written since 1969 by Paul Hersey and Ken Blanchard called *Situational Leadership*. We all know that many great coaches happen to be great communicators. What this means is they have the ability as the seniors in a dyadic relationship to communicate effectively with the subordinates or the players to get things done. Interpersonal communication at the dyadic level (one-on-one) is critical. Obviously, coaches communicate to units and groups as well, which requires more complex leader skills.

Leadership is one of the most talked about concepts in social science and probably one of the least understood. There are over 300 definitions of what it is to be a leader. Management, leadership, and supervision are clearly different concepts. Management is a process of working with and through individuals and groups as well as other resources such as equipment and facilities to accomplish organizational goals. Generally, the goals of a football organization are to win first and to teach second. Tangential to that is to grow and develop young people. Management applies to organizations, whatever the type, and they require their management personnel to have interpersonal skills. Supervision is a permutation to management, but leadership is the essence of influencing your subordinates to where you wish them to go. Although management and leadership are often thought of as one and the same, they have important distinctions between them. Leadership is a much broader concept than management. Management is a special kind of leadership in which the achieving of organizational goals is paramount. Leadership, however, occurs whenever one person attempts to influence the behavior of another individual or a group. Leadership is an influencing process, where management is an attempt to achieve a goal. If leaders can influence subordinates to move toward the goals of the organizations in which they are a part and obtain

congruence between the behavior of the players and the goals of the organization, then they use leadership to obtain their management ends. Leaders seek to get every member of the organization, every part of the team in synchrony and to influence them toward those goals. This is accomplished through the influencing process of leading.

Situational Leadership is one model of the many in the leadership field which can be positioned as a simple "how to" model to deal with the performance behavior of football players. There is in fact a model to describe how one would optimally behave to influence or to lead a subordinate where you wish them to go. More importantly, it can be used to lead them where they would wish to go if those objectives could be made congruent. A coach might ask what is in this for me and my team? The answer might be shaving fractions of seconds off of a time, growing talent as quickly and as efficiently as possible, providing a common language for discussing performance, improving morale, dealing with performance regression, and obtaining more success in the form of wins and enhanced performances.

An entire body of thought has been dedicated to studying traits, attitudes, values, and thoughts, all of which are extremely important, but these affect us only internally. They evoke no reality. If we as coaches are to have an effect on the performance of our players, we must first change our own behavior, and then we can change the behavior of others. Situational Leadership describes and details out a model from which we can do this. What coaches need is a leadership model to help them function more effectively as leaders. The expanded situational leadership model that follows describes the behaviors of the coach in terms of leadership that would elicit the optimal responsiveness from the followers depending on where they were in their state of readiness or maturity. This model which comes from a body of knowledge called Situationalism means that we, as coaches, understand as leaders that we must be adaptive in our styles as to how we communicate clearly with subordinates. It should not be lost on us that over the last 50 years we are operating in an increasingly democratic and liberal culture. This makes leadership more difficult because leaders have less power. Relating to the modern player as a subordinate and to effectively communicate with them to optimize on eliciting from them their best performance is our goal. The Situational Leadership model out of situationalism describes a way to do that. Simply, it enables you as the coach to more fully empower your team. The model follows:

TASK BEHAVIOR-

The extent to which the leader engages in defining roles i.e. telling what, how, when, where and if more than one person who is to do what in
Goal-Settion
Organizing
Establishing Time
Directing
Controlling

RELATIONSHIP BEHAVIOR-

The extent to which a leader engeges in two-way (multi-way) communication listening facilitating behaviors socioemotional support:
Giving Support
Facilitating
Interactions
Active Listening
Providing Feedback

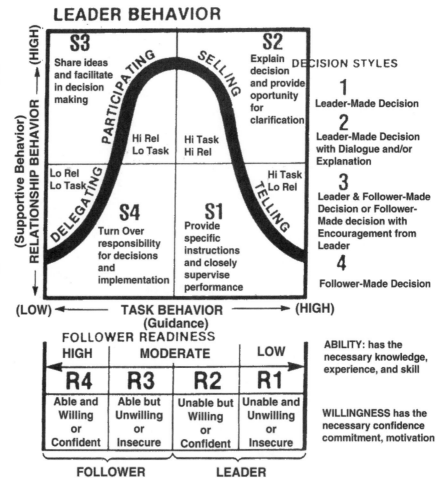

Expanded Situational Leadership Model

Old-school traditional or even classical thinking does not have to be sold out nor compromised away to do this. What the model represents is how many great coaches of days past have behaved situationally. They learned to be flexible and adaptive as authority figures rather than compromising on their values. Simply, if we see every problem as a nail, the only tool that we may have is a hammer. We know there are lots of ways to skin a cat. The more adaptive and flexible that we are, the more effective we can become. We must learn to appeal to the situational nature of the subordinate and the situation that we are in. Now study the model and we can look at the four-celled matrix where four basic styles of leader behavior emerge. If you will study the figure of the expanded situational leadership model, you can see that there are two types of behavior for leaders. Running horizontally is task behavior, moving from low to high, left to right. Task behavior is the extent to which a leader engages in defining roles for subordinates. This is where coaches tell people what to do, how to do it, when to do it, where to do it, and under what circumstances to do it. This natural style for coaches employs goal setting, organizing, establishing timelines, directing, and controlling. These behaviors come naturally to many coaches as they are task-oriented and task-specific. The second type of major leader behavior is relational or supportive behavior which runs vertically on the four-celled matrix from low to high. Relationship behavior is the extent to which the leader engages in two-way communication where he listens, facilitates, gives socio-emotional support, interacts, displays active listening, and provides feedback. There is a higher order nurturing component to this sort of behavior than to the task-driven and logical task behavior on the other axis.

The interaction of leader task behavior with leader relationship behavior plotted out on the four-celled matrix of leader behavior then describes four basic styles which leaders may use. For example, in the lower right quadrant where task behavior is very high and relationship behavior is lower, style one describes a high task, low relationship "telling style" where the coach provides specific in-structions and closely supervises performance. At the extreme ends of style one behavior would be military drill instructors and highly intense offensive line coaches who would rant and rave in a highly intense instructional mode with little room for affect. Put in another way, highly authoritarian styles of leaders often operate in style one. Looking at the right side of the model on decision style, these are leader-made decisions. As relationship behavior increases, moving up the bell-shaped curve into the style two quadrant, it introduces high task and high relationship coaching styles. The term "selling" can be used to describe this style of leadership and it has also been referred to as "coaching." This is where the senior in the dyadic relationship spends more time relating to the subordinate as well as providing instruction, feedback and direction. Style two embodies explaining decisions and providing opportunity for clarification, therefore this decision-making style is a leader-made decision with dialogue and/or explanation and more room for interpersonal communication. Style two is really what coaching is.

Situational Leadership as a model would suggest that if coaches can implement a style as defined by this model that is most appropriate for the level of readiness or maturity in which the individual player is behaving, then you have a leader style and a readiness match. The condition optimizes on communication and mitigates towards optimal behavior on the part of the subordinate. When styles mismatch with readiness by more than two cells on the matrix, there is very little effective communication going on. You should not scream (style one) at your quarterback (generally R4).

Moving along the bell-shaped curve to the style three quadrant is where we have high relationship but lower task behavior. This cell has been designated "participating." As a coach, this is where you share ideas and facilitate in decision making. Such coaching behavior is more low task and high relationship. Envisioning this style of behavior on the practice field is where the coach might be in a team practice session observing in the secondary, making encouraging comments and observing as the team conducts more on its own initiative the executing of a play script. The behaviors of the coach would be participative in nature where he would share ideas and interact on an as-needed basis. The players would be more independent than in different settings. Moving down to style four, where delegating is the descriptive term, task behavior in style four is now lower as well as relationship behavior. This leader style is referring to leaders' low-task and low-relationship behavior where the senior has turned over responsibility for decisions and the implementation is handled by the players. The coach (leader) is now in a more passive role of delegating, observing, and providing feedback on an as-needed basis. In looking at the parabolic curve that runs through the four cells of the leader behavior matrix, we then have style one "telling," style two "selling" or "coaching," style three "participating," and style four "delegating." The parabolic curve which runs through the four cells describe styles of leadership in these four basic ways which can be used by any leader. When a leader's behavior is matched appropriately with the subordinate at a corresponding level of readiness, this is called a high probability match. We see descriptors on the figure that is useful in understanding what the four styles are. Style one is telling, guiding, directing, and establishing timelines, goals and objectives. Style two, which becomes more socio-emotional in nature, involves selling, explaining, clarifying, persuading, and leaving more room for clarification and interaction within the dyadic relationship. Style three is more participative where encouraging, collaborating, committing, and supportive sorts of behaviors emerge to the forefront. Style four or delegating, involves observing, monitoring, fulfilling, and turning over responsibility for decisions as mature followers implement them.

Focusing on the follower as part of this dyadic relationship, look at the follower readiness scale underneath the four cells of leader styles. This represents the other side of the leader-follower relationship where an insightful leader who fully understands his capability of having a range of leader behavior styles can now interact with the follower or the player where he is. Follower readiness, which

has been called maturity, crosses from right to left, low to high. The two basic components that describe follower readiness are ability and willingness. There are numerous components in the subordinates to pinpoint them in terms of their readiness, but for simplicity, let us call ability the necessary knowledge, experience and skill, which includes talent and willingness as the necessary confidence, commitment, and motivation. Looking at the first cell of follower readiness R-1, which we call low readiness, where the player is unable and unwilling or insecure in carrying out the desired task. Such low readiness is most optimally dealt with from the leadership style one telling behavior. Moving up the follower readiness continuum to R-2 or low to moderate readiness, the player may be unable but willing or unable and confident which still requires some leader-directed behavior, but more socio-emotional support. Obviously, as players move up their own spectrum of readiness, coaches should respond accordingly by moving up the parabolic curve to a more advanced and more appropriate style of leader behavior. R-2 would have a higher probability match of optimal response if the coach were selling or coaching using both high-task and high-relationship behavior in such a situation. As players become higher in readiness as shown by R-3 and are able but perhaps unwilling or able but perhaps insecure, coaches need to instruct less and emotionally support more. Parents work similarly. Here we become more follower-directed than leader-directed because there is more power resting with the followers or the subordinates. Coaches then should spend more time and energy sharing ideas and facilitating in decision making, being more socially and emotionally supportive, and giving less instructions to achieve a higher probability match of communication. As followers or players become most able, willing, and confident, and at the higher levels of follower-directedness, (R-4) the most appropriate leader behavior then is style four or delegating. This is the point where we turn over more and more responsibility for decision and implementation to the subordinates. Again, this achieves a higher probability match that the things we are seeking will occur because the communication style is optimally matched with leader behavior and follower readiness. Again, we have stated that if we are more than two cells apart in leader behavior and follower readiness, communication is very low and productivity suffers.

The situational leadership model is incident by incident in nature. What that means is all of us have basic styles that we would gravitate to by personality and makeup and yet we must interact with our subordinates on an incident-by-incident basis. Ken Blanchard in his book, *The One Minute Manager*, captures this in the title of the book. It is minute-by-minute that we interact with our subordinates. Although each subordinate also has a general readiness and maturity description how they behave, only a minute-by-minute basis is what matters. That is why as coaches, parents, and teachers, we must respond in the "here and now" and not in general sorts of ways. Readiness can apply to your coaching staff, your assistant coaches, your trainers, and your players. Readiness is an interactive and continuous variable that shapes the style the leader will optimally use to get the most out of the subordinate. If the leader can match up the appropriate leader style, regarding how much task and how much relationship behavior to use, so that it fits with the level of readiness or maturity where the subordinate is behaving, a high probability match is achieved. This was the heart of the study I conducted on Coach Bobby Bowden's football team at Florida State in the mid-1980s. The leadership style of the coaches was measured, categorized, and defined, and we presented it to the players where their maturity was measured to see if the appropriate leader style actually made a difference in terms of responsiveness. The data was found to be statistically significant, which suggests that situational leadership as a model is effective in the football environment. Coaches' leadership style matters.

Let's take a real football example and try to operationalize the model in the real world. At readiness level two, here is a player who is unable to do something. In other words, he cannot block his opponent, but he wants to. The player is willing to, he believes that he can, but he seems to

not be getting the job done. Your job as an offensive line coach, is to teach him a little bit more about how to do this. Your player may be anxious. He may be excited, but is he interested? If he is responsive, receptive to input, is attentive, and is enthusiastic, support this. You do not want to destroy this, you want to capture it because the player is willing. So using a "selling" or "coaching" style, where you give more task input but you are also socio-emotionally supportive and encouraging is the most appropriate leader style here. Just screaming (Style 1 – negative) is not the answer. Contrast this with the readiness level three where the player is able but may be unwilling or insecure. They have showed that they can do it and they have showed that they can play. But perhaps they are hesitant or maybe they don't want to take the next step or maybe they are a bit insecure. Dealing with this may require more relationship behavior and less task behavior. Maybe they want some feedback from you. This is someone who is able but because of insecurity or unwillingness, must be dealt with in a different way. Challenging them positively can be style three. This is the essence of the leader discerning where the players are and reaching them with an adaptive and flexible style. Effective leadership is not just one style.

When your quarterback comes off the field and you ask him what is going on, and he says, "Coach, they are doing exactly what we said they were doing in the films on Tuesday, you just can't see it from here." You now have a chance as a coach to respond appropriately. If you scream at your quarterback using your style one leadership, you may destroy his motivation. If, on the other hand, you are composed enough to recognize what he is saying may be correct, you will respond in a higher order leader behavior which will have a higher probability match and lead to a continued positive interaction. Responding to where a subordinate finds himself is critical to being an effective leader. The quarterback, as your leader on the field, is in a leverage position just like you are as a coach. The quarterback can regress down his own performance curve toward a lower level of incident by incident readiness. As a result, this calls for different leadership because leadership is an incident-by-incident affair. Leadership is not a general thing, it is a specific thing. This is the idea from One-Minute Management which strikes the essence of situationalism. How someone behaves today at this moment in time is how you should respond to them as a leader. If your quarterback regresses to level one readiness, gets sloppy, and feels sorry for himself, and then you yell at him because that is what he deserves, this is what his readiness level might require. Quarterbacks, most of the time, don't respond to this because they act at higher levels of readiness. The trick here is to be discerning and insightful enough in diagnosing where people are in terms of their own personal readiness on an incident-by-incident basis to call up the right leadership response from yourself.

Our wetware, that is our brain, is wired as such that we can hold on to only four or five elements at any time. This is evidenced by telephone number and social security number groupings. Leadership is no different in that we need a simple model of how to lead. The situational leadership model hopefully provides a simple conceptual model for us as coaches on how to lead. Looking at the expanded situational leadership model and its parabolic curve which defines the readiness level of the followers and the task and relationship behavior creates four styles and gives us a few elements of leadership. This is a simple model of how you lead. The model may be likened to a compass or a lens in that we can write the whole thing on the back of a business card. I must be careful here to manage both my own and your expectations because this brief explanation is only an introduction. I have often said that the most important skill that a coach can have is knowledge as to how to be an effective leader. Such skills require a lot more work. Coaches have to look at themselves as shaping instruments. You are a teaching mechanism, you are an adaptive reinforcer, and you are a very, very strong authority figure in the football environment. You are an influencer, and can be so much more effective using the situational leadership model as one of your tools. I

might add that understanding yourself better through this model will make you more effective as a father and a husband and a son in your own family. You have the capability based on how you relate to the young people as your subordinates and players to shape them and to influence them in any number of directions. I think as coaches, you have to look at yourself and using this model as a tool to adapting your own behavior, you can clearly accomplish a great deal. If you don't do this, you are leaving an awful lot of yourself on the table.

The situational leadership model gives us the ability to get into alignment both our walk and our talk. Our leadership intentions and our actual leadership behaviors must be congruent if we are to be perceived as credible. As we have learned from the model, our leadership behaviors must optimally match up with the readiness level of our subordinates. How we intend to be seen is often radically different than how we are actually perceived. It is the perceptions of others, in this case the players, that is reality on the field and in the locker room. Remember that reality is perception as perceived by the subordinates of who you are as a leader. What you think is not nearly so important as to what you do. Therefore, you must walk your talk because if there is incongruence, you will not be perceived as real and their behavior will certainly not be optimized toward what you want them to do.

So often, there is a disconnect as to why we are so effective with some players sometimes and so widely ineffective at other times. This can simply be described as failing to lead in a style that is appropriate to where the player is readinesswise. In coming to terms with this, we can begin to grow as leaders all the more excellently. Coaches within the confines of appropriate style as married to player readiness can also behave in both hindering and helping roles. Again, a dissection of these two modes within each style is beyond the scope of this discussion but it suggests how much we can learn about being leaders as coaches and effectively drawing the most out of the potential of our subordinates, our players. You see the key concept of leadership as a coach is to attempt to always match your leader behavior to the readiness level of an individual player, an element of the squad, or the whole team. Individual leadership and group leadership have their differences but in any case, a leader-subordinate match feels like the reward and a mismatch feels like punishment. It becomes clear to us that the consequence of mismatches are that we develop people more slowly, we lose people, we failed to optimize on potentiality and capability, and ultimately we lose games. Football games are won or lost based on the interplay of a team's ability and willingness to execute it. Task behavior speaks to the needs around ability while relationship behavior speaks to the needs around willingness. The disconnect between the tensions of a leader and their behavior often come from a failure to discern what is required. What we do know is that we often provide a coaching style that people want and not what they need in a particular moment on a particular task. We know that our coaching styles are often shaped significantly by our mentors and what our experience has taught us in that we emulate it. Many times this may be inappropriate particularly as the total environment of society has changed. Generals certainly cannot win the next war by using the tactics and strategies of the past and coaches cannot, either. We cannot afford to use certain styles which are comfortable to us with specific tasks and ignore diagnosing where a specific individual or a group is in the here and now. Although I may have a go-to style that is more comfortable for me, it may not be the best one to use. Additionally, leadership is very much a here and now in the present type of event. How you respond and how you adjust situationally will determine how the subordinate player will respond to you. The irony of all of this is that many times if we learn to adapt our own style, we empower the subordinate. They may not know that, and you may not know that, but this is what happens. Even if you don't understand or know the model, if you act accordingly, it will manifest itself. Many excellent leaders use the situational leadership model and don't even know it.

The sum of the situational leadership model tells us about the need for coaches to be adaptive and flexible. If you remember nothing else from this discussion today, know that there is no one style of leadership that is effective for all individuals and for all situations. Know that there is no one best leadership style. Each individual is different and each situation is different. You, as a coach, can not be locked into just one style. If all you do is yell at your players, or in the words of the psychologist, negatively reinforce and punish, and if you don't ever exhort and don't ever uplift, you are your own worst enemy. We must learn to move outside of our primary or "go-to" style and work from it situationally. Using the situational leadership model, which can be inscribed on the back of a business card, gives us a simple model of how to lead which deals largely with modified behavior. We must learn to match and move within this model if we are to win. Excellence requires that we make optimal use of the intellectual resources we have at hand. To be adaptive and flexible is key. This leadership model describes a critical element of our behavior as coaches if we are to succeed.

While knowing the X's and O's of football is required of all coaches, it is equally important as a personal quality that you understand how to be a leader. Please write to me and ask me what books might be helpful. Thank you so much for your kind attention and I'll be glad to field questions as long as it takes.

Thom Park, Ph.D., is Courtesy Associate Professor at Florida State University and he serves as a consultant to the football industry. He has been involved in the game since 1958 as a player, coach, recruiter, administrator, scholar, businessman, agent, and player's father. Write to him at 3515 O'Ffaly Court, Tallahassee, Florida, 32308-3141.

PLAY PACKAGING AT THE LINE OF SCRIMMAGE

NORTH PENN HIGH SCHOOL, PENNSYLVANIA

My topic today is Play Packaging. We run a Multiple Offense at North Penn High School. I think we have really helped our team a lot with the things we have done at the line of scrimmage. I do not expect you to stop everything you are doing on offense and switch to this type of offense. In fact, we only use this offense about 30 percent of the time.

There are a lot of X's and O's in this package, but I want you to look at it more as a concept and as a framework of your own offense. The point is how to adjust and how to change and adjust. I know a lot of teams run the Wing-T in this area and I feel this would work in very well with that offense.

The starting point is this: Why do we want to package plays? When your kids step up to the line of scrimmage you want to maximize the chances for a successful offensive play. That is the bottom line. There is no perfect defense. If there was, everyone would be running it. Every defense has a weakness. I have listed several reasons why we want to package plays.

1. Make the defense wrong – attack the weakness.
2. Force defenses to be gap sound – they can not load up or gamble as much.
3. Can be successful versus multiple defensive looks – run best play versus certain front.
4. Remove some of the guesswork from play calling.
5. Take advantage of personnel matchups – run at / behind / away from a certain player.
6. Minimize effectiveness of opponent scouting – makes some or your tendencies invalid.
7. Make things easier on your linemen – usually blocking certain schemes versus same look.
8. Allows use of multiple formations.

Defensive coordinators are getting very smart. They are playing more multiple fronts on defense. If a team plays the same defensive look down after down we can take advantage of that situation. Teams mix up the defenses more and more today.

The next question we ask is this: When to package plays?

1. When your team can handle it mentally. We use the **Sponge Theory**. How much can your players absorb? I learned this from my dad several years ago when I first got into coaching. If you combine your teams brain power you can think of them as a sponge. You can just keep throwing water and soon it will hit a point where it is saturated. That is when your players stop retaining what you are teaching them. Every team that I have worked with over the last few years the players were very smart. We were able to do a lot at the line of scrimmage. This coming year we may not be able to do as much. If your team can handle it, do it. If they can't you will have to scale back and do the simple things.

2. When your opponent does not give you the same front or the same coverage every play.

3. When your opponents flip-flop personnel to match up with your personnel.

4. When your opponent likes to gamble defensively – unsound fronts, blitzes, etc.

Next I want to talk about the types of packages. This first package is a base package. It is **Check With Me**. All we are going to do is to take a particular play and package it with its mirrored play. For example we look at the Fullback Iso in the Right B Gap. It is packaged with the Fullback Iso in the

Left B Gap. We call 34 SLASH. That is our Fullback Iso in the Right B Gap. We are going to package with the Fullback Iso in the left B Gap. That is the first thing we teach the quarterback to read. For us it is a very common sense read. We want to run to a soft spot or to the bubble.

The read can also be at a specific opponent. You want to find a defender and run right at him. Or you may want to find a defender and run away from him. There are going to be times when the quarterback gets to a point in the game and is not sure what to do. This is a common thing through the reads. We do not want to burn a timeout. We always have a default read. It is only one way to go. Usually when it is a Check With Me, we are going to go to one side or the other, depending on which side of the line is better. Usually our default read is to go behind our best linemen.

Something we have gotten into recently has been to read from the sideline. We have been able to signal in to the quarterback the play we feel we should run. If the quarterback is not sure he can look to our sideline for help and we hand signal the play we want to run. We point up if we want to run the play called in the huddle. If we want to change the play I point down.

How do we communicate the play? We make the huddle call – "34 Slash – Check With Me." Our Cadence is simple. "Set, Hut, Number, Color, Number, Ready, Go." We assign two colors. One to represent the original play called and the second color to designate its mirrored companion. GREEN – Go with it. RED – Change it.

The quarterback makes the read. If he wants to stay with the play called, 34 Slash which is the original call this is what he calls. "Set, Hut, Green 80, Green 80, Ready Go." We run the 34 Slash. If he wants to change the play and run the opposite play, 33 Slash this is what he calls. "Set, Hut, Red 80, Red 80, Ready Go." Now we run 33 Slash.

Let me go over the Coaching Points on this. When installing the base run (Slash), teach it as "Check

With Me." Walk through the installations throughout the off-season – reps, Reps, REPS!!! During film study, constantly ask the quarterback what he would call, (Green or Red.) We have our JV program use at least one "Check With Me" play so those players are familiar with the concept when they move up.

On our 34 Slash Check With Me this is how we read it. On the Straight Setup we have a softer B Gap to the Right. We run Green in our cadence and run 34 Slash.

STRAIGHT SETUP
34 SLASH CHECK WITH ME

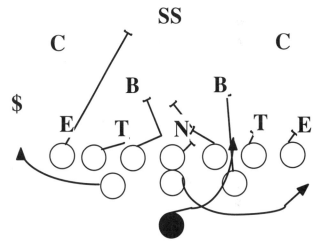

In our Blue Right Weak the softer B Gap is to the left. We call Red in our cadence and change to 33 Slash.

BLUE RIGHT WEAK
34 SLASH CHECK WITH ME

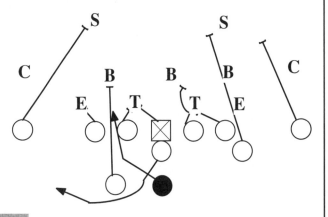

In the Straight Setup against a balanced front we run behind our best linemen. Our best linemen are to our right. We use Green in our cadence and run the play to the right.

STRAIGHT SETUP
34 SLASH CHECK WITH ME

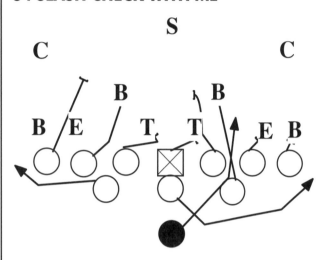

I have other examples of Check With Me. If we go up against a team that runs the 4-3 defense and set their front one way or the other. They will give you one edge softer than the other. We run 58 Toss Check With Me. If we run the 58 Toss from our Flanker Right Far, we like the blocking angles on the side of the Flanker we call Green. If we see the ends block to the left would be easier we will motion the Flanker over and have him seal inside and run the play to the left with a "Red 57." When we run the Toss "Check With Me" he looks to see which of our ends has the easier block. I am not as interested in the X's and O's as I am the concept.

Another example would be our 18 Speed Option "Check With Me." We can run it out of different formations. We want to find the Strong Safety and run away from him. We motion our opposite back toward the play side. We want to force the defense to check the coverage. If they do not check the coverage you will have a great play when the motion back gets the outside angle.

If we have the blocking angles to the left we call "Red" and run 17 Speed Option. If it is a balanced defense we call our "Green" and run the play we called in the huddle. That is the "Check With Me" concept. We take a Mirrored Play and packaging it with its companion play.

Next we have a couple of Base Run Packages. The first package is our Midline Fullback Trap. It is a Fullback Trap in either A Gap and it is packaged with the Fullback Wedge. We run this against teams that are not disciplined up front. We like this play against teams that do not do a good job of squeezing down. You do not see this play with much success in college or pro level because the linemen are taught to squeeze down so well. When we get a team out in the middle of the field the Trap is a great play.

We can run the trap to the easier side and that is usually to the wider tackle. We can run the play with the Fullback, Tailback, and we also have a Quarterback Trap. We can trap with either guard. We also package the Trap with the Wedge Scheme. We run the play just like we run the blocking on the quarterback sneak. We seal everyone inside and block any inside movement.

There are a couple of fronts that are difficult to trap. We are better off running away from those schemes. That is why we throw that into the package. We could not call "Trap – Check With Me." The front I am talking about is two B Gap linemen and two A Gap linebackers. It is very difficult to trap that scheme. However, this gives you a soft middle and we can run the "Wedge" in that area.

This is how we communicate the play. We can not go on the Color. Now we have to use the Numbers. This is the Huddle Call – "Fullback Trap Package." Cadence – "Set, Hut, Color, Number, Color, Number, Ready Go." We use numbers to indicate the desired play. Color and 1st digit are meaningless. The 2nd digit designates the play. If we call "81" we trap in the 1 hole. If we call "82" we trap in the 2 hole. If we all "80" we run the Wedge in the 0 hole. If the quarterback wants to run the Fullback Trap to the Right A Gap this is what he calls. "Set, Hut, Blue, 82, Blue 82 – Ready

Go." We trap the <u>2</u> hole. If he wants to run the Fullback Trap in the Left A Gap this is how he calls it. "Set, Hut, Blue, <u>91</u>, Blue <u>91</u> Ready Go." We trap the <u>1</u> hole. If the quarterback want to run the Fullback Wedge in the <u>0</u> hole this is what he calls. "Set, Hut, Blue 7<u>0</u>, Blue 7<u>0</u>, Ready Go." We run the 30 Wedge.

Again, we can signal the plays in from the sideline. We have the quarterback wear a wrist band. We signal in the number that we want the quarterback to run.

Here are the coaching points. To avoid collisions between guards, in the beginning have your smarter guard make a "Me" call or a "You" call to designate the trapper. Have them make dummy "Me" and "You" calls to avoid tipping off the trap plays. When installing the base run, (Trap) teach it as a PACKAGE. Walk through the installations throughout the off-season; reps, Reps, REPS!!! During film study, constantly ask the quarterbacks for what he would call; 0, 1, or 2. Have the JV program run the Fullback Trap Package so those players are familiar with he concept when they move up.

PRO RIGHT WEAK – FB TRAP PACKAGE

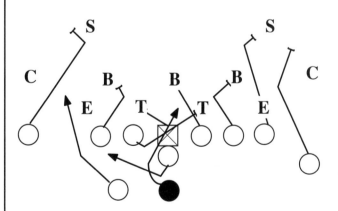

Against the 4-3 shaded front we trap the widest defensive tackle. (3 Technique) We use the "2" as the 2nd digit – we run 32 Fullback Trap.

SLOT LEFT I – FB TRAP PACKAGE

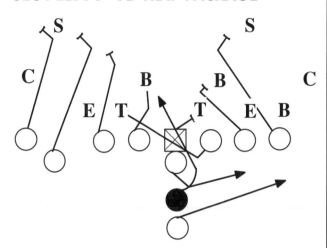

Against the "Split" – 52 shaded front we trap the widest defensive tackle. (3 Technique) We use the "1" as the second digit. We run the 31 Fullback Trap.

KING LEFT – FB TRAP PACKAGE

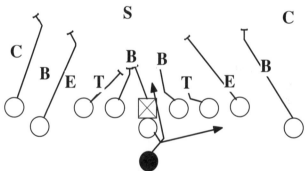

Against two B Gap defensive tackles and two A Gap linebackers we know it is tough to run the trap. But they have a soft middle. We use the "0" as the second digit. We run the 30 Wedge.

We run the Trap Play several different ways. We do not have to run it with the fullback all of the time. We can run it with the other backs. We can run it with either running back or the quarterback.

We have two Base Run Packages. The first package is the Trap Package. The other is the ISO Package. With some good linemen and a good tailback we ran a tailback oriented offense. He made a lot of big plays for us. We package four plays. We can run the Tailback, Fullback Iso in either A Gaps or either B Gaps. This evolved from the Check With Me. If we called the Iso in either of the two B Gaps and the defense gave us a balanced front they could take away both B Gaps. If they gave us two B Gap tackles we were in trouble. We always want to run into the bubble. The way teams set their fronts today we are not sure where we are going to get it. Rarely do we see a front that can take away all four Iso's.

We tell the quarterback to run the Iso at the largest bubble. He must determine which gap or gaps will not be occupied by the defensive tackle after the snap. We have a pre-determined order of priority for a particular week based on the scouting report. We tell them to check the right side first. He checks A and B Gaps on the right side. If neither of these are open, he works to the left side. We can tell him to work the B Gaps first. If the B Gaps are not open then look at the A Gaps. Or, we can tell him to check the A Gaps first. If they are not open then he looks at the B Gaps.

We can also be opponent specific. If a particular linebacker or defensive tackle is weaker we can run at them. We always have a default read. If any doubt we go a certain way. It is usually behind our best drive blocker. Again, we can help the quarterback by calling the plays from the sideline.

How do we communicate the play? Huddle Call – Iso Package. Cadence – "Set, Hut, Color, Number, Color, Number, Ready Go." We use numbers to indicate the desired play. Again, the 2nd digit designates the play. The Color and first digit are meaningless. The second digit determines the play: 8$\underline{1}$ – TB Iso in the $\underline{1}$ hole, 8$\underline{2}$ – TB Iso in the $\underline{2}$ hole, 8$\underline{3}$ – TB Iso in the $\underline{3}$ hole, 8$\underline{4}$ – TB Iso in the $\underline{4}$ hole.

"Set, Hut, Blue 81, blue 81, Ready Go." We run the A gap which is the 1 hole. We can run all four of the gaps.

The coaching points here are very important. We vary the formations. You don't always have to be in the I Formation. We can offset the FB and we

can use Near and Far motion We can use 2 players as lead blockers. Left side 1, 3 holes. Right side 2, 4 holes. When installing Isos teach them all individually then teach them as a package. Walk through installations throughout the off-season; reps, Rep, REPS!!! During film study, constantly ask the quarterbacks for what he would call, 1, 2, 3, or 4. Have the JV program run Iso Package so those players are familiar with the concept when they move up.

PRO RIGHT I – ISO PACKAGE

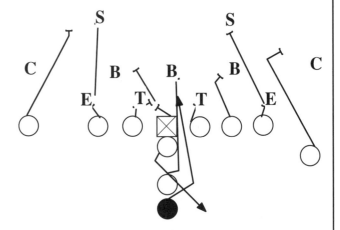

We have two open Bubbles – the 2 hole or 3 hole. Game plan decision. Assume the better match-up is in the 2 hole. Use "2" as 2nd digit – we run the 52 BOB. (Back On Backer)

KNIGHT LEFT NEAR – ISO PACKAGE

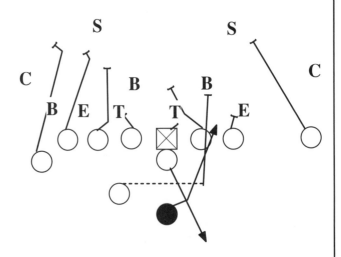

We have two open Bubbles – 1 hole and the 4 hole. Game plan decision. Assume better matchup in the 4 hole. Use "4" as second digit – we run 54 Slash. (Fullback motions Across)

DIAMOND RIGHT – ISO PACKAGE

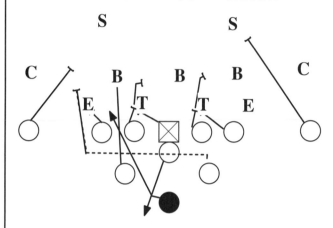

We have 2 open Bubbles – 2 hole or 3 hole. Game plan decision. Assume better match-up in 3 hole. Use "3" as second digit – we run 53 Slash. Opposite Fullback Motions Out)

We have one Passing Package that we use. We call it our Drop Back Package. Basically, what we are doing is to take three drop-back routes and combining them together. We call it from Queens – we are in four wideouts and we are in the Shotgun. We run routes based on what the coverages show. We do not get a lot of disguise coverages in our league. What the defense lines up in is what they are going to play. All we have to do is to distinguish between Cover 2, Cover 3, or some type of Man Coverage. Our quarterback signals the coverage. Against Cover 2 or any type of 4 across look we run our Double Hitch Corner. The two outside receivers run 5-yard Stop routes with the two inside receivers running Corner routes.

Against Cover 3 we run All Out Routes. All of the receivers run Go Routes. It is our 4 Vertical Routes. Against Cover 0, 1, or any form of Man Coverage we run Double Slant Flat. The two outside receivers run Slant routes with the two inside receivers running Flat Routes. Those are Arrow Routes. This

is where the natural pick occurs. There is no change for the offensive line. All three plays are Drop Back Pass Protection rules. We always have a default read. If we have any doubt we go this way. (Usually All Go – pick an outside mismatch. Can help with read from sideline with hand signals.)

How do we communicate the play? Huddle Call – "Drop Back Package" Cadence – we can use any cadence. Use hand signs to communicate route combination to receivers. The 1 fist means 3 Deep look – run All Go. The 2 fist means 2 or 4 deep look – "Double Hitch Corner." Bang two fist together means Man to Man look – "Double Slant Flat."

Coaching points include making sure the QB and wide receivers occasionally use dummy hand signs. When packaging patterns teach them all individually then teach them as a Package. You can package whatever route you want based on what coverages you see the most. Practice this during seven-on-seven throughout the off-season; reps, Reps, REPS!!! During the film study, constantly ask the quarterbacks what he would call. (1, 2, or Man)

QUEEN RIGHT GUN/DROP-BACK PACKAGE

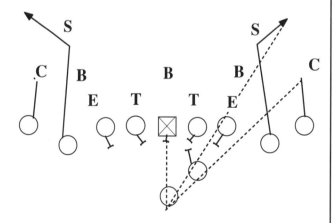

Against Cover 2 look – run Double Hitch Corner. The QB signals 2 fist. Pick one side to work. Read the corner. Throw the ball high or low.

QUEEN RIGHT
GUN/DROP-BACK PACKAGE

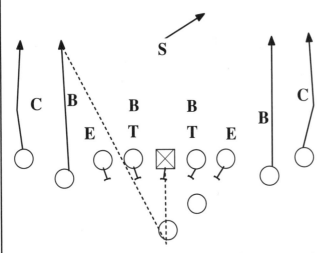

Against Cover 3 – run All Go. The QB signals 1 fist. Look off FS to one side and throw inside Go Route to the other side.

QUEEN RIGHT
GUN/DROP BACK PACKAGE

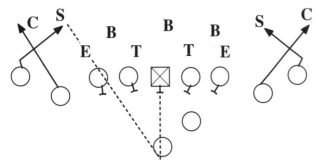

Against Man Coverage look – run Double Slant Flat. The QB bangs 2 fist together. Pick one side to work, throw the Slant as the receiver is clearing the Flat route.

Next we package Multiple Plays. We package plays based on our defensive scouting reports. We study our opponents' tapes and decide on plays to package that will go against their base looks. We pick plays that are difficult to defend because of their common looks. We pick formations we haven't shown – one we think can give the opponent some alignment/assignment problems. We make decisions based on our scouting report. You want to make sure you look at your pervious games versus this opponent.

We package a higher risk play with a lower risk play. We use a Reverse, Option, Naked Boot, etc. with a lower risk play say a Power or Iso, or Trap. We want to determine which defense the higher risk play will go against and have the quarterback run the lower risk play versus any other look.

In teaching the reads we give the quarterback one or two basic players to read their alignment. For example we have him read the alignment of the defensive end on our tight end side. If the defensive end is inside we run the first play. If the defensive end is outside we run the second play. We always have a default read. If any doubt we go this way. (Usually the safest play). Again, we can help with the read from the sideline with our hand signals.

How do we communicate the play? In the Huddle we call – "56 Post Check 58 Pitch." Cadence – "Set, Hut, Color, Number, Color, Number, Ready Go." We use numbers to indicate the desired play. Again, the color and 1st digit are meaningless. The 2nd digit designates the play. If the QB wants to run 56 Post: "Set, Hut, Blue 26, Blue 26, Ready Go." We run 56 Post. If the QB want to run 58 Pitch – "Set, Hut, Blue 28, Blue 28, Ready Go." We run 58 Pitch.

Install all plays individually then teach them as a package at the beginning of a particular game week. You can even take plays and package them during games as halftime adjustments. During film study constantly ask the quarterbacks what they would call.

We may package our Iso Package with the Check 90 All Hitch. We either run the Iso or the 90 All Hitch. This is good against 4-3 teams. We line up in a 3 wide look. The defense must decide how many men they are going to keep in the box. If they only keep 6 men in the box we run our Iso play. If they keep more than 6 in the box we run the All Hitch play. If the QB calls a 2 or 3 we run the Iso. If he calls the 9 we run the All Hitch play. Our 90 Series is our three step protection.

The other plays we package together are our Toss Reverse Left Check 30 Wedge. All we do is have the QB check the edges. If nothing is threating from the corners we go ahead and run the reverse. If we see that the defense is running a blitz into the reverse we check out and run the Wedge play. When you are behind late in the game you do not want to package the Wedge with a Reverse play. You may want to run a play that has a better chance of making a big gain. If you run the Wedge the crowd may get on you. It is a better package early in the game.

If we want to package a play to one particular receiver we run 58 Veer Check 52 Go Pass, P60. The QB looks at our split end. If we have a favorable matchup he will check to the 52 Go Pass. The P60 indicates our protection. If we do not like the matchup with the split end we run the 58 Veer. Again, we are packaging a high-risk play with a low-risk play.

Our last package is our QB Trap Package. We run it with our Check 90 All Seam Routes. The inside men run Seams and the outside men run Hitch Routes. If the defense is scrambling around we run the QB Trap Package. It is the same as before. If the defense does not cover all receivers we throw the pass. You can also run the Trap Package on this. If they line up in a blitz look we run the 90 Seam. We are looking for the mismatch.

Here are some additional points on packaging.

1. Go on first sound enough with your other plays to discourage teams from shifting fronts or coverages late in the count. Force teams to line up in what they are going to lay.

2. Use a variety of numbers and colors in your cadence to avoid tipping off a smart defense.

3. Have offensive linemen utilize "dummy calls" to avoid tipping off a smart defense.

4. After the QB makes first color – number call, allow offensive linemen sufficient time to recognize play and make appropriate line calls.

5. REP-REP-REP!!! We install / walk through base packages in the summer and continue to rep through out the season.

6. Offensive line coach has extensive (minimum 15 minutes) prepractice walk through.

7. Constantly quiz the QB's during film study regarding what read to make on particular plays.

8. Use two-a-days to master physical techniques – majority of the playbook should already be installed before you put on the pads.

9. DO NOT LOSE SIGHT OF THE FUNDAMENTALS – If your players cannot COME OFF THE BALL AND BLOCK the best scheme in the world is worthless!

NORTH PENN PROGRAM PHILOSOPHY
1. NEVER GET OUTWORKED.

2. Must have a strict attendance policy – lifting is a privilege!

3. Must have a program to improve football speed and agility.

4. Must do a significant amount of X and O work in the off-season and in summer passing league and our 7 on 7.

5. NEVER GET OUTWORKED!

6. Be versatile. Develop your offensive and defensive systems around your kids. Don't try to fit your kids to the system.

7. Be demanding of your players – mentally and physically. If you ask for a lot and don't quite get, it still beats asking for a little and getting what your ask for.

8. Team motto: DO YOUR JOB AND GOOD THINGS WILL HAPPEN!!!

9. NEVER GET OUTWORKED!!!

We are fortunate to have a full-time TV studio in our school. I get a lot from them. They do a great job with our videotapes.

LEADERSHIP AND MOTIVATION

KANSAS STATE UNIVERSITY

I appreciate the opportunity to be here. I appreciate the high school coaches here. I was a high school coach for a considerable amount of time. I appreciate what you are doing. I am especially proud of the way high schools have been able to serve young people. Young people in this day and age need a lot of help and assistance. I think a lot of that help comes from the high school coaches who provide leadership in our school systems.

I actually coached for nine years in high school. I was born and raised in St. Joseph, Missouri. I went to William Jewel College. I was short-lived as an athlete in college football so to speak. But I do have great appreciation for what I experienced as a high school coach.

When I left William Jewell College I coached in a small town called Gallup, Missouri, for one year. I went back to college as a grad assistant. I went to Eastern New Mexico University. From there I went to Indio, California, for two different stints for a total of five years as a high school coach. I was a grad assistant at Southern Cal after that. I went back to high school coaching after that at Foothills High School in Santa Ana in California for five years. Then I went into college coaching at a NAIA school in Sherman, Texas, at Austin College. From there I went to North Texas State University for three years. From there I went to the University of Iowa for 10 years. I have been the head coach at Kansas State University for the last 11 years. So, you can see I have been at a lot of places. All of this equates to 39 years of coaching. Nine of those years were at the high school level.

When I lived in southern California I attended the Coach of the Year Clinic regularly. I went to clinics continuously throughout the year. In that area there were clinics every week of the year. I loved attending clinics. I learned a lot at those clinics. I had a chance to meet and to listen to some of the great, great names of coaching of that particular era. I did that for the seven years I was in southern California. One thing that was important for me when I attended those clinics was to listen to all of the X's and O's. I wanted to know how to block certain plays, what the pass routes were, and what stunts to run with each defense. I learned a lot doing that. As time went on and I became more active in coaching and started to understand more about my college coaching career. I realized there were some other things that were extremely important in coaching that seemed to be tied to the success or the failure of prominent coaches that I had an opportunity to listen to.

The thing I found out was this. The principles that involve achieving success, dealing with people, understanding people, and caring about people, and the intrinsic values we all teach to young people, seemed to be the things, along with organization and leadership, that truly set aside those coaches that were successful and perhaps those that were unsuccessful. I always had a great appreciation of this from that point on.

I have a room in our basement that is filled with boxes of all of those notes that I took at those clinics. My wife threatens to throw them out each year. I accumulated so much by going to those clinics. It was very worthwhile to me. I learned a lot about football. I learned about techniques, and I learned the X's and O's. The thing that kept coming back to me was the intrinsic values of being able to guide and to direct and lead people to give them the best opportunity to be successful in the things they did. That is what I appreciate about what I have learned from the very fine coaches.

I think we all have some things in common. One is dealing with young people. The other thing is that everyone in this room, myself included, wants to be successful in whatever adventures we are involved in life. The common point here is the fact it is in coaching. I have an appreciation for wanting to be successful. That is extremely important. It is being able to have that sensitivity to want to be the very best we can possibly be. This is true in all facets of coaching.

The things I am going to share with you are things that were important to me when I coached at the high school level, when I was an assistant coach at Austin College, and when I was an assistant coach at Iowa. But these things have come even more into focus having become the head coach at Kansas State University.

When I was a high school coach I thought there was such a big difference in high school coaching and college coaching. Obviously there are certain things that are different. There are things that none of us can control. But, it is so similar coaching at both levels. There are only a few things that we do at Kansas State that you could not do at the high school level. Now, do we have a better quarterback? Do we have bigger players and faster players? That may be true, but by and large, things that are important in our program are also important at the high school level. It does not matter what level you are coaching at.

As the head coach you have the opportunity to implement certain things into your program. Assistant coaches can have the input to allow it to happen. We did that when I was an assistant coach as well. But the real issues are how you implement your program and how you deal with people.

I think the first thing we all should be concerned with is related to academics. Do we really have a genuine concern about academics? We give lip service to it very easily. Many of you look at the college level and say you cannot do the things we do academically. My belief is this. Young people are a lot smarter today. It is easy to say to a young per-

son, "We really care about how you do in the classroom, and we care about you as a person, and we care about what your character is all about." But we do not always prove that is the case. We read things in the newspapers all of the time about problems in athletics. Look at the NFL. They are going through some hard times and there is some turmoil there. There is a character issue involved there. There is a character issue on college campuses. There are character issues in our program and there are character issues in your program. There are academic issues involved here. It is easy for me to say, or for you to say, "We really care about how you do in the classroom." But, what do we do? Kids are smart enough to know if you are "Talking or Walking." You are doing it or you are not doing it. That is the whole deal.

You may say we are coaching at a university and we have a learning center. You may not have that in your program, but I am not saying you need it. We have tutors and mentors, and we have study tables. You may say we can do that because we have the personnel to do it. But think about it for a little while. It really depends on this. Do you really want to back up your word. You can do all of those things. Do you need a Taj Mahal to have a study table? I go to a lot of high schools and I know there are a lot of schools that have study tables. I think this is important. Not only does it send a message to young people in your program, but it also sends a message to the people you work with. It sends a message to faculty members as well. It is important for those faculty members to understand that you have the same interest they do in trying to educate those young people.

You may say colleges can hire tutors to help the student athletes. That is true, but you can find the right people to help you with the young people in your program. You can arrange help if it is important enough to you.

We have a mentor program. We do not pay the faculty members in this program. They spend quality time with our athletes, especially our freshmen when they come into our program. You can do the same thing. You could get faculty members to assist you.

I think it is important for the young people to understand about their growth and character. You understand it and you do not like it when they make bad decisions. You do not like it when there is a flaw in their character. Why? Probably because it embarrasses you. We have been embarrassed when things happen with young people making bad decisions. But we should be concerned with those that make the mistake.

I visit with our assistants on a regular basis on this subject. The easiest thing in the world when someone does something wrong is to say, "That is it, you do not play for us anymore." I look at things in terms of making decisions in our football program as it deals with discipline this way. We have an extremely disciplined program. I do not believe you can find good programs at all levels that are good that do not have good discipline. Not only do they have self-discipline within the staff and players, but they also have the willingness to discipline young people. It is easy to just say, "Get out of my way." It is easy to say, "Go home, go play basketball, go do something else." What kind of an asset have we been to those young people when we do that? Probably not very much. Can we help them? Yes we can help. We can help a great deal. That is an important thing for you to consider. The thing to ask yourself is this: "How can I help young people?" Certainly we would like to nip the problem in the bud. We would like to portray the kind of character in a role model for young people so they will always make the right decision. We are living in the dark ages if we think that is the way it is going to take place. This is something we have to work at. It is a lot different today than it was 20 years ago. Things have changed dramatically. All you have to do is to watch TV or read the newspaper and you will know what I am talking about. You had the tragedy in Colorado. You have tragedy all over the country. It does not surprise me at all. We are living in a tough society today for young people. Young people need our help and guidance. They need your direction.

You can do this at the high school level in you program. We have what we call a Freshman Transition Class. Eleven years ago, when I took the job at Kansas State, I was the only head coach that taught a class. It was not one of those "Basket Weaving" type courses. We put everyone of our freshmen in that class. At first it was a one-semester class. Now it is four semesters. I do not teach the class anymore. We hired some people to come in and teach the class out of our student academic programs. We bring in people that address certain issues to young people. I think you can do this at the high school level. I did this when I was coaching in high school but not to the degree that we do now.

In my experiences I have learned a lot and I have paid attention. I have learned a lot about young people when they make a transition, in our case, from a senior in high school to a freshman in college. In your case it could be a variety of differences. It could be going from the eighth grade to the ninth grade. It could be going from the 10th grade to the next grade. It could be just be a young person 15, 16, or 17 years old.

I share this information with you because I think you can do the same thing. If I were back in high school coaching this is one of the first things I would do. I feel your superintendent, principal, faculty representative, or whoever you report to, would love to see this program implemented. Our president has asked me each year to help him implement this program for the entire student body at Kansas State University.

Very briefly, the class deals with all issues that young people have to deal with in being a student athlete. It deals with being away from home. How to deal with a newfound freedom. It deals with associations that you and I and parents are concerned about from all over the country. It deals with sexual issues. It deals with substance abuse issues. Alcohol is a big-time problem all across our country. We deal with those issues.

We deal with communication skills, reading skills, writing skills, and you name it, we are addressing it. We cover how to conduct yourself among your peers, and how to conduct yourself with adults. There are an enormous amount of subjects you can study. You can draw up your own study in that regard. Our guys have to go to that class. We bring people in to discuss all of those issues.

The NCAA has this program at the university level. It is called Life Skills. They try to encourage all universities to have certain people to address certain issues. Say they come in and address substance abuse. They advertise they are going to have a speaker come in on a certain date and speak from 7 p.m. to 10 p.m. Now, our guys have a lot to do with their time. They go to class, go to practice, and they have to study. It is not easy to make those sessions. But my question is this. If a person has a problem with drugs are you going to be able to solve it in those three hours? You can't do it in three hours. It is something that must go on over a period of time.

Our program is an ongoing program. Our players go to that class. That special program is important, but we are going to cover that same issue in our class. They hear this for the entire week, for the entire year. It is not just a one-shot, three-hour deal. But, think about that type of class for your situation. I do not think it is that difficult to do. It all depends on how important it is to you. How important is it to you for your young people to become better citizens and to find out what this life is all about? Believe me, as good of a role model we may try to be, they are not paying that much attention to us.

In regards to the talent level, yes it is a little different as to where we are and where you are. How do you address this issue. One way is for you to get on the field and for your coaches to coach hard. You can teach the fundamentals and techniques. We all can look down our depth charts and find positions where we are not very good at certain positions. You may not have very good athletes in those positions. Most of us realize, if we have 11 that play on offense and 11 on defense, that what we really want are good athletes in those positions.

Size and strength is good, but we like to have athletes at all of those positions. You want to have offensive linemen that can run, sure. You like them big and strong, but you want them to have some athletic ability.

I am not sure what the state high school associations allow you to do in each state but this is what we did when I was coaching in high school in California. We had an Athletics Skills Clinic that we promoted to our high school. We brought into our high school the fourth-, fifth-, sixth-, seventh-, and eighth-grade students to that clinic. Our school started at the ninth grade. Every summer we brought those young kids in to our clinic. We had two facets of the clinic. One of the phases was strictly for athletic skills. When I say athletic skills it did not have anything do with football, basketball, or baseball, or any other sports. It was just purely athletic skills. It was movement, agility, changing directions, and understanding a speed school type clinic. It was for skills that would allow you to develop athletic ability. For a lot of people speed is a gift from the good Lord. But for young people, they need to develop athletic skills. Again, this all goes back to you. How important is this to you to be able to develop kids at that early age? They are eventually going to go to high school. Are you interested in developing them at that early age to become better athletes?

The other phase of the clinic was to take all certain "Skilled Positions" and try to develop the skills with them. We introduced a program where they could develop their skills. For example, we worked with the Punter, Place Kickers, and Quarterback. We took a look at those young kids to see who in that group would be able to develop the skills to become a quarterback in our program in the future. I am a firm believer that if you have a strong quarterback or a good Tailback, you have a chance to have a good offense. If you one of the good athletes at quarterback or Tailback you have a good chance for success. We attempted to develop quarterbacks through a system in this way. We covered the techniques of a quarterback and passing skills.

This is the way we did it. Now, this was awhile back and video was just coming on the scene. This is what we did. After we taught the skills we would ask the parents to come in for a meeting. We gave the parents a workout schedule and drills for them to put the kids through. The parents would video-tape those workouts. Then the parents would provide that videotape to one of our assistants. He would make out correction sheets and give them back to the parents. In a sense the parents were coaching their sons. It had quite an impact. At the time we did not have seventh- and eighth-grade football. It all started at the ninth-grade level. But, we were helping to develop them before they got to us. It was productive for us.

I know what may be running through some of your minds. You may say if we are going to start at that young age I may not be the coach when they get in high school. This leads me into something I learned a long time ago. You learn things by having certain experiences. There was a time when I was coaching with one foot in and one foot out. What I mean by that is that I was coaching where I was and I was trying to be someplace else. I wanted to be a college coach. I wanted to go as far as I could go in the profession. There is nothing wrong with this. But the problem was this. I was trying to get there without paying enough attention to my job where I was as I should. I learned after awhile. I was not a very good football coach to be honest with you. I was good at going to the clinics. I was good at taking the notes. I had a lot of things running around in my head that I thought was pretty good. I was a grad assistant at Southern Cal when John McKay was the head coach. I tried to pattern myself after him. I tried to be like him. I tried to walk like he did, and I tried to talk like he did.

I learned two things from that experience. One was Be Where You Are. Now, wherever I happen to be, that is it. I have not shown an interest in other jobs. I have been totally focused on where I am. When I was in Texas I was totally focused. When I was at the University of Iowa I was totally focused on what I was doing there. Since I have been at Kansas State I have done exactly the same thing.

The feeling is that I want to do the very best I can do here and to do justice to the program that I am in. If something happens then something happens.

A young coach asked me a few minutes ago this question: "How do I get into college coaching?" My answer was this: "Do well where you are." That makes a big difference. That was important to me because it made me a better coach. Today we hear about the Five-Year Plan. Coaches talk about having their own recruits in five years. I have never been able to understand that, but I do believe this. If you go to a new school and you feel that you must have a plan, make it a 10-year plan. You may want to make it a 15-year plan. Put it out there so you will be developing a program that has a firm foundation. If you are there to get someplace else the foundation is not going to be there. If the foundation is not sound I doubt if you have done justice to the program you were involved with.

The other thing I learned was to "Be Who You Are." I tried to be John McKay. Whoever you are, be good. You can be good. You can be a good football coach if that is what you want to be. You can do it your way. You do not have to do it someone else's way.

When I left USC I went back to Indio High School as the head coach. I was the assistant before I went to USC. While I was at USC I saw that everyone worked hard. I said that was the first thing we were going to do. We were going to work hard. I wore them out. I flat wore them out. The players, coaches, and everyone else hated me. We were down on the desert. When everyone else was going two-a-day we were practicing three-a-day. When the sun is up it gets up to 115 degrees. When the sun goes down it gets down to 105. Our players were falling out like you can't believe. After everyone left I would keep those assistant coaches there until 2 a.m. They would be back at 6 a.m. and we were going over all of the things we had learned. I was trying to be someone else. I thought that was the way they would have done the job. Just Be Who You Are. You can do fine by being who you are.

Another thing I share with our players in our program, and I buy into this myself. I share this with you and my own children. It relates back to what I said a minute ago. One of common things we all want is to be successful. This is what I tell players and coaches. One of the first things that may be of importance to you is this. Surround yourself with people who genuinely want to make a difference in your life. Be around people that care. Be around people that want to have an impact on your life. Be around people that really want to make your life better. Think about that for a minute.

That is what I share with our players. "We know there are people out there that do not give a darn. They do not care about your life one way or another. You are going to be around people that want to pull you down, and they will pull you down. Every high school coach knows they have a player someplace that will pull down someone in your program. They probably want to pull them down. But, there are a number of people that will help make life better for you."

This is true for you and I, just like it is also true for the young people we work with. I think it is a tremendous message to try to convince young people to buy into this.

I ask our players to do this. I ask our players to make a list. I ask them to identify who are those people in their life that totally want to make your life better. We sit down and discuss this list. I ask them why they can't spend more time with them. "Why can't you seek them out? Look for those people and spend time with them."

Now I ask them who the people are that do not want to make life better for them. "Why would you want to spend time with them?" If you want to be successful then you need to be around the right people. Be around great people. It makes a big difference. We have talked to CEO's from across this country. The first thing they will tell you is that they have been around great people. I can tell you that I would not have been able to do the things I have been able to do in my life if I had not been

around great people in my life. I have been fortunate to have been around great people. But I can tell you something. You can select those people you are around. The players can do the same thing. I think it is important for them to be able to do that.

You have a system about goals in your program. I do not know what it is, but you have a goals program. It is really amazing about achieving goals. In our program we believe this is important. But what I see all across the country, in sports, and other phases of life is that people give lip service to this. I can give you a perfect example. I do not know how many of you are as old as I am. But I can think back to a period of time when New Year's resolutions were a big thing. Now, there were two things that happen in the course of the day that you look forward to. These two things both fell on the same day and that was the first of January. One was that you got to watch all of the bowl games on TV. The second thing was that you got to make your New Year's Resolutions. What were the resolutions? They were always self-help things. You were going to stop smoking. For some reason people had to wait until January 1st to do it. Other resolutions included the following: stop eating fatty foods, stop drinking as much, start exercising more. So we had all of these self-help things that we were going to do. We were setting goals.

Now, think back if you ever set New Year's Resolutions. What happened? Hopefully you were successful. People that I saw were not very successful. They could make it through January and everything was good. By the time March came around they started to taper off a little. Then April and May came and the people were back where they started. They were back eating fatty foods, or they were back drinking alcohol, or they were back smoking.

What was the problem? Those were all goals. They set goals but they did not achieve them. To me it is important to be able to achieve the goals you set for yourself. We have a lot of goals in our program. But we break them down differently. We have goals by position. We have goals by units. We have goals by offense, defense, and kicking game. We have collective team goals. These are not just things you write down and put up on a bulletin board. I understand, and our coaches understand, that if we are going to have goals we are going to do more than just pay lip service to them. We are going to get our players involved and we are going to spend time establishing the goals. Then we are going to move on where we can achieve those goals.

I tell our players this. When we set goals we are no different than anyone else. We know that 100 percent of our society sets goals for themselves. Very, very few achieve the goals they set. We tell our coaches and players that the second step in setting goals is to have a well-thought-out plan of how you are going to achieve those goals.

At times my assistants get a little upset with me. We have staff meetings and some of them what to talk X's and O's. I want to talk about what I know will make us successful. I know if we set goals and we do not achieve them we are not going to be successful. So I want to know how we are going to achieve our goals. It is important to have a step-by-step plan for achieving every single goal we set. We spend a lot of time planning step-by-step how we are going to achieve our goals.

I would say this. Less than half of the people that set goals have a plan of how they are going to achieve those goals. Most people will tell you they are going to work hard to reach a goal. I ask our players how they are going to achieve their goals and they tell me they are going to work hard. That may be part of it but that is not the answer. I can work my fanny off but still not reach my goals. Why? Because I do not have a step-by-step plan to achieve success.

This is a NIKE Clinic. I always share the third thing in goal setting with our players. NIKE has a slogan that I always liked. I think it is neat. That is the other step that sets up the whole deal. **JUST DO IT**! Carry out the plans. Just do the things you planned on doing to achieve those goals. It is hard for young people to understand that. It may be even harder for those in our profession to understand it.

I go to see a lot of schools and visit a lot of people. I talk to a lot of coaches about goals. It may be goals you want to achieve in each game. Our offensive and defensive coaches have set goals that they want their units to achieve in the course of a ballgame. On Monday our staff goes through those goals to determine if we have achieved them or not. They mark off the things they achieved and acknowledge those they did not achieve. To me this is not what you need to do. You are still looking at your goal sheet and it says you have not achieved some of them. How can you be successful if you are not achieving the goals if your goals are directly related to you being success in your program. The message is to *Have A Plan*.

A lot of motivational experts express it this way. They say, "Keep your eyes on the goal." I have some concern with this. If you are keeping your eyes on the goal you are overlooking the steps you need to take to get to where that goal is. This does not have to as complicated as many try to make it sound. A lot of people out there making a lot of money will stand up in front of a microphones and talk with people about motivational subjects and particularly about goals. To me it is not worth paying five hundred dollars to go to one of those seminars just to find out that what you need to do is to have a PLAN.

Everyone in here is smart enough to develop a plan in order to achieve the goals that you want to achieve. I could spend some time talking about this. I hope you have plans for all of your goals. My experience has been that many people do not have a plan for the goals that they want to achieve.

In our program this is one of our goals. We do not have those goals that say we are going to win nine games or 10 games or 11 games or a championship or any of that. I am not saying that is wrong. I am just saying we don't do that. I can't say that my players don't have those goals But I can tell you that we have 16 goals. We established those 16 goals 11 years ago when we came to Kansas State and they have not changed. All of those 16 goals are intrinsic things. They are intrinsic goals.

The top of the list is to improve. That is simple and you probably hear that a lot in coaches' dialog. We spend a lot of time trying to sell our players on trying to become better every single day. This is the way I can convey it to the team and it fits right in with Kansas State football over the last 11 years.

We ask our players to do this. *Find a way every single day of your life to become a better person, a better student, a better football athlete, and be better with your faith, and be better with your family*. Why do I pick those words? Because I tell them I think it is important that they understand what their priorities are while they are at Kansas State University. Their priorities would be different than yours to a certain degree. They would be different than the players you have in your program. Whatever those priorities happen to be, that is what needs to be established. Make those priorities in the areas that you want to make improvement in. Those are the five things we hope they will choose at Kansas State as their priority. Therefore, we hope that they will find a way every single day of their life, 365 days a year, to get better at.

What I share with our players I will share with you. Take any one of those and find a way today to get a little better at it. To be a better football athlete, how hard is it to find a way today? When you think of one of your players, would it be hard for one of your players to become a better player today? I am not talking about gigantic strides; just a little better. How hard would it be for him to become a better person? If he worked at it, it would not be very hard at all. It is easy to identify what to do, and it is probably easy to do it. It may just be going to film study. It is that easily done.

I tell our players to just envision what may happen with this. You are going to be at Kansas State University for X number of weeks or months or years. If you can make a little improvement each day just envision the success you can have in a month, a year, two, three, four, or five years.

In our program we have 115 to 120 young people. If we can put those successes and those areas or improvements together over that same period of time, just envision how good your football team can be. Envision what they can do collectively as athletes, as people, and as students.

Have we lost? You bet we have. Have we lost ballgames? Yes we have. Have we had any young guys get into trouble? Yes we have. But, I believe we are making a lot of headway. This does not mean that we stop trying just because we have someone who goes in the wrong direction.

Improvement is important. That is what all of us want. Every time you get up and talk on a microphone that is what you talk about. But, do we do anything other than just talk about it? This is what I do. After every single practice I go into the locker room and walk around. Players will answer the question before I get to them. My question is this. *"DID YOU GET BETTER TODAY? DID YOU IMPROVE TODAY?"* They will respond, "Yes I did, Coach!" I ask them what did they get better at. They do not have to be better in everything that they did that day. Every day our players go to practice with an area of improvement in mind that they are going to focus on in order to become a better player. Our position coaches have a one-hour meeting with the players just before they go on the practice field. At the end of that meeting they come together on one area that they are going work on to get better for that practice. When I go around to see the players they all have an answer for me. "Coach, I got better at this today." Could they fall back on this skill later? Sure. But the point is they are thinking about getting better. It is on their mind because we keep it on their mind. When they cross that line to go on the field they know they are going out there to get better. Does that mean we do not have some players that do not always improve. Of course we do. But improvement is on their mind everyday. If you have a group of players, whatever your numbers are, if you can get your players to focus on getting a little better each given day then your team is going to get better. Your football team will get better. You can go hide in a closet and they will get better.

If you can convince those youngsters to do this you will get better. When they see the progress in football you can convince them the other facets of their life can be handled exactly the same way. This is true for their classroom work, and their personal lives.

Look at Kansas State University. It was mentioned that it was not a winning program for decades. Now, some of you are young and it is tough for you to think back 11 years ago. Kansas State did not just rise out of the sand like Las Vegas did. There had never been a time prior to the last 11 years that Kansas State had done anything special. It has been step-by-step, a little at a time. We have gotten a little better. When we look back and look at it has been exactly that way. In my first year at Kansas State we won one game. We were 1-10. If you have not had any fun lately let me tell you about going 1-10. But, ever since that time we have gotten better and better. The record indicates this. In the last three years we have won 11 games each year. We have improved from that 1-10 year each year. We won one the first year, won five the next year, seven the next year, and on and on. It was never all of a sudden we were there. It shows we were trying hard to do what we were preaching about. We wanted to get a little bit better as we go along. I attribute our success to exactly that. It is easy to say, "Coach, you have a lot better players now than what you had in 1989." Yes we do. But we got better players a little bit at a time.

All of these things are easy concepts. The game is not as hard as we want to make it sometimes. You know the same things. If you have motivated on the field you are probably are going to do well. But, we do not always know how that motivation takes place. I may sound like one of those speakers on a motivational tape and I understand that.

When I first went to Kansas State University as the head coach I asked someone in the athletic department to contact the 22 seniors that had used up their eligibility to come to see me. I asked them to come in and sit down with me and spend one hour with me. All 22 of those players came in and visited with me for one hour. That is a whole story in itself. Of those 22 players, not a single one of them had ever played in a college football game that they had won. They would never play for Kansas State again. They had tied one game. Their time was up. There is some sadness to that, isn't there?

I was concerned about those 22 young guys. I felt their lives had been tramped down. They saw themselves as failures. Failure has a dramatic impact on people. A dramatic impact, not because they did not win at football, but they see themselves as failures in so many facets of their lives. Those 22 players told me they would not wear their letter jackets. They did not want to be identified with the football team. Their grades had suffered dramatically. It went on and on.

It was an interesting time visiting with them. But the point is this. There is a persistence about making sure things take place and that things happen. You have problems in your program. I have problems in our program. Sonny Lubick has problems in his program. We all have problems. If your program is big like ours you realize that you have problems every single day. You are dealing with young people that are 15, 16, 17 years old and the whole world is available to them. It does not make any difference if you live in rural Kansas or Denver, Colorado, the whole world is at your feet. Anything and everything that is out there is accessible to them. So, you are going to have problems. There has to be a persistence of how you attack those things. These problems can flat wear you out. There are a lot of people in coaching that have stopped coaching because of this. There are those or you here that will look back and ask why you did a certain thing. There are a lot of guys that coach football that get in deep real quick in some form or fashion. It takes a persistence that is just unbelievable.

Football is unlike anything else that takes place in our society. It is as good as it can be if we treat it the right way. There is something special about this game of football. But, there is something very special about the people that play the game of football, because they are our young people. How we impact their lives is as dramatic as anything.

By persistence I mean you have to fight it every single day. The easy thing is to turn your back on it. It is easy to turn your back on a kid when he irritates you to no end.

We have what we call Responsibility Running. That is the consequences for certain violations or problems. We do not tolerate being tardy. We do not tolerate missing a class. We have a lot of things where if the players do not do well they have to suffer the consequences for. But this is not the total answer.

A lot of the time the assistant coaches want the players he works with to be his friends. They want the players he works with to be better. The head coach goes nuts because sometimes the discipline is avoided. I address our staff with that all of the time. I think this is important. An assistant coach needs to discipline his young people enough so they will not get into trouble or at least they are going to think very strongly before they do. I am not telling you that physical punishment is going to get the message across to young people. That is not the case. But it does take the persistence that you have to persevere through so many things. So that is what we have done for 11 years at Kansas State University.

One story I relate to the young people is this. I use this because they all have read the story about Abraham Lincoln. Abraham Lincoln failed at eight attempts at public office. He went bankrupt after those eight attempts. Then in the very next election he became President of the United States. He had a plan and he carried it out. He had perseverance. The story goes on and on.

I told you I coached at Southern California. You all have heard of Steven Spielberg. His movies have influenced your lives and my life. He made great movies. He may be one of the greatest producers ever in history of the business. Supposedly, USC is the best film-producing college in the world. The

story that was told to me was this. Steven Spielberg applied for admission at the film school at USC and was not admitted because of his grades. I do not know what they called the school of film making then but I know want they call it now. They named it after Steve Spielberg. He could not go to school there but they named the school after him.

Why was he successful? Because he has perseverance. He had a plan. He carried his plan out and he persevered and he had great success.

Let me address a couple more thoughts here. We have all heard this term. We all have heard people talking about a football team and say that they have great Expectations. When you hear that it means you are expected to have a pretty good team. People will say that this team has great expectations. The expectations are high. It is something that I think is important. You need the types of players in a program that are quality people. You need people that are good enough so the expectations are high. Our players are never under as much expectation by the media as they are within the program. We have great expectations.

This is how we address this issue. We address it in two ways. One is this. If you are the head coach it relates to the assistants, or if you are the assistant it relates to your players. That is you had better have great expectations of yourself before you can expect great things of the people you are working with or for. If you have great expectations for your capacity to achieve success and work toward that end, then that puts you on solid ground to have great expectations of the young people or assistant coaches.

It is so easy to say, "Coach, you are asking me to do too much. Remember, this is just a game. I can only do so much. You are asking a lot." Yes you are! I share it with our players this way. I tell them if they can do it once, then I know they can do it. I will say the same thing to our coaches. All you have to do is to do it once. Just prove one time that you can do it. When they do it once they are in serious trouble. I am going to expect them to do it that way every time. If you do it right once you have proven you can do it.

The other side of this coin is a word called limitations. This is what concerns me more than anything else. I refer back to those 22 seniors that I interviewed that had finished their eligibility. They had placed great limitations on their abilities to achieve success. I was not there to place blame on any of those 22 players. They were anxious to volunteer information on their situation. I still keep in touch with those 22 players.

In that meeting one of those 22 players asked me this question. That past football season Iowa played at Kansas State. This is the question he asked me: "Coach, in our game this year the score was very close at halftime. Iowa won the game going away the second half. Why did that happen?" I assured him that was a great question and I had a simple answer. It was because of Iowa's expectations. It was their ability to achieve success. I say that not just because it is a word to throw out. I believe personally in our program, it is important not to allow young people to place limitations on their ability to achieve successes on the things that are important in their lives. Football is one, their skill level is another, and there are certainly a lot more that are more important.

The last thing that I will share with you has to do with decision making. We all talk about making decisions for young people. If the people you work with are like the young people we work with, they have heard choices and decisions for the last 15 years of their lives. When you start talking about making decisions they close up. It goes in one ear and out the other. How many times have they heard someone say "make the right choice or make the right decision"? I do not try to tell the players that this is the right decision or this is the wrong decision. For me I have found in our program it is important to have a process where you can make decisions yourself. As a football coach, I have to cross that when I am going to make decisions. When I have a chance to make a decision, I am not going to make hasty decisions. I am not saying it is good

or bad to make quick decisions. Sometimes it can be good and sometimes it can be bad. I am going to take all the time I need to make the decision.

One of the first things I am going to ask myself is this: If I chose to do this will it help our program become better in all of the areas that are important to our program? If the answer is YES we are going to do it. If the answer is NO we are not going to do it. When I say program, this is important. There are a lot of decisions you or I will have to make that deal with individuals within our program. I still ask myself the same question. I am not asking myself if this is better for this young man. I would like to ask that question. If he were not a part of our football team that is exactly what I would ask. But if he is with our football program I am going to ask myself that question.

If I chose to do this, regardless of how it will impact that young man, will this be in the very best interest of our football program? Will it make us— and remember what our priorities are—a better football team, a better group of young people, better students, better representatives of this university? Will it make us better with our faith and with our family? If the answer is yes we are going to do it. If the answer is no we are not going to do it.

When it comes time for young people to make decisions this is what I share with them. Our process may not be best for you, but have a process, and have a way to go to make decisions. Have a way about making decisions. Young people make those quick decisions. You know it and I know this. Young people make quick, bad decisions and regret it. You regret it and their families regret it, if they have family. If they just had a process to make decisions.

I ask our players to do this. I ask them to consider this and try to buy into it. When the opportunity arises for a 20-year-old to make a decision they need to have a process to help them make those decisions. They are going to have to make a lot of decisions every day that are going to be nothing in their lives. It is not going to make a difference one way or the other. There are a few decisions that they will make that will have a moderate impact on their life. There are a few decisions they will have to make that will have a dramatic impact on the rest of their lives. I ask our players to take 10 seconds out of their lives and to step back, regardless of the incident, and ask themselves this question. Again, this is based on what your priorities are. *If I choose to do this will it help me with my faith, will it help me with my family, and will it help me be a better person, a better student, or a better football athlete*? If the answer is YES to any one of those then DO IT. If the answer is NO then DON'T DO IT. Make the decision to do what is in front of you. If the answer is no, why do you want to do it.

There are a lot of ways and a lot of processes you can have to make a decision. But you have to have a process by which you can choose to make decisions. Do all of our guys make great decisions? NO! Do we have guys that make bad decisions? We do. But I would suggest that we have more and more making better decisions all of the time.

I would appreciate this from you. There are a lot of you that are here that I have your attention. I appreciate that a great deal. I would like to believe that you truly recognize what is important in your coaching career. If it is coaching for you, that is fine. But, the real value of this coaching thing is not the wins and loses. Now, I would not be the coach at Kansas State if we were not winning ballgames. I know that as well. But the point is, the real value is that we are doing something for others. There is an old adage about the good things we receive when we do something for others. You are doing something for others. I appreciate you because of that. It would be very easy for you to get up and leave the room. I am not talking about a quarterback or the running game. I am not talking about pass patterns. I am not talking about a blitz

package. Some coaches think they are not going to learn if we do not talk about the X's and O's. If you feel that way it tells me one thing. It tells me that your interest in not in the right place. I think the coaches that feel that way are going to have trouble being successful. If you understand how to deal with people and you understand how to help young people, you are going to have the greatest opportunity to have success. You will have a feeling that comes from it that is beyond belief.

I will appreciate you because you provide that kind of leadership, direction, and guidance to the young people that need it. This is the toughest time in the history of our society for young people. If you don't believe it, go read the newspaper.

If you put a pin in the middle of the USA it would be in Manhattan, Kansas. There is not a lot going on there. We used to say that all of the problems of the cities do not go on in the small rural towns of the Midwest. But we know better now. It happens anywhere in this country.

A lot of you may say that you are doing what you can to help the young people in your area. But I will tell you this. You are in a position where you can do more than what you are doing. That would be my challenge to you now. You are in the community and you are in the school You only have under your supervision a few student and a few athletes. But, you have access to everyone in that school. You can help in a lot of different ways. You can do the same thing in your community.

I appreciate your attention. These are the things I feel are important. These are the things that have allowed Kansas State to have a winning program. We believe in these things. That is true of our players and coaches. Thank you very much.

SECONDARY SUPPORT IN THE EAGLE FRONT

UNIVERSITY OF OKLAHOMA

Thank you very much. Well, you must be the last guys standing. I appreciate you being here this morning. I want to start out by letting you know how much I respect you guys and appreciate the job you do. Coaching football at whatever level is all relative. My father was a high school coach in Ohio for 30 years. I've got an older brother who coaches high school ball. I've got an uncle who has been a longtime high school coach and now coaches at Youngstown State.

I have a great appreciation for what you guys do for young people in the way you help direct them and influence their lives. I appreciate your dedication after a hard weekend. You are still rolling and trying to learn some football.

I'm going to share with you some ideas we have implemented at Oklahoma. These are defensive strategies and philosophies that we started developing at Kansas State University. I carried it with me to Florida and now to Oklahoma. I think everything starts with your philosophy. This is not just clinic talk. I make sure when we start off every spring and fall camp, our players understand our philosophy.

We are not "a bend but don't break defense." We shoot for stopping the offense right now. We want to:

1) Stop the offense immediately. We want to set our offense up with field position and score points defensively. We do that by getting turnovers or having a three-and-out series. During the season we averaged 4.5 plays for possession, and about 50 percent on three-and-out.

2) Our defense starts with dominating the running game. We are going to do everything we can to outnumber you at the point of attack. We want to do everything we can to take away the balance of the offense in pass and run. The most difficult offense to defend is an offense that can both pass and run.

3) We want to force the offense to throw the ball. After we do that we want to pressure the quarterback. We play a lot of bump man-to-man and have a variety of blitzes we use. We want the quarterback feeling pressure and unsure of what he is getting. We want to create some uneasiness in his demeanor.

4) We are going to concentrate on taking away the offense's strengths. We want to be strong on percentages of the things they do in down and distance, and formations. We want to know and understand the offense's personalities. We have to get those things across to our players. It doesn't matter what the coach knows, it is what the players know.

5) We are going to spend a lot of time in practice on critical situations. The third down is a critical situation. We work on third-and-short, medium, and long yardage. Our players have a good feel for what is coming in those situations. We concentrate hard on Red Zone and Goal Line areas. We want to stop people 50 percent of the time in third-and-short, and 75 percent of the time in third-and-long. If an offense gets the ball in a first-and-goal situation, we want to force the field goal 80 percent of the time. If you force field goals you have a much better chance to win.

There are other factors that we believe are critical in playing good defense. We harp on it and make sure our players understand them. The first thing is to be *great hitters* and *tacklers*. We design a lot of beautiful schemes to stop people. It has happened more than once, when you have run the correct defense, have a player right there, and he doesn't make the tackle. Nothing is more frustrating for a coach. We spend a lot of time emphasizing tackling. We do all the drills, get in live situations in practice, and work on this phase. Nothing takes the place of being a great tackling team. It makes a big difference.

The second thing in this section is *great effort*. We grade effort. After we go through the tape and grade for technique, alignment, and so forth, we'll go back and grade for effort. We want to know who is playing hard and who isn't. We have penalty runs after practice for guys who get caught loafing. It becomes a pride issue. They don't want to see their names on the **Loaf Chart**. They want to give 100 percent effort.

We want to be *physical* and *aggressive*. We want to attack the offense. That has to do with not being a bend and break defense. If we make an error, we want it to be from being too aggressive. That is opposed to sitting back and letting the offense have all the fun.

The thing I emphasize on our offense as well as our defense is being *disciplined* in our *responsibility* and our *technique*. I emphasize to our kids all the time that no one should play smarter, harder, or more physical than us. It takes absolutely no talent to do those three things. If you do those three things better than your opponent, you will usually win that game.

You have to be able to depend on one another. The thing that drives me crazy the fastest is a player that doesn't know or understand what to do. There is no excuse for it. You spend time in meetings and practice things during the week. When it comes to a situation in the game when he is supposed to do something and doesn't do it, there is no excuse for it. That is where players have to take responsibility for winning and losing. If something comes up that we haven't covered, that is a different story. Our players understand that.

As coaches we want to make sure we *acknowledge performance* and *not potential*. We all have had those guys that look beautiful in that uniform. He is the one you want the other team to see. But when the ball is snapped, they can't make a play. The other guy looks terrible, but for some reason he makes all the plays. That is all we care about and our players know it. The media blows so much smoke up these kids' butts, that they think they are great. You have to be careful you don't read all that and think he is. The other guy who you signed in the last week of recruiting is the one who makes All-American, because he makes plays.

We tell our players we want to see it every day in practice, in live scrimmages, and games. In those situations we will find out who the players are. If you make the most plays, you are going to play.

I caution my assistant coaches not to get too comfortable with a lineup. If the guy playing behind the starter outworks him during the week, he plays. It all depends on the depth you have, but you want to push players and motivate them.

We want to be *consistent* with our *teaching* and our *philosophy*. We want to improve from day to day, teaching the same techniques and the same defense throughout the year. There are a lot of different ways to play defense. You have to know what you are, stick with it, and do it well. Players know you are not going to start off the year in this defense and in the middle of the year go to something else. If you are consistent, the kids know what is expected of them and they grow in your philosophy. I know that every year you have slight changes that evolve from your defense, but the structure doesn't change.

These are the things we start with every year in spring ball and every fall when we start practice. I believe in them and our players understand what is expected of them.

From there let's get into our base structure. We are primarily an **Eagle Defense**. We have a 6 technique Sam linebacker, the ends are in 5 techniques, the nose tackle is in a 0 shade to the tight-end side, and the open-side tackle is in a 3 technique. Our Will linebacker is in the A-Gap to the open side and the Mike linebacker is in the B-Gap to the tight-end side. We move the nose tackle from the nose to a G technique occasionally. We move the 3 technique tackle into a 4I some also. What my talk is going to be today is involving the secondary with the reduced front.

EAGLE DEFENSE

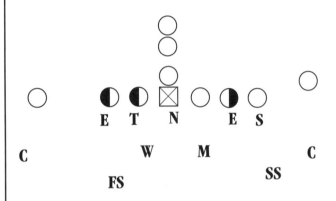

If you play the 4-3 defense you have to use the secondary to get to an eight-man front. When we play some teams and we don't respect the passing game, we will play up with both of our safeties in the box. That gives us nine guys ready to come. Our strong safety is going to align 1-4 yards outside the tight end and 8 yards deep. The free safety is aligned on the outside edge of the open-side tackle, 8 yards deep. We seesaw the safeties back and forth depending on who is coming down in the run game. On the snap one safety will be down and the other up.

That matters because that tells us how we are going to play our linebackers. If you get the isolation play to the Mike linebacker, he is going to spill the ball to the strong safety. He is going to take the inside of the block and spill the ball to the strong safety in the B-Gap. That lets the Will linebacker sit back for the cutback run.

ISOLATION SPILL TO SS

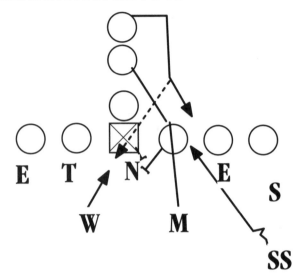

If the free safety is down, the Mike linebacker attacks the blocker on the outside and forces the ball back into the Will linebacker who is fast flowing over the top. The free safety fills the backside A-Gap for the cut back run. The nose tackle is going to receiver a double team block from the strong guard and center, with one of them trying to get to the Will linebacker. If that happens the nose tackle should cancel the gap and force the ball to the free safety.

ISOLATION SPILL TO WILL LINEBACKER

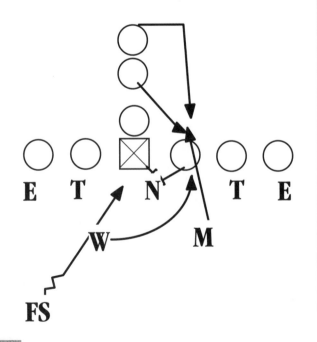

There are different ways we can play this defense. The Mike linebacker may walk up and fire. If he does, the strong safety is the replacement guy on all runs. If we fire the Will linebacker, the free safety replaces the Will linebacker and becomes the scrape linebacker. We are going to do everything we can to outnumber the offense in the run game.

In our coverage we are like everyone else. We can sink out and play quarter coverage. The strong safety is playing the tight end, which we call the number 2 receiver. If the tight end releases vertical he is on him. If the tight end goes to the flat, the Sam linebacker takes him. The strong safety works out to double the number 1 receiver coming inside. If the tight end runs a crossing patter, the Will linebacker takes him, and the strong safety move out to double number 1.

The free safety is going to double on number 1 his side from the inside out. The corners are squeezing from the outside in over the top. At times we bump the corners to man coverage, and play everyone else the same way. They know they have help to the inside. When we bump the corners we usually push our free safety right to the middle. The strong safety is still playing robber. If the tight end is a factor, he'll play him. If he is not a factor, he slides into the middle hole and watches the quarterback's eyes for a square in coming from either side to help the corners. The corners are man; the free safety pushes to the middle, the Sam and Will linebackers go to the flats, and the Mike linebacker sits in the hook zone for the tight end.

EAGLE DEFENSE VS TWINS

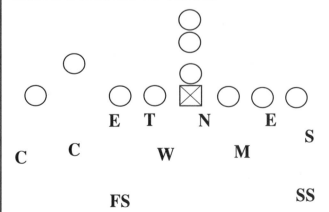

If the offense motions to twins or lines up in twins, the corner comes over with the wide receiver. That gives us both corners on the same side covering their wide receivers. The reason I like to do this is to keep the run support the same. Usually our safeties are better tacklers than our corners. The real advantage is that everyone is doing the same thing over and over. If they run the isolation we have the same fits as we did with the pro set.

People always ask how we play the outside plays. We don't wrong-arm the play or try to keep it inside. We tell our guys to go hit the pulling guard or fullback as hard as he can and penetrate. We want them to go attack the fullback or guard in the knee area. If you tell the guy to spill the play, everything starts to get too shallow and it becomes an easy corner to get around. If you tell them to keep it inside. They start to jump outside and get kicked out too easy. Our whole deal is for anybody that is taking on a kick-out block, go get it. If you are on either side getting bounced either way, you are not doing your job. We attack the thigh boards and drive through the knee area, as opposed to bracing yourself. We want to cut through the knee area and penetrate whatever is coming on us.

If you go back and look at the film cutups over the year, when we cut through the knee area and penetrate, usually the play is over. If you do it the other way the offense gets a successful play. It is hard to practice because you are cutting your scout team personnel or your lineman. But we have to do it on certain days.

The compliment coverage with the corners over is 3 deep. The outside corner plays the flat, the Will linebacker plays the curl, and the Mike and Sam linebackers play hook and flat. The free safety is in the middle third and the strong safety is in the outside third.

If we play man coverage, the corners are manned on the split receiver and the free safety is free in the middle. The strong safety takes the tight end if he is a threat to get deep. If he goes outside one of the linebackers will pick him up, and the strong safety drifts and looks to help on the speed side.

The linebackers are playing run first like everyone. Once they see pass Sam goes to the flat, Mike works for the tight-end hook area, and Will starts to expand to the flat, but in a twin set he goes to the curl. It is a simple coverage.

If they were to run the isolation weak, the tackle stays outside. The end squeezes outside. The Will linebacker hits the fullback on the outside, if we had strong safety support on. The offense doubles the nose tackle, and the Mike linebacker flies over the top to cancel the gap the fullback is taking. The strong safety runs through the cutback gap. The nose tackle keeps pushing the A-Gap when the double-team comes off on the Mike linebacker.

ISOLATION WEAK VS. SS UP

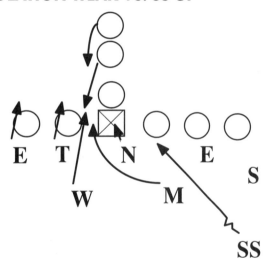

When people start to offset the fullback. We don't worry if they offset him strong. But if they offset him into the offset weak, we're in trouble. In our base structure the Will linebacker has the flat. The offset back has leverage on the Will linebacker, which is going to cause us to widen the Will linebacker. If the offense runs the zone play, they have the A-Gap. What we do is leave the Will linebacker in place, walk our free safety down, and change up our support. We treat the back weak like they were in a one-back with a slot. The free safety is going to protect the Will linebacker in the flat. The corners are in thirds and the strong safety is in the middle third. The free safety and Sam linebacker are in the flats, and the Will linebacker is in the curl area.

If we man up everyone takes a man. The strong safety is free and either the Mike or Will linebacker will be free, depending on whether number 3 comes out and which way he goes. If he goes toward the Will linebacker, he takes him. The Mike linebacker takes him going the other way.

ADJUSTMENT TO WEAK OFFSET

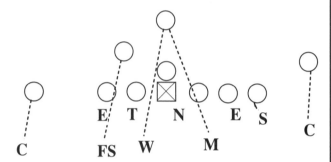

It gets back to the same philosophy of not being outnumbered in the box. When they start moving that fullback around, they are trying to out-gap you or get leverage on you. If they were to motion the fullback out strong, the strong safety would come down and the free safety would go up. If we were blitzing the Will linebacker, the free safety would have the back coming out that side because he is replacing the Will linebacker. That is just a different way to change up our support.

ADJUSTMENT TO MOTION

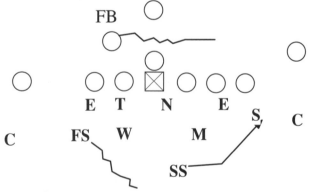

You don't want to become predictable in your support. If you are bring the strong safety down every time to the tight-end side, people will read that. They have become so good at running the strong-side isolation, they can bend the play back on you.

They will block out on your nose tackle and 3 technique. That leaves a pretty sizeable gap for the Will linebacker to play. We don't like the tailback knowing all the time where the hole is going to be when he gets the ball. That is why we work hard on disguising where the support is going to come from.

ATTACK THE SS DOWN

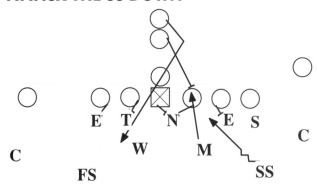

Let's cover the double tight end with two backs, on how we keep our numbers good in the box. All we do is move the defensive end from a 5 to a 7 technique. The corner comes down with the second tight end. Everything else in the defense stays the same. The free and strong safety support has not changed and we have been consistent in our adjustments.

DOUBLE TIGHT END SET

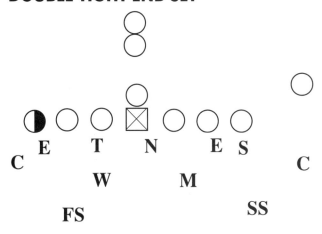

Another thing we face is the three-wide-receiver set with an I formation. They all want to see you walk your Sam linebacker out on the two-receiver side. By alignment they have stretched you out. If you move the Sam linebacker you have become weak inside. We move the strong safety out on

the second receiver. If they run the isolation strong, the Mike linebacker attacks the fullback on the inside and bounces the tailback outside to the Sam linebacker. The Will linebacker takes the cutback. If they run the play weak, the Will linebacker will attack the fullback from the outside position. The Mike linebacker goes over the top to cancel the play. The Sam linebacker cancels the bend cutback into the A-Gap. Again we have them outnumbered.

3 WIDE RECEIVERS

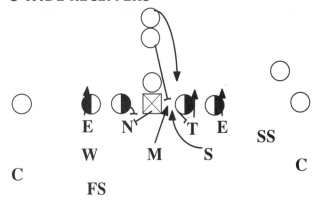

The coverage we could use against this set can vary. We could use man coverage with the free safety in the middle. The linebackers will take the two remaining backs out of the backfield. One of the three will be free. We could bail the corners out and play three deep with Will in the flat, Mike and Sam in the curls, and the strong safety in the flat. We could also blitz one of the linebackers and play man free.

We kick our linebackers away from the strong safety. You have to be careful with the Will linebacker. If you get him too wide, he could get cut off from the cutback run. We want to stack them for option and those kinds of things so he can escape and contain. But with the inside run game he has to get inside and cancel gaps as well.

If the offense came out in a pro left with an I formation in the backfield, we would reduce to the tight end. If they shifted the fullback into the weakside slot position outside the tackle we would adjust two ways. The end would move from a 5 to 7 technique. The free safety would walk down on the outside shoulder of the fullback. If the strong safety is into the wide field, he will stay on the tight end. As the ball gets centered up in the field, he moves more to the middle of the set.

FULLBACK WEAK SLOT

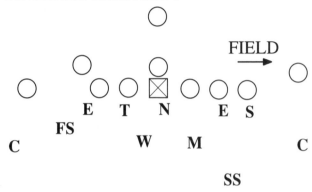

Along with our base quarters, 3 deep, and man coverage, it is simple for us to run a zone blitz from this position. We rip our end inside, the Sam linebacker comes off the edge, and the Mike linebacker fires outside the end's rip. The nose tackle slants across the center's face. The 3 technique loops outside and the 5 technique end goes to the flat. The free safety rotates back to the middle third, the strong safety comes down, and plays the flat. The Will linebacker is the hole player in the middle. The corners drop and we play 3 deep.

ZONE BLITZ TO FIELD

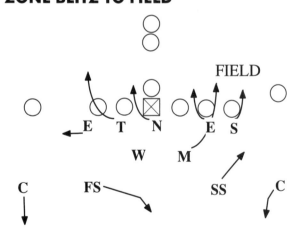

The other zone blitz we like to run to the field is this one. We could be in man coverage once in a while, but most of the time we end up in 3 deep. If we call *Dog* that is the Sam and Mike linebackers. If we call *Fire* that is the Will and Mike linebackers.

We put the nose tackle in a G alignment on the guard. He fires the B-Gap. The Mike linebacker blows the weak-side A-Gap and the Will linebacker fires up the strong-side A-Gap.

The 3 technique tackle loops for contain and the 5 technique end has the strong-side contain. The Sam linebacker and the 5 technique end has the flat coverage on pass. The free safety is replacing the Will linebacker and is the support player and hole player in the middle. The hole player always slides underneath the number 2 receiver if he comes to the inside. The corners are squeezing the number 1 receiver to the outside thirds and the strong safety is the middle third player. If the backs stay in and block, the Sam and end slide underneath the number 1 receivers to the outside. They stay under number 1 until something takes them to the flat.

ZONE BLITZ FIRE

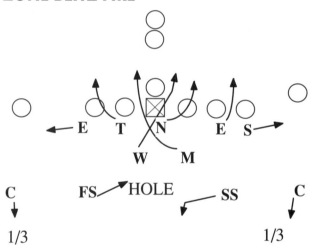

The strong safety is reading the tight end. Even though his responsibility is to the middle third, if the tight end blocks, he is coming to support. These zone blitzes are good run stunts also. We just don't run them in passing situations. It gives the quarterback a different look and they are easy to run and are safe.

When we shade players we are in wide shades. It almost looks like we are in gaps. We are reading the ball, jumping, and reading the shoulders of the offensive linemen. We want to get off on the snap.

If we played a trips set from our pressure front we would probably be in man coverage. Both corners lock up on the wide receivers. The free safety comes down on the third receiver. The Sam linebacker has the tight end and the strong safety is our free player. The Mike and Will linebackers have the remaining back. If he is set toward the trips, the first thing we think is sprint out to the trips. The Will linebacker aligns on top of the adjusted back. On the snap, if the offense sprints, the Will linebacker is coming right now. The end is going to attack the back, and the Will linebacker is coming straight for the quarterback. The Mike linebacker flows and is ready to help.

TRIPS TO THE FIELD

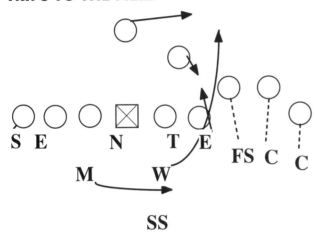

If we want to play a zone with this we play a regular defense against it. We can run the zone Dog against it and get the same thing type of pressure. Now the corner will be on the tight end to the weak side. The free safety is in the middle. The strong safety and corner are on the outside receivers. The Sam linebacker is on the third receiver. On the snap of the ball if there is a pass the strong safety is in the flat, the corner is in the third, and the Will linebacker has to hustle to get over the third receiver to that side.

DOG VS. TRIPS

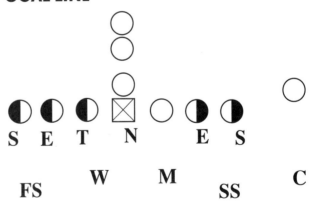

I've got some tape to show, that will make it clearer about what I've been talking about. After that I'll open it up for questions. Okay, that's it for the tape, are there questions you would like to ask?

The first question is about our goal line. Basically what we do with our goal line is replace one of our corners with another Sam linebacker. The adjustment is similar to the way we play two tight ends with our regular defense. Everything else remains the same. The safeties are tighter because of the nature of the position of the field. We don't spend a lot of time on goal-line defense because it is not that much different from our regular defense.

GOAL LINE

STRATEGIES OF THE MIDLINE VEER

UNIVERSITY OF THE SOUTH

I really appreciate you being here. This has been a long day for many of you. I really enjoy coaching clinics. It seems that you can always get something out of the presentation regardless of the subject or the speaker. You may hear a speaker and realize that you may do something a little better than they do, or you may get something that will be new to your program. I really enjoy the opportunity to be here.

Option football and the Midline Option has been a big part of my coaching career for a long time. I was fortunate to do some things when we were running the Wishbone offense in 1985 and 1986. We actually ran the Split Backs Veer when I was at UK. When I went to Texas A&M we got away from it. At Northern Illinois we were a true Wishbone team. The Inside Veer and Zone Double Option were the two plays that we ran. We tried to be as innovative with those schemes. We had a lot of success. In football, when you have success you get a lot of other opportunities. Our unfortunate opportunity was that we got to go to Oregon State. That was a great opportunity and we tried to make the most of it. We were in a tough situation there. From that experience we were able to grow and to develop the offense in a lot of ways.

In 1993 I had the opportunity to visit spring practice with the University of North Carolina. I studied some of their offense. I looked at their G-Option and Trap Option, and plays of that nature. Mack Brown was the head coach at that time. I stayed there a week and watched their practices. I stood behind their offensive huddle and watched them the entire week. The were running a Trap Option that was very similar to what Syracuse was running at that time with George DeLeone as offensive coordinator. I kept watching the Tight Dive or the Midline Dive by the fullback. I saw what that did to the linebackers. I

was equating this with the problems we had with the Inside Veer. This was especially true against the 40 Front with a 3 technique crease problem we were having. We were getting a lot of real fast flow linebackers. It is about a four-hour flight from Raleigh-Durham to Portland, Oregon. I was writing on every napkin the flight attendant had. I was going through all of the options the Tight Dive by the fullback added to what we could do. I looked at all of the possibilities of changing the read on the Inside Veer from being the first down lineman from the B-Gap to actually reading that 3 technique we were having so much trouble with. In option football we have always followed the principle that if a defender was hard to block he would be easy to read. If a defender was the type that gave our linemen a hard time blocking him, we could let our quarterback handle him a lot easier. So we applied this principle to the 3 technique. That 3 technique problem was a serious problem at that time. We were playing against some teams in the PAC 10 that we were having a tough time blocking that 3 technique. That necessity led us to the Midline Veer Option.

I believe in a concept on offense that is related to a core group of plays. One of the things I took from a lecture by Coach Woody Hayes 20 years ago was this. He said you need to have a good offense. The importance or doing that, regardless of what scheme you used, was that you had a repetition for doing something well. If you developed that repetition of doing something well, every team that would play you would know that was what they had to stop. If you could do that, all of your offense would branch out from that.

This is our running game. For lack of a better term it ends up being a triangle of the Inside Veer and Triple Option, Double Option, and the Midline Veer Option. Those three schemes together are so opposed to each other if you set a defense to stop one or two of the three, you create opportunities in the other phase of the offense. That was really the missing ingredient in what we have been trying to put together as an offensive package. We started with the Inside Veer as the core play. The Inside Veer as a core play is a great play. It may be the best running play ever devised in football because you are going to attack the defense at its weakest point. You can attack with the fullback, the quarterback, or the pitchout. But, if that is all you have on offense it will not take the defense long to bait you into giving the ball to the fullback. You have the linebackers blowing up inside and you can't knock them out of the holes. They may force you to pull the ball from the fullback and to pitch the ball and they have everyone flying to the pitch. You could create some opportunities, but basically the defense is going to dictate what you are going to be able to do.

The Zone Double Option gave us the opportunity to do this. If the defense wanted to play those kinds of games with the Triple Option we could Zone the line of scrimmage and get the ball to the perimeter very quickly. That took a lot of the Triple-Option Stunts away from the defense.

We started to see a lot of 6-1 fronts and a lot of expanded defenses on the corner. Still, if we ran the Triple Option they were forcing us to hand the ball off inside. When we ran Zone Double they had perimeter leverage and we were pitching the ball outside into a lot of defenders.

We needed a way to attack the defense that was not conventional. Conventional defenses absorb the fullback, and outside of that they have a corner player to absorb the quarterback, and a pitch player that plays outside. Every defensive coach that got on the chalkboard would draw up the defensive scheme like this: "This man has the fullback, the man outside of him has the quarterback, and the outside man has the pitch." We were trying to break that conventional wisdom. This is what happened when the Midline came along. We were able to put our quarterback in a position where the defense

was not able to handle him. That was mainly in the C Gap right outside the fullback read.

As this play fits into an offensive package it fits in as one of the core plays, but certainly not the core play, because there is not enough flexibility for this play to sustain an entire offense.

In terms of option principles, there are some things we try to do whenever we are putting these schemes together. They will always be coordinated. It is easy to get into a staff room and say something like this. "Hey, why not do this, or this, or why can't we change this?" As long as we maintain certain core principles we know that we have a solid play.

Here are the Midline Principles. We are going to read the first down lineman from the A-Gap outside. This is a departure from the Inside Veer thinking. In a 40 defense the 5 technique defensive end is always going to be the read key. Defensive teams spend the entire week teaching that end how he can read the quarterback, or how he can get across the line and box the shoulders to try to screw up the quarterback's read. They do not spend that time with the 3 technique, or the 2 technique or the I technique. So, by changing the read key from the normal Inside Veer to the first down lineman out, we create a lot of problems for the defense. Usually the defense will take their biggest, slowest, defensive lineman that they put inside just to take up space, and now we turn him into the read. That generally makes a good play for us.

One thing I will mention about this play is this. A lot of teams run this play as a predetermined play and not a read play. We only spend about 1 percent with our quarterback and fullback on this Midline read. This is opposed to the enormous amount of time we spend with the Inside Veer read. It is not difficult on the Midline read because the down lineman is not going to be able to do many things. The quarterback is in a position if it is a gray read where he can clean all of that up because of his position.

We always want to have two blockers on the play-side linebacker. That holds true for all of the options we run. You will see that on all of our schemes throughout.

The give for us on the Triple Option is a "Give" read. We coach the quarterback to hand the ball off. He is only going to pull it if the read key turns his shoulders and comes flat down the line of scrimmage. There are two things that have to happen. We teach him the difference in And-Or. Two things have to happen; he has to turn his shoulders and he has to come down the line of scrimmage. This read is different for the quarterback. If the 3 technique, or read on the Midline leans on the fullback, we want the quarterback to disconnect. Because of the lean, we feel the quarterback can get around that man and still get outside.

We will throw a Hot call on the back side on some plays. When we talk about schemes later I will show you the reason why. Everyone is kind of a product of the bad things that have happened to them. We were playing Southern California one year and we were driving for the winning score late in the game. We got down to the 5-yard line and ran this play. We got hit from the back side and lost the game. That has always been something we have always been concerned with.

Let me talk about the advantages of running this play. There are a thousand advantages. When we first started running this play in college in 1993 we were the only team running it. There may have been some high school teams using it. It seems that things always filter up in football. After we had a lot of success with it in 1993 I went to visit the Air Force Academy. They were excited about running this play. Later we went to West Point and talked to their staff. Now, a lot of teams are using this scheme because they see the versatility of what is happening. These are the reasons we want to run the Midline.

We were an Inside Veer team and the 3 technique was a problem for us. We had to use two blockers to block that 3 technique. This left the linebacker free on the Inside Veer and that was not a good situation. If our guards could not get any kind of movement in the crease that stopped the Inside

Veer. A hard-to-block 3 technique was one of the big reasons we went to this play. We were looking for something to find some answers. That man is easier to read than he is to block.

Another advantage is that we are going to freeze linebacker pursuit. Most of the Wishbone teams have generated out of that formation into some kind of double slot, or wing and slot formations. That involves motion to get the pitch back in the pitch relationship. A lot of defenses are starting to key on that motion. They fly linebacker and secondary guys to that motion. This play, because there is not a directional force with the fullback, because he is heading right over the center, freezes the linebackers. Defensive linebackers have been taught from the beginning of time if the center blocks back and the fullback comes at you, the play is going to be a Trap. "Step up and take on the Trap." That is what we are trying to take advantage of with this play.

A lot of teams were trying to defend us with a lot of leverage on the perimeter. If you are a strong option team, or if it is only a part of what you do, a lot of teams will fly defenders outside and force you into some type of arc block with the halfback. They know they have a 50-50 chance of beating you on the arc block to give you a lost yardage play. This play cuts off that outside leverage. We are going to draw a line at the tight-end box and base wall that end down the line of scrimmage outside and tuck the quarterback up underneath that block. They can line up 15 guys outside the tight end and be solid out there against any option we run, but we are going to cut those outside guys off and not let them be a factor in what we are doing.

Being able to attack the defense with a quarterback from inside the normal defensive reads ends up being a much bigger deal that we ever thought it would be when we first started running this play. I don't know of any defense that is designed to take care of the quarterback in the C-Gap. When we first started running this play there were plays when there was no one on defense from the holes in the 3 technique, who had squeezed down to take the fullback, all the way outside to the 7 technique who had stayed outside. It really shocked us that we had that big of a hole.

Now, what happens is this. The more you start running this play the more the hole restricts. The more that area restricts and the tougher it gets inside, what has this done to all of that level 1 leverage? It brings all that back inside. It opens up the Zone Double Option and opens up some of our outside plays. That is why, as I said, these plays are in that triangle, and these plays work in companion with each other.

We can run the play from a variety of formations. That is one of the reasons I have gone around and lectured on this play. Generally, I would not speak on schemes. If you are not running this type of offense, or if you are not running these formations, then this is all meaningless to you. But, the advantage of this play, especially with the Fan Load Play that we will get into in just a minute, you do not need a pitch-back for that play. It is a quarterback/fullback-type deal. You can run the play out of Trips, Spread, or out of any formation you want as long as you have a quarterback and fullback in the backfield. You do not have to be an option football team to run this play. This is especially true for the teams that are throwing the ball because the defense is running up the field.

The ability to option without motion became a serious concept for us because everything we were doing was out of the Double Slot or a Wing and a Slot. We had to bring a back in motion to get him in pitch relationship. Against Oregon and against Cal and some of the real good defensive teams in the PAC 10, they would line up with Inverted Safety Men over both slots. As soon as we would send a man in motion those safeties would slingshot down to the motion. It was worse than the old Cover 3 where the safety in the alley would come running downhill to the ball in the slot. We did have a running start on them but now they were starting to take advantage of that.

With this play we are able to option with motion or without motion. We can use the motion to carry the defense away from the point of attack. By using the scheme that way we were able to generate a lot more running room, not only in the C-Gap, but outside when we ran the Arc Option as well. That ended up being a big advantage.

Let me give you an idea on the schemes that we run. These plays all have numbers for us, but they do not really mean anything. I will just give them names so we all can be on the same page. The Midline Fan Load is the quarterback in the C-Gap play. We are going to mesh and read the first down lineman from the A-Gap outside. If we get a disconnect the quarterback is going to duck into the C-Gap. That is Fan Load. We are going to fan the line of scrimmage and load on the linebacker, and duck the quarterback up in the C-Gap. Off of that scheme we have taken the play three or four steps beyond. This was because of some problems and some advantages that developed. Fan Blast, Fold Load, Fan "COG", and G Load are some examples of how this play has branched out from what we did originally and how it has developed. That is one whole section of plays—the Fan Load Scheme.

Another scheme that was part of the original play in all of this, but a lot of people are not running it, is the Arc Option part of it. The Arc Option part is broken down into two segments. They are the Arc Double and the Arc Triple. You can read the Triple to get the ball outside. We kind of migrated into running it as a Double Option scheme the last two years because we have advantages outside. If we are going to Arc we want to get the ball outside instead of running it as a Triple and getting it handed off inside to the fullback.

I like to cover the rules on the play because I will only be able to show the play against one or two defenses. By having rules it allows you to put them in against all defenses. Our backside tackle is going to cut off anything from a 4I outside. He is going to high-pressure control from inside out. He is going to take a stab step and work himself inside high. We are not going to scoop the back side. We need to make sure we control the back side so that guy does not collapse with the quarterback. When we mesh with the quarterback, he is not moving away from the line of scrimmage like he is on the Inside Veer. He is moving away from the back side. He is going to be frozen to his back side. Protection to the back side is going to be important. If the tackle is uncovered he is going to fan the back side. The backside guard is going to inside cutoff from a shade technique outside. A shade ends up being a slight problem, but I will put up some answers for you. His technique is also pressure control. He is not trying to scope through. He is trying to lock on. If he is uncovered he is going to block the first linebacker head up to outside. That would be against a 50 defense.

The center is going to base block the man on him in a 50 look. If he is uncovered he has the backside A-Gap, to the backside linebacker.

The play-side guard is going to veer. He is going to block the first linebacker to the inside. The play-side tackle is going to fan the first thing from a 5 technique outside. Those rules hold true, especially from the guard back for every scheme that we run. So this is a very simple scheme for the offensive line. Their rules do not change except for a very few exceptions.

Let me cover line splits. We are split 3 feet at guards and 4 feet at the tackles. That is generally what we do on the Inside Veer. The closest we would ever be would be 3 feet all the way across when we are in our Zone Plays or Play-Action Plays. It is not much of a departure from what we normally do.

Against a 4-4 defense or some type of Split look this is what it looks like. This is out of Trips but it can be drawn up with any look. The backside tackle is going to pressure control anything from a 4I outside. He locks on right there so that the backside man cannot close down on us.

The backside guard is going to cut off the first thing from a shade outside. He is using a high-pressure control. If the man is a 1 technique the guard will get help from the center if he is uncovered. The guard is going to keep that man out of the hole. If

that man is in a 3 technique it is going to be an easy block for him.

The center has backside A-Gap to backside linebacker. If you have heavy A-Gap pressure the center will power up and try to keep his shoulders square up as he works up to the linebacker. That helps the guard generate a real good hole in that area.

The onside guard is going to veer. He has the first linebacker head up to inside. If the linebacker walked up into the A-Gap, obviously that would be his man. That veer release is the same release we teach with the Inside Veer. He is going to step hard with a gap lead step down inside. He is keeping his shoulders square. He dips his inside shoulder to try to reduce the friction. He tries to get a vertical push. If the read key climbs him, we will just wash him out all the way into the A-Gap knowing the ball will be pulled.

The onside tackle is going to fan anything from a 5 technique to outside. That is what we call a Base-Wall Technique. He steps to Base, and then throws his inside arm and Walls the man off and works toward the goal line as he gets locked up into the block.

The halfback has the first man head up to inside. All he is going to do is step around the tackle and block down. You talk about an easy block to execute, that linebacker has a lot of things he is looking at. This is something we have had a lot of success with. We will cut the man if he is lined up in the hole. If he is moving we will stay on him and ride him in the direction he is moving. If he is attacking we are going to cut him. If you can't cut him, you can still step inside and block him high. We would block him just like the fullback does on Iso.

On the outside we would just lock on and base the man on the outside. If we were not in Trips and we had a slot on the back side we would send him in motion to try to draw the coverage away from us. We are trying to occupy those defenders outside.

What we are trying to do is to create a wall. We feel we can create that wall because we have the angles on the defense. We can create a wall on the back side that is going to stay solid. If we get a *Give* read by our *Read Key*, then we have the advantage. We have the numbers and the angles in the A-Gap. Our fullback will be able to take advantage of that. We want to create that wall with our center and our two guards. It is the same on the Fan Block on the outside. We are going to block the rest of the defense outside and create a wall outside. Now we have gap by angles and by numbers that we take care of. The only defender inside that wall is the read key that we know we are going to eliminate one way or the other. We eliminate him by the fullback or the quarterback. We have a blocker for the linebacker. We are trying to isolate the linebacker and put a blocker on him, and the 3 technique can go wherever he wants to go.

The fullback has a Midline tract. He is going to line up with his hands in his stance at 6 feet behind the quarterback heels. That may be a different way of saying it for the alignment, but that ends up about 4½ yards distance between them. The thing that makes a difference to us about his depth is the speed of the hands of the quarterback. As the quarterback meshes he must be able to get his hands fully extended back before he has to start coming forward. If he is swinging the ball backward as the fullback is meeting him then the fullback is too close. If he steps back and has to wait, and wait, for the fullback, then the fullback is too deep. As soon as the ball is set in the give position the quarterback is ready to rock back forward so he is not swinging the ball in the fullback as he comes forward.

MIDLINE OPTION

On the mesh of the quarterback, he is going to step back with his opposite foot. If we are running the ball to my right I am going to step back with my left foot. I am going to get off the midline with that foot. As I step back I am bringing the ball directly back, and I bring my right leg back and get off the midline. When I set up I should be able to stand up with a camera and see directly down the midline. The quarterback should not be in that path. If you want to fumble this play you let the quarterback take the steps he wants to take.

He will get back and line up in the midline and the fullback will smash into him and the ball will go flying out of there. The detail of the play is that the quarterback must get back off the midline and then extend the ball. One thing the quarterback will do once he takes his steps is to lean over in the midline. Make sure they stay back off the midline so the fullback can clear and they can have a smooth mesh. It is not a long ride by any stretch of the imagination.

This is not anything like the Inside Veer read. It goes very fast. It is a real quick mesh point. The read for the quarterback is determined by what that 3 technique does. If he leans on the fullback we are going to disconnect. He can step around the fullback and it is a great read.

If the quarterback gets tackled at that point I will pat him on the back and ask him what he thinks he should have done in that situation. "I should have handed the ball to the fullback." Okay! What made you think that? "I thought the 3 technique was leaning a little too far toward the fullback." Now you know. That is how we approach them with this read.

The first time we ran this play was against Arizona State. They had a 310-pound defender playing the 3 technique. He was an All-Conference player. When we ran the play the first time he fell flat on his face. He thought he was going to take on a blocker and he fell flat on his face. It ends up being a real simple read for the quarterback.

If we get the read key leaning on the play we are going to disconnect and put the quarterback up in the C-Gap. It is a very difficult place for the defense to handle the quarterback. The only player that can handle him is the free safety and he has to be looking for it. If the free safety gets motion or anything that tips off that we are running an option, he is going to be flying to the alley to be a second run support outside on the pitch. You will break that man's ankles by having him trying to stop to come back to take the quarterback inside. That ends up adding another advantage to the play that we had not anticipated. It slows the free safety in the alley. Now he has to check the C-Gap quarterback run-through before he heads outside on the pitch.

We never predetermine the Fan Load play because we want to take advantage of getting the 3 technique out of there without blocking him. That was part of the reason we went to run the play to begin with. If we predetermine the pull by the quarterback then someone will have to block the 3 technique. If we are going to do that we would rather be running the Inside Veer.

After a couple of years after we started running the Midline I knew we had a good play. In the *American Football Quarterly*, Larry MacDuff and Rich Ellerson, two defensive coaches at Arizona, wrote a big article about how to stop the Midline. I knew if those guys were starting to write about the play then we had something pretty good.

What Arizona was doing to stop us was to stop some of their normal defensive tendencies of what they were teaching the middle linebacker. What they would do was to squeeze with the 3 technique and then when we pulled the ball they would scrape the middle linebacker over the top of the 3 technique. Now we had two linebackers sitting in the C-Gap instead of one. That generated some problems for us because we only had the one halfback coming inside to block that man.

We did two or three things to counter that move by the middle linebacker. I will show you a couple of different ways to attack that. You can change the defense by use of formations or you can assign blockers to that area.

The first thing we did was to add a Blast to the play. We got in the I formation. The I Slot was a part of our package. When that linebacker scraped outside, we told our I-back to run that path. We were still going to mesh with the quarterback and the fullback. We were still going to read the 3 technique. If the quarterback disconnected now we had a blocker for the Mike linebacker. The halfback still steps under the tackle for his linebacker. Now we had a blocker for both of those defenders. Our quarterback was still able to get into the C-Gap and get in a real good seam.

MIDLINE OPTION – I SLOT BLAST

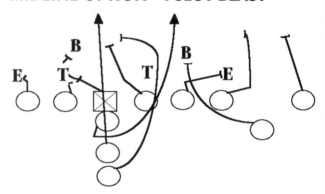

We are running this from the tight-end set. This is to the tight-end side. One of the advantages of running this with the tight end is this. The tight end is going to step outside the number of the 7 technique and work himself up to the second level. What that looks like to the 7 technique is a reach block. He thinks he is getting reached by the tight end like he would on a Toss Sweep or a Zone Option. As soon as our tight end steps outside, the 7 technique is taking him on. Now, that just takes that 7 technique out wider and stretches the play wider for us. I will talk about companion plays later. That is one of the key issues of this play. As the 7 technique expands the C-Gap it is the area we want to run.

As the play develops you will see the safety start to roll up. That is what the tight end is for, to keep him out of the play. Now we have everyone accounted for and we have them all blocked.

We can motion the back to get him to the same area to block on the middle linebacker. The motion man takes the place of the deep back on the seal on the middle linebacker.

MIDLINE OPTION – BLAST – MOTION

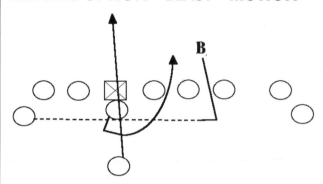

You can get the blocker on the middle linebacker to come from several different sets. It is a matter of using you imagination on the play. It depends on what fits in with your package. We have done all of these things so we could take advantage of two linebackers in the C-Gap.

The other way teams have run this play is to Fold Block on the tight-end side. They block the tackle outside and fold the tight end underneath. That may work on some of the formations you are using. The downside of that is this. When you fold the tight end back underneath to block the linebacker you do not get the stretch we got before. You have the halfback block the Mike linebacker. But that restricts what you are trying to do. That makes the 7 technique lean hard in the C-Gap. It forces them back down inside. It makes the alley a lot tighter. We are trying to expand that area as much as we can. The Fold Scheme is a way to run the play but it makes it hard to get up in there. But, based on your formations that may be the way you want to do it. You may not want to send your halfback up inside to block the middle linebacker.

By using motion we are able to draw the secondary in the direction we want them to go. We can get them past the C-Gap and get them out of the play.

Against linebackers that walk up on the line of scrimmage this really gives us an advantage on this play. We can block them down inside and still keep our

read key the same. We can get them eliminated and get the ball to the second level.

We spend a lot of time with the fullback on his first step on the inside veer tract. The fullback steps with his play-side foot down the A Frame to get to his aiming point. When we started running this play with the fullback we were stepping with our play-side foot right down the midline. What happened was the fullback started to drift away from the quarterback. At first we could not figure out why it was happening. We had trained him to run down the A Frame so much he kept drifting away from it. Now, and you can see this on our film, our fullback will start with his opposite foot. If we are running to the right he will start with his left foot. This keeps him hugging tight on the midline.

What do you do if against a Shade technique? For a number of years we would just check opposite the Shade. We found out that was not such a great answer. We would have to Zone or single block the Shade. Either block allowed the defense to squeeze the A-Gap. Then we had a hard time getting a blocker on the linebacker. So what we started doing was this to check it off to the 3 technique all of the time. We do not do that anymore. A lot of the time in our game plan we will check it to the 1 technique. We know on our presnap what the read is going to be most of the time. We felt our quarterback had a better chance of making yards than our fullback did. So it really did not matter that much to us which side we run the play. A lot of the time we will check it to the 1 technique. However, we do not like to run it into the Shade unless we make a call. We call C O G which means Center and Guard. We are going to double-team the Shade and take the read off the play. We know the Shade is going to be an inside player anyway. We do not want to get screwed up on who the read is and who the fan is. We are doing the exact same thing on the back side. The center is going to keep his shoulders square if he gets a backside linebacker run-through. But, the guard and center are going to vaporize the Shade. They are going to take him as far down the field as they can in the direction the guard is pushing the Shade.

MIDLINE OPTION VS. SHADE NOSE

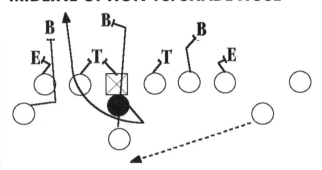

When we call *COG* it takes the read away. Now, the fullback is going to work himself around the double-team block and he takes the middle linebacker. When the fullback hears the quarterback call *COG* he knows he is going to mesh, work his way around the double-team block, and take the middle linebacker. Now it is an automatic disconnect for the quarterback. He lets the fullback clear and he gets downhill in the C-Gap seam. So the question about predetermining our play, we would only do it as a call against a shaded nose.

Let me cover what we do against the 50 defense. For several years we did not run this play against a 50 defense. We did not want to run our fullback on top of the center that was covered by a defender. We have used this play as an inside companion play against the 50 look. We looped the guard and tackle and left the center to cut off the nose guard in the A-Gap. Our success depended on how good our center was. If the defensive line was slanting, our center could not keep that nose man out of the A-Gap. That was a perfect reason to switch from the Inside Veer to the Midline play. Because the nose guard was slanting into the A-Gap our center could lock onto him and run him out of the play.

If the nose guard was a stuff-type player and was just going to take us on one-on-one we would run Inside Veer. Now the center could cut the nose guard off and the fullback could get inside on the veer path. The blocking is the same for everyone.

FAN LOAD VS. 50 DEFENSE

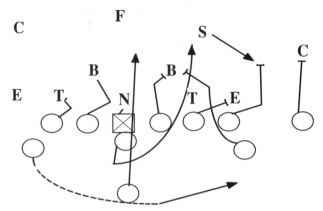

A play that Nebraska has used with this play is interesting. To take it one step further they are pulling the backside guard on the play. They are trying to log the read key. They would try to run G-Log with the guard on the read key. Against the 40 look they would log the 3 technique. You do not want the 3 technique getting upfield. The pulling guard wants to get to him before he gets upfield. It is more difficult to run the play this way, and it is a way to run the play without a read. This is how it looks against a 50 defense. It is not a read play. The quarterback is in an automatic disconnect mode.

NEBRASKA G-LOG

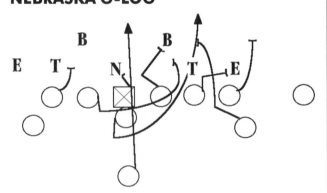

Nebraska is a heavy trap team. If you like the fullback trap, then the Midline is a good play to run especially against a 4-3 defense. If you have both the Trap and Midline it is a dangerous combination. Let me show you one play that is a companion to the Midline. We tie this in with the rest of our offense The Zone Double Option is the easiest play known to man. Everyone zones on the line of scrimmage We capture the end of the line of scrimmage with our tight end. We put our fullback and half-back outside for pursuit. The quarterback is going to get to a level 2 option key which would be the safety rolling down in the alley.

After we have run the Midline the defense starts coaching the defensive end to play the quarterback in the C-Gap. He slants down inside. That is the tip for us to run the Zone Option. Now the tackle and tight end take the defensive end down the line. It is an easy block if the end is coming inside. So we took an expanded look and ran the Midline to draw the defense back into us. When they squeeze the C Gap to stop the Midline we have the Double Zone Option to run.

DOUBLE ZONE OPTION

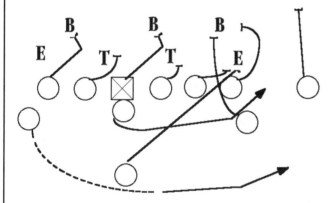

The fullback has the penetration. If a linebacker comes on a blitz inside he checks penetration. Then he has pursuit which would be the first linebacker he sees. If our halfback does not block the line-backer our fullback will pick him up to the free safety. His rule is penetration, pursuit, free safety.

The quarterback does not ride the fullback on the play. We want him free to take off outside. We reverse the quarterback out on the play just to get the quarterback off the line of scrimmage a little more to get him downhill more on the option.

On the Arc Option the blocking is the same on the backside. Now we have the quarterback read the first man outside the A-Gap. We are going to pitch off the next man outside the man in the A-Gap. We still get the veer release. The only thing different is for our play-side tackle. He is not going to fan. He has the first linebacker to inside. Our tight end has the linebacker if he scrapes. Remember the rule when we first started. We want two linemen on the play-side linebacker. The tackle takes him if he plugs, and the tight end takes him if he scrapes.

One of the advantages of this play is that we are able to use Counter Motion. This is good especially against Invert Safeties. The corners are man-to-man outside. The safeties roll with the motion. The play has allowed us to get the play outside without all of the pursuit chasing us. We have given them a Counter Motion, and we have given them a Midline fake to hold all of the linebackers in place. The quarterback is going to take two steps and pitch it outside.

Against the 4-3 it is a great play. We have two blockers on the linebacker. It is the same action. We have Counter Motion and Arc blocking.

ARC TRIPLE OPTION

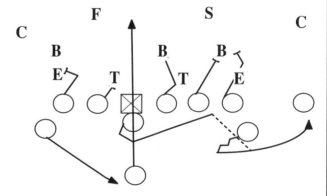

I have had a great time here. I appreciate being here. Thank you.

MULTIPLE BLITZ PACKAGE

UNIVERSITY OF ARKANSAS

Thank you. Today I am going to show you some things that are unique in a blitz configuration. They are things that are unique in how we do them. I want to take you through WHAT, we are doing on defense. I want to take you through HOW and WHY we are doing it. It will be a mixture of something we have been doing the last couple of years. It will be how we take some of the things we have done over the years and have mixed them with other packages.

What we are doing at Arkansas now is this. We are taking what Arkansas did before and making very few changes to fit this package. The big thing is to take this Blitz System and make it fit into what they have done before.

I would much rather talk about drills and fundamentals, especially at this time of the year. But what this will do for you is this. You can take this package and work it into what you are doing with your package no matter what you are using now. It does not matter if you run a 50, 4-3, or an eight-man front, you can take some of the things we are doing and integrate it into what you are doing. I want to gear this lecture toward that.

I will cover individual linebacker blitzes first and then I will give you a Blitz Package out of an Okie Front that we are using. There are some reasons why we use this scheme.

When we were at Southern Mississippi a few years ago we decided we had to have a defense that would match up against a lot of different offenses. We played four or five games each year where we knew we were going to be outmanned. We had a few games where we felt we would be as good as our opponents. But we had those games where we knew we would be outmanned and we felt we had

to do something that was unique on defense. It had to be a little more creative. We wanted to give the offense some different looks and something different to work on.

We wanted our defense to be unique. We wanted it to be on defense what the Wishbone attack was for the offense. We wanted a defense that would be difficult to prepare for in a short work week. The scout team would have a hard time duplicating the defense. We want our defense to be UNIQUE. Hopefully we would force the offenses to change some of their offensive game plan just because of our defense.

With that in mind we decided we this. We wanted to attack *players* – not *coaches*. We decided we would try to beat the quarterback and not the defensive coordinator. We wanted to work on the offensive linemen and not on the offensive line coaches. When you put the tape on and break down the defense you will see it is really simple. With everything mixed in with what we do we feel we can make it difficult on an offensive line, receivers, running backs, and quarterbacks.

We wanted to be able to disrupt any kind of offensive rules and recognition. If we could give the offense a look that would break the offensive lineman's rules that would make them bastardize their sets, or do something different, then we felt we had an advantage by doing that.

The next thing we wanted to do was to make it fit our system. We wanted it to fit our previous system again. We were coming from a 4-3 defensive set. We were not playing a 4-3 at Southern Miss. At Arkansas, more than anything else, we are lining up in an Eight-Man Front. We are going to stay with that Eight-Man Front. But, what I am going to show you today will fit in with the Eight-Man Front.

We will continue to use that front. We want it to fit our progression and multiplicity package. By that we mean this: we believe in a teaching progression. We want to build a foundation that allows growth of the defense. We must have something we can hang our hat on. If we can do that we are in control. We could take experienced, older players and they could execute our defense. We could take younger inexperienced players and they could play early. We could have more talented players and they could do a little more with the defense.

We wanted the flexibility to adjust and change weekly. That is one of the most important points for any defense. You need to have the ability to adjust on the sideline, to adjust weekly, and to be able to adjust from season to season.

I mentioned this earlier. We want to make sure we build from a foundation that allows for growth of the defense at all levels. We want to have a defense that allows us to do that at all levels and with all types of players and talent.

Let me cover some of the *Why Points* we felt were important in setting up our defense. *We wanted to take the quarterback out of his comfort zone.* We did not want it to be passive for the quarterback. We want him to be real uncomfortable. We were going to try to keep him off balance the entire game.

TAKE QUARTERBACK
OUT OF HIS COMFORT ZONE
A. Disrupt Rhythm Of Passing Game.
    1. Blitz – bring more than they expect or more than they can block.
    2. We wanted HITS and KNOCKDOWNS.

B. Illusion of Blitz.
    1. Bluff, Prowls, Stems – NO ROBOTS.
    2. Force poor decisions by offensive players.
    3. Limits play calling – keep them guessing.
C. Disguise where fourth, fifth sixth, or seventh rusher comes from.
    1. Force offense to protect perfectly.
    2. Limit number of backs and receivers in route.

D. Mix and Disguise Coverages.
    1. Force Receiver and quarterback to think quickly.
    2. Force route adjustments after ball is snapped.

E. Freedom to Defense – To Out-Athlete OL.
    1. Force the OL to react to speed, quickness, and agility.
    2. Unorthodox alignments, Stems, and movements to make the offense less aggressive.

We put this package together a few years ago when we were getting ready to play Florida. We went back and looked at Florida's last 15 games on films. We tried to take the best things all of the teams did in those 15 games against Florida. They had a great Two-Back run offense. They had a great No-Back throwing game. They did everything in between. We felt if we could match those things to our system and play Florida we would be in good shape. We hoped to do this by disrupting the quarterback and by Blitzing. At times you have to bring more than the offense can block. At times you have to play Man Coverage. We do not do that very often.

What I am going to show you today is mostly out of a Four-Man and a Five-Man Package. They are simple to pick up. I could draw up each of the blitzes and you would say that you have a protection package that will take care of that. But when we mix it all in and we are able to bring in the pure blitz, then the illusion of the Blitz becomes important. We want to *Prowl*. What we mean by prowl is this. You are like a burglar walking around looking in the window. You are just creeping around. A *Stem* to us is when you move from one alignment to another. At times we have *Individual Stems* and at times we have *Team Stems*. There are some defenses where we will move every snap. There are some defenses where we do not want to move at all. We start with the defense moving. But there are times when we have to play pure fast ball and line up and be hard nose. We do not Stem on those situations.

We wanted to be able to force poor decisions out of the offense. We want to disguise our coverages. We do not feel that running backs and wide receivers study the films as much as offensive linemen and quarterbacks. We do not think we can fool offensive coordinators or any offensive coach. But we feel we can get to the running backs and receivers. If we get to them then perhaps we can get to the quarterback. But we do not feel we can fool the quarterback a lot. We do not even try to fool him a lot. We just want him to feel uncomfortable by worrying where the defense is coming from.

If two guys were a threat to hit me, and I did not know which one was going to hit me I may get hit if I go one way or the other. But if I knew which one was going to hit me I may be able to avoid it. We want to disguise where the fourth guy is coming from. Then when we can bring five men we are a lot better off.

We force the offense to protect perfectly. We want to limit the number of backs and receivers in a route. We see a lot two- and three-man routes. The offense will leave the backs or tight end in to block. When they do that we can play a lot better coverage.

We want to keep our coverage disguised and we want to keep it mixed up. We have to be able to call a lot of different coverages and to keep them mixed up.

No doubt, and most of the time they are, but our defensive players should be better athletes than the offensive linemen. We want to make the offensive linemen react to our athleticism. We show them the unorthodox alignments, stems, and movements to keep the offense off balance and less aggressive. We have so many teams that are calling the play after they get to the line of scrimmage. They get the personnel on the field, or it comes on the field late. The play caller on the sideline looks at the defense and then signals the play in. Most of the offenses we play try to some of this. (FILM)

When do we go to that defense? We make sure we stop the run first. We will not get to any of those looks until we have totally stopped the run. That is a big key in doing what we are doing. We are not trying to fool ourselves by going out and playing a lot of wild looks. We want to stop the run first.

STOP THE RUN FIRST
A. Cannot Blitz effective if you do not stop the run.

B. Commit whatever it takes to STOP the RUN.
 1. Eight- or Nine-Man Fronts
 2. Overload Line of Scrimmage
 3. 7 Defenders vs. 6 Blockers
 4. 8 Defenders vs. 7 blockers

We have always been concerned when we were in a 4-3 look if we had enough men up front to stop the run. We were always trying to get another man down in the Eight-Man Front. We were looking to get another linebacker in the game, or another man in the game to take care of all of those gaps. Out of the Eight-Man Front, which we are going to line up in, we think we have that.

We do not think you can Blitz effectively until you do stop the run. Our base defense may well be an Eight-Man Front. We are going to overload the line of scrimmage depending on the number of people you have in the set. If you are in a two-back set with a tight end, we are more than likely going to be in an Eight-Man Front. If you break the formation and go to one tight end and one back we are going to give you a mixture of some things.

C. Force the offense to throw – when they should run. (Down and Distance control.)
 1. Effect the offense:
  a. Confidence
  b. Frustration level
  c. Morale
 2. Creative Negative plays

We want to force the offense to throw when they should be running the football. We want to make them execute. When we do that we think we can affect the offensive team's confidence. If you can't run your base play and we shut down the run you have some doubt about the offense. (FILM)

Next is the WHEN. When are we going to use the Blitz Package? After our Firm Foundation is set. After we are satisfied with the Eight-Man Front or the 4-3 defense and we have all the gaps covered. It is after we have our base defense in.

FIRM FOUNDATION ESTABLISHED FIRST – BASE

A. Communication System
   1. Teaching Progression
   2. Terms / Words
   3. Building Process

We want to make sure all of our communication fits what we are doing. That is what we are doing now at Arkansas. We are going to change as little as possible and make what we have and make it fit. You must make the terms and words you use be the same. If you call the looks a lot of different things you are not giving the players a chance to learn. But if you can package it and put it into concepts it makes it easier to learn. Then it can grow and get bigger and bigger.

B. Organized Method of Teaching.
   1. PLAN – Time/presentation.
   2. REASON – Is it effective?
   3. PURPOSE – What does it accomplish?

We take a lot of time in organizing our method of teaching. We believe in having a Plan, Reason, and Purpose. We are not just trying to put another defense in when we add something.

In spring practice and two-a-days we put in more Packages and Concepts. Then when we get into a game we pull out certain phases of that package. We spend a lot of time on what kind of handouts were are going to give our players, what type of videotapes they are going to get to see. One of the best things we have done is to make a Video Playbook. We took two or three clips of each defense and we meshed it with our installation plans. Instead of just putting everything up on the chalkboard we could show them what we wanted. In the summer we gave each player a tape and made them accountable for what was in the tape. This was a real success.

C. WHOLE (All)
   PART (Break it down)
   WHOLE (Total Package)
   1. Force-Feed Information
   2. Installation Plan
   3. Keep Progressing / Moving
     a. Pressure on teacher

The Whole-Part-Whole idea is this. At first you put as much on them as you can. It is like a car. You take all of the parts out of the car and then you put them all back together. If you know how the engine works you can do that. In the beginning you may not know how it works. It is the Whole-Part-Whole System. A lot of people say we "throw a lot of mud on the wall and see what sticks." We are not doing that. We are teaching more concepts than anything else. With each grouping it all fits into one package

It keeps the pressure on the coaches to make sure the defense makes progress. At times you may want to keep playing a defense if you are having success. But you MUST have a plan and stick to that plan.

D. THE ONLY LIMITS ARE IMAGINATION AND COURAGE.

I put courage on this because some of this looks different. You have to tell the players it is going to be different. Your imagination and courage will be tested. But the packages I am going to show you have no boundary and have no limits. We must make sure it is effective. We do not put in any defense that we do not feel we can be effective out of. That is true for any blitz or any defense we use.

E. GAME PLAN
   1. Down/Distance/Field Position.
   2. Scripts

We keep a Down and Distance and Field Position Chart. It is no different than what other teams use.

1st and 10
2nd and Short
2nd and Medium

2nd and Long
3rd and Short
3rd and Medium
3rd and Long

We grid the chart out. There should be 42 sections on the chart. We break an offense down in each of those situations. We break it down where it is first-and-10 from the minus 10-yard line. We are going to get your tendencies in that area. If it is second-and-long from the plus 40 to the plus 20 we are going to get your tendencies in that area. Then we develop a game plan for each of those areas. We are going to have a call for each of those areas. Most of them are going to be the same thing. We are going to take the entire field and study you from goal line to goal line and make sure we have something for the offense.

The way we do this is each coach breaks down a Down and Distance. Everyone gets involved and everyone learns the defense. Everyone has a say-so. By Wednesday morning we will talk through all of this. I am not talking about the game-plan sheet, I am talking about this: "Here is what we are going to run when it is first-and-10 when they have the ball on the 30-yard line. When the ball is backed up, here is what we are going to run."

The next thing we do is to Script the play. We go on Normal Downs and Long Downs. We will go from one to 25 calls in normal downs. Then we go from one to 25 on long downs. It may only be 12 or 15 plays. We will talk about the order we want to run the defense in. A lot of this is still going to be based on personnel. We do not have to stick with this for all of the plays but everyone knows what we are going to do on the first play. On Wednesday we are able to sell them on what the first *Normal* call is and what the first *Long* call is going to be. We usually stay with the script for the first seven or eight plays.

You get to practice the plays and work on them. The coaches all agree on the calls and the players know what we are going to do. That is a big deal for us.

Now I want to get into *what* we do and *how* we do it. Let me put this on the overhead.

1. Our Blitz fronts and stunts are taught by numbered series and individual linebacker stunts. We can call a 30, 40, 50, 60, or 70. We can play all of those by alignments by numbers. This gives them an alignment but it also puts them in an attitude. I think we have to teach attitude as much as anything else. This tells the linemen if they hear a number they are coming. They are in a pass-rush attitude. My alignment may not change that much. They have an attitude. "Ole' Coach has called this for a reason. That quarterback thinks he is going to throw the ball. I am thinking I am going to get the sack."

2. Any linebacker Stunt can be run with any series.
   a. Carryover of terms and alignments.
   b. Same calls (repetitions) but different look to offense.

You can put this in the defense in a 15-minute meeting. We make the same calls but it is a different look for the offense and we feel this is important. We want to be a multiple defense. But at no time do we feel any kind of a defense is going to win the game. *Alignees* win the games, not the *Alignments*. We win on the practice field. We sell that to our players.

3. Take advantage of individual defender.
   a. Special talent (Pass Rush, Anchor, etc.)
   b. Playmaker/Awareness

If you have a special talent we want to take advantage of it. You have wreck havoc-type players. Your best player may be a tackle or a linebacker. This system will allow you to accentuate that player. You can put him into position where they have to find him to block him.

4. Create any personnel matchups along the offensive line.
   a. Best vs. worst.
   b. Ends vs. guards/centers.
   c. Attack protections.

You can create any type of matchups. You can attack protections. You study the pass protection. Bill Johnson is our defensive line coach and I think he is the best in the country. He studies individuals better than anyone I know. He is going to find out where you are stepping. If you are stepping too wide or too deep we are going to get a pass rush on you. By studying the personnel we are able to match up the way it will help us the most.

30 – OKIE – ANY LB WILD

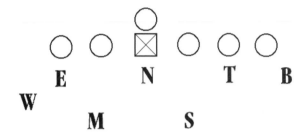

Our 30 package is what we call our Okie Package. Any of the linebackers can be *wild*. Most of the time we are going to bring a combination of two of the linebackers. We have a separate package where we give them numbers to do that. The nose and end are rushing.

If we call 40 it tells the front four that they are free to rush the passer. It gets them in the pass-rush mode. Any linebacker is wild. If we tag one of the linebackers he becomes a rusher. Now we have five men coming on the rush.

40 – STACK – ANY LB WILD

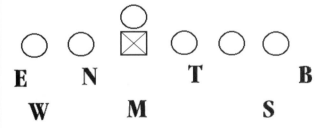

Out of the 50 package we take advantage of the Bandit linebacker. The Bandit is *wild*. He can line up anywhere we want him to. If the nose hears "50" he knows he lines up over center. He is listening for a strong or weak call. He is going to rush in that area when he gets the call. When the Bandit

hears 50 he knows he is the free man. We tell him where to line up. We use even numbers to the call, and odd numbers away from the call.

50 – BANDIT WILD

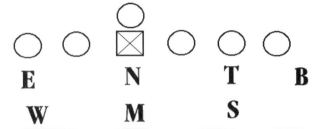

On 60 we do it with the end. The end may be a better pass rusher. We can put him in that end position and rush the passer. He is the wild card. The other players have not had to learn anything new. We use the same terminology to plug him in. If we call 61 he lines up over the guard on the weak side. If we call 62 he lines up over the strong-side guard. If we call 68 he lines up to the strong side out wide. If we call 67 he lines up outside weak.

60 – END WILD

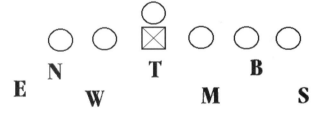

On our 70 package the tackle is wild. If we want to move the tackle around we can. The end, nose, and bandit are rushing. Now the tackle can be the fourth rusher.

70 – TACKLE WILD

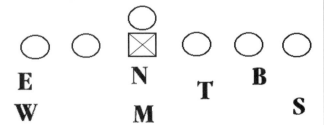

Here is how we call our **Stunts** out of our **Numbered Fronts**. Each linebacker has a name for a specific Gap. Each Stunt's *name begins* with the *letter of the position* running the Stunt first. Each Gap will have a trigger term applied to the Stunt. Let me put up some examples.

If I am the Mike linebacker the calls to the called side or the strong side will be BOYS' names; Andy, Bob, Charley. If it is to the weak side the calls are Alice, Betty, Carol; GIRLS' names.

MIKE LINEBACKER – (MIDDLE)

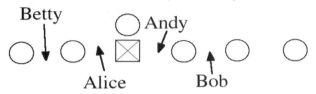

For the Stinger or Sam linebacker any stunt starts with the letter S. For A-Gap we call s*A*il; for B-Gap we call sta*B*. For the C-Gap we call it sti*C*k.

STINGER (SAM)

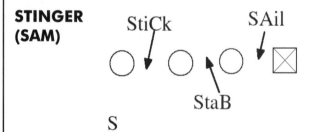

For the Wolf or Will linebacker the stunt starts with the letter W. We call Wand*A*, Willie *B*, and Wi*C*k.

WOLF (WILL)

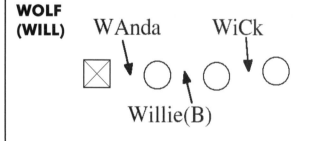

For the Bandit it is ba*G* if we want him to blitz over the Guard. It is ba*T* for the tackle hole. If we want him to go outside the end it is ba*D*.

BANDIT (OLB) – WILD

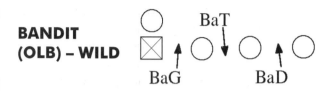

We can match any individual linebacker stunt with the "30" or "40" Fonts. Let me give you some examples. If we call 30 Stab we sent the Sam linebacker in the B-Gap. It is a three-man rush with the front tackle, nose and end. We make it a four-man rush with the Stinger going in the B-Gap

30 STAB

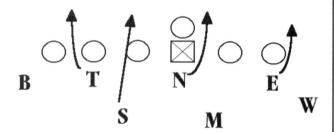

If we call 30 Willie there is no change for the front three rushers. The Will linebacker rushes the B-Gap. We have a four-man rush.

30 WILLIE

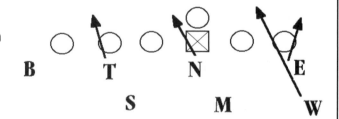

If we go 30 Bat it is the tackle that is rushing. It is the same for the front three.

30 BAT

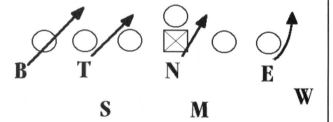

On 30 Andy we send the Mike linebacker. Everything else is the same. All of those rushes are Four-Man Rushes. But, we have been able to bring a different defender to make it a four-man rush. It is easy to put any of these calls in. To put them in all together takes a little more time.

30 ANDY

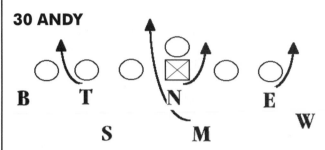

All of these could be good run blitzes. We do not run all of these all of the time. We put them in our package and then decide who we want to bring and who we do not want to rush. It comes down to who we want to cover and who we want to blitz.

If we call 40 the Bandit, Tackle, Nose, and End all know they are coming when they hear 40. If we call 40 Stab we turn into a five-man pressure team. The Stinger rushes the B-Gap. The front learned what 30 and 40 meant a long time ago. The Stab stays the same.

40 STAB

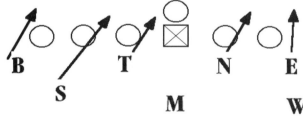

40 WILLIE

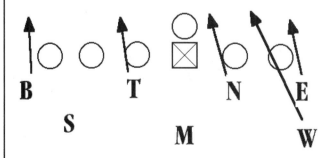

40 ANDY

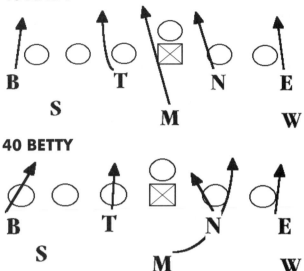

40 BETTY

Now you can see how your package can grow. First you put in the alignments for the 30, 40, 50, 60, and 70 and then put in the linebacker Stunts.

Here is what we run most of the time our of our Okie Package. Our players pick this up quicker than most coaches. When we go through this with the coaches they see the whole picture. The players look at it only from the position they play. If you look at it from only one position it is real simple. If you look at the total package it may take you a couple of minutes to get it. We use a Numbered System for the Gaps we want to Blitz. The Call Side is EVEN Numbers and the ODD Numbers are Away from the Call.

NUMBER SYSTEM/ OKIE BLITZ PACKAGE

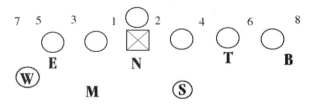

We take the four linebackers, the Stinger, Will, Bandit, and Mike, and run combinations with them. There are 6 Combos that we can run in this package. The first digit called is for the first linebacker called in the Combo. The second number is for the second linebacker in the Combo. If we call BAM it is a stunt between the Bandit and Mike linebackers. Here is the System for the Designated Blitzers.

BAM – BANDIT AND MIKE
BASS – BANDIT AND STINGER
BOW – BANDIT AND WOLF
SAM – STINGER AND MIKE
SAW – STINGER AND WOLF
MOW – MIKE AND WOLF

If we call BAM 81 the Bandit runs the 8 Gap and the Mike runs the 1 Gap. There are 108 different combinations we can run. But this can be put in your package in 25 minutes. Now, some of these stunts are not very good and some of them are better than others.

We do have Containment and Gap Rules. The tackle has to know if he hears an 8 call he is free to rush. If he does not hear an 8 he has to contain. The nose runs the 1 or 2 Gap. If he hears number 1 he runs the opposite gap which is 2. If he hears 2 he runs 1. If he does not hear either a 1 or a 2 he has a free rush. If the end hears a 7 he knows he has a free rush. If he does not hear a 7 he has contain. We have changed the names of some of the front seven to go along with what Arkansas has been calling them. But it is all going to look the same.

Here are some easy stunts that will give you a good idea of what we are doing.

BAM 82

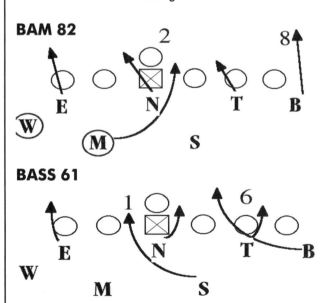

BASS 61

BOW 43

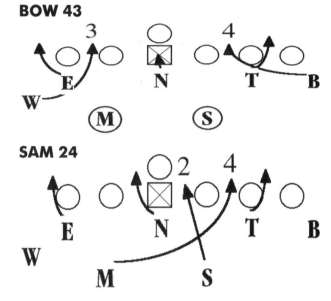

SAM 24

SAW 17

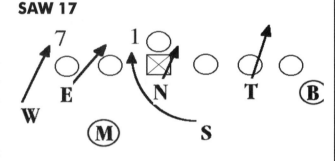

MOW 33

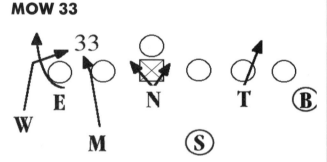

I think you get the idea. I am not going to go over all 108 of them. The two linebackers not involved in the stunt are in the Coverage. They may be your run players, or they may be better cover-type players. If you want you can drop them into a Zone Coverage. We are bringing five rushers.

A lot of you can look at this and say, "We have that stunt in our package." Some of you may be thinking you could pick that stunt up. I am sure you could. But, when we run four stunts one week, four the last week, and then we run two from last week and two from the week before, you have a lot of stunts to get ready for. That quarterback has a lot of different blitzes to look at. Let me show what some of these blitzes look like. (FILM)

I want to spend the rest of the time I have on how we practice all of this. We do a walk-through in a regular-size room. You do not have to have a lot of space to do it. We set up chairs in the room to simulate the front five on offense. We divide up into two groups. We have defensive line and linebackers on one side and defensive backs and linebackers on the other side. We call out our stunts against a particular set. We do not have them get down in position. All we want them to do is to get their feet lined up where they are supposed to be lined up. Then we have them take a couple of steps on the snap. We do the same with each group. There is no yelling and screaming We are coaching. We never go more than 20 minutes total. We change and put the second group in after the first

10 minutes. The linebackers get to work with each group. We work on the calls we are going to be using that game or for that day.

When we go to the field we upscale the tempo. We use 50-gallon barrels on our field. All we do is to line up and run through our blitzes. We put cones in the area we want the blitz man to rush to. He goes 3 or 4 yards deep in the backfield to the cone. We may move the cones to make him chase the quarterback. It is full speed to the cones.

We run our Blitzes in the Pass Skeleton Drills. We get our coverage and take two or three steps and we stop. We know we are not sacking anyone. We do not run the stunts against our Scout Team. We could sack them every time if we did. We try to run our stunts against the Running Game. We spend more time with our blitzes in the Running Game. We want them to see how it should look.

If you want Multiplicity in you defense there is a way to do it. However, you must make it fit your system. But this defense has caused people some problems. This system lets you play faster. It takes the robots out of them. The guys enjoy playing the game in this system. It is fun to call the defense in this system. You can get pressure on the passer but you have to stop the run first.

Thank you for your attention.

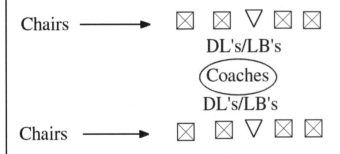

TURNING A PROGRAM AROUND

UNIVERSITY OF ILLINOIS

It is great to be here representing the University of Illinois. It is good to be speaking for Nike. I appreciate you leaving those tables and coming in to hear me. It is great to be here.

I get asked all the time how we turned the program around at Illinois. We were 0-11 in our first year, and 3-8 the next year. This year we won eight games including the bowl game. People ask me what we did to turn the program around and what did we do differently. My answer to that is this. The guys asking those questions must not be football coaches. They must be media people. We all know how much the media knows about football. They all want to know what we did differently. The key is the fact that we did not do anything differently. I really believe that is the key. We did make some slight adjustments along the way, but to me the key is the fact that we did not do things differently. We stayed with what we believe in. We did the same things we did when we were 0-11. We told the guys they were good, and we told them the way we did things were good, and the way we practiced was good. We told them the offense and defense we ran was good and we were going to get better in due time. In the course of going 0-11 everyone is looking at you. We continued to stick with what we had been doing. I think that was one of our keys to having a successful year this past season. I am going to talk about some of those things today.

There are four things that come to mind when I start talking about turning a program around. I am not sure what the best order is for these four elements. I think you have to have these four elements to be successful. This is true not only for turning a program around, but for maintaining a program once it is successful. As you know, that may be more difficult than just turning a program around and getting over the hump.

The first element is that you must have a plan. That is crucial. It sounds simple and many people say they have a plan. But I am not sure everyone does. I am not sure everyone has *A Plan* for what they want to do.

The next key element is to have a vision of where you want to go with that plan. You need a sense of direction of where you are going and how you are going to get there. You must have a clear path to how you are going to carry out your plan.

You must be willing to stick with your plan once you have set out on it. When you are 0-11 and 3-8 back-to-back it is easy to start to change when the alumni start to grumble. The tough part is to stick with what you have been doing. If you have a plan and you believe in that plan you will stick with it through tough times. Not many people saw the progress we were making in our program. Most of the people picked up the paper on Sunday and saw the scores and did not think we were getting better. But our players and our administration and support staff saw what we were doing and knew that we had a plan and that we were sticking with that plan. We sold the fact to our guys that we were not going to waver from our plan. I kept telling them if they would stick with it things would work out for us.

You have to have a plan to build confidence. When we were playing and not winning games we had to find ways to be creative to build the confidence of our players. The way we did that was by selling our plan. We told them what we were doing and that it was our way of doing things. We told them we were going to focus on ourselves and no one else. That was the way we were going to build confidence.

I am real big on goals. The longer I coach the more I have gotten into goals. It is important to have goals and to have them clearly defined and lay them out to the team and for everyone involved. You can have one, two, or three goals. This past year we laid out one goal. We had some steps that fit that goal that we felt was important. That one goal was to *Have A Winning Season*. That was our goal this year on our team. We had not had a winning season at Illinois is five years.

Some of the players felt we were selling them short. They told me they wanted to have more than a winning season. I assured them I knew that. I told them let's get to a winning season and then we can readjust our goals and go from there. We had a Five-Step Plan of how we were going to have our winning season. Those steps were what we had to do to achieve that one goal that we had.

Discipline is critical in developing goals. Discipline has to be a big factor in your plan. That was the biggest thing that we had to address on our football team. We had to work on discipline in all areas. One of the things I will address here is that I believe there has to be a single source of authority. Most of you will say that the head coach has to handle the discipline. It is not always that way.

When I got to Illinois our trainer handled the discipline in the training room. If someone did not show up for treatment, or did not get taped the trainer handled that individual however he wanted to handle it. Our strength and conditioning coach handled the discipline in the weight room the way he wanted to handle it. When I got there I wanted all discipline to come through me. It did not matter how minor the infraction or problem, I wanted to know about it. It might be a minor problem to our strength coach but if that same kid is doing the same thing in three or four areas it can turn out to be a major problem. I want to know all about the problems.

A big part of discipline has to involve communication. A lot of the times a head coach knows the plan and the assistant coaches know the plan, but that is about it. The players may know the plan.

We felt we had to communicate our plan with everyone involved. Everyone is important and everyone had a role. The trainer, the academic person, the strength coach, the lady who cooks our food, and the people that serve out food were involved. I meet with anyone that has any contact with our players on a regular basic to let them know where we are going. I do not want anyone involved with our program to be negative with our players. I do not want them on a different page than what we are on. You have to have a plan and you need to communicate it.

Another step in the process is Attitude. This was huge for us. We had to change the attitude of everyone in a lot of ways. We had to get our players to understand what it takes to be successful. This is especially true in a conference like the Big 10. We had to get them to see what it takes to be successful in the best football conference in the country. We had to communicate to them the kind of commitment it takes.

The players must learn to be unselfish. The players must understand this. It does not matter how good they must learn to be a team player. They must understand what it takes to be a team player. We had to get the players to change their attitude. We want them to have the "Count On Me" attitude.

Around our place you hear a couple of words used a lot. They are *Finish* and *Focus*. We talk about being focused. Most of the time we are staying focused on ourselves. When we get ready to play Michigan or Ohio State we did not talk about them much except to say here is what they do defensively, and here are the fronts they use. Here is what they do on offense and special teams. That was it. All of the rest of the focus was on ourselves. We tried to do what we do better than what they do. That is all we focused on. It is important to understand that.

The other word we stress is finish. Everything we talk about is Finish. Finish the play, the drill, finish what you are doing. Eventually they would learn how to finish off games.

Another big factor was getting our guys to believe. When we first came in I wanted to get them to believe in me. I wanted them to believe in the coaches. I wanted them to believe in the plan that we had. We wanted them to believe in the system on offense and defense. You have no chance if they do not believe in those things. They must believe in themselves and in each other.

The last point about attitude is this. You can't do anything successful if you do not have a passion for what you are doing. Have a passion for what you do. When we got there they did not have a passion for what they were doing and they did not have a passion for playing football. Going to parties was more important to them. The went to the parties and had a hell of a time and then went out and hoped they could win the game on Saturday. Win or lose on Saturday they were going to go out and have a good time.

They did not have a passion for what they were doing and they did not have a lot of success. Now our football has a passion for the game and they go out and have a lot of fun.

You must have players to win. Players are critical. You must have players. We can go out and recruit better players. As high school coaches you cannot do that. But, I think that is one element of turning a program around. It is important as far as the talent level you have and the players you get. I think there are a lot of other things that are important. A lot of times these things get overlooked, especially at our level. That is developing the players that you DO HAVE. It does not matter how big they are, or how fast they are, they can be developed and become better players. If they have a passion and are willing to work at it they can become better.

I coached in the NFL for four years and 16 years in college. At all of those places where I coached before we did not do a very good job of developing young players. When I came to Illinois I talked to the staff about this. I told them we were going to redshirt some players and develop them. This past year we brought in 20 freshman and we were able to redshirt 15 of them.

I told the staff when we come back in March for spring practice I want those 15 freshmen to be a lot better players than they are right now and when they report in August. I do not think that will happen if they spend their entire time on the scout team and not get to run our offense or our defense. Of course, they are going to run the scout teams and they need to do that. That is a part of their development. But we felt we could do more to develop them.

This is what we did to help develop those redshirt freshmen. On each Sunday we would have a scrimmage for the players that did not get into the game or only played a few snaps. The players started loving this. We have a light practice on Sunday. We have a 40-minute workout for the guys that played in the game and then the other guys came out in pads. They would scrimmage and they really got into this plan. They even called it the "Buster Bowl." I am not sure where that came from, but I am sure it has some meaning. We ended up having a Buster Super Bowl at the end of the season. They really got into the game. We gave them 25 to 35 plays every Sunday during the season. If you add all of those plays up it is a lot of plays. We did that for 11 games. If you go to a bowl game it is 12 games. We took films of the Sunday scrimmages and then we came in and watched the film. They got an opportunity to get better.

Another thing we did with the players that were not playing in the games and the redshirt freshmen was to keep them after practice for 20 minutes on Tuesday, Wednesday, and Thursday. Each position coach would work them for 20 minutes on techniques and fundamentals. They were working on blocking, tackling, throwing the ball, running routes, or whatever. They worked on techniques and fundamentals. Again, 20 minutes three times a week is one hour a week. For 12 weeks that is a lot of skill time and a lot of development for them that they would not be getting. This really helped to develop these guys. In your own program you can find ways to develop your young players.

I am going to talk briefly on our Indoor Program. I really believe in what we are doing. We have 6 a.m. workouts. We have stations that we work on for agilities, and quickness, and speed development. These are things we have developed over the years and I think they are outstanding. That has been a big key for us. It has helped us develop an attitude, develop toughness, and to get better in the fundamentals of playing the game.

The utilization of personnel is very important. This is the number 1 thing I learned when I was with the Chicago Bears. You must maximize your strength and minimize their weaknesses. Don't put someone in a position to do something they can't do. We have all done that and we have seen people do that. If a kid can't do something, don't ask him to do it and then chew his butt out when he doesn't do it. Ask them to do things they can do.

We work real hard to come up with ways to utilize the strengths of the players of our football team. We put them into position to do what they do best. This helps build the confidence that we talked about earlier because they are doing things they can do. We help develop them in the other areas of the game. We are trying to build self-esteem and to get the players to play up to their capabilities. This all goes together.

Continuity is a key for any program. Obviously the number 1 way is to keep the staff intact and to continue to do what you are doing. But we are going to lose coaches and you are going to lose coaches. But you can still keep the continuity. Keep the philosophy the same. Get everyone to understand what the plan is and you can keep the continuity. You can do this with the sports staff, the administration, and the players, and the staff, and everyone involved in the program.

I think there were some key things that happened in our program that allowed us to win seven games this season and to go on to win the bowl game this year. These things did not start in September. These things started three years ago when we started building the foundation and started changing the

attitude. Here are some events leading up to our success for the 1999 season.

It started right after November 22, 1998, when we were getting ready to play Michigan State. We came to East Lansing and we played terrible and got our butts kicked. On the next Monday we had a team meeting. For the first time since I had been at Illinois players stood up and wanted to express their views. They talked about commitment. They talked about where we were going. They talked about being tired of losing and what they were going to do to keep from losing. Not only did they talk about it they started doing the things they said they would do. They started doing something about turning the program around. They made the commitment to have a winning season. That was our one goal and that is where it came from.

About January 10 a lot of our players came back early to start the indoor program. Our students were not back in school. We could not ask our kids to come back before January 20. That is when our Off-Season Program started officially. We had at least 75 percent of our players come back early and start working out in the weight room without the coaches. Many of them were sophomores that lived in a dorm. They had to bunk in with their teammates that had a place to stay. They did this to get back to school and to start working. To us that was a commitment. That was a big step in achieving that one goal that we set.

In our Off-Season Program we did the same things we had been doing. We had those 6 a.m. workouts. We break everything down into three phases. The third phase is the 6 a.m. workouts. We do that for three weeks. We get after it in that program. Before some of the players would come in late. Some players would not show up. All of that was involved in the discipline we talked about earlier. But this year we could start our workouts by 5:50 a.m. because everyone was there on time ready to go. When they all showed up we started. It was a different sense of purpose than it had been in the past.

In spring practice it was the same thing. It was a different feeling and the players had a little more of a bounce to their step. They were out there practicing to get better. They were practicing to win and not just to go through the motions. They were preparing to win.

In our summer workouts it was the same thing. We had a 7 a.m. running group that was run by our strength coach. We had a 5:15 p.m. running group. Then they had a 7-on-7 drill. They did their drills in an orderly fashion. It looked like an organized practice without coaches out there. They were not just out there. They were out there with a sense of purpose.

One of the biggest things that happened was that they went to a Volunteer Experiential Session on July 24. This man came in and talked with me. They train swat teams, military groups, collegiate academies, and other groups of that nature. I presented this to our seniors and they decided they would do it.

This was big for us. We had 53 players sign up for the program. It cost them 60 dollars each to attend and they had to provide their own transportation. That was about 30 miles away. The coaches did not have anything do with the program. They had to get there and they had to pay their own way and they had to organize the program.

It was 110 degrees heat index and it was a 24-hour program. They showed up at 6 a.m. and it ended at 7 a.m. the next morning. It actually went for 25 hours. It was 110 heat index all through the night. I am not sure you could do something like this, but anything you can think of that will create togetherness, trust, and belief in each other is very big in building a program.

We go to an old Air Force Base for summer camp. It is about 25 miles from campus. I have been to a lot of training camps over the years but this was the best camp I had ever been around. I said that right after the camp. I did not wait until we won eight games. It was great as far as focus, attitude, and as far as determination that our guys had. The commitment they showed was real.

In May four of our seniors came to see me. They said they want to put in a rule where our players could not go to parties through the week during the football season. They did not say anything about Saturday, because they wanted to keep it open. They said during the week, "No Bars and No Parties during the season." I told them that it was up to the players. If they wanted to put that in they would have to come up with the consequences for anyone that violates the rule. The 22 seniors got together and they put it to a vote of the team. It was accepted unanimous.

If you have been on college campuses recently you know what it is like. Thursday and Friday nights are the biggest party nights. The other nights are not bad either. Our players made a commitment not to go to those parties during the week. When I got to Illinois I think a big part of the team had those parties as the number 1 thing in their life, and the second thing was the football team. At a Big 10 school that may be shocking. But that truly was the case.

At Illinois the parties are unbelievable. But when our players made that commitment, I knew we had a chance to win. I knew we were headed in the right direction and they stuck with it.

Those are some keys to our success. I think those things are important in turning around a program or to keep a program on top. You must have that commitment.

THE ARIZONA FLEX DEFENSIVE PACKAGE

UNIVERSITY OF ARIZONA

Thank you. Guys it's great to be back home. I really consider this home. My wife came along and we're coming back this summer. I really love it here in Hawaii. Coach Tomey sends his regards. There are five of us at Arizona who have ties going back 18 years here in Hawaii.

One of the coaches on our staff asked me the other day the difference between being a head coach and an assistant coach. I told him there were a lot fewer headaches being an assistant. I really mean that.

The first year I was at Arizona we went 12-1 and were ranked fourth in the country. I thought this was a piece of cake. This year we went 6-6. We got hurt early and never recovered. We lost some good players and the guys coming up couldn't quite replace them. A year ago all our juniors and seniors had their best years. That didn't happen this year.

I was happy however, to see UH do well. I spent 19 years in this program. It was good to see them get back on track and have a great year. It's great to see people in this program that you know. I know June Jones did one heck of a job this past year.

I got a couple of books for Christmas and on the way over I read some of them. The John Wooden book, I thought was excellent. It summarizes his coaching philosophy throughout his life. I really enjoyed it. This is the time of year where I have a little more time and I try to do some reading, go to clinics, and grow professionally.

My topic today is the Arizona Flex Defense. Let me give you a little background. In 1987 Rich Elision joined our staff at UH as defensive coordinator. That was the first year I was head coach here. He was trying to carry on the things we had done. He came to me and wanted to talk about what they had done

in the CFL with Don Matthews. I told him to go ahead. It looked really sound to me. We led our league a couple of years with it.

He went to Arizona and put it in there. Their talent level was better than ours and over night it became the defense to run. It became known as the **Desert Storm** defense. It became a really hot defense. I'm going to show you some of our alignments we have made with the defense.

Our base front is similar to the Bear Front. In our base front we have a Stud end and an End who can play up or down. The Stud goes to the strong side or field side and the End plays the weak side or boundary side. We play two tackles, which we call Nose and Tackle. We slide them up and down the line on the shade of the center and guards. We have Mike and Rover linebackers that we play inside. The Whip linebacker is our flex linebacker, who we play on the strong or weak side. We have a boundary and field corner and a free safety. The Kat is our strong safety.

BASE

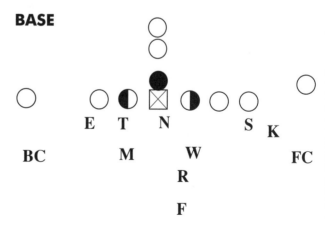

In this defense we match personnel quite a bit. That minimizes the adjustments we have to make with motion and shifting sets. Our Stud should be our best pass rusher. We put him into the field or to the strong side. The End is not the same type of pass rusher that the Stud is. The Whip linebacker is more of a true plugger-type linebacker. The Mike linebacker stays in the box. He is the middle linebacker. Our Rover linebacker is like a half strong safety and half linebacker. The adjustments we make to an offset back are made by the Rover linebacker. The Mike linebacker stays in the middle. If they motion that back, Rover is the one who adjusts to him. If he goes in motion past the tight end, we may bump out to the defensive backs and Rover would take the tight end.

STRONG

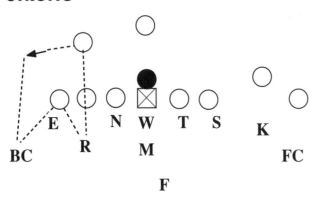

In the one-back set the Kat will play toward the formation in the middle of the field and toward the field with the ball on the hash mark. The Rover linebacker plays opposite the Kat. The Kat will play the number 2 receiver to the strong side. Stud plays into the field or formation and the End plays opposite. We can do different things with our tackles and flex linebacker. For clinic talk I'll put the tackles in 2I's slanting to the tight end. The Whip is in a stack weak with the Mike linebacker in the middle.

ONE BACK

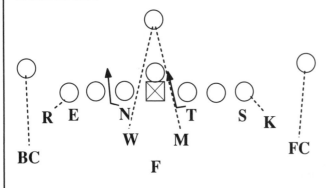

Our linebackers in the balanced two-back set or I formation have their toes at 5 yards from the line of scrimmage. We play deep and laterally. We cancel all the inside gaps with our people up front. Against the single back or offset back the Mike linebacker aligns at 6 yards deep. Against split backs the Kat goes to the formation side. The Rover adjusts to the split back strong. The Mike linebacker adjusts to the split back weak. The Stud plays the formation side with the End opposite. The Whip linebacker plays weak with the tackles adjusted toward the formation.

SPLIT BACKS AND RECEIVERS

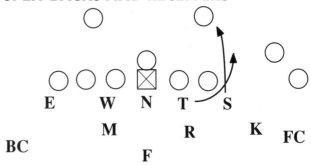

If we get what we call **Y-Trips** or tight-end trips set, the Kat plays the number 2 receiver strong. The Rover comes over into what we call an Outlaw position. He aligns over the tight end. From there we can play zone or man pass coverage. The Stud moves out to a 9 wide technique, which is a good pass rush position for him. He can also contain better from that position, because people like to sprint toward the trips. The End to the opposite side moves into a 3 technique and the Whip linebacker steps outside of him. The Mike linebacker stays in the middle.

Y-TRIPS

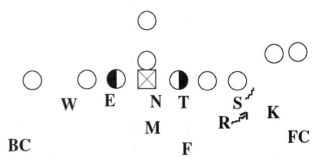

In our **Kat Front** or 40 we play 2 techniques with our Tackle and Nose or we can play shade on the center. The Whip linebacker aligns in the middle a yard and a half off the ball. His toes are going to clear the heels of the defensive linemen. If the tackles are in 2 techniques he is on the center. If they are shaded, the Whip linebacker is in a stack position behind the nose tackle. He steps opposite the direction of the nose tackle on the snap of the ball. The techniques you play with the tackle depend on the personnel you have. If they don't move very well you might want to play more 2 techniques. If they can move you might want to angle them. We stem our front a lot. We always get quite a few procedure penalties when the offensive line jumps with our stem. We double move and angle with our tackles. When I show you the film it will show you what I'm talking about.

KAT FRONT

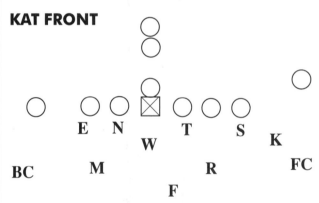

Our linebackers' keying system is pretty simple. It gives our guys a chance to be athletes. They can run and play the defense. We can change up our keys based on who we are playing and what they are doing. In our base defense the Whip linebacker is keying the tailback in the I formation. The Rover and Mike linebackers key the fullback. They key the tip of the pad to their side. If the Whip linebacker is keying the fullback then the Mike and Rover linebackers are on the tailback. I'll get into how that ties into the coverage later. In our base defensive the Stud has his inside arm free and is supposed to kick the tight end's ass. If we get both backs to the strong side, the Kat attacks and bounces everything outside. The Rover linebacker leverages the play and the Mike linebacker is the scrape player. He is the killer on the play.

Our **White Coverage** is a base three-deep four-under zone. The Whip and Kat are playing curl to flat zones. The Mike and Rover are playing hook to curl zones. The corners and free safety are playing three deep zone. We see so much play action pass on first down that this defensive coverage has not been that effective. When people threw the ball against this coverage they completed it. We play this coverage in running situations or long yardage situations. It is a change up coverage for us.

WHITE COVERAGE

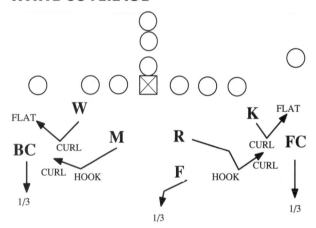

If we see the offset back we have an adjustment we like in that case. Our End moves out on the tight end to the weak side. The Whip and Rover linebacker exchange responsibilities in their coverage. The Rover would play the curl to flat and the Whip would take the hook to curl. Everything else would be the same.

If they came out in a one-back set with the tight end weak and the tailback split wide, the Rover linebacker would move out and take the curl-to-flat coverage. The Whip linebacker would stay inside and take the hook to curl.

In our base defense with the Whip linebacker so close to the line of scrimmage, we feel like the offense has to protect against 5 instead of 4. The Whip may not be coming, but the offense has to account for him in their protection scheme.

The next thing I want to talk about is our **O Coverage.** I've got a tape of this, which will make this explanation mean a lot more. This is a switch coverage, which has real good run controls. The free safety is free. The boundary corner is playing aggressive on the number 1 receiver from the outside in. He has a hole player to his inside short, and a deep safety over the top for the inside post move. The field corner is on an island. He is inside number 1 and has to play over the top on any inside move. In our O Coverage most people read nickel coverage. On first-and-10 we feel we have a healthy front vs. the run and a solid defense vs. the pass.

The Whip linebacker has the tailback man-to-man in this situation. As a rule the Rover linebacker can't be out-leveraged by the tailback if he comes his way. If that happens Rover picks him up and the Whip will fall off on the back closest to him. If both backs went toward the Rover, the Mike linebacker becomes the hole player, or zone player, in the middle of the defense. The free safety is going to split the difference between number 2 strong and number 1 weak.

The Kat is going to combo coverage with the backside linebacker. In this case with full flow toward the Rover, it would be the Mike linebacker. If the tight end releases inside, the Kat is forcing the play. The tight end coming across the field is now picked up by the Mike linebacker.

If full flow went toward the Mike linebacker the combo coverage would be between the Kat and Rover. If the tight end released inside, the Rover

O – COVERAGE

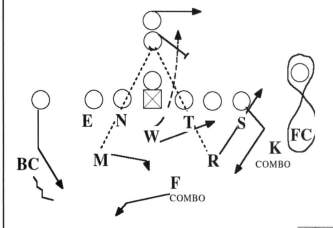

picks him up and the Kat becomes the hole player in the middle.

On full flow toward the Rover, if the tailback ends up the widest back, the Rover has the leverage run and takes the tailback. Usually, the fullback is the blocker to that side, and the Whip linebacker will be free in the lane.

If the tailback offsets to the weak side, the Rover linebacker takes him man-to-man. The Whip linebacker takes the fullback and the Mike linebacker and boundary corner combo coverages on the tight end. The End is playing heavy on the tight end and makes it hard for him to release inside.

O VS. OFFSET

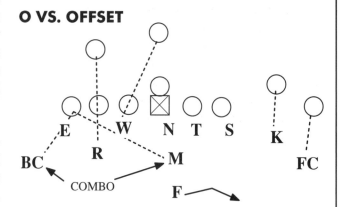

If we get a one-back set with a tight end and a flanker to the weak side, the Rover linebacker becomes the leverage player to the weak side. The boundary corner has the number 1 receiver inside out and over the top. The Rover and Mike linebacker have the combo on the tight end. The Whip linebacker is man-to-man on the one back. The Kat and field corner has number 1 and number 2 strong with the free safety over the top.

If the offense gives us a formation into the sideline with split backs, we adjust accordingly. The Whip moves to the field side and takes the back to his side man-to-man. The Mike linebacker stays in the middle and takes the other split back into the sideline man-to-man. The Kat goes to the sideline side and combos with the Rover linebacker on the tight end. The boundary and field corners play normal and the free safety is in the middle over the top.

O VS. FORMATION TO SIDELINE

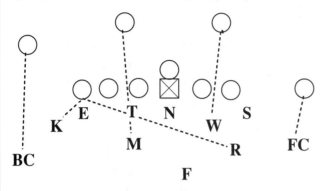

One of the change-ups we may go to comes from a Trips set. We attach the **Slam** to the coverage call. The field corner is playing tight man with help deep. The Kat and Rover have number 2 and number 3 strong. The Mike linebacker is man-to-man on the remaining back. The boundary corner is playing inside-out man. He is playing high on position. That means he is not going to get in a footrace deep. The Whip linebacker is running underneath number 1 weak. This would be an adjustment to a run-and-shoot team. That gives you a 2-on-1 back side and a 4-on-3 to the strong side. The Rover and Kat can play in and out man depending on the splits of the receivers. That means if the receivers crossed, Kat would take the receiver coming out and Rover would take the one coming in.

O – SLAM

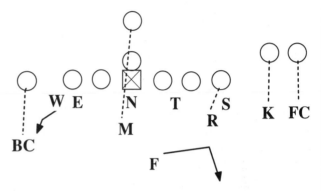

Hopefully that gives you a good overview of what we do. These were the basic things we have in the defense. I'll be around and in and out all weekend. I hope to see a lot of you guys because I haven't seen you in a while. Thanks for the opportunity.

THE MSU LEAD DRAW SERIES

MICHIGAN STATE UNIVERSITY

Thank you George. I tell you this. Coach Perles is a great man. Coach Perles brought me to Michigan State 10 years ago. I have been in Michigan for 16 years. I started out at Eastern Michigan University. I was there for five years. I got to know the Michigan State program and coaches very well. I developed a relationship with them. I went to Kansas for about three months. Then George Perles called me to join the Michigan State staff. I did not have time to unload the moving van until I was turning around and heading back to Michigan.

I have been coming to this coaching clinic for 16 years. I used to head out to Grand Rapids to hear all of the great speakers Don Lessner and his staff put together. It is a thrill for me to be here today as the head coach at Michigan State to talk to the high school coaches of the state of Michigan. You are our life blood. You are very important to our program. One thing we try to emphasize and that is to recruit the state of Michigan first. We will continue to do that.

The last few months have been a whirlwind for me. Going from an assistant coach to head coach and then going to a bowl game, organizing and recruiting a new class, playing the bowl game, and finishing up with the recruiting. Now I have gone through the process of losing a couple of assistant coaches. We lost two assistants to the pros. But we have replaced them and we look forward to spring practice.

I am going to talk to you about a very simple play that we run at Michigan State. It is a Series. We have the run play and we set up the pass off the run. It is a Series that we have had a lot of fun with. It is our **Lead Draw Series**. It is the number 1 play in our offense. We look to take this series into every game we play no matter what defense we are going to face.

The thing we like to do on this series is to run it from a lot of different formations. We change up with motions, and different personnel groupings. We can run it from regular personnel groupings which is the Two-Back Set, with one tight end and two wide receivers. We can run it from a Two-Back Set with two tight ends and one wide receiver. We can run it from the One-Back Set with two tight ends and two wide receivers. We will get into all types of formations. The most traditional way to run the play is from the Two-Back Set with one tight end and two wide receivers.

We will get into a situation where we will call the play in a base set and then we will check it, based on how we want to run it in our game plan. The base concept of the run and the pass is exactly the same. On the run play we show pass and block down and lead through. On the pass we show pass and block down and lead through. It is the same concept. The series is excellent to run on any down. You can run it on first, second, or third down depending on the situation.

When we talk about running this play we want to be in situations where we can run it against any front. Anytime we get in our Two-Back Set we are going to see an Eight-Man Front. Teams try to run their safeties down on us based on the backfield flow. One of the most important things on the play is how you block the back side. We change up the backside blocking depending where the backside linebacker is lined up. It depends if he is lined up in the A-Gap or if he is in a stacked position or if he is in a true stack over our tackle. We make different calls on the blocking.

We turn back with the center on the nose. We tell the fullback to shuffle and lead through on the inside linebacker. The tailback shuffles over, presses the A-Gap, and reads the first covered lineman. We tell him to stay in the A-Gap and to press the hole. At times they have a tendency to get two wide and do not see the cutback. The play has a three-way go.

Against this flow the strong safety usually runs down to the outside hole. They rotate the two-deep man toward the flow. We try to dig those defenders out with our wide receivers. That is the most basic way to run this play.

WITH ZONE COVERAGE

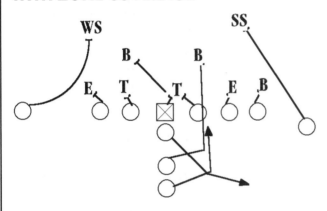

If we get Man Coverage we will set the formations to the boundary and motion the wide receiver over. Usually that will cause some type of rotation. They may play matchup and run the corner over, or they may rotate the safety down. Most teams play us in matchup so they can stay in their Eight-Man Front. They bring the corner over and bring the strong safety down to play in the alley in the Eight-Man Front.

WITH MAN COVERAGE

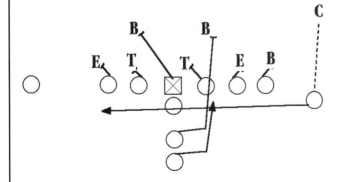

Another way we can run it is with a wide slot with an offset back to the strong side. The defense is going to play a zone and roll toward our slot. Now we use the fullback on motion on the linebacker.

SLOT - MOTION WITH THE FULLBACK

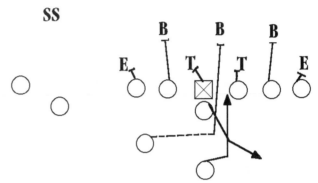

OFFSET – MOTION WITH THE FULLBACK

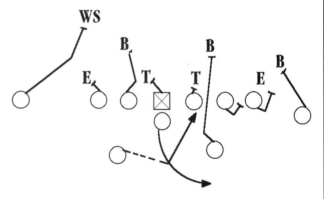

Those are the basic ways to run this play. Now, it gets a little more interesting. Now we start changing up with our personnel grouping. As soon as you bring in two tight ends and one back into the game the mentality of the defense changes. Now it is a little tougher for them to get into their Eight-Man Front. They may still run their safeties down in the alley, rotate, bring blitzes, and play Man Coverage. This is a called play. This is the same blocking scheme. We have two tight ends in the game. We bring the wide Y end in motion and he blocks the gap between the guard and tackle.

Y MOTIONS VS. MAN COVERAGE

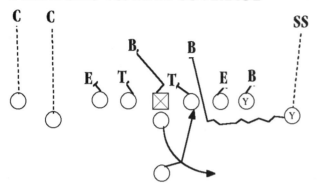

You could also put the same tight end over on the other side in Trips and bring him back in motion and run the same play. You can put him in a Wing Set and motion him over and block it the same way.

Y SLOT MOTION VS. ZONE COVERAGE

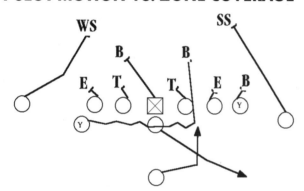

Now we want to be able to check this play to the best possible way we can run it the exact same way. There are two ways we can do that. We can go ahead and set the two tight ends off the line of scrimmage and two wide receivers on the line of scrimmage. We have one back. We have done this two different ways. Our favorite way to do this is to run it to the 1 technique. We want to find the 1 technique in the center guard gap and run at him.

DOUBLE SLOT RT. Y MOTION

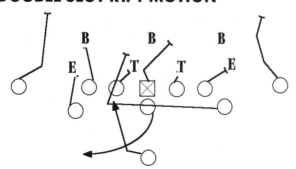

I have a videotape I will show later and you will see that we get a lot of mileage out of this.

We can run this play out of Split Backs. If we are in a passing situation and we may to run the Lead Draw. I talked about running the play on third down. The defense may bring in a nickel back on third down. They may keep their regular personnel in the game, it does not matter. If you want to run the ball on third down this is a safe play to run. It is a simple play to run. You can use motion, use slots to the field, and you can use a base set. On third down it is a good passing down and it is very soft in the middle area. You can get a lot of mileage out of this play.

We get a lot of movement by the defense. Very seldom will a defense sit back and let us run this play at them all of the time. They know going into the game this is one play they will have to stop. Everyone in the Big 10 runs this stunt. They slant the line one way and scrape the linebacker the other way. They roll to Cover 3 on the play. This is an excellent play against this movement.

RUN VS. MOVEMENT

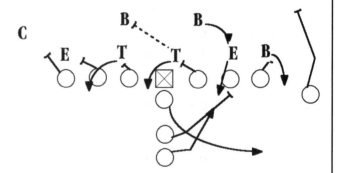

Say we get the A-Gap Blitz. This is another common blitz we see. They will blitz the A-Gap and try to scrape the other linebacker over the top. They try to free that linebacker. Most teams will buzz the strong safety down inside the box. They will have someone to buzz the box from one side or the other based on whatever coverage they are going to play. You are going to have someone buzz the box to replace the linebackers and play Zone Coverage behind them.

LINEBACKER BLITZ

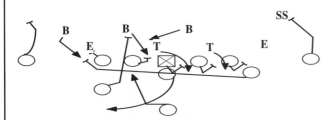

Off the Lead Draw we have our Play-Action Passes. The backs are the key to making this play go. We have two different types of protection on the play. This is the first way we run it. The fullback is aggressive to the Middle linebacker. He runs as if we were going to run the Lead Draw inside. The tailback is going to fake the Draw and check the outside linebacker.

The other way we run it is to switch the backs up. We send the fullback aggressive on the outside linebacker. The tailback fakes and leads through on the middle linebacker. Our offensive line has the down four linemen and the weak-side linebacker. It is turn-back protection. If you are running the Lead Draw successfully and you are running it over and over it sets this pass up.

We have a variety of routes we run with the play. I will not be able to cover all of them but I will give you some you can take with you. All of the formations I showed you how we run the Lead Draw, you can run the pass plays with the same personnel groupings as well.

I am going to show you some of the passes we use on the play. Again, we run the play two ways with the fullback and tailback switching responsibilities. I like the fullback up inside with the tailback out on the edge.

We can run the pass or the run from different formations and with different personnel groups.

RT. – 626 CURL Z POST

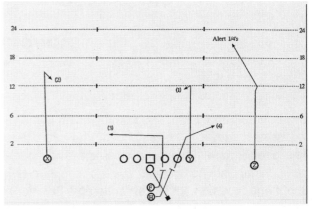

KING LOUIE FAR FLEX – 606 SCAT Z / X CROSS

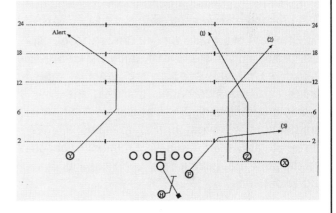

Those are some of the things we do in our Lead Draw Series. It is very simple and you can have a lot of fun with it. Have your base formations set and then change them up a little. Move your personnel around on the play. You can get a lot of miles out of the Lead Draw Series.

Our strength at Michigan State is running the football. When we make up our minds to throw the ball it is the play-action pass. We are not a great Drop-Back Passing Team. We like to feed off the fact that we are going to be able to run the football. Once we get the defense playing the run we are going to fake the run and throw the ball down the field.

Thank you for you attention. I hope you got something out of it.

KICKOFF TECHNIQUES AND DRILLS

STANFORD UNIVERSITY

Thank you. I appreciate you coming out this morning to hear me. It is certainly beautiful over here. The people here have been so warm and hospitable. What I am going to do this morning is to talk about and focus on our kickoff coverage. But moreover I want to talk about special teams practice. You have to put time into the special teams and make it more than just something you have to do as part of a football game.

At Stanford we made a commitment to our special teams and it starts with our head coach. He has given me the freedom and practice time to make sure the kids understood that the special teams are important. He wants them to know we are going to win with our special teams. We were fortunate at Stanford to have a number of coaches on the staff that have a lot of special teams coaching experience.

At Stanford all our coaches are involved with the special teams program. I have a lead coach for every special team. I am the lead coach on the punt and kickoff teams. But I am the facilitator for the special teams program. It is impossible for me to do everything. The coaching staff shares the responsibility for coaching the teams. I basically organize everything and am involved in the personnel on those teams and their motivation.

Special teams play makes up a third of the game of football. We are always going to try to win that phase of the game. We have a special teams meeting a half hour before the team meeting on Friday night. We talk about it, we highlight it, and make sure the kids understand it is important.

One of the things I struggled with when I started coaching the kicking game was how to practice it. What do you do other than running down the field under a kickoff to teach techniques? We began to highlight some specific techniques that happen on the way to covering a kickoff.

What I am going to do is take you through the things we thought about that we felt were important when it came to the kicking game. I'm going to show you how we set up our practice structure and some drills that we use to teach the skills needed in covering kicks. These drill are unique to us at Stanford.

The first thing we have to talk about is focusing on the fundamentals. Alignment and stance is the geneses of anything you do in football. The next things we talk about are *time-ups*, *get-off*, and *lanes*. That is basically your coordination of your kicker, his alignment, how you expand the field, his approach on the ball, and everyone working in unison. When the ball is kicked we want everyone moving forward. Everyone has defined lanes and we will talk about that later.

The next thing is what we call attack technique. On the way to the ball there are some attack techniques the coverage will be using. We have come up with little words and phrases that speak to that. The first thing we say is the kickoff is a *40-yard dash*. It is a sprint. I am expecting our kickoff team to be at the 30-yard line when the ball is caught. The second word we use is *avoid*. This is a term I use as I am in my lane coming down the field. When someone comes to block me, I am going to avoid him to the right or left. The third thing is what we call *Two-Gap*. This is a technique where I have encountered a blocker and I don't know which side the ball is coming. It is shedding the block and making the tackle.

The next technique is called *Shoot-and-Run*. This is a combination technique where the cover man is sprinting down the field, encounters a block, gets his hands out, and walks the block back into the ball carrier. We use the term *Wedge Split*, to describe the technique we want used on a double-team or wedge alignment by the blockers. *Skins* are basically for our outside coverage people. They are coming off the edges of the wedge. We want them to skin nice and tight and keep their shoulders square.

For any coverage team to be successful, you have to *Tackle* well. We are highlighting these things and we are going to focus the majority of our work around them.

Let's go into our structure in a practice situation. The first thing we cover is our *alignment principles* and our *huddle procedures*. Because of our makeup on the defensive staff, I am in the press box on game day. That presents a small problem in the coordination of the special teams. One thing that was a problem before we got there was making sure we had 11 people on the field.

We make a big deal out of our huddle procedures. When we practice, and even in a game situation, we use two huddles. We have an A huddle and a B huddle. The A huddle organizes at the 50-yard line and the B huddle is on the 40-yard line. When the A huddle organizes, if there is a problem we don't know about, we can substitute right from the other huddle. We make a concerted effort to make sure our huddle discipline is there.

On our player count we count from the outside in. The guy on the sideline is number 5 and the guy next to the ball is number I. We have a Right and Left side. Our Right side is considered our strong

HUDDLE ALIGNMENT

R5	R4	R3	R2	R1	25
L1	L2	L3	L4	L5	30
		K			
		X			35

side. The Left side is considered our quick side. The kicker faces the huddle. We have a two-line huddle with the left side on the front row and the right side on the back row.

The field is divided into three zones. The right, middle, and left are places we could kick the ball from. We kick the ball either right or left. We don't kick it down the middle. The cover zones are 1 to the right and 3 to the left. An example of our huddle call would be *Strong Right-Right-Cover 3*, *Run-Hit*. That means we are putting our strong side right. We are going to kick from the right hash mark. And we are going to kick the ball into the right corner of the field. The Run Hit signals everyone to clap and reminds them why they are on the field. If I call *Strong Left-Middle-Cover 1*, our strong side would align left, the kick is from the middle of the field, and the ball is going to the left side. That lets me move my strong side around. That doesn't mean I'll always kick to the strong side. The problem with sending the strong side to both sides, is our huddle. If we call strong left, our huddle has to realign for the dispersion of the players. Sometimes that can get confusing. Most of the time where we align depends on what the opponent is trying to do with his return game.

We line up on the 25 yard line facing inward toward the kicker. Our front foot should be on the line and our hands on our knees. The kicker puts his hand up when he is ready. The official will blow the whistle. When the kicker puts his hand down to his thigh, he counts 1001, 1002, 1003, and then approaches the ball. Everyone should be within 1 yard of the ball or the 35 yard line when the ball is kicked.

Your alignment comes off the number 5 men. We want the five guys to align 5 yards from the sideline and everyone aligns about 5 yards apart from the outside. That was pretty standard until the rules changed. Now everyone must be inside the numbers until the whistle blows. Because of that our alignments come from the R1 and R2, since we are kicking for the right hash mark on this diagram. The R1 aligns 2½ yards inside the hash mark. The

R2 aligns 2½ yards outside the hash mark. The rest of the team aligns off those guys alignments. When the whistle blows our number 4's are on the numbers and our number 5's are 4-5 yards from the sidelines.

I am generally going to kick the ball to my strong side. I put linebacker types on the strong side. The quick side has faster types in its makeup. I am going to take the strong side into the place where I think the wedge or point of attack is going to be. I want to turn the return back to my quick side. If I put the ball in the middle I can use a *check with me* call as to where the ball is going. In that case the ball may be kicked to the quick side.

Let's go into some of our drill work. We came up with what we call a *Kickoff Cycle*. We have four coaches involved, with each of them having a particular position. We split the kickoff team into fourths. We have an A, B, C, and D group which we rotate around to each individual station. We take half the football field. We put two drills on each side of the field at the 20-yard line and two drills at the 40-yard line. When we teach this, there is about three minutes at each station. Once we get the teaching done, we only spend about five minutes for the entire drill. That works out to about 45 seconds at each station and 15 seconds to rotate around. We do it quickly.

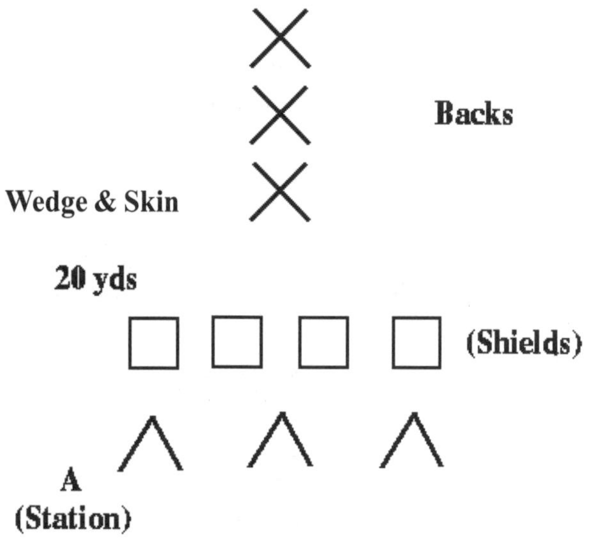

The first station is station A. That is our *wedge and skin* station. We get our defensive line guys to hold some shields. We put four shields up. We put three guys covering the kick. The guys on the outside work on skinning around the shields, and the guy in the middle splits the wedge. We want them to turn the shoulder and take the wedge on with the right or left shoulder.

Never try to split a wedge with square shoulders. They don't drop their heads when they attack the wedge. Once they split the wedge they square up the shoulders once again. We put our extra backs about 10 yards behind the shields. As the guys come through the shield they make a form tackle. The other two guys are working on striping the ball. We rotate around on the skin and wedge positions.

The second station is our *2 Gap drill*. We have four guys with shields and four coverage guys. They are four ball carriers behind the shields. The coverage attacks the shields, uses their hands to shed, and goes to make a form tackle. The coach will give the ball carriers a direction to go, so the coverage guys can shed to that side. When we do this drill we concentrate on keeping the feet moving. We don't stop the feet to shed

KICKOFF CYCLE – A

Backs

Wedge & Skin

20 yds

(Shields)

A
(Station)

KICKOFF CYCLE – B

2 Gap
Ball Carriers

(Shields)

40 yds

B
(Station)

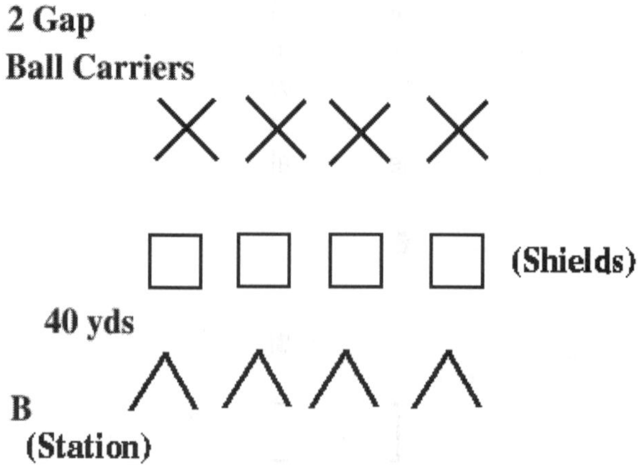

At station C we work on *avoid and 2 gap drill*. We use popup dummies for the coverage people to avoid. We have people holding the shields. The coach again gives the backs a direction for them to

go. The coverage people avoid the pop-up dummies using rip techniques, attack the shields, walk them back, shed, and make a form tackle.

KICKOFF CYCLE – C

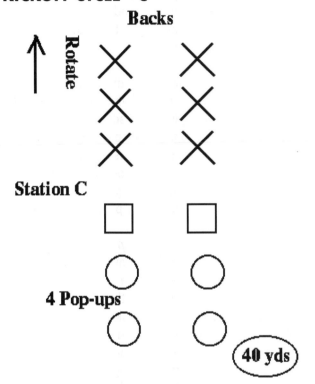

The last station is a *shoot-and-press drill*. We have three people holding shields and three coverage guys. They attack the shields and walk them back 10 yards before they shed them. They work the form tackle and strip techniques in the drill also. Notice in each drill we are working in our tackling techniques. All our kickers take part in these drills also. We expect them to make tackles.

KICKOFF CYCLE – D

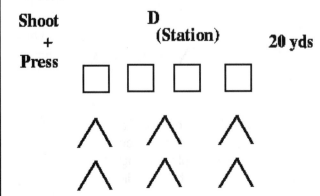

The next thing we use is called *Kickoff Gauntlet*. This is where we put all the techniques together. We have two groups going. I put groups A and B on one side and groups C and D on the other. We start out with three popup dummies. Behind them are the shields. After that we have three tube dummies to step over. At the end we have a cone with a coach behind it. Five yards away on a 45-degree angle we have two standup dummies.

The coverage man starts out. He weaves in and out of the popup dummies using his avoid technique. He rips right-left-right or left-right-left. He

KICKOFF GAUNTLET

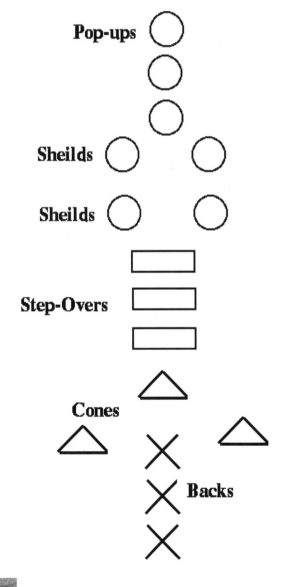

attacks the shields using his right shoulder on the first group to split and his left shoulder on the second group. He steps over the three tube dummies. In this area I want them working their hands like a shoot-and-run technique. After that he sprints to the cone. The coach gives him a direction and he performs a run-through and tackles one of the standup dummies. These are techniques on the run.

Obviously this takes some time to set up. I only have 10 minutes for my special teams period. While I am working on the punt game or something else, the managers are on another field setting up the cycle or gauntlet drill. We don't use practice time to do that. When we finish whatever drill we were working on and sprint over to this field. When we come to the drill it is set up and all they have to do is run it.

When we use the gauntlet we have anyone who is on any kind of coverage team in the drill. Our punt coverage team is also doing this drill. They have the same techniques that carry over from one to the next. Again, the kickers are in this drill. I grade the drill, show it to the kids, and make a big deal out of it.

The next things I am going to talk about are coverage rules, keys, ball placement, and things like that. These are some general rules and principles we talk to with the kids. Kickoff coverage is an all-out sprint. Speed and desire are important. Speed is important, but we have to have guys who want to be out there. It is not always the fastest guys who are the most effective. It is the guys who understand what we are doing and use their techniques. We want them to stay in their assigned lane if at all possible. If they get forced out of their lane, they want to get back and fill in a vacate lane. If you are knocked down, recover as quickly as possible and get back in your lane. If the man in front of you gets knocked down, try to fill his lane. It is not a shame to get knocked down, but it is a crime to stay down. To be on the kickoff team it helps to be wild and crazy. We want people that are kamikaze types. Don't overrun the ball and take proper angles.

Tackles should never be made by one man. We want to gang tackle. Everything starts with a good kicker. The ball has to be kicked where it is supposed to be. It has to be kicked deep with proper hang time. Our goal is to always keep the ball inside the 20-yard line.

A ball that travels 10 yards is a live ball. Never assume the ball is not going to be run back out of the end zone. Anytime we kick the ball into or out of the end zone our whole coverage team sprints all the way to the goal line. That is something we feel is important. If we see guys not doing that, we are on their butt about it. Our three keys are **Desire**, **Recognition**, and **Technique**.

We have visual keys for all our guys. The inside people, which are our 1's and 2's, keys are going to be what we define as the left and right wedge setters. The 3's, 4's, and 5's keys are the right and left ends, respectively.

If the opponent is using one fullback in the middle as their wedge setter, we call that a Diamond Set. The 1's and 2's would key him.

We want to anticipate where the ball is going. That gets us into what we call *Points of Departure*. The point of departure is the point at which the coverage people would hit the wedge. The vision keys take the coverage people to their points of departure. If we were playing a middle wedge, I want to sprint to the 35-yard line before I start to squeeze to my point. If it is a middle wedge, everyone has a point on that wedge that they hit. The R1 and L1 hit the inside shoulders of their respective wedge setters. The R2 and L2 hit the outside shoulder of that wedge setter. The R3 and L3, and the R4 and L4, hit the inside and outside shoulder of their ends. There is an NR in the diagram. That stands for Non-Return man. If the NR committed to the strong side, the R4 can hit the inside shoulder of the NR to his side because he has an R5 outside of him for contain. If the NR committed to the quick side, the L4 has to play 2-gap through the outside shoulder of the NR. The R5 and the kicker are on the hash marks about 8 yards behind the coverage as the safeties. We play physical and aggressive. If someone breaks, I want our safeties right on them. That is our point of departure versus the middle wedge.

P.O.D VS. MIDDLE WEDGE

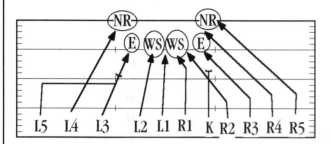

This is all about recognizing on the run. The ball is kicked and I am looking at my visual key. I see the wedge setter and I am working to converge on my point. On the way to his point he is using the techniques we just talked about.

If we get a right or left wedge our points change a little bit. Now we end up with what we call single points. As our guys are running down they have to understand the body language of the returner. If, though, the ball is kicked left and the blockers start to form the wedge right, you have to adjust your lanes accordingly. If the ball is kicked to our right there is a returner and a nonreturner. If the nonreturner works to the right, R5 skins and contains through the outside shoulder of the nonreturner. He uses a shoot-and-run technique through the upfield shoulder. The R4 splits through the outside shoulder of the right wedge setter. The R3 hits the inside shoulder of the right wedge setter. The R2 splits through the inside shoulder of the left wedge setter. The R1 skins the outside shoulder of the left end. The coverage guys away from the wedge direction have a slightly different technique. Hopefully the strong side will force the ball back toward the middle. If that happens, the L1, 2, 3, and 4 uses a *Run-Through* technique, where they skin behind the wedge and make the tackle. If the ball, however, has broken to the side, they have what is called a *Linebacker Fold*. When the ball breaks to the sideline, they come over the top like a linebacker. The L1 shoots and runs through

or uses the linebacker fold. The L2 and L3 run through or use the linebacker fold between the right and left ends. The L4 skins the outside shoulder of the left end and contains. The L5 and kicker keep the ball on their inside shoulders and use their lane progression. The kicker sprints to around the 35-yard line and than presses the area in between R3 and R4. The L5, once he recognizes the return to the right, rotates halfway to the middle of the field. If he needs to he comes over the top to make the tackle.

RIGHT WEDGE

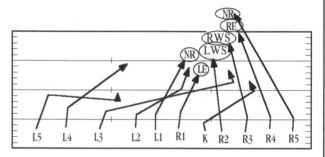

There was a question asked. Do you kick away from good returners? That answer is absolutely. I hate to do it because there are a lot of other variables that come into it. If we have the wind and I think we can kick the ball into or out of the end zone, than I'll kick to anyone. If we are kicking into the wind, I'll probably put the kicker in the middle of the field and go *check with me*. Then we directional kick the ball away from the good returner. People that see you doing that line their returners up in an I on the goal line. The good returner may get the ball but he is going to have to run to get it. On our kickoff team we use our first-line guys.

Here is a coaching point for R4 and R5. We are trying to kick the ball into the right side of the field between the hash mark and the numbers. If we can get it outside the numbers that is all the better. If we get it outside the numbers, R5 forces the ball back into the wedge. The reason for this is our coverage is concentrating on their points of departure. The coverage is focused on the blocking, not necessarily the position of the ball. When we have bad returns against us, it is because guys are watching the ball instead of their points. Those guys have to funnel the ball into the rest of the coverage.

If the ball is kicked into the right side of the field but the return is coming into the quick side, we have to redirect. The L4 skins through the outside shoulder of the left end or nonreturner for contain. The L3 splits through the outside shoulder of the left wedge setter. The L2 splits through the inside shoulder of right wedge setter.

The L1 split through the inside shoulder of the right end. The R1 skins off the outside shoulder of the right end. The R2, 3, and 4, linebacker fold between the left and right ends. The R5 has to make sure he pushes the ball into the coverage. The L5 keeps the ball on his inside shoulder, uses his lane progression, and presses the area between L4 and L3. As the ball starts to run to the left wedge, R4 and R5 keep the ball on their inside and outside shoulders respectively. They funnel him into the coverage and if he tries to cut back they are playing on his inside and outside shoulder.

LEFT WEDGE

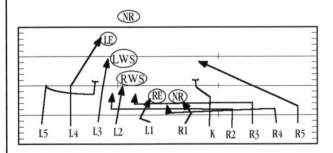

Everyone doesn't run the same types of returns. These are examples of what we do each week to play our opponents. People can give you false keys. We work each week on this part of the game. We go over it to the point that we know what we are supposed to do game day. We change the points

of departure based on the type of return the opponent has.

When we work on this in practice we kick the ball, but we are not watching it. We are looking at our points. The thing we have to guard against is breaking out of the lanes too quickly. As we come down we don't have to kill the guys in the wedge, but we want them working to their points.

We have a kind of grading system we use on coverage. We have A, B, and F positions. The A position is based on the avoid and body position. If the ball and his key are working right, then his hat should be on the right side. The B position is when the coverage man isn't sure where the ball has defined itself. He is thinking about shooting and running through his man. The F position means the cover guys took a course right and the return and key went left. The A is good, B is acceptable, and F is unacceptable. Sometimes a guy runs the opposite side of the avoid, but I expect to see him skin back to the ball quickly. If I see a guy violate his lane and his key, I know he is looking at the ball as opposed to recognizing his keys.

Hopefully that gives you some insight into the coverage. Maybe you can use some techniques to help with the way you cover. We have won so many games with our special teams. That is the hidden yardage in football.

A lot of times a special team can change the momentum of a game. It can work both ways on you. If you make a mistake in the kicking game it can hurt. How many times have you worked like hell to drive the ball down the field and score, only to have the football run all the way back on the kickoff for a touchdown? In a matter of seconds, the opponent has stolen what it took you so long to gain. If you need help I would be glad to share some of these things with you. Thank you very much.

COACH OF THE YEAR CLINIC FOOTBALL MANUAL

01. **ALPERT, BOB** – DUNCANVILLE HIGH SCHOOL, TEXAS: Option Football
02. **BEAMER, FRANK** – VIRGINIA TECH: Principles of Punt Blocking And Returns
03. **BEST, ROB** – APPALACHIAN STATE UNIV.: Inside And Outside Zone Stretch
04. **BILLINGS, TIM** – MARSHALL UNIVERSITY: Coaching The Defensive Tackle
05. **BURTON, RON** – INDIANA UNIV.: Linebacker Techniques And Fundamentals
06. **CHANDLER, CHARLES** – UNIV. LOUISVILLE: Running Back Techniques & Drills
07. **CHAVIS JOHN** – UNIV. OF TENNESSEE: The Tennessee Defensive Package
08. **COLE, JIM** – ALMA COLLEGE: Attacking With The Spread Offense
09. **DIMEL, DANA** – UNIVERSITY OF WYOMING: The Inside Running Game
10. **DONNAN, JIM** - UNIVERSITY OF GEORGIA : Coaching The Offense
11. **DuBOSE, MIKE** –UNIVERSITY OF ALABAMA: Defensive Line Play
12. **FRANCHIONE, DENNIS** – TCU.: Find A Way To Move The Football
13. **GREGORY, BOB** – UNIV. OF OREGON: Man To Man Secondary Coverages
14. **HACKETT, PAUL** – UNIV. SO. CALIFORNIA: Coaching The Young Quarterback
15. **HAYES, JAY** – UNIVERSITY OF WISCONSIN: Tight Eagle Defensive Look
16. **HEACOCK, JON** – INDIANA UNIVERSITY: Defensive Secondary Zone Blitz
17. **HODAKIEVIC, KERRY** – McKINLEY HIGH SCHOOL, OHIO: Efficient Practice Organization
18. **HOLT, NICK** – UNIVERSITY OF LOUISVILLE: Development Of Defensive Linemen
19. **JOHNSON, LARRY** – PENN STATE UNIV. : Special Teams Kickoff Coverage
20. **JONES , JUNE** – UNIVERSITY OF HAWAII: The Run And Shoot Offense
21. **KEANE, TIM** – UNIVERSITY OF KENTUCKY: Defensive Secondary Play
22. **KLAUSING, CHUCK** – GUEST COACH: Views On The Wing-T, Blocking, And Tackling
23. **LANG, WADE** – WOFFORD COLLEGE: Combining The Wing-T And Option Series
24. **LENTI, FRANK** – MOUNT CARMEL H. S., IL.: Setting The Tone For The Season
25. **MATTISON, GREG** – UNIVERSITY OF NOTRE DAME: The Bench Reduction Defense
26. **McCALL, MICK** – MULLEN HIGH SCHOOL, CO.: A Flexible Multiple Offense
27. **MUELLER, DALE** – HIGHLANDS H. S., KY.: The Shotgun Offense Running Game
28. **MUMME, HAL** – UNIV. OF KENTUCKY: Teaching Pass Patterns And Drills
29. **OLSON, GREG** – PURDUE UNIVERSITY: The Bubble Screen Pass
30. **PAGAC, FRED** – OHIO STATE UNIVERSITY: Linebacker Play And Defensive Fronts
31. **PARK, THOM** – FORMER COACH: Managing Your Football Coaching Career
32. **ROCCO, FRANK** – SHALER AREA H. S., PA.: Quarterback Techniques And Reads
33. **ROMANO, AL** – ADRIAN H. S., MI.: Strategy In Stopping The Wing-T
34. **RUEL, PAT** – MICHIGAN STATE UNIV.: Blocking Stunting Defenses
35. **SANDERS, RANDY**, UNIV. OF TENNESSEE: The Tennessee Offensive Package
36. **SANDUSKY, JERRY** – PENN STATE UNIVERSITY: Linebacker Techniques And Drills
37. **SIMMONS, BOB** – OKLAHOMA STATE UNIVERSITY: Utilizing Multiple Formations
38. **SMITH, LARRY** – UNIV. OF MISSOURI: Building A Program From The Bottom Up
39. **SPENCER, GLENN** – STATE U. WEST GEORGIA.: The 4-3 Defense And Blitz Package
40. **WIDENHOFER, WOODY** – VANDERBILT U.: The Commodores Defensive Package

ALL THE ABOVE LECTURES IN ONE SUPER CLINIC MANUAL